COLERIDGE'S PHILOSOPHY

Coleridge's Philosophy

The Logos as Unifying Principle

MARY ANNE PERKINS

CLARENDON PRESS · OXFORD
1994

Oxford University Press, Walton Street, Oxford OX2 6DP
Oxford New York Toronto
Delhi Bombay Calcutta Madras Karachi
Kuala Lumpur Singapore Hong Kong Tokyo
Nairobi Dar es Salaam Cape Town
Melbourne Auckland Madrid
and associated companies in
Berlin Ibadan

Oxford is a trade mark of Oxford University Press

Published in the United States
by Oxford University Press Inc., New York

British Library Cataloguing in Publication Data
Data available

Library of Congress Cataloging in Publication Data
Perkins, Mary Anne.
Coleridge's philosophy : the Logos as unifying principle / Mary Anne Perkins.
Includes bibliographical references and index.
1. Coleridge, Samuel Taylor, 1772–1834—Contributions in doctrine of the
Logos. 2. Logos—History of doctrines—20th century.
I. Title.
B1583.Z7P47 1994 821'.7—dc20 93–43259
ISBN 0–19–824075–9

1 3 5 7 9 10 8 6 4 2

Typeset by Best-set Typesetter Ltd., Hong Kong
Printed in Great Britain
on acid-free paper by
Bookcraft (Bath) Ltd.
Midsomer Norton, Avon

ACKNOWLEDGEMENTS

Since this study was first conceived (then in the form of a Ph.D. thesis), it has received generous encouragement, help, and support from many friends and colleagues. First, I would particularly like to express my deep gratitude to the supervisor of my Ph.D. studies, Bruno Brinkman, who never failed to provide the stimulus of penetrating criticism combined with a belief that the project was worth while, and could and would be successfully completed. Secondly, thanks are due to the British Academy, who provided the studentship award which enabled me to undertake the Ph.D. out of which this book emerged. To many fellow Coleridgeans I owe much thanks; particularly to Lorna Arnold for all her invaluable help with Coleridge's wayward Greek, to John Beer and Tim Fulford for reading and commenting on the script at an earlier stage, to Heather and Robin Jackson for their continued interest and for hospitality and help during my research trip to Toronto, to Anthony Harding for crucial encouragement when the 'Idea' was at a very embryonic and vulnerable stage and for support through all the various stages of development. I would also like to give especial thanks to Robert Brandeis and the staff of the E. J. Pratt Library at Victoria University, Toronto, for all their help during my studies there and for the welcome they gave me. To the examiners of my thesis, Colin Gunton and David Jasper, I give grateful thanks for their recommendations. Thanks, too, to Mark and Anya Taylor for giving me an especial 'boost' in the last stages before the book was accepted for publication; to John Clarke and Peter Conradi at Kingston University for their advice, and to John Ibbett for help with correction of last-minute errors. Finally, to my daughter Jo, for her patience, acceptance, and practical support, for cooking meals which otherwise would never have appeared, for preventing violent destruction of word-processors by solving technical problems in a moment!

CONTENTS

ABBREVIATIONS

Coleridge's Works

AP   *Anima Poetae: From the Unpublished Notebooks of S. T. Coleridge*, ed. E. H. Coleridge (London, 1895).

AR   *Aids to Reflection* (1825); 2nd edn. (London, 1831); ed. James Marsh (Burlington, Vt., 1840).

BL   *Biographia Literaria* (1817); ed. James Engell and W. Jackson Bate, 2 vols., *The Collected Works of Samuel Taylor Coleridge*, Bollingen Series, vii (London and Princeton, NJ, 1983).

C & S   *On the Constitution of the Church and State*, ed. John Colmer, *The Collected Works of Samuel Taylor Coleridge*, Bollingen Series, x (London and Princeton, NJ, 1976).

CIS   *Confessions of an Inquiring Spirit*, ed. H. N. Coleridge (London, 1840).

CL   *Collected Letters of Samuel Taylor Coleridge*, ed. E. L. Griggs, 6 vols. (Oxford, 1966–71).

CM   *Marginalia*, ed. George Whalley, 3 vols. to date, *The Collected Works of Samuel Taylor Coleridge*, Bollingen Series, xii (London and Princeton, NJ, 1980–).

CN   *The Notebooks of Samuel Taylor Coleridge*, ed. K. Coburn and Merle Christenson (London and Princeton, NJ, 1957–).

Friend *The Friend* (1809–10), ed. Barbara E. Rooke, 2 vols., *The Collected Works of Samuel Taylor Coleridge*, Bollingen Series, iv (Princeton, 1969).

LPR   *Lectures (1795) on Politics and Religion*, ed. Lewis Patton and Peter Mann, *The Collected Works of Samuel Taylor Coleridge*, Bollingen Series, i (London and Princeton, NJ, 1971).

LR   *Literary Remains*, ed. H. N. Coleridge, 4 vols. (London, 1836–9).

SM: LS *The Statesman's Manual* in *Lay Sermons*, ed. R. J. White, *The Collected Works of Samuel Taylor Coleridge*, Bollingen Series, v (London and Princeton, NJ, 1972).

N   Notebook (unpublished).

NED   *Notes on English Divines*, ed. Derwent Coleridge, 2 vols. (London, 1853).

ODI   'On the Divine Ideas', intended as part of OM, MS, Huntington Library, San Marino, Calif., HM 8195.

OM   'Opus Maximum', 3 sections, VCL MS. (I have kept to the original numbering of the vol., though it is likely that

Coleridge intended vols. ii and iii to be numbered in reverse order).

PL   *Philosophical Lectures (1818–19)*, ed. K. Coburn (London, 1949).

TL   *Hints towards the Formation of a more Comprehensive Theory of Life*, ed. S. B. Watson (London, 1848).

TT   *Table Talk*, ed. Carl Woodring, 2 vols., *The Collected Works of Samuel Taylor Coleridge*, Bollingen Series, xiv (London and Princeton, NJ, 1990).

Other Abbreviations

BL   British Library.

VCL   Victoria (University) College Library, Toronto.

EXPLANATORY NOTES ON THE TEXT

I have capitalized words such as Logos, Reason, and Idea when using them in the specific sense in which Coleridge used them, that is, as seminal themes and realities expounded in his 'logo-sophic' system. It has not always been possible to be completely consistent, since Coleridge himself is not; he sometimes uses these terms in a way which blurs the distinction between tran-scendent principle and the normal usage of the term to express a finite concept (this is consistent with his view of the Logos as the mediation between transcendent principle and finite form).

When using *logos* in the context of Greek philosophy it is transliterated and italicized as are any other Greek words or phrases in my own text. When representing some aspect of Coleridge's idea of the divine principle, Logos is transliterated in roman type, as it is when referring to Coleridge's concept of the image of this principle in the human logos. I have, however, chosen *not* to transliterate Λόγος and Νοῦς in Chapter 3.1, since I am here specifically exploring Coleridge's distinction between the Greek terms, and the application of their philosophical associ-ations to the theology of Logos. Consistency is here again almost impossible, not only because Coleridge is inconsistent in his own usage of the term, but because of the different traditions and associations of *logos* which I have attempted to represent.

In order accurately to represent Coleridge's thought and the traditions on which he drew, I have deemed it appropriate to use the generic term 'man' throughout (for example, in Ch. 4.1), especially since the terms 'person' and 'individual', which might today be seen as preferable, are used by Coleridge in a particular and specific sense.

CITATIONS OF COLERIDGE

Coleridge's unpublished notebooks and other MSS often contain errors, which, on the whole, I have left uncorrected unless this completely confuses the sense of the passage, in which case '[*sic*]' is given. Sometimes the errors take the form of unusual punctuation, sometimes of incorrect Greek and Latin, and sometimes of inconsistent spelling. Where this is very likely to cause confusion as regards the sense of a passage, I have supplied punctuation in square brackets. In transcribing Coleridge's Greek from MSS, breathings and accents have been omitted; in all the passages quoted here, he follows his normal practice of using them sporadically and with a tendency to follow rules of his own making (though he could, when transcribing a passage for print, be reasonably accurate). In Coleridge's day there was, in any case, some controversy about their desirability and the ancient authority for them; he evidently was not taught to use them at school, and some books even published by Oxford University Press dispensed with them. Henry Nelson Coleridge is responsible for adding them when editing Coleridge's work; in *CL*, on the other hand, they are normalized. Since Coleridge is not responsible for the breathings and accents in these published works I have chosen to maintain consistency by omitting them. In my own occasional use of Greek without transliteration, I have used breathing and accents.

Square brackets are used where my own letters or words have been inserted in Coleridge's text, for the sake of coherence or presentation. Angle brackets are also given as found in the published edition of Coleridge's Notebooks. Where a word is difficult to read or unreadable in Coleridge's MSS I have used square brackets and preceded the word by a question mark: [? . . .].

In quoting from unpublished MSS, I have always given the folio number as it is represented in the top right-hand corner, whether Coleridge's own, or added later in an attempt to bring order to the notes and fragments.

FOOTNOTES

Quotations from Philo in English translation are taken from the Loeb Classical Library edition of his works.

Bibliographical details of works from ancient and classical texts are only given where a specific and/or non-standard version has been quoted. For example, the particular edition of Origen's work *Scholia in Apocalypsin*, referred to in the notes to Appendix B, is included in the bibliography.

Introduction

Much of Samuel Taylor Coleridge's work has been published for the first time in recent years. In the light of new revelations consequent upon this and upon the availability of the new critical editions of works previously published, his place in the history of ideas is being reassessed.[1] It is one of the aims of this book to contribute to this process, to suggest that Coleridge's importance is even now underestimated, and that he developed, on the ground of the Logos principle and in his 'logosophic' system, a framework for the reconciliation of thought, faith, and experience which is potentially as generative of critical thought in the areas of psychology, philosophy, and religion as, for example, the systems of F. W. J. Schelling and G. W. F. Hegel.

In his own time, Coleridge's erudition and critical insights were valued by many philosophers, literati, scientists, and prominent social figures.[2] Charles Sanders has explored his important influence in the latter half of the nineteenth century in the development of the Broad Church movement through the work of liberal Churchmen and theologians such as J. Hare, F. J. A. Hort, and F. D. Maurice.[3] Yet many castigated Coleridge for obscurity or

[1] See e.g. *The Collected Works of Samuel Taylor Coleridge* (yet to be completed), 16 vols., Bollingen Series (Princeton, NJ, Princeton University Press). This contains much previously unpublished material.
[2] e.g. Humphry Davy (see Davy's letter to Coleridge in Mar. 1804 (*CL* ii. 1103): 'you are to be the historian of the Philosophy of feeling . . . your *spirit* . . . will appear to *all men* . . . as a fair and permanent *light*'); Gladstone (*C & S* 55 n.); and J. S. Mill (*Essay on Bentham and Coleridge*, ed. F. R. Leavis (London, 1967)). Coleridge was known and respected by German philosophers, among them Tieck and Solger. There is at least one report that Schelling too knew of his work, though the tone of Schelling's remark is (perhaps deliberately) ambiguous. Benjamin Jowett wrote that he had spoken to him 'about C.'s plagiarism; he seemed very good-natured about it, and said that C. had expressed many things better than he could himself, that in one word he had comprised a whole essay, saying that mythology was not allegorical but tautegorical' (see E. Abbott and L. Campbell, *The Life and Letters of Benjamin Jowett, M.A.*, 2 vols. (London, 1897), i. 146; quoted in *SM: LS* 30 n. 3).
[3] C. R. Sanders, *Coleridge and the Broad Church Movement* (Durham, NC, 1942).

plagiarism,[4] and many who at one time had supported him (for example, Joseph Cottle, John Thelwall, the Wedgwood family, and Wordsworth) lost patience with his melancholy, his religious intensity, the self-abuse of his opium addiction, and his seeming incapacity with regard to personal, domestic, and financial affairs. That he was acutely aware of such opprobrium and criticism, often feeling betrayed by his friends, is evident from letters and notebook entries.

Today, Coleridge's claims to have developed a philosophical system are still rarely taken seriously. Perhaps J. S. Mill's assessment of his thought as beyond the comprehension of his contemporaries is still relevant.[5] Certainly Coleridge held a pessimistic view of the philosopher's audience in Britain:

The Philosopher must seek an Audience elsewhere than Great Britain, or submit for the vast majority of his Hearers to enact the not very flattering part of 'Old True-penny in the Cellar', and by a sort of melancholy Self-survivorship to sink into a subterranean, posthumous vox et præterea Nihil!* (N 56, fo. 8)

[* 'a voice and nothing besides']

It is reported that he remarked to two young Cambridge students who visited him 'I am a poor poet in England, but I am a great philosopher in America';[6] an opinion which appears to have been confirmed by the attentions of James Marsh,[7] and the founding of the University of Vermont on Coleridgean principles.

Coleridge planned to set out his philosophical system in one great work. The plans for his projected *magnum opus* or 'Opus Maximum' were many and various.[8] It was to be entitled, significantly, 'Logosophia'. In almost every description of this system

---

[4] For a detailed analysis of this aspect of Coleridge's reputation, see T. McFarland, *Coleridge and the Pantheist Tradition* (Oxford, 1969). See also Thomas Carlyle's scathing attack (*Life of John Sterling* (London, 1852), 67–85); and that of J. F. Ferrier ('The Plagiarisms of S. T. Coleridge', *Blackwood's Edinburgh Magazine*, 47 (1840), 287–99). 'Coleridge with all his logosophy was no philosopher,' wrote James Stirling (*The Secret of Hegel* (Edinburgh, 1865), 28).

[5] See Mill, *Bentham and Coleridge*.

[6] T. Reid, *The Life, Letters, and Friendships of Richard Monckton Milnes* (London, 1890), ii. 432.

[7] James Marsh was President of the University of Vermont (1826–33), which he attempted to run on Coleridgean principles. He published his own edition of *AR* with 'Preliminary Essay' in 1829.

[8] T. McFarland details some of these ('Coleridge's *Magnum Opus*', in *Romanticism and the Forms of Ruin* (Princeton, NJ, 1981), 359–61).

the term 'Logos' features prominently.[9] It is my aim here to show that the Logos is the unifying factor of Coleridge's 'system' (for such he claimed to have established) and the 'key' to understanding every area of his thought after 1805.

In comparison with the huge volume of articles and books on Coleridge's poetry and on aspects of his contribution to literary criticism, there have been relatively few studies of his religious thought. There are even fewer which have explored his attempted reconciliation of philosophy and religion through the concept of Logos.

J. H. Muirhead, in *Coleridge as Philosopher*, has explored Coleridge's 'theological Platonism' and provides a chapter on the Idea and the personal Being of God in Coleridge's philosophy of religion; but he gives little specific attention to the Logos concept.[10] In contrast to J. D. Boulger's study *Coleridge as Religious Thinker*, which focuses on the integration in Coleridge's thought of the Platonic tradition with Christian doctrine, and refers to 'the rationality of the Logos',[11] my own study emphasizes the influence of, for example, *Gefühlsphilosophie*[12] and the differences between Coleridge's concept of Logos and that of the Platonic tradition. While the Logos is for Boulger a peripheral theme, my own study takes it as the centre and circumference of Coleridge's system. J. Robert Barth states that he has not attempted to follow Boulger in taking the relation of philosophy to religion in Coleridge's thought as his focus;[13] rather, he is concerned with the latter's treatment of Christian doctrine and belief. Hence, for example, in referring to the Logos, Barth

[9] See e.g. his letter to Frances Langham (*CL* vi. 736, 5 June 1817); see also *BL* i. 302.
[10] J. H. Muirhead, *Coleridge as Philosopher* (London, 1930), 110, 217–55.
[11] J. D. Boulger, *Coleridge as Religious Thinker* (New Haven, Conn., 1961), 141.
[12] The term '*Gefühlsphilosophie*' may be translated as 'the philosophy of feeling'; this in the double sense of the emotions (sensibility) *and* of sensation, i.e. the ground of all experience, accepted here as the basis of human knowledge. J. G. Hamann (1730–88) and F. H. Jacobi (1743–1819) were two of the leading exponents of this movement in thought. They delighted in Hume's subversion of a priori foundations of human reason, on which rationalist philosophies had been constructed, but developed his empiricism in quite different directions from that which Hume himself had envisaged. Human reason, they insisted, rightly included the activity of the whole personality; that is, sensation, emotion, belief or faith, love, and conscience.
[13] J. R. Barth, *Coleridge and Christian Doctrine* (New York, 1987), p. vii.

concentrates on the Logos of the Fourth Gospel. In contrast, my emphasis has been on Coleridge's attempted reconciliation of religion with philosophy. The idea of the Logos is as much a philosophical principle as a focus of religious faith. I suggest that any treatment of the Logos theme which ignores this polarity must fail to do justice to his thought. My own study covers a wider range of his writings and ideas than that taken by David Pym in *The Religious Thought of Samuel Taylor Coleridge*, the steady focus of which is Coleridge's theology.[14]

David Jasper's study *Coleridge as Poet and Religious Thinker* recognizes the importance of the Logos theme,[15] but his treatment of it is necessarily brief since his main focus is the relationship between Coleridge's literary and religious thought. While exploring Coleridge's logocentricity in his philosophy of language and in his concept of symbol, I have, in contrast, deliberately paid little attention here to his poetry or to his place in the field of literary criticism. David Newsome has dedicated a chapter to a useful exploration of the Logos theme in *Two Classes of Men*, and Stephen Prickett acknowledges, in *Romanticism and Religion*, that he owes to Newsome his own brief exposition of the Logos. In *Words and the Word* he explores Coleridge's theme of the divine Word of God in creation linking this to the 'logos' of the 'arbitrary language of humanity' which 'evolves and *desynonymizes*'.[16] The focus is on the divine Word of the Bible, on theories of the imagination, on 'logos' as a prominent literary and poetic theme. Relatively little attention is given to Coleridge's use of Logos as a unifying philosophical, psychological or 'theanthropic' principle. My study differs from these in three important respects: firstly, in the centrality which it gives to the Logos idea; secondly, in suggesting that this idea is the 'key' to an understanding of Coleridge's claim to have established a unified system of thought and experience; and finally, in that I take the approach of a historian of ideas.

Within the last decade, books and articles have appeared which have included reference to the importance of Coleridge's Logos

---

[14] D. Pym, *The Religious Thought of Samuel Taylor Coleridge* (Gerrards Cross, 1970).

[15] D. Jasper, *Coleridge as Poet and Religious Thinker* (London, 1985), 140–3.

[16] D. Newsome, *Two Classes of Men* (London, 1974), 79–80; S. Prickett, *Romanticism and Religion* (Cambridge, 1976), 25; *Words and the Word* (Cambridge, 1986), 133–9.

idea in the context of his concept of nature,[17] in the light of his
treatment of the Christian Trinity,[18] and in the context of the
related concept of polarity.[19] Two studies in particular have re-
cently given more attention to the Logos theme: James Clayton
has explored Coleridge's concept of the Logos as Reason, espec-
ially in the light of Kant's influence,[20] and Graham Davidson's
book *Coleridge's Career* explores both Coleridge's Christology
and the relation of this to the latter's concept of history.[21] There
are significant points of disagreement between Clayton's reading
of the Logos theme and my own; for example, between Clayton's
claim that 'Coleridge always thinks of reason in Platonic terms as
the power of mind to apprehend eternal reality beyond what is
accessible to the physical senses',[22] and my own emphasis on the
difference between Coleridge's view of Reason and that of the
Platonic tradition.[23] My approach differs from that of Davidson
too, in that I have explored the Logos theme from the point of
view of Coleridge's place in the history of ideas and as a response
to philosophical as well as moral dilemmas.

Here, Coleridge's 'logosophic' system is explored in the con-
text of the thought of his contemporaries and of those seminal
thinkers in the Western intellectual tradition who most influenced
his work. He himself believed that his was 'the only attempt I
know, ever made to reduce all knowledges into harmony' (*TT* i.
248). This claim provides the background against which my study
is drawn. As a history of ideas, it will take an expository and
comparative form rather than that of a critique of Coleridge's
philosophical principles or method. An attempt to trace the
unifying principle of the Logos idea will, I hope, give a new
perspective on his thought and show it to be of a more coherent
nature than has generally been allowed. The Logos principle acts
as a 'decoder' of his work, especially of the more fragmentary
notes and annotations; that is, it illuminates obscure connections
of thought and explains what, if it is not understood, appear as

[17] R. Modiano, *Coleridge and the Concept of Nature* (London, 1985).
[18] D. Hardy, 'Coleridge on the Trinity', *Anglican Theological Review*, 69 (1987),
145–55.
[19] J. S. Cutsinger, 'Coleridgean Polarity and Theological Vision', *Harvard
Theological Review*, 76 (1983), 91–108.
[20] J. Clayton, 'Coleridge and the Logos: The Trinitarian Unity of Conscious-
ness and Culture', *Journal of Religion*, 70 (1990), 213–40.
[21] G. Davidson, *Coleridge's Career* (London, 1990), 152–79 and 218–47.
[22] Clayton, 'Coleridge and the Logos', 214.
[23] See below, Chs. 3.2 and 4.1.

eccentric assumptions or muddled reasoning. I will suggest that his criticisms and corrections of past and contemporary thinkers are more easily comprehended in the light of the logocentricity[24] of his own work. I will pay special attention to Coleridge's philosophical and religious thought (one of his chief aims was to show the unity of philosophy and religion through the logosophic system); particularly to those later writings (*c.* 1826–34) in which his ideas were most fully developed.

Since Coleridge's thought not only covered an extraordinarily wide range of disciplines and subject-matter, but was also stimulated by his extensive reading in the whole history of Western thought, the scope of this study might be recognized as problematical. The Logos idea has, however, provided the necessary framework of selection and connection here. In many respects, his Logos is typical of a 'unit idea';[25] he believed it recurred in different guises and could be traced through the history of religious and philosophical thought. His own treatment of the subject drew extensively on this history. Reading Coleridge, particularly his unpublished notes and annotations, presents problems. It might be described, perhaps, as not only an acquired taste, but an acquired art. Taken out of context, his thought can appear either banal or eccentric. Because much of his work, published or unpublished, is in the form of annotations or notes, irritatingly oblique or esoteric references are frequently made without further clarification. The length of his sentences, the frequent parentheses and digressions, all make the task of following his thought a difficult one. One of the aims of this book is to show that his thought can best be understood *as a whole*; that is, in the light of the connecting themes which appear, disappear,

---

[24] The term 'logocentricity' is not reducible here to that aspect of Western thought which Derrida so powerfully criticizes (see e.g. 'Dialogues with Jacques Derrida', in Richard Kearney, *Dialogues with Contemporary Continental Thinkers* (Manchester, 1984), 108): it merely reflects Coleridge's own description of the underlying ethos of his work and its main theme.

[25] A. O. Lovejoy's concept of 'unit ideas', ideas which can be traced through various modifications in history, such as the idea of God, or freedom (*Essays in the History of Ideas* (Baltimore, Md., 1948)), perhaps risks neglecting the uniqueness of historical, social, and cultural contexts. In many respects, however, Coleridge's Logos is typical of a 'unit idea'; there is no doubt that Coleridge *does* take the idea of Logos to be one which recurs in different guises and is traceable through the history of religious and philosophical thought. His own treatment of the subject draws on this history.

and reappear, running through his whole output of notes, annotations, letters, fragments, and published works. Often, his brief annotation of a certain work will shed light on a perplexing passage in a notebook, and vice versa; what had previously seemed obscure and vaguely mystical will then appear as part of a lucid and creatively rational process.

Coleridge was often critical of those thinkers of whose influence on his own thought he was most aware. Through a process of dialectical thinking,[26] he proposed a method and system which, he believed, identified the sources and offered a possible resolution of problems, dichotomies, and failures within the philosophical and theological conventions of his time. He believed he had found a solution to what he saw as an increasing fragmentation and alienation in human thought and experience. His work was both greatly enriched by the relational emphasis[27] out of which this solution emerged, and yet also hampered by the inevitable complexities arising from such an approach. The proposed 'Logosophia' or 'Opus Maximum' may itself have suffered from the difficulty of deciding upon a starting-point in what was a closely woven methodological circle. The frequent changes which appear in the various lists of intended subjects, and in his own preoccupations, are a consequence of his struggle to find a principle (one which would incorporate, but not be constrained by, the forms of the speculative intellect) through which ontological, epistemological, and existential unity might be established.

A close reading reveals significant themes related to the nature and function of the Logos which recur frequently in every area of Coleridge's thought. His method, which, because of the incomplete nature of his system, is not always easy to identify, is in many ways similar to that of Immanuel Kant, whom he greatly admired. Coleridge too began his philosophical explorations by acknowledging the interdependence of experience and ideas, and

---

[26] Here 'dialectical' signifies a process of thought or internal argument through oppositions or polarities (Coleridge always distinguished these from contradictions) in a manner which is developed in Kant's antinomies of reason. However, it should be said that Coleridge believed these oppositions to be not merely regulative of our concepts but living, dynamic, and productive both logically and ontologically. In this sense, his thought has more in common with Hegel.

[27] My use of this phrase will, I hope, become clear. It relates to the importance of polarity, of triunity, of the I–Thou relation in every aspect of Coleridge's work, and to the Logos as the principle of relationship.

searched for the antecedent unity which he, with Kant, believed
to be the condition of both. Unlike Kant, we shall see, he believed
that the source of this unity could be encountered and known.
Again, his thought is often developed dialectically, through
oppositions, connections, and relationships which have much in
common with those explored by Hegel. Coleridge reworked the
ideas, theories, and critiques both of classical theology and of
contemporary philosophy into his own scheme. He developed his
themes across a whole range of disciplines and subject areas,
sometimes showing a deep awareness of historical and cultural
context, sometimes disregarding this and leaping with discon-
certing ease from the fifth century BC to the Renaissance, and
from thence to the preoccupations common to many in his own
time.[28] His work offers a positive hermeneutic which recognizes
the psychological and epistemological questions underlying issues
of interpretation and method.[29] The epistemological and psy-
chological principles on which his 'logosophic' system is based
reflect Kant's emphasis on the synthesis of the unity of appercep-
tion and the latter's theory of the rational will.[30] Coleridge also
drew on the insights of J. G. Fichte and F. W. J. Schelling,
blending these in his exposition of an 'ideal Realism' in which the
ideal is never opposed to the real, and in which ideas are their
own evidence and *constitutive* of reality (N 37, fo. 44ᵛ). He
adopted F. H. Jacobi's emphasis on conscience, feeling, and faith
as the necessary condition of every act of knowledge.[31]

The exposition which I give of the logocentric theme in
Coleridge's writings does not follow a chronological order. Such
an arrangement would, I think, be misleading in the light of the
dialectical and sometimes recapitulatory way in which he devel-
oped his ideas, especially in the notebooks. One focus of his

---

[28] Coleridge's notebooks and annotations of the works of others give evidence
of this wide range of thought. In notebook NQ, for example, Coleridge moved
from Newton and Laplace (fo. 23), to John Wycliff (fos. 5 ff.), to Thomas Fuller
(fo. 36), to Southey's Naval History (fo. 59), to Homer (fo. 70) and Aristotle (fo.
79).
[29] This hermeneutical aspect of Coleridge's work has been explored in E. S.
Schaffer's article 'The Hermeneutic Community: Coleridge and Schleiermacher',
in R. Gravil and M. Lefebure (eds.), *The Coleridge Connection* (London, 1990),
200–9. See also Coleridge's notebook NQ, where he gives notes on reading a text
and the psychological factors involved (e.g. fos. 15ᵛ, 67).
[30] See below, e.g. Chs. 3.4 and 4.3.
[31] See below, e.g. Chs. 3.2 and 4.3.

interest would inspire another which then led him back to a reappraisal and modification of the first. He often abandoned a theme only to take it up with renewed vigour months or even years later. This study acknowledges the pattern of Coleridge's own thought in which a starting-point of argument or exposition, or a radically new development, is often hard to identify since each topic or theme is inextricably bound up with those others which form together the whole context of his thought. Thus the chapter headings, representing what I take to be the principal aspects of his idea of Logos, do not belong exclusively to any one particular period, but provided the framework of coherence in his thought from the early years of the nineteenth century.

The 'logosophic' system is both dynamic and relational. It goes beyond formal logic (though Coleridge takes to task any philosopher whose logic is weak), making use of the tool of Kant's 'transcendental logic', and of a concept of reason which includes conscience, faith and imagination. Coleridge maintained that human reason reflects the nature of the divine Logos, communicated to humanity. We shall find that the concept of divine *perichoresis*[32] is mirrored in his system; in the themes of distinction-in-unity, of interpersonal relations, and of dynamic polarities as methodological tools. In the notes for the 'Opus Maximum', for example, the thesis–antithesis–synthesis progression (as explored by Kant, Fichte, and Schelling) is constantly in evidence, though in modified form. The main themes of Coleridge's thought are constantly reassessed and modified, yet despite their organic and relational nature he asserted, as their ground, an unchanging Prothetic reality. The archetypal reality which he represented by the *tetractys* figure[33]

---

[32] *'Perichoresis'* is used here in the sense of dynamic, reciprocal indwelling as in the relationships of the Trinity. Stephen H. Ford has briefly explored this concept in Coleridge's thought ('Perichoresis and Interpenetration: Samuel Taylor Coleridge's Trinitarian Conception of Unity', *Theology*, 89 (1986), 20–4): 'we are indebted to Samuel Taylor Coleridge . . . for contributing to English-speaking theology the technical trinitarian term "interpenetration", the equivalent of "perichoresis"'. Ford finds this idea in Coleridge's *Theory of Life* where ' "interpenetrate" is synonymous with "coinherence" ("perichoresis")' (p. 22); and shows how Coleridge explores prayer as the expression of *perichoresis*. He emphasizes that, for Coleridge, 'intercirculating love unites without blending' (ibid.).

[33] The 'prothesis' is the highest term in Coleridge's four-termed *tetractys* figure. He adopts this Pythagorean symbol (see e.g. *PL* 108–9; *CN* iii, § 4427) as a

not only provided the object, goal, and content of his thought, but also the pattern and inspiration of his method.

There were, I will suggest, only two major shifts in his perspective: one in 1805, and another towards the end of the second decade of the nineteenth century, the latter provoked by his growing dissatisfaction with Schelling's philosophy. Both of these I take to be directly or indirectly attributable to the development of the Logos theme. Otherwise there are few clear divisions in his thought. On the contrary, it evolves not in linear fashion, but in a manner reminiscent of Hegel: more like the progressive describing of a circle in which the circumference is always related to its centre; here, the Logos. Despite the many and various currents of thought and emphases which assume centrality at different periods, then lapse and later re-emerge, Coleridge's thought is, taken as a whole, integrated and coherent.

The Logos Theme

The chapter headings, providing a framework within which the exploration of his ideas can be structured, are drawn from significant words and phrases constantly used by Coleridge to represent the second person of the Christian Trinity, the Logos, the Creator and Communicator of God to Man. His Logos idea was drawn from the meanings and functions of the term *'logos'* in Greek philosophy and from the Logos of the Christian tradition, based on the Fourth Gospel. We shall see that, in many respects,

dynamic expression of the supreme divine reality and of the life principle within finite reality. The Pythagorean *tetractys* has a base of the number four, and yet contains all numbers up to ten, thus symbolizing the whole of reality. It represents, according to Coleridge, not only thesis, antithesis, and synthesis, but the source and end of these: 'prothesis'. It expresses polarity, movement and relation, proportion and creative power (see also below, Ch. 1.2). Two of the secondary sources in which Coleridge would have found this symbol explored are: W. G. Tennemann, *Geschichte der Philosophie*, 12 vols. (Leipzig, 1798–1819), i. 107 (some of Coleridge's marginal notes are to be found on this page); and T. Stanley, *History of Philosophy*, 4th edn. (London, 1743), 433. Stanley wrote: 'The Tetrad connects all Beings, of Elements, Numbers, Seasons of the Year, Coaevous Society; neither can we name anything which depends not on the Tetractys, as its Root and Principle: for it is as we said, the Maker and Cause of all things; Intelligible God, Author of celestial and sensible Good.'

his thought reflects the Logos idea of Heraclitus,[34] which, as W. K. C. Guthrie writes, 'seems so puzzlingly to be at the same time the word he utters, the truth which it contains, and the external reality which he conceives himself to be describing':[35] a description which might almost equally well fit Coleridge's exposition of Logos. Perhaps even more important in the 'logosophic' theme is the development of what the latter took to be the prophetic visionary themes of Philo's Logos idea; these he found had much in common with the Fourth Gospel.[36] A further influence was Plotinus' recognition of the divine principle of distinction-in-unity; though Coleridge is, on other counts, critical of Plotinus and of Neoplatonism generally.

He was well read in Patristic theology: there are, we shall see, striking parallels between his theme and, for example, Origen's concept of Logos.[37] His system owes much, too, to his reading of Augustine, of Scholastic and Reformation theology, and to the work of the English divines of the seventeenth century.[38]

[34] In his published works and in many of the unpublished notes Coleridge frequently cites Heraclitus. His knowledge of Heraclitus was probably derived mostly from Tennemann (*Geschichte der Philosophie*, i. 209–39), from Stanley (*History of Philosophy*, 499–506), and from F. D. E. Schleiermacher (*Herakleitos der dunkle, von Ephesos, dargestellt aus den Trümmern seines Werkes und den Zeugnissen der Alten*, in *Museum der Alterthums-Wissenschaft*, eds. F. A. Wolf and P. Buttman, 2 vols. (Berlin, 1807–10), I. iv. 315–533; see *CN* iii, § 3656 n.). Coleridge intends his 'dynamic system' to be a reworking of the Heraclitean philosophy in which the idea of *logos* is so central, an exposition of 'the very rudiments of "Heraclitus redivivus"' (*CL* iv. 775).

[35] W. K. C. Guthrie, *The Greek Philosophers from Thales to Plato* (London, 1967), 14.

[36] An important source of Coleridge's knowledge of Philo's idea of Logos was John Whitaker's *The Origins of Arianism Disclosed* (London, 1791). Coleridge heavily annotated several pages of Whitaker's discussion of the origins of the Logos term in Philo and its concurrence with St John (pp. 34–41). Coleridge's marginal notes explore the historical and religious context of Philo's writings and their relation to the cabbala and to Greek philosophy. Many of the particular aspects of the Logos theme of Philo became central elements of Coleridge's own 'logosophic' system; most of these aspects are also discussed by Whitaker. It is clear that Coleridge was not an unequivocal admirer of Whitaker's interpretation: he described Whitaker's 'absolute naked Tritheism' (pp. 132, 266). However, it is not clear at what date this criticism was added: Coleridge, in a marginal note commenting on his own earlier annotations, made clear the 'many years' which had elapsed between his first and his later use of this source. For an indication that Coleridge read Philo himself see N 42, fo. 15.

[37] The parallels between the Logos themes of Origen and Coleridge are explored below; see e.g. Chs. 1.3 and 4.1. and App. B.

[38] See below, Chs. 1.1, 1.2, and 4.1.; also *CM* ii. 291, 319.

The writings of the Christian mystics, especially those of Jacob
Böhme,[39] provided another source of inspiration for the develop-
ment of his theme. He also draws on the metaphysical poets
(Donne and Milton) and the Christian Platonists (Henry More).[40]
Finally, Coleridge found a model for his 'Logosophia' in the
German philosophies of self-consciousness (in Kant, Fichte, and
Schelling). These provided him with a stimulus towards the de-
velopment of a unified system in which thought and being, the
life of the imagination and the life of nature, the experience of
positive good and evil, might be reconciled.[41]

Coleridge himself constantly reaffirmed that the Logos of the
Prologue to the Fourth Gospel was an essential and fundamental
ground of his system. James Gillman wrote that: 'he continued
attached to the writings of St John and St Paul for thirty-four
years of his life'.[42] This indicates that Coleridge became 'attached'
to the Fourth Gospel at around the turn of the century, the time
when, as his notebooks and letters show, he was becoming dis-
satisfied with Unitarianism and the 'necessitarian' philosophies of
David Hartley and Joseph Priestley. If, as this suggests, the
Fourth Gospel was an important factor in the change which was
firmly established in 1805, it seems the Logos of the Prologue
convinced him finally that the Trinity could be accepted not
merely as an intellectual representation, but in faith and con-
science. He set out to discover 'if Christ be that Logos or Word
that *was in the beginning*, by whom all things *became*; if it was the
same Christ who said, *Let there be Light*: who in and by the
creation commenced that great redemptive process, the history of
life which begins in its detachment from Nature and is to end in
its union with God' (*CM* iii. 919). Coleridge came to believe that
the Logos of (as he thought) St John, was the most perfect
expression of the divine Word, who is also Light and Life, both
Son of God and Son of Man. These characteristics of Logos were
to be, in Coleridgean terminology, the 'Ideas' (an echo of Plato's

[39] His annotations of Böhme often contain references to the Logos theme and
to Böhme's own rendering of it (e.g. *CM* i. 583, 591).

[40] For Coleridge's identification of the Logos with Christ see his annotations on
Henry More's *Theological Works* (1708) (e.g. *CM* iii. 919).

[41] The influence of Kant, Fichte, and Schelling will be constantly referred to
and explored throughout this thesis in relation to all the different aspects of
Coleridge's Logos idea. See e.g. nn. 12 and 26 above.

[42] J. Gillman, *Life of S. T. Coleridge* (London, 1838), 317.

living spiritual and intellectual realities) on which his philosophy was based and the foci around which it developed. We shall trace these Ideas in their thematic course through his various writings.

Within each of the themes presented under these chapter headings, I have outlined the network of philosophical and hermeneutical relationships which Coleridge described. The first chapter explores his idea of Logos as Word; an exposition of Logos as the foundation of etymology, linguistic philosophy, of symbol and imagination, and of revelation. The next chapter examines his identification of Logos as 'Light and Life', the source of the powers and products of nature and the key to the proper understanding of the physical sciences. Following this, his concept of Reason is examined (Logos as Idea, as Law, and as the unity of Reason and Will). Finally, I trace Coleridge's concept of Logos as the divine Humanity or Idea of Man; not only, as in classical theology, the archetype or pattern of universal humanity, but also the idea of Self and of Person. The Appendices risk wider and more speculative comparisons than seemed appropriate in the main body of the text. Here parallels are traced between aspects of Coleridge's Logos idea and themes in the work of his contemporaries (that is, of Wilhelm von Humboldt and Hegel). I also suggest that the Logos idea in some sense bridges the vast historical distance between the thought of Coleridge, that of Origen in the third century, and that of Teilhard de Chardin in the twentieth.

In order to do justice to the inclusive and relational nature of the Logos idea this study involves an integrated approach to different disciplines. In establishing a methodological and hermeneutical framework, it has been necessary to 'juggle' with the disciplines of literary critical theory, theology, and the history of ideas. The first has frequently provided the background for Coleridge scholarship, but, while valuing the insights which it provides, I have not made it the focus of this study. The second has been important both as an aid to my own understanding of the background to Coleridge's religious thought and to my assessment of the interest and significance of the Logos theme. It has also allowed me to take seriously his basic premiss: that intelligibility presupposes a unity of distinctions, and that all human knowledge, communication, life, and experience may comprise a unified whole which could be knowable only through

the reconciliation of reason, will, faith, and conscience. The third
has provided the broad angle of approach which is necessary to
cope with the enormous range and scope of his reading, his
criticism, and his ideas, and through which it is possible to find
that perspective which has led to my proposal of the Logos as the
central 'key'.

Coleridge agreed with idealist philosophy (for example, with
the emphasis on ideal reality in Fichte, Schelling, and Hegel) in
so far as he too asserted an ultimate unity of Being and Mind
which provided the correspondence of mind with objective reality.
I will suggest that he quite consciously and deliberately built his
system on the Logos as unifying principle and that, consequently,
this is the 'key' element by which its intelligibility and coherence
are established. He maintained both the possibility and the
necessity of seeking out those underlying laws of consciousness
which are the ground and explanation of all knowledge. His
'system', however, is one which involves paradox and polarity;
it is never one of exclusion or rigidity. The Logos as Word,
Reason, 'alterity' (distinction), form, combines with *Sophia*, the
Spirit of love and energy, the dynamic principle of organic unity.
This was to be the basis of the 'Logosophia'.

The reconstruction inherent in any reading of a text[43] involves
not only dangers but also, one hopes, the possibility of a positive
contribution. I have taken Coleridge's expressed intentions as
more than merely the manifestation of 'a hidden agenda', and,
with reservations, I have accepted that it is possible to encounter
something of the *real* Coleridge through a critical attention to his
writings. To this encounter I have attributed a certain autonomy.
I have found the study of his thought enlightening, provoking,
and exciting. Such an involvement, I believe, need not be un-
critical (though, I have said, this study is not primarily a critique
of Coleridge's philosophy), and is to some extent necessary in
any act of interpretation. I remain convinced (and here I would
claim allegiance with such as Leo Spitzer, R. Bultmann, H.-G.

---

[43] Reconstruction must be distinguished from Collingwood's *reproduction* of
the past: 'the historian must re-enact the past in his own mind . . . re-thinking for
himself the thought of his author' (R. G. Collingwood, *The Idea of History*
(Oxford, 1946), 282–3).

Gadamer, M. Polanyi, and Stanley Fish[44]) that not only is the exclusion of all empathy and emotional response probably impossible, but that such a reading would be impoverished. The grounds on which Coleridge rejected Spinoza's suggestion that the 'I' should be set aside in the philosophical task[45] are convincing.

The preformed questions with which I came to this study were modified by my reading, which in turn provoked new questions. The extent to which these are the 'real' questions, and the extent to which the answers I have found are a true representation of Coleridge's thought, are issues which involve a complexity of critical theory from which I have here deliberately remained detached. For example, while valuing the Deconstructionist critique which reveals every reading as in some sense misleading, and Paul de Man's metaphorical suggestion that it may be only the blind who (fortuitously) have insight,[46] as a useful piece of 'grit' in the 'oyster', both for a reading of Coleridge and as a critique of my own work, I yet remain suspicious of what often appears to be a variety of the self-referential paradox. This is manifest in an incompatibility between, on the one hand, the necessary, implicit, and inescapable belief in the genuineness and 'good faith' of his or her own criticism on the part of the Deconstructionist, and, on the other, an insistence on the hidden agendas and unacknowledged motives of all texts. Deconstruction, in this way, presents its own unacknowledged metaphysic of truth and falsity, which appears to me to surpass in its audacity any Coleridgean claim.

---

[44] See L. Spitzer, *A Method of Interpreting Literature* (Mensha, Wis., 1949), 5, 20; R. Bultmann has argued for 'demythologization' and the recognition that God's revelation of himself (in this case, in Scripture) takes place by and through the context of our own culture, historical situation, and personal experience; see *Faith and Understanding*, ed. R. W. Funk, tr. L. Pettibone Smith (London, 1969), 300–11. Hans-Georg Gadamer has suggested that it is neither necessary nor helpful to seek to establish a pure, objective 'neutrality' in the approach to a text; *Wahrheit und Methode* (Tübingen, 1960); tr. from 2nd edn. by W. Glen-Doepel as *Truth and Method* (London, 1975), 285. For M. Polanyi's position see n. 59 below; see also S. Fish, *Is there a Text in this Class?* (Cambridge, Mass., 1980), 42–52.

[45] BL MS Egerton 2801, fo. 11.

[46] Paul de Man has suggested that the very blindness which prevents critics from noticing the 'gap' between their statements *about* the nature of literature and the results of their own criticism in fact leads to valuable insights; *Blindness and Insight: Essays in the Rhetoric of Contemporary Criticism* (London, 1983).

The Logosophic System: An Introductory Overview

'The Logos', wrote Thomas Ashe in the late nineteenth century, 'is Coleridge's fetish.'[47] Whether or not it may be described as obsessional, there is no doubt that, from 1805 on, the Logos theme constantly and emphatically recurred. Earlier, as the 1795 Lectures show, Coleridge had agreed with Joseph Priestley's Unitarian conception of the Logos as an expression of an attribute of God; of the divine power and intelligence which *was* God (*LPR* 200 and n). This intelligence had been imparted to the man Jesus 'by immediate Inspiration'. With Priestley, Coleridge mocked the Gnostics' mystical conception of the relation of Christ to the Logos (*LPR* 199). He noted that Plato had represented the Intelligence which is manifested in the visible world as *'o Λογος'* (the Logos). He found Plato 'quaint' and endearing at this stage, and no doubt considered his use of the term merely another example of '[t]he sunny mist, the luminous gloom of Plato' (*CN* i. 528).

Yet the Logos became the cause of Coleridge's rejection of Unitarianism, the means by which he was finally able 'to reconcile personality with infinity' (*BL* i. 201) and by which the philosophical acceptance of triunity was transformed into Trinitarian faith in a God who revealed himself in the Person of the Logos who is Christ. In February 1805, after reading 'Horsley's Letters in Rep. to Dr P.',[48] Coleridge had a sudden revelation of 'an awful Truth. . . . No Christ, No God!' (*CN* ii, § 2448). An earlier notebook entry shows him to have been pondering, in the light of Bishop Samuel Horsley's (1733–1806) work, the idea of Logos in the writings of the 'Platonic Fathers' of the Church: 'Reason, Proportion, communicable Intelligibility intelligent and communicant, the WORD' (*CN* ii, § 2445). From this point on, he was intellectually convinced; but the idea of Logos was to become much more than a philosophic principle. The desire for a fuller and richer experience of the truth which he believed he had found, and of the consequent error of the Unitarian position, was present even then: 'O that this Conviction may work upon me

---

[47] 'On the Prometheus of Aeschylus', in S. T. Coleridge, *Miscellanies, Aesthetic and Literary*, ed. T. Ashe (London, 1885), 59. Ashe writes this impatient footnote to Coleridge's mention of the Logos.

[48] S. Horsley, *Tracts in Controversy with Dr Priestley*, 2nd edn. (Gloucester, 1789).

and in me / and that my mind may be made up as to the character of Jesus, and of historical Christianity, as clearly as it is of the Logos and intellectual or spiritual Christianity—that I may be made to know either their especial and peculiar Union, or their absolute disunion in any peculiar Sense' (*CN* ii, § 2448). Coleridge pursued this inner conviction; it led him to an understanding of the Logos as the 'Jehovah-Word'[49] of the Hebrews, as the historical Jesus, and as the Providence and Idea of all history.

He had arrived at a philosophical recognition of the fundamental value of the concept of triunity before his conversion to orthodox Trinitarian Christianity. He described his position at the time of his attempts to procure subscribers to the *Watchman* (1796): 'I was at that time and long after, though a Trinitarian (i.e. *ad normam Platonis* [following the manner of Plato]) in philosophy, yet a zealous Unitarian in religion.' His education, like that of most young gentlemen of the time, had included an intensive study of classics of Greek and Roman literature, and he had supplemented this from his own wide reading of, for example, Cudworth's *True Intellectual System of the Universe* (1678) and James Burnet's *Antient Metaphysics*.[50] He wrote to Thelwall in November 1796 ordering the works of Proclus, Plotinus, and Porphyry among others, no doubt to increase

---

[49] Coleridge uses the term 'Jehovah' or 'Jehova' frequently, in common with most of the religious writers of his own time. He appeared to suggest that 'Jehovah' is a variant representation of the Greek O ΩN—which he translated as 'The Being or God' (*TT* ii. 237).

[50] Coleridge only rarely mentions the work of James Burnet (Lord Monboddo) (see e.g. *CL* ii. 679); but his interests suggest that he had probably read Burnet's *Antient Metaphysics* (6 vols. (London, 1779–99)) and also Burnet's *Of the Origin and Progress of Language* (6 vols. (Edinburgh, 1773–92)). Burnet traces the development of language and speculates about its origins. Coleridge's concerns seem to echo those of Burnet; the latter also, for example, speculated about whether language was a gift from God or whether it was a purely natural development (*Of the Origin and Progress of Language*, II. ii., pp. 182–94). Like Coleridge, he pondered the question 'which was most necessary, language for the institution of society, or society of the invention of language' (ibid. I. ii. 196), though his conclusion is different from Coleridge's assertion that 'language and a state of Society mutually presuppose each other . . . neither can be the first—neither can be said to begin. . . . Language was taught and at the same time the Social State instituted by *God*' (N 33, fos. 2ᵛ–3). Burnet believed that society must have been first (*Of the Origin and Progress of Language*, I. ii. 197). Another interesting parallel is Burnet's emphasis on *logos*, and on the distinction between λόγος ἐνδιάθετος (unspoken, inner word or thought) and λόγος προϑορικός (expressed or uttered word) (ibid. I. i. 7 n.). This theme was later taken up by Coleridge too (see below, Ch. 1.3).

his first-hand knowledge of their work. His earliest works (for example, the 1795 *Lectures*) show his familiarity with Plato, though his admiration increased greatly with maturity. His reference to Plato in connection with his own philosophical and ontological acceptance of Trinity indicates that he had, before the turn of the century, absorbed the latter's triunity of sameness, difference, and unity.[51] Coleridge was familiar with the adoption of this Platonic theme into Christian theology: 'I considered the *idea* of the Trinity a fair scholastic inference from the being of God, as a creative intelligence; and that it was therefore entitled to the rank of an *esoteric* doctrine of natural religion. But seeing in the same no practical or moral bearing, I confined it to the schools of philosophy' (*BL* i. 204). At this point, the Logos could be accepted as a hypostasis, as a self-sufficient substance or 'Person'; but Coleridge could not identify the Logos with the historical Jesus. He was unable, for example, to accept the vicarious atonement of the Cross as compatible with a beneficent God. He had, however, accepted the Pythagorean and Platonic concepts of a triune reality of dynamic form, distinction, and relation (*CN* iii. 3814). It is from this basis that he was later able to recognize the Logos as the principle of distinction, of 'alterity' (*LR* iv. 2) as *Deus alter et idem*.

Coleridge believed the completion and perfection of philosophy was to be found in its transformation from the role of the abstract and analytical understanding to an 'ideal Realism' (*BL* i. 303).[52] He had become convinced that the Trinity was not merely an intellectual solution, but provided the only way in which human being and experience could be understood. In May 1810 he wrote: 'The doctrine of Sin & Redemption first authorized by practically necessitating the doctrine of the Trinity—before that Time it [the Trinity] was a pure Philosopheme tho' most beautiful

[51] Coleridge used the terms 'triune' and 'triunity' recurrently. See *SM: LS* 62 and n. He also thought it possible, if not probable, that Plato postulated supreme reality in triune form, see e.g. his notes on Robert Robinson's *Miscellaneous Works* (Harlow, 1807), iii. 130.

[52] Coleridge described his 'ideal Realism' in a letter to Wordsworth: 'Facts elevated into Theory—Theory into Laws—& Laws into living & intelligent Powers—true Idealism necessarily perfecting itself in Realism, & Realism refining itself into Idealism' (*CL* iv. 575); see also *BL* i. 260–3. Schelling expressed his own concept of 'ideal-realism' in his *System des transcendentalen Idealismus* (Leipzig, 1800); tr. Peter Heath as *System of Transcendental Idealism* (Charlottesville, Va., 1978), 41.

and accurate' (*CN* iii, §3814). Concerning the Trinity, 'the scholastic value, the theological necessity, of this doctrine consists in its exhibiting an idea of God, which rescues our faith from both extremes, Cabalo-Pantheism,[53] and Anthropomorphism' (*NED* ii. 263). It rescued faith, on the one hand, from the abstractions of the identity systems of Spinoza and Schelling, and from the mysticisms of the cabbala and of Böhme, and, on the other, from religious 'enthusiasm' which could see God only in terms of human characteristics and attributes. Unless the Logos were recognized as coequal and coeternal, as distinct and self-subsistent, the idea of God could not, Coleridge thought, be rescued from either a mystical abstract identity (in which the idea that '*all is God*' led inevitably to the idea that '*God is not*'), or from some kind of anthropomorphic projection which had no basis in reason.

So Coleridge's acceptance of triunity as a fundamental principle of philosophy was gradually transformed in the first few years of the nineteenth century into religious faith. He found a compatibility of personality and infinity in the very concept of the coequal Logos begotten by perfect Will and existing in a complete and perfect love relation of distinction-in-unity. The central Christian doctrine of the eternal Logos, coequal as the Son of God with the Father, the Logos who is Christ, pre-existent and incarnate, became the centre of a committed search for philosophical and theological reconciliation. This search was not merely intellectual: it was always related to the concrete reality of his own experience and to his perception of human experience in general. We shall see that it was based upon the idea of *person* and of interpersonal relationship between God and man.

Coleridge claimed that 'the historical dogmas, namely, of the incarnation of the creative Logos, and his becoming a personal agent, are themselves founded in philosophical necessity';[54] it was his constant aim to show how philosophy could be reconciled with the concrete historical experience of human beings and with religious truth. He maintained a distinction (always insisting that distinction was not to be confused with division) between the

---

[53] Coleridge is sometimes suspicious of cabbalistic mysticism; here he links it to a mystical emphasis on the divine unity of all things which he rejects.
[54] The *logosophic* system attempts to justify this claim.

philosophic *principle* of Logos, and the Logos as *Person*, so that there is always a kind of internal polarity in the theme. He attempted to establish the Logos as unifying principle (natural, moral, psychological, and aesthetic) and as the symbol which best communicated the underlying reality of the powers and forms of the physical world. He argued that the Logos reality was the unity of true self-consciousness (that is, of the rational will) which is the human ideal, the condition of imagination (as opposed to 'fancy') and of the poet's art. Through the Logos idea, the whole of life and thought were both realized and recognized as a harmonious whole. For example, the Logos was the life and form of language and symbolism, and also of the processes, relations, and institutions of the ideal nation and the state. In the language of Judaeo-Christian symbolism, the Christian Logos was the 'Jehovah-Word' revealed in the Old Testament as 'the Crusher of the Serpent's Head, the Shiloh, the Desiderium of the Nations, the Saviour of mankind, of Adam, of the Patriarchs' (N 26, fo. 53).[55] The interweaving of these philosophical and religious ideas around the Logos theme provided the foundation of Coleridge's system. This was the basis of his response to what he saw as the loss of the human ideal and the alienation within thought and within individual and social experience produced by the extremes of dualism and monism which either divided physical from metaphysical or spiritual reality, or subsumed these distinctions in an undifferentiated identity. The intellectual, psychological, and spiritual preoccupations which M. H. Abrams has identified as themes common to the Romantics and which he suggests are causally related to revolutionary political and social change;[56] these Coleridge consciously and deliberately adopted. He accepted Fichte's final and joyful conclusion in *The Vocation of*

[55] Coleridge is using 'Shiloh' in the sense in which the phrase 'until Shiloh come' (Genesis 49: 10) appears to have been interpreted by the Targums (Onkelos, Jerusalem, and pseudo-Jonathan), that is, as referring to the Messiah. This is not, however, the interpretation given by the ancient versions of the text, which suggest instead that this refers either to (*a*) the final conquest achieved by the Israelites and their meeting at the place Shiloh; or to (*b*) 'shiloh' as 'his progeny' (Late Hebrew, *'shilyah'*, 'afterbirth'); or to (*c*) a lost Hebrew cognate of the Arkkadian *'silu'*, 'ruler'. The verse obviously reflects the ascendancy of the House of David, but finds an eschatological Messianic interpretation only later in the Targums. See under 'Shiloh' in J. Hastings (ed.), *Dictionary of the Bible*, rev. and reset for 2nd edn. by F. C. Grant and H. H. Rowley (Edinburgh, 1963).

[56] M. H. Abrams, *Natural Supernaturalism* (New York, 1971).

Man, a response to the question whether, given the powerful
and unanswerable claims of scepticism, the 'inner voice' which
positively tells him he thinks, feels, and knows should be ignored.
Fichte's answer is 'I will not'; each of these words having a
special and peculiar significance in the context of his philosophy
of moral freedom.[57] The voice is not to be ignored. Like Fichte,
Coleridge comes to the radical conclusion that rationality itself is
dependent upon acts of faith and conscience from which all
knowledge of every kind commences, and on which every in-
tellectual claim is based, consciously or unconsciously. His con-
tribution is not a 'secularized theology' (Abrams); his primary
object is not to save the Christian religion at all costs: 'He who
begins by loving Christianity better than Truth, will proceed by
loving his own Sect or Church better than Christianity, and end
in loving himself better than all' (*AR* 96). Instead, he offers a
'theanthropology' born of a genuine attempt to meet and to
resolve the problems raised by the German idealists; an attempt
at a unified system based upon the reconciliation of intellect and
faith, and consistent with human nature and experience.

A Response to Alienation

Coleridge, like Hegel, perceived a fundamental malaise in many
areas of thought and experience in his own time. In the eighteenth
century David Hume had reduced reason (and therefore the
whole philosophic endeavour) to the slave of the passions, and
of nature and the senses. Neither the materialist nor idealist
responses which had followed seemed adequate to Coleridge.
Philosophy appeared to him to have become impoverished either
by an empiricism which totally neglected noumenal reality, or
by assertions of the unknowability of the noumenal (Kant), or,
again, by an abstract idealism which was unable to maintain a
proper balance between the reality of the objective 'outer' and
the subjective 'inner' worlds, between 'it is' and 'I am' (Fichte
and Schelling).[58] He argued that the reality of Logos provided
a mediation not only between idealism and atomistic material-
ism or 'mechanistic' philosophy, but between all oppositions

---

[57] J. G. Fichte, *Die Bestimmung des Menschen* (Berlin, 1800); tr. Peter Preuss
as *The Vocation of Man* (Indianapolis, 1987), 67–71.
[58] See below, Chs. 3.2, 3.3 and 4.3.

which had been misinterpreted as contradictions, or as mutually exclusive.

The Logos as unifying principle provided, Coleridge believed, an intersubjectivity of communication without loss of objective reality; it transcended the requirements of system because the communication of the Logos is interpersonal.[59] Both the essence and the ideal existence of humanity were to be found in the Logos as Principle and Person; true philosophy must therefore be both logocentric and anthropocentric.[60] He believed he could show Logos to be the supreme philosophical principle through which the reality of life and mind could be communicated. The external world *in* which humanity finds itself, and the world of thought *through* which it finds itself, share the same source. In answer to the materialist philosophy prevalent in his own time (this, he believed, had developed out of an obsession with the empirical method as propounded by Newton, Locke, and Hume), he claimed that a principle of life must be presupposed as the ground of all phenomena; this principle was Logos. In answer, on the other hand, to the spread of pantheism which he saw in the work of such as Wordsworth and Schelling, he argued that reality presupposes 'otherness' or 'alterity' and that God, though immanent, remains transcendent; only through the 'key' of the Logos concept was this paradox intelligible.

Religion, Coleridge (and Hegel) believed, had become distorted and lifeless either through excessive rationalism (this is the basis of his criticism of Deism and of German 'Higher Criticism') or by an 'enthusiasm' which set it against reason.[61] He saw

---

[59] In recent years T. F. Torrance has emphasized the integrative, intuitive, and personal element in all knowledge (*Transformation and Convergence in the Frame of Knowledge* (Grand Rapids, Mich., 1984)). M. Polanyi rejects objectivism (see *Personal Knowledge* (London, 1958), 15, 214, 286, 323). Echoing Augustine's 'nisi credideritis, non intelligetis' ('unless you believe, you will not understand'; *De Libero Arbitrio*, i. 4), he writes 'while our acceptance of this framework is the condition for having any knowledge, this matrix can claim no self-evidence. . . . Our mind lives in action, and any attempt to specify its presuppositions produces a set of axioms which cannot tell us why we should accept them' (*Personal Knowledge*, 266). This theme of the necessity and even the fruitfulness of the subjective act of faith in all knowledge is important throughout Coleridge's writings (e.g. *LS: SM* 97).

[60] See below, Ch. 4.3.

[61] See 'Mystics and Mysticism', in *AR* 383 ff. Coleridge wrote in his marginal notes on John Donne's *Sermons* (*CM* ii. 291), 'Since the Revolution in 1688 our Church has been chilled and starved too generally by Preachers & Reasoners,

the work of the 'neological' theologians engaged in the 'Higher Criticism' of the Bible (they applied to its interpretation the same rules as those applied to other historical or literary writings) as a valuable antidote to 'bibliolatry' and one from which he himself gained useful insights and greater understanding. Yet, too often, they had reduced the written Word to a dead script. They had failed, he believed, both to take into account the need for spiritual illumination, and, more importantly, to recognize the reality of immediate and intuitive knowledge; the direct *experience* of the truth of Scripture. They had neglected its 'finding' power, which, Coleridge claimed, is *sensed*. As sensation it is impossible, he said, to define, since definition is synthetic and our sensations are simple.[62]

The inconsistencies in the Christian writers of the New Testament seemed to Coleridge 'a work of Providence, in order to preserve the necessity of internal evidence, of individual illumination and inward experience and the whole Fact of Christianity in the broad scale of History as the main supports of its credibility' (N 34, fo. 26). On the other hand, those 'enthusiasts' who separated the good from the true, paying little attention to reason, appeared to make God an arbitrary tyrant. Religion had become separated from actual and factual experience and from the realities of human nature. If Christianity were true religion— if it were the perfection of human intellect (*AR*, p. x) and the fulfilment of personality—it must be shown to be adequate to the whole human situation, to every area of life and thought: 'every theological scheme must [?fail] which appeals only to some one or more of the Qualities & Faculties of Man.—The infallible Test of Gospel Faith is that it appeals to all the constituents of our present Humanity, & brings them all to an equilibrium—to a

---

Stoic or Epicurean—first, a sort of pagan Morality, = Virtue, substituted for the Righteousness by faith, & lastly, Prudence, Paleyianism, substituted for Morality.'

[62] VCL S MS 5, card 9. In this, Coleridge followed Kant (*Critique of Pure Reason* (1781); tr. Norman Kemp Smith (London, 1989)): 'The concept itself is always *a priori* in origin, and so likewise are the synthetic principles or formulas derived from such concepts; but their employment and their relation to their professed objects can in the end be sought nowhere but in experience, of whose possibility they contain the formal conditions.' Kant says the same is true of 'all categories and the principles derived from them. . . . We cannot define any one of them in any real fashion, that is, make the possibility of their object understandable, without at once descending to the conditions of sensibility, and so to the form of appearances' (A 240).

Beauty of Holiness' (N 48, fo. 30ᵛ). Coleridge believed that, through the idea of Logos as divine *Humanity*, the Christian religion fulfilled this essential demand.

He was concerned, too, with what he saw as the failure of political and social institutions to maintain truly human and moral principles. Either progressive tendencies threatened to sacrifice principle to expediency and to the uninformed opinion of the majority, bringing about so-called reforms which betrayed the human ideal, or else the old unjust ways prevailed against much-needed genuine reform and social evolution. Coleridge placed enormous faith in his 'logosophic' system. He believed it offered a potential for the resolution of dilemmas, tensions, and alienations within society and between individuals, communities, and nations. He was convinced that he had found in the Logos the ground, root, and living principle of humanity, whether of individuals, families, or nations. We shall now turn to the Logos theme in the context of his particular concerns and as the unifying principle of his work.

I

Logos: The Word

1.1. 'LOGOS . . . COMMUNICATIVE INTELLIGENCE'

Life and language are alike sacred. Homicide and *verbicide*—
that is, violent treatment of a word with fatal results to its
legitimate meaning, which is its life—are alike forbidden.

(Oliver Wendell Holmes)

'In the beginning was the Word' (John 1: 1). This first declaration
of the Fourth Gospel is the focus of Coleridge's 'logosophic'
system. He constantly echoed and explored it from the time of
his full adoption of a Trinitarian faith (*circa* 1805). That he found
'Word' (Logos) to be a supremely fitting analogy to communicate
the reality of the Idea of God is consistent with his own character,
interests, and talents. His fascination with words was lifelong. In
his childhood he was, by his own admission, 'a playless Day-
dreamer, an Helluo Librorum' (N Fo, fo. 91), and in his youth, a
'library-cormorant' (*CL* i. 260). Although his reading was at first
indiscriminate, he developed a keen sense of the power of words
and of the significance of their use or misuse in all forms of
human discourse. Increasingly, not only that which the words
conveyed, but also words themselves, their history, and their
relationship to thought and things, attracted his attention.

Coleridge, in 1805, accepted WORD as a living God-given power:
'the profoundest and most comprehensive Energy of the human
Mind' (*CN* ii, § 2445). From this time on, he had no hesitation in
identifying this energy of intellect as having its source in the
divine Logos. He described the 'sublime metaphor (*plusquam
metaphora*) of "THE WORD": the representation by which of the
Son of God is the sublimest Thought that ever entered the Soul of
man, the purest Form of Intuition—"eine mehr als geometrischen
[*sic*] Anschauung [a more than geometrical insight]"' (*CM* i.
568). This metaphor perfectly represented 'the Divine Alterity,
the Deus Alter et idem [God Other and the same] of Philo;

Deitas Objectiva [Objective Deity]' (*C & S* 84). Coleridge's 'science of words' was developed out of his idea of the essential connection between words and the Word. His emphasis on Logos as *Word*, and the consequent attention which he gives to a philosophy and history of language, distinguish his thought from the arch-rationalism of which Hegel has (perhaps unjustly) been accused. This connection was, for Coleridge, the ground of all human discourse and communication. Many of the plans which he outlined for his projected 'Logosophia' or 'Opus Maximum' give details of etymological and grammatical studies and linguistic analyses which were to be included. Much of this work appears in the *Logic*, which he intended to be one part of the whole.

Coleridge's etymological researches, his theory of symbol, and his concept of revelation are all linked through the polysemy of Logos or Word. For him, Logos was the source and living power of language. On this basis, he associated moral degeneration with the misuse of words, a consequence of the failure to recognize the relation between the Word and words. This was the basis, too, of his analysis of the forms and relations of words in the laws of self-conscious mind as the ground of grammar, of logic, and of philosophy. These forms and relations, he claimed, reflect the nature, purpose, and power of the divine Logos.

He believed that human language reflected those characteristics and qualities which are attributed to the Logos in the Greek–Hebrew synthesis of Philo, and in the Fourth Gospel, that is, the principles of form, distinction, and relationship (Logos as 'alterity'), the 'communicative intellect in Man and Deity' (*BL* i. 302), and of power: 'Words . . . are the great mighty instruments by which thoughts are excited and by which alone they can be ⟨*expressed*⟩ in a remembered form' (*PL* 201). His interest in the study of all aspects of language, and his attempt to show how these reflected the divine Word, increased proportionately with his commitment to Christian orthodoxy. He maintained that laxity in the use of language was the result of failure to perceive that its origin must have been superhuman; this failure led to philo-sophical error and to disastrous moral consequences.[1] Philosophy, as the love and pursuit of wisdom, was dependent upon a veridical

---

[1] See below.

use of language. This in turn was dependent upon the recognition and restoration of the true relation of Word and words.

Logos: Source and Life of Language

Since language and society presuppose each other and since neither can be thought to have existed eternally, it must be, Coleridge maintained, that language was preceded and inspired by some *gift* of communication, supernaturally revealed.[2] God 'supplied the place of Father, Guardian, and Instructor' to the first human beings. The divine 'I AM' supernaturally inspired its human reflection; εἰμί—the 'verb substantive' as the root of human language.[3] From this root, Coleridge believed, by a process of separation and distinction in the development of human reason, languages gradually evolved through human history. The process of polarity is to be found, he claimed, in the generation of language just as it is in the life processes of the natural world;[4]

---

[2] N 33, fo. 4; see also OM iii, fos. 16–17, where Coleridge admits that the conventions of language as systems 'of cypher & of shorthand' are formed by agreement, but claims that: 'Convention itself, nay even the very condition and materials of all convention[,] a society of communicants[,] presupposes a language.' It may be, he agreed, that the 'grounds and causes' of language exist in the human mind 'just as the faculties of the adult body exist potentially in the new born infant', but just as there is the necessity 'of the pre-existence of an adult or of some cause equivalent in order to explain the infant's own existence', so 'it is as inconceivable that language should have been given to a mind that did not contain in itself the grounds and principles of language, as that these grounds and principles should ever emerge from latency, had not a language in its rudiments at least have been previously given'.

[3] Coleridge had read and annotated both J. G. J. Hermann's *De Emendenda Ratione Graecae Grammaticae* (Leipzig, 1801) and William Vincent's *The Greek Verb Analyzed: An Hypothesis* (London, 1795). Many grammatical philosophers of the time, like these, accepted in some form that all verbs are grounded on the verb 'to be'. Vincent, like Coleridge, believed that language as a whole had developed from the original root of εἰμί as the root of human language. He wrote: '[the old grammarians] call Εἰμι, the verb substantive, because, as they say, it can stand alone, and all other verbs they call adjectives, because, in their opinion, they all comprehend the verb Εἰμι, or depend upon it for support. . . . What then is the sense of Εἰμι? It is the verb that represents *existence* and this so pre-eminently, that it is applied with particular energy and propriety to the Deity as Self-existent' (*The Origination of the Greek Verb: An Hypothesis* (London, 1794), 9).

[4] Coleridge argued that, through the Logos, the Self-who-is-Other, God is self-realized as *Deus alter et idem* and the reality of distinction-in-unity is established. Following the mysterious primal apostasy of will, the divine Logos transformed contradiction into a fruitful and dynamic polarity, both in the act of creation and

the Logos is the source of both the language of nature and of humankind. The primal word, the 'verb substantive', split off into verb and noun, and from these into all the other parts of speech. The unfolding of human consciousness took place through this separative and distinguishing process in human language. Words, he declared, are powers; they are linked to the life and creative power of ideas and are thus not only regulative of reality but also are the tools through which this reality is constituted and communicated (*LS: SM* 114).[5] Words which are unconnected to ideas are mere sound and meaningless. 'Without the *Idea* present to the mind of the Speaker or Hearer what can *Words* be, but articulated Sound, vox et præterea nihil?' (N 35, fo. 42^v).

Coleridge hypothesized that, as the process which he called 'desynonymization' continued, distinctions emerged which were transformative of thought itself. This developmental process of language, he argued, must be encouraged and restored where it had been neglected. He described the growth of language thus: 'As society introduces new relations it introduces new distinctions, and either new words are introduced or different pronounciation. Now the duty of a philosopher is to aid and complete this process as his subject demands, and a distinction THAT has perhaps already begun IN an adjective to carry on INTO a substantive' (*PL* 369). Coleridge, no doubt, saw himself as contributing significantly to this process; he himself coined many new words, which have since become part of the English language, believing that 'Unusual and new coined words are doubtless an evil; but vagueness, confusion and imperfect conveyance of our thoughts, are far greater.'[6]

He argued that the restoration of words to a true relation with their roots, and with each other, was dependent upon the recognition that they are not to be confused with mechanistic structures as signs attached to things, but have a life and power of their own. He argued that whereas, for example, 'technical grammar' (that of the exclusive and static forms of the understanding) suggests that words govern the words which follow

in the act of re-creation, that is, of moral regeneration through the truth of Ideas and the redemption of the will (see below, Ch. 3.3 and 3.4). Thus, for Coleridge, the Logos *is* the principle of polarity.

[5] On this point, Coleridge disagreed with Kant, who maintained that ideas are regulative only (*Critique of Pure Reason*, A 643–5, 664; B 672, 692; see also Ch. 3.3, below).

[6] See the list of coined words in *BL* ii. 319.

them, 'historical' or 'philosophical grammar' recognizes that words are self-governed (N 46, fo. 37); that each has, in its own right, a character which both reflects and is instrumental in the evolution of individual and social consciousness. Human language, Coleridge declared, participates in the 'communicative intellect of man and Deity' (*BL* i. 302), the life and power of the divine Word. Just as, in Christian doctrine, the Logos remains eternally with the Father, and yet goes out to create, reveal, and redeem, so words, while they remain as thought with the speaker or hearer, yet go out as utterance (or 'Outerance') and, in this sense, have independent existence.

Coleridge was familiar with the work of G. B. Vico and of J. G. Herder, and therefore with the concept of language as evolutionary and dynamic. He was critical of Herder's naturalism (*CM* ii. 1051). Herder had attacked the notion that speech was originally communicated from God to man, and insisted that all history, including that of language, is the product of a purely natural evolution of human actions, desires, and faculties modified by the context of the particularity of time and place.[7] Coleridge himself recognized an evolutionary element in language which reflected the life of the nation,[8] but insisted, as we have seen, that the source of this process can only have been *super*natural, the gift and inspiration of language.

He had studied Vico's *Principj di Scienza Nuovo* and *Vita*,[9] and at one time proposed to write a work entitled 'Biographical Memorials of Revolutionary Minds', in which Vico was to be included as one of the 'Heroes' of Italy.[10] Coleridge admired the latter's important proposition that the structures and evolution of the human mind itself are interdependent with the evolution of language. The cognizance of external reality takes place conjointly with language, through which it is ordered and shaped. Vico suggested that the genesis of language, manifested in monosyllables, reflects 'the principles of universal nature, by

[7] J. G. von Herder, *Ueber den Ursprung der Sprache* (Berlin, 1772); for Coleridge's further criticisms of Herder, see e.g. *CN* iv, § 5336.

[8] See *AR* 234.

[9] Sometime in 1825 Coleridge began to read an edition of Vico's *Principj di Scienza Nuova* which also contained the *Vita* (Milan, 1816); see *CN* iv, § 5205.

[10] See Coleridge's note on *The Works of the Late Reverend Mr. Samuel Johnson, Sometime Chaplain to the Right Honourable William, Lord Russell*, 2 vols. (London, 1710); in *CM* iii. 142.

which the elements of all things, out of which they are composed and into which they are bound to be resolved, are indivisible; and also with the principles of human nature in particular. . . . So much the more must we deem the first men of the nations to have [begun with monosyllables], for their organs were extremely obdurate'.[11] Coleridge's view of the development of language from roots such as 'Sum', 'the root of all supersensuous terms' (*CN* iv, § 5232) has much in common with Vico's view.[12]

Seen in another light, his demand for the restoration of a purity and veracity of language reflects his admiration for Reformation theology[13] with its emphasis on the primary revelation of the Bible, which 'speaks' to the heart of the individual, and the consequent importance which it attaches to exegesis and interpretation. Evident in his notes is an interest in William of Ockham and in the implications of Nominalist philosophy for theories of language.[14] These notes also reflect his fascination with a much older concept of linguistic mysticism associated with the occult traditions. Coleridge knew that Hermetic and cabbalistic doctrines supported belief in a single primal tongue. This 'Adamic' language was derived from the divine Word. Cabbalists and Hermeticists had concerned themselves with the search for the original language, by some (notably the Jewish Gnostics) thought

[11] Vico, *Principj di Scienza Nuova*, tr. from 3rd edn. by T. G. Bergin and M. H. Fisch as *The New Science of Giambattista Vico*, rev. and abridged (Ithaca, NY, 1970), 110.

[12] Nigel Leask has explored Vico's influence on Coleridge in *The Politics of the Imagination in Coleridge's Critical Thought* (Basingstoke, 1988).

[13] See R. L. Entzinger, *Divine Word: Milton and the Redemption of Language* (Pittsburgh, 1985). Entzinger quotes Luther's letter 'To the Councilmen of All Cities in Germany That They Establish and Maintain Christian Schools' (1524); from *Luther's Works*, ed. Jaroslav Pelikan and Helmut T. Lehmann (Philadelphia, 1958), 360, 362: 'And let us be sure of this: we will not long preserve the gospel without the languages. The languages are the sheath in which this sword of the Spirit is contained. . . . If through our neglect we let the languages go (which God forbid!), we shall not only lose the gospel, but the time will come when we shall be unable either to speak or write a correct Latin or German.' Entzinger gives an account of the post-Reformation sense of the 'fall' of language and of the necessity for its redemption. Coleridge shared this view of language which was an important theme in Milton's work; for example, in *Paradise Lost* and *Samson Agonistes*: '*Samson Agonistes* recapitulates the importance of the doctrine of the Word and reaffirms the appropriateness of human language as an instrument capable of redeemed use' (Entzinger, *Divine Word*, 19–20).

[14] See e.g. his marginalia on John Scotus Eriugena's *De Divisione Naturae* (Oxford, 1681), 205 ff. in *CM* iii. 135–6.

to be most closely represented by Hebrew. All that was called into being by God was called by *name* (Genesis 2: 19–20). This primal naming was, because of its association with the divine Word, not merely the ideal form of communication but had the closest possible congruence with reality. Man's speech thus imitated and participated in the functions of the divine Word of power.[15]

Coleridge was deeply interested in the Hebrew language, in which each word and phrase has an ontological and spiritual significance beyond its merely designatory function.[16] This fascination with the cabbalistic traditions was fostered by his reading of Jacob Böhme, whose work drew extensively on cabbalistic imagery and thought. He responded eagerly to Böhme's emphasis on the sacred power of speech and to his exploration of the origins of language; as his marginalia show, these stimulated an abundance of fruitful ideas, criticisms, and conclusions in response. Another source of his interest in the cabbala was the work of Henry More; here again, his marginalia and notes frequently invoke More directly, or reveal the latter's influence.[17]  Coleridge's friendship with Hyman Hurwitz also contributed insights into Jewish history and culture, both ancient and of his own time. Here again the link was language; they collaborated to

---

[15] Coleridge describes the process through which the whole creation is redeemed through Word and words: 'as Man finds his redemption . . . so . . . does the whole inferior Creation, which fell not willingly, seek yea, yearn and groan (i.e. significantly, tho' inarticulately, utter its desire) for Redemption in the Human Animal. In Man is the solution of their dark Enigma: for the Word, the Son of God, has become the Son of Man, the living Sacrifice, and the perpetual Sin-offering. . . . In Man, the Vowels have been found, the hidden Letters have become Consonants—the Sound there of is heard, and the interpretation is made. So it is even now in the outward Man—but in the inward and in the World of History which is its Phænomenon, Man is to the Idea Man as the inferior Creatures to their Co-organization in the Human Frame' (*CN* iv, § 4984).

[16] See below, Ch. 1.2; e.g. n. 78.

[17] Probably Henry More's *Conjectura Cabbalistica* (London, 1653) contributed to Coleridge's interest in the cabbala. According to his notebook entries, Coleridge appears to have been particularly closely studying and annotating Henry More's *Theological Works* (1708) between 1823 and 1824 (see *CN* iv, §§ 5066–8 and *CM* iii. 918–29). His inclusion of references to More in *AR* suggest that the latter was an influence here too. Another source for Coleridge's knowledge of the cabbala was J. J. Brucker, *Historia Critica Philosophiae*, 2nd edn. (Leipzig, 1767), ii. 919–1072; see e.g. *CN* iv, § 5121; *CL* i. 323.

produce a work on Hebrew and its influence on the development of etymology and syntax.[18]

The Fall and Redemption of Language

Coleridge believed that the restoration of the veracity of 'living words' must be an integral part of the regeneration of human nature by the Word. The idea of the fallenness and imperfection of words together with their potential redemptive power had been emphasized by one of the theologians he most admired, Augustine of Hippo. The Reformers (especially Luther) had carried forward, among many other of Augustine's teachings, a concept that language reflects the fallenness of man and is therefore imperfect. Yet it was found by Augustine, as Andrew Louth shows, to be both 'disabled' *and* 'redemptive'.[19] Following the Reformation, especially in the seventeenth century when its influence had become widespread, the concept of an ideal original language, given to Adam but distorted and lost in man's subsequent Fall with all its consequences, became a topic of much literary and philosophical speculation. The poetry of John Milton (a subject to which Coleridge frequently returns) explores this idea of a linguistic Fall, its consequences, the final restoration of language, and, through language, of man's reason and relationship with God.[20] Coleridge looked back to this period with a sense of loss, believing that before the Restoration, theology had been linked to the truth of Ideas, through close attention to the correct

---

[18] Hyman Hurwitz, *The Etymology and Syntax, in continuation of The Elements of the Hebrew Language* (London, 1831). Coleridge frequently consulted Hurwitz (1770–1844), a Jew, on Hebrew language, history, and culture. Hurwitz also made use of Coleridge's theories of language (see *CL* vi. 816). He became Professor of Hebrew at University College London in 1829. Coleridge wrote of him: 'Mr Hurwitz, whom it would be no flattery to name the English MENDELSSOHN, is the first Hebrew and Rabbinical Scholar in the kingdom; and among the first in the Languages of the Hither East—I mean the ancient and modern Arabic, the Syriac, Chaldaic and Syro-Chaldaic' (*CL* v. 440).

[19] A. Louth, 'Augustine on Language', *Literature and Theology*, 3 (1989), 151–8: 'Augustine's scepticism about language is overcome by his grasp of the reality of redemption through the Word—the Word Incarnate and the word preached. Language itself frustrates communication, producing an illusory community of meaning, to some extent fortunately, given the nature of fallen man. But it can also be a means of redemption, and then in some mysterious way language is healed and healing' (p. 158).

[20] See above, n. 13.

use of words, and that this had been reflected in the work of the poets and divines of the period.[21] He adopted the view that the 'I am'—for him the birth of reason[22]—is in fact linked inseparably to the root of language; that the distortion and misuse of language is associated with a loss of self and a consequent all-pervading moral and philosophical corruption.

Coleridge believed, with Augustine and Milton, that human language always fails to comprehend God (OM ii, fo. 244); but the *divine* Word reveals what is hidden. He shared Milton's sense of the Fall of language, but linked it with the corruption which was a consequence of the particular misuse of words by individuals. He affirmed the value and incorruption of language in so far as its development reflected the life of the nation. He emphasized the evil consequences of its misuse, which led to false convictions and to philosophical and moral degeneration. Just as Milton's *Paradise Lost* suggests that the restoration of the divine–human relationship is accompanied by a restoration of language as the communication of truth and love, so Coleridge believed that the veracity of words and language, and their correspondence with reality, are inseparably connected with religion and morality. This is consistent with the primacy which he gave to the Logos theme.

Two centuries earlier, the idea of a fall of language had also been the subject of philosophical speculation by Francis Bacon (1561–1626), for whom Coleridge frequently expressed his admiration.[23] Bacon's anticipation of those logical and philosophical distinctions, which Coleridge himself deemed necessary to the pursuit of reason, included an emphasis on the importance of precise word definition and on the significance for philosophy of linguistic origins, development, and structure. In his 1818–19 lectures on the history of philosophy, Coleridge had remarked on the value of Bacon's Idols. These included the 'Idols of the Market Place,' Bacon's expression for the 'intercourse and association of men with each other' through common traditions of discourse in which 'words are imposed according to the apprehension of the vulgar' leading to their devaluation: 'and therefore the ill and

---

[21] See BL Add. MS 34225, fo. 21.
[22] See below, Ch. 3.2.
[23] See e.g. *Logic*, ed.'s app. B: 'Preliminary Outline of the *Logic*', 283; *CL* vi. 676 (1827).

unfit choice of words wonderfully obstructs the understanding . . .
words plainly force and overrule the understanding, and throw all
into confusion, and lead men away into numberless empty con-
troversies and idle fancies'.[24]

The Socratic and Platonic emphasis on the definition of words
as the first step in the pursuit of true knowledge had been given a
different emphasis through Nominalist philosophy and Refor-
mation theology. Thomas Hobbes had insisted that 'in the right
definition of names lies the first use of speech; which is the
acquisition of science: and in wrong or no definitions, lies the first
abuse; from which proceed all false and senseless tenets.'[25]
Leibniz later developed this critical awareness of the role of
language in human learning through his pursuit of the '*charac-
teristica universalis*' ('universal system of characters'). It is the
basis of his exploration of the relationship of religious faith and
language.[26] Nobody, he insisted, is able to judge of the truth of
'things' unless they are able to understand exactly what the words
mean that signify those things: 'It is impossible to perceive
the truth of a proposition if the meanings of its words are not
perceived.'[27] Though Coleridge was not an uncritical admirer of
Leibniz, and disliked Hobbes's philosophy, his work reflects their
influence and contains many similar assertions. Throughout *Aids
to Reflection*, the view that the development of reason depends
on the correct use of language is clearly expressed.[28]

Coleridge's interest in Greek philosophy, in Hebrew thought,
and in the synthesis of these in Christianity, was often focused on
the analogy drawn in all these traditions, between the divine
Word (expressed by Heraclitus and Plato as *logos* and in the
Jewish tradition, as, for example, *memra*) and human language
and speech. Asserting the sound/form, subjective/objective

---

[24] Francis Bacon, *Novum Organum*, or *The New Organum*, ed. F. H. Anderson
(Indianapolis, repr. 1980), 49.

[25] *The English Works of Thomas Hobbes*, ed. William Molesworth, 11 vols.
(London, 1839–45), iii. 24.

[26] See G. W. Leibniz, 'Commentatiuncula de Judice Controversiarum, seu
trutinâ rationis et norma textus' (On the Judge of Controversies) in *Sämtliche
Schriften und Briefe*, ed. Deutschen Akademie der Wissenschaften, 11 vols.
(Berlin, 1950), VI. i. 548–59, §§ 9–13. M. Dascal quotes from this text in *Leibniz,
Language, Signs and Thought* (Amsterdam, 1987), 99.

[27] Leibniz, *Sämtliche Schriften und Briefe*, VI. ii. 409.

[28] See e.g. *AR*, pp. xi, 114–15, 199 n., 309 n.

dualities of the nature of 'word' (which term he extended beyond its normal use to, for example, the forms of nature, and of art and architecture[29]), he appears to echo the ancient distinction (used, for example, by Heraclitus, by the Stoics, and by Augustine) between the inner and outer word.[30] Heraclitus had suggested that there is both an inner and an outer truth of *logos*—the inner gives strength and sustenance to the powers of human thought; the outer is the life in all things and the living power of the universe.

Augustine, himself steeped in the later tradition of Neoplatonism, had taught that the spoken word (for example, that of the preacher) reflects the quality of the speaker's inner life. Not only is all human rational discourse dependent on the divine Logos, but this inner activity of grace, of the communication of life and of the light of reason, should be the main focus of attention: 'The word which sounds without is a sign of the word that shines within, to which the name of word more properly belongs'.[31] Coleridge explored both the inner reality of words in their relation to thoughts and also their objective, 'outer' reality, their self-subsistence. We find him describing the divine Logos as the 'Outerance' of the divine Will (*CN* iv, § 4870), and the products of nature as phenomenal 'words'.

In *Aids to Reflection*, he quoted Heraclitus: 'To discourse

[29] 'No man can be a philosopher or Critic of the Fine Arts who has not yet come to understand *Word* in sensu generalissimo, as an organism of sound & forms objective-subjective. A grand strain of Music, a Cathedral, a painting of Michael Angelo are in this sense *Words*, and to him each integral part a vowel or syllable' (NQ, fo. 15^V).

[30] Coleridge would have known of the Patristic distinction between *logos endiathetos* and *logos prophorikos*. J. N. D. Kelly traces this distinction between 'immanent logos' and 'expressed logos' to the Stoics (*Early Christian Doctrines*, 3rd edn. (London, 1965), 13 ff.). He shows that 'the Stoics' Logos (which also means reason or plan) was the rational principle immanent in reality, giving form and meaning to it; at the same time reality was comprehensible to men because of the presence of Logos in them' (p. 21). Philo made a similar distinction (see *De Vita Mosis*, ii. 127); Kelly describes Philo's view thus: the Logos is 'first of all the ideas or thoughts of God's mind, and is then projected into formless unreal matter, making it into a real and rational universe' (*Early Christian Doctrines*, 21–2). As will be seen, Coleridge's understanding of the Logos as both indwelling and transcendent in all areas of life and mind develops this distinction. Augustine's understanding of the difference between the indwelling and the expressed word is further explored below (Ch. 1.3 and n. 9).

[31] Augustine, *De Trinitate*, xv. 11. 20; tr. S. McKenna, as *Augustine: The Trinity* (Washington, DC, 1970), 476–7.

rationally it behoves us to derive strength from that which is
common to all men: for all human understandings are nourished
by the one DIVINE WORD'. He drew attention to the likeness
between this and the Christian doctrine of 'Logos, or co-eternal
Filial Word'.[32] The Greeks' use of the concept of inspiration
through *logos*—of, for example, Heraclitus' description of the
power in nature and in mind as the 'ever-living fire through the
disposing WORD' (*SM: LS* 95)—these, for him, are flawed but
insightful anticipations of the truth fully revealed in the Christian
Logos. Coleridge's own definition of language, in a letter to John
Murray in 1814, has a Heraclitean tone. Language, he wrote, 'is
the Sacred Fire in the Temple of Humanity' (*CL* iii. 522).

It was his judgement that this living, dynamic power of language
had been neglected in the 'Higher Criticism' of German theology.
In applying the criteria used for the interpretation of secular texts
to the analysis and exegesis of the Scriptures, 'Higher Criticism'
was particularly influenced by those social and cultural factors in
linguistic development to which Herder had drawn attention.
Coleridge believed that there had been an over-correction of the
errors of 'bibliolatry' (the literal interpretation which appeared to
idolize the letter of Scripture) in the work of these 'neologians'.[33]
Theologians engaged in this work failed to acknowledge that
language itself is not only the *product* of the evolution of thought
and experience, but is *constitutive* of it—a creative and living
process. In studying the written Word as a mere mechanism of
words, they had lost touch with its life and power.

This criticism reflects Coleridge's own intense reflection on the

[32] Heraclitus had asserted a general lack of comprehension concerning the
logos; that even though the words of revelation are heard, men are not 'awake' to
their real and deepest meaning: 'Of the logos that is given in my book, men are
always uncomprehending. They do not understand it before they hear it from me,
or when they first hear it. For, although everything happens in accordance with
this logos, men have no cognizance of this, even though they have encountered
the words and things I put before them, as I dissect each thing according to its
real nature and show forth how it really is. Other men are not aware what they do
when they awake, just as they are forgetful of what they do in their sleep' (DK
BI; tr. David Wiggins, 'Flux, Fire and Material Persistence', in Malcolm Schofield
and Martha Nussbaum (eds.), *Language and Logos: Studies in Ancient Greek
Philosophy* (Cambridge, 1982), 21).

[33] Coleridge, having studied the work of J. Eichhorn, concluded that the latter
was 'no philosopher—a sensible Conceptualist, but who contemplated nothing in
the light of the *Idea*' (*CM* ii. 478 and n.; see also N 44, fos. 25–29^v; and *CM* ii.
155).

power of the poetic impulse and the imagination. Language is not merely a product of the relativity of national cultures, but, as a power, is the antecedent condition of these. The logocentric theme is maintained. Just as the Logos is both Creator and the life within the evolving forms of his creation, so words and language are both constitutive and the evolved products of man's life in community. Coleridge saw an intimate relationship between the divine Word and the words of human language. On this ground, etymology and linguistics must be recognized as of fundamental concern to the issues of the Christian faith.

The 'Distinctivity' of Words

Coleridge gave as the most important aim and object of *Aids to Reflection*: 'To direct the Reader's attention to the value of the Science of Words, their use and abuse, and the incalculable advantages attached to the habit of using them appropriately, and with a distinct knowledge of their primary, derivative, and metaphorical senses' (*AR* xi). This was necessary not only that error and sophism might be rooted out, but also, he believed, because the power and the life of words is in some sense sacred, because it images the activity of the Logos. Again, he emphasized the *moral* significance of language. He quoted the title of Horne Tooke's etymological work: '*Επεα πτεροεντα*, Winged Words: or Language, not only the *Vehicle* of Thought but the *Wheels*'[34] and proceeded to amend it in order more accurately to express his own approach and interest: 'With my convictions and views, for *επεα* I should substitute *λογοι*, that is, Words *select* and *determinate*, and for *πτεροεντα ζωοντες*, that is, *living* Words.' Words are not only instrumental to the communication of intelligence: they are part of the living process of thought.

The nature and activity of the Logos, Coleridge declared, is reflected in the creative and distinguishing power of words. When we learn to distinguish carefully each word from others by focusing on its true meaning, it is recognized as a living power in its own right and communicates its own unique revelation of reality. In giving attention to the true nature and use of language we are able

---

[34] *Επεα πτερόεντα; or, The Diversions of Purley*, 2nd edn. (London, 1798). *Επεαπτερόεντα* is a classical phrase used by, for example, Homer and Hesiod.

to participate in the activity of the Logos, who is the archetypal principle of distinction, form, and limit, the 'forma formans' of the creation. We are able to recognize words as 'LIVING POWERS, by which the things of most importance to mankind are actuated, combined and humanized' (*AR*, p. xv).

The Logos is (in this, Coleridge develops the Logos theology of the early Church Fathers) the communication of form, of organization, and, particularly, of distinction: 'the *Word* in *forms*, distinguishes, articulates, organizes' (N 41, fo. 83). Again, this is characteristic of the Logos both as the Creator and indwelling Life of nature and as the Light of mind. If a transcendent and universal Logos is once accepted, a unifying systematic principle is found. Coleridge sets out his concept of the relationship between the divine Word and human words in a notebook entry:

Reason, Proportion, communicable Intelligibility intelligent and communicant, the Word—which last expression strikes me as the profoundest and most comprehensive Energy of the human Mind, if indeed it be not in some distinct sense ενεργημα θεοπαραδοτον [God-given energy] . . . [T]he moment we conceive the divine energy, that moment we coconceive the Λογος; . . . the redeemed & sanctified become finally themselves Words of the *Word*—even as articulate sounds are made by the Reason to represent Forms, in the mind, and Forms are a language of the notions. (*CN* ii, § 2445)

He likened redeemed human individuals to living words, which are the instruments through which truth is communicated, and which, while 'self-governing', are nevertheless dependent (if this potential is to be fulfilled) upon the relationship of context, as parts of a whole (a sentence, or phrase). The man or woman enlightened by Logos becomes in his or her own being an image of the divine 'I am'; that is, a distinct member of a wider community, creating and communicating truth in a network of relationships mirroring those of the Trinity. Just as the activity of the Spirit and the Word creates and imparts form and life, individuation and unity,[35] so the Logos is reflected in the human logos. The analogy between Word and words is thus appropriate. Words 'call forth and bring to the birth what Words could neither

---

[35] See below, Ch. 2.2.

ingraft or beget' (N 44, fos. 66ᵛ). They bring to consciousness the truth already implanted by the Logos.

An enlightened use of language, in Coleridge's view, is that which acknowledges the importance of distinction, the means of 'desynonymization' by which the development of language towards abstract thought progresses. Interpreting, according to his symbolic theory, the language of Christianity, which represents the divine Word as that of God the Father, sent forth, Coleridge is drawn to the archetypal pattern of distinction-in-unity, a concept which became a central focus of his thought.[36] He declared this principle to be essential to etymology, grammar, logic, and therefore philosophy. The failure to apply it resulted not only in the distortion of knowledge and learning, but in moral corruption. He was convinced that the existence of true synonyms in a language witnessed to a nation's moral decline (OM iii, fo. 59), for these denied to words the living power which characterized each in its own right and by which each reflected the distinctive power of the divine Word. In notes written in 1814 (while staying with Josiah Wade in Bristol), Coleridge expressed his belief that the careless use of words without attention to their true and distinct meaning led to all manner of depravity:

the early Habit of using words without meaning is too likely to make way for that of using words with a false meaning . . . Lying, Duplicity, Equivocation, Lip-worship, Superstition, and Inflammability of the Passions by the vague Watch-words and blind Phrases of political or religious Fanaticism, have not seldom commenced, and must always have been risked, by the early and long-continued Practice of uttering words by Rote: in short . . . Intellectual accuracy is the Faithful Friend and next-door Neighbour of Moral Veracity, so that both are comprised in the one term, Truth. (*CN* iii, § 4210)

Here again there are echoes of the theme of a Fall of language. *Aids to Reflection* later picks up a similar theme:

---

[36] Distinction-in-unity is the very foundation of Coleridge's system—the Logos is the principle of distinction or 'alterity' and must be understood within the idea of the Trinity. In this theory of life, of mind, and of human nature Coleridge constantly builds on this principle, and sees the failure to recognize it (whether in German idealism or in Christian heresies such as Socinianism and Arianism) as the source of dangerous error. The *tetractys* (see below, Ch. 1.2) is, for him, its most perfect expression.

In questions of Philosophy or Divinity, that have occupied the Learned and been the subjects of many successive Controversies, for one instance of mere Logomachy I could bring ten instances of *Logodaedaly*, or verbal Legerdemain, which have perilously confirmed Prejudices and withstood the advancement of Truth in consequence of the neglect of *verbal debate*, i.e. strict discussion of Terms. (*AR* 114–15).

In this respect at least, Coleridge's theory and practice are consistent. James Marsh[37] noted that he 'uses words uniformly with astonishing precision, and that language becomes, in his use of it—in a degree, of which few writers can give us a conception—a living power, "consubstantial" with the power of thought, that gave birth to it, and awakening and calling into action a corresponding energy in our own minds'.

For the purpose of encouraging the restoration of the accurate use and understanding of words, Coleridge proposed in June 1814 to write 'a Greek and English Lexicon, on philosophical Principles, in which the *one sole* meaning or original sensuous Image, of each Word, will be first given, and then the different applications of this one meaning developed and explained' (*CN* iii, § 4210). Again, the emphasis is on accurate definition and the recognition of distinctions. As for synonyms, where the term refers to words 'having precisely the same definition', these 'cannot exist in an original and homogenous language except through the degeneracy of the nation' (Coleridge here gives an example from modern Greek); in a language of mixed origin, they are 'defects'. They are not simply unnecessary encumbrances but harmful to thought and to the relation of thought of things: 'While they remain they are not merely excrescences, but those in which all the bad humours lurk and obtain a semblance of organisation' (OM iii, fo. 60). They must be thought of only as material for 'future appropriation'; that is, they will be absorbed usefully into the language, desynonymized, 'when in the progress of intellectual development new distinctions are brought into consciousness' (ibid.).

Human language is always imperfect, but it has a divine origin and therefore 'Language, (as the embodied and articulated Spirit of the Race, as the growth and emanation of a People, and not the work of any individual Wit or Will) is often inadequate,

---

[37] A note in his 'Preliminary Essay' to his own edition of *AR*.

sometimes deficient, but never false or delusive' (*AR* 234 n.).
According to Coleridge, we have but to find the true definition of
a word and to use it accordingly, to release its creative, com-
municative power: 'We have only to master the true origin and
original import of any native and abiding word, to find in it, if not
the *solution* of the facts expressed by it, yet a finger-mark pointing
to the road on which this solution is to be sought' (ibid.). From
the ideas of our infancy which are really more like instincts,
language leads us 'from the vague to the distinct, from the im-
perfect to the full and finished form'.[38] Again, we are reminded
that language is formative of consciousness, reflecting the activity
of the divine Word; it is the process, and not only the product, of
thought.

Logos: From Word(s) to Reason

Aids to Reflection demonstrates Coleridge's continual questioning
and redefinition of words in pursuit of that 'PERFECTION OF HUMAN
INTELLIGENCE' (*AR*, p. x), which, he believed, was to be achieved
by the reconciliation of reason and faith. He drew attention to
distinctions, such as that between 'thought' and 'attention' (*AR*
4 n.), between 'virtue' and 'righteousness' (*AR* 8 n.), and, most
importantly, between the 'Reason' and the 'Understanding', the
latter being, in his opinion, the most crucial distinction for both
philosophy and theology (*AR* 214–27). In a notebook entry, he
developed his idea of the importance of desynonymizing further
through such examples as the neglected distinction and therefore
misuse of 'vivaciousness' and 'vivacity': '1. passive—the vivacious-
ness of the Turtle; 2. active—the vivacity of the Sky-lark' (N 59,
fo. 11).

The harm that resulted from failure to distinguish words
adequately was well illustrated, so Coleridge asserted in his 'Opus
Maximum' notes (OM iii, fos. 59–60), by Thomas Hobbes's
confusion of 'compulsion' and 'obligation', and thus of 'must' and
'should', a defect which distorted the latter's whole philosophy.
Similarly, David Hartley and Joseph Priestley had distorted

---

[38] General Introduction 'On the Principles of Method', in *Encyclopedia
Metropolitana* (London, 1845); separately published as *A Treatise on Method*
(London, 1818), 4.

reasoning by confusing 'necessity' (which Coleridge claimed to be, in its ideal form, one with perfect liberty) with 'compulsion proper'. On this falsity of language the 'necessitarian systems' were founded. In Coleridge's insistence on the importance of distinction, there is a hint of his rejection of the errors of Socinian, Arian, and Unitarian views, and of their denial that God self-realized is a unity of distinct Persons.

Frequently, when annotating the works he was studying, Coleridge commented on these errors in word definition or usage. Richard Baxter, whose work he greatly admired, he none the less criticized for imprecise language which distorted reasoning (*CM* i. 237–8). One particular failure in this direction was frequently noted—it concerned the lack of recognition of the essential difference between Reason and Understanding.[39] For this Joseph Butler too was castigated in Coleridge's notes on Butler's *Analogy of Religion* (1736): 'The excellent sense of this passage is rendered less perspicuous by the common error in our language of using Reason and Understanding (Vernunft & Verstand) as perfect synonymes. Reason & Virtue naturally involve and imply, each the other—which is not the case with understanding, an extraordinary power of which is sometimes instanced in the malignity of madmen' (*CM* i. 869).

Coleridge maintained that, where words are abused, false convictions follow. His *Logic* makes clear the importance of a correct understanding of the relationship between word, thought, and thing; of the distinction between 'Word' as expressing the form of ideal reality and word as sound; of the relation of words to the Word:

For should there be another and higher meaning, namely the meaning itself, should the word differ from the mind only as the breeze differs from the air—should it, I say, mean the truth, contemplated as conveyed and communicated, and the truth itself be a living power, or, to bring all to one point, should two diverse things be included in the term 'definition', which in the one therefore must be the essence of the thing and in the other the mere accident, namely an articulated sound or its visual representative, should the *ρηματα* (flowing sounds) which are not *λογοι* (intelligible words) be distinguished from the latter, whether appearing with the accident of the former or otherwise, and, lastly, should

---

[39] See below, Ch. 3.1.

all words have their ground and highest source in the 'Word' that was from the beginning, it might appear that a dispute . . . concerning words is the most important subject on which the mind of man could exert its reasoning powers. (*Logic*, 119–20)

A notebook entry confirming language as imaging Logos stresses that the analogy of Word and words is necessarily imperfect, but of great value:

Contemplated in its eminence and Absolute⟨ness⟩, Speech (Sermo, Verbum, Logos sensu infinito) denotes the essence of the filial Deity; but in its finite and derivative existence, it is the act, attribute, and in the most ancient languages the name of the *human* Understanding—i.e. the Understanding as distinct from Reason but not, as in inferior Natures, *contra*-distinguished therefrom. Divinely and in the fullness of Inspiration did the Evangelist affirm—In the Beginning was THE WORD: and the Word, God of God, became the Mediator between God and Man, and the Redeemer of Man. (*CN* iv, § 4984)

Words and Relations

The principle of distinction (Logos, 'alterity') in the supreme reality and unity of the Godhead is, Coleridge argued, reflected in every process of thought and being. It is the condition of all communication and of all relationship. From the time of his adoption of orthodox Christianity, he maintained that reality was most adequately expressed and communicated in terms of relationality, whether in the form of triunity or polarity, or as symbolized by geometrical figures, for example, in the circle and the *tetractys*, the pentad and the heptad. In language too, words, in their relation to reality (particularly to the reality of abstract thought), should imitate the perfect relationship between God and his self-manifestation in the Logos. To Coleridge, words were distinctions within an underlying unity of thought. They were not simply accumulated end to end, but each had its own distinct reality and yet was part of a whole (for example, in the sentence). Similarly, sentences followed this pattern of connection and relationship, which mirrored the Logos principle of distinction-in-unity.

He valued Scholastic philosophy for its clarification of the dependence of meaning on the relations of words; for its precise definitions, and avoidance of the common abuses of language

(*PL* 291). He bemoaned what he described as the failure of English thinkers, particularly in the eighteenth century, to maintain the valuable contribution of the Scholastics regarding this relational aspect of language. The former had given up the gains of the latter and removed 'as an offence all the marks of connexion, to make each sentence an independent one, easily indeed understood, but still more easily forgotten' (*PL* 290).

In grammar—at once the birth and the expression of self-consciousness (*Logic*, 18)—and also in logic, the ground of intellectual speculation and discourse, Coleridge claimed that the human logos reflects the activity of its divine pattern. It brings order to what would otherwise be merely a chaos of articulate sounds. Grammar and logic are, he claimed, the first two of the 'Pure Sciences' which deal with the relation which the Ideas or Laws of the mind have to one another. Grammar, for example,

apart from the mere material consideration of the sound of words, or the shape of letters, and regarding speech only as a thing significant, teaches that there are certain laws regulating that signification; laws which are immutable in their very nature; for the relation which a noun bore to a verb, or a substantive to an adjective, was the same in the earliest days μεροπων ανθρωπων, in the first intelligible conversation of men, as it is now; not can it ever vary so long as the powers of thought remain the same in the Human Mind. This, then, is a Pure Science proceeding from a simple or elementary Idea of the form necessary for the conveyance of a single thought, and thence spreading and diffusing itself over all the relations of significant Language.[40]

[* of articulate-speaking men]

Both grammar and logic are here defined as products of immutable laws according to which the human mind functions. These laws of the human logos reflect the '*forma formans*', a transcendent reality of Intellect. They are themselves the ground and condition of human thought, and are presupposed by it. Coleridge declared their source to be metaphysical; thus all the pure sciences which are concerned with form and law, as soon as these are recognized to be the conditions of reality, lead to metaphysics and, ultimately, to theology:

as we advance from form to reality, the Sciences of *Metaphysics* and *Morals* first present themselves to view, and these lead us forward to the

[40] *Treatise on Method*, 35.

summit of Human Knowledge; for at the head of all Pure Science stands *Theology*, of which the great fountain is Revelation. It is obvious that both Metaphysics and Morals are conversant solely about these relations which we have called Relations of Law.[41]

He emphasized the derivation of the term 'logic' from 'logos' in the outline plan for his own *Logic*:

IV. The etymological history of the Word (Logos) from which the Science, that treats of words in relation to connected Thoughts, derives its *technical* Name—and the several successive meanings of the word from the visual image, its simplest and primary signification, to its last and highest sense in the Christian Theology.[42]

Grammar, Coleridge argued, has its foundation in the origin of language, the 'verb substantive', that from which both nouns and verbs are derived. This 'I am' is the first principle of the philosophies of self-consciousness, from that of Descartes to those of Kant and Fichte. Like Fichte and Jacobi, Coleridge believed that to recognize this a priori self-conscious principle necessitated the acknowledgement that it must have a transcendent source. The name of God is given in the Old Testament as 'I AM THAT I AM' (Exodus 3: 14); this he believed to be the representation of ultimate reality in which language, and therefore philosophy, ought to be grounded.

In establishing the primary polarity of noun and verb and of subject and object, grammar reflects and gives substance to the polarity of act and being in all finite reality. Coleridge described grammar as 'thoughts in connexion or connected language, and the primary distinction of identity and alterity, of essence and form, of act and being, constituting the ground-work and as it were the metaphysical contents and pure conditions of logic' (OM iii, fo. 76). Grammar derives its form from the 'form of all forms' and its ontological connection from language, which begins with the divine act of self-begetting and self-affirmation:

In Grammar, the Nomen, or Substantive, corresponds to the Subject, Object or Thing in Logic; and the Verb to the *Act* of the Logicians. . . . The *Identity* of the Noun and Verb, viz. that which is both in one not by *synthesis*, whether it be mere juxtaposition or mechanical union . . . [but

---

[41] Ibid. 36.
[42] BL MS Egerton 2801, fos. 34^v–5.

rather by] Identity, which means One containing the power of *two* as their radical *antecedent*, or as a point *producing* itself into a bi-polar Line but contemplated as anterior to this production, and *containing* the two Poles or Opposites in unevolved cöinherence . . . this Co-inherence of Act and Being is the I AM IN THAT I WILL TO BE, of Moses, the Absolute I AM, and it's grammatical correspondent is the VERB SUBSTANTIVE. (*CN* iv, § 4644, 26–7)

Coleridge claimed that the first principle of his philosophical system was contained in an act and that this could be discerned in grammatical form: 'in the language of the grammarians I begin with the verb, but the act involves its reality—it is an act of being, a verb substantive, of which, as the radix containing both as in one, the substantive and the verb are the two poles' (OM iii, fo. 136).

Again, the 'act' which 'involves its reality' reflects the act by which the eternal Word is begotten as self-subsistent Being. Perhaps Coleridge's clearest statement of the relation between 'philosophical Grammar' and the Logos is given in a notebook entry of 1820–1: 'We should commence with the aweful Supreme Reality, of which the radical forms of Speech are the faint types, or reflexes, with the living I Am, the eternal *Word!*' (*CN* iv, § 4784).

His concern was not with merely logical, grammatical, or functional relations in language. In their reflection of (and participation in) the divine Word, he believed that human words act as communicative intelligence and participate potentially in the redemptive work of love, the act of the Word sent from God.[43] However convincing his argument, Coleridge's sense of the power of words to awaken, to transform, to enlighten, and to empower is evident in his poetry, his puns, and in the many notes which play with the sound and forms of words in various languages (*CN* iv, § 4832), conjuring with the constitutive nature of the relationship between thought and language and the creativity of symbols. We shall see that it is in his theory of symbol that Coleridge most fully expressed his view of the participation of human language in the divine Word.

The initial premiss of his theory of language is an underlying act of faith. It is difficult, given the work of twentieth-century

---

[43] See App. A.

hermeneutical theory, to maintain that this act of faith should be regarded as a weakness. If it is, it is one which is present in every act of interpretation, be it of 'text' in the widest sense, or of experience. Perhaps one of Coleridge's strengths is his anticipation of the inescapability of this. But we shall see that he recognizes the need to support his act of faith by both rational argument and appeal to experience.

1.2. THE ARCHETYPAL SYMBOL

There are already many analyses and evaluations of Coleridge's idea of the symbol;[44] and these often explore it in the context of nineteenth-century aesthetics, for he was not alone in his fascination with the symbol's nature and function. J. W. von Goethe and F. W. J. Schelling, Ludwig Tieck, and Karl Solgar, for example, were developing theories which had much in common with his own, and from which he benefited.[45] Like Coleridge, they rejected Kant's view of the symbol as representation which cannot put us in touch directly with noumenal reality, only with material for reflection; though this itself, Kant admitted, transfers 'our reflection upon an object of intuition to quite a new concept, and one with which perhaps no intuition can ever directly correspond'.[46] Kant had concluded that 'all our knowledge of God is merely symbolic'. Schelling, Goethe, and Coleridge would have thought the word 'merely' a mistake. Here we are not so much concerned with the symbol's place in literary or aesthetic theory as with the interdependence of Coleridge's whole theory of symbol with his understanding of Christian theology as an integral part of his 'logosophic' plan.

His concept of the imagination as 'the living Power and prime

---

[44] See e.g. Modiano, *Coleridge and the Concept of Nature*; J. R. Barth, *The Symbolic Imagination* (Princeton, NJ, 1977); John Beer, *Coleridge's Poetic Intelligence* (London, 1977); M. J. Swiatecka, *The Idea of Symbol: Some Nineteenth Century Comparisons with Coleridge* (Cambridge, 1980).

[45] David Jasper has explored the similarities between Coleridge's theory of symbol and those of Solgar and Tieck: 'Some Romantic Theories on Religious Symbolic Language', *Heythrop Journal*, 28 (1987), 31–9.

[46] I. Kant, *Kritik der Urtheilskraft* (Berlin, 1790), I, § 59; tr. W. S. Pluhar, as *The Critique of Judgement* (Indianapolis, 1987), 228.

Agent of all human perception . . . a repetition in the finite mind
of the eternal act of creation in the infinite I AM' (*BL* i. 304) has
been explored as aesthetic principle. The symbol is, paradoxically,
the awakening source of this power, its mediatory channel and its
product, that which reveals the universal in the particular (*SM:
LS* 30) and which is often the means of raising human con-
sciousness to the contemplation of spiritual truth.[47] This has
a parallel in Goethe's definition: 'That is true symbolism, where
the more particular represents the more general, not as a
dream or shade, but as a vivid, instantaneous revelation of the
Inscrutable.'[48] Schelling's influence on this aspect of the partici-
pation of symbol in both the suprasensual and the sensual worlds
reflects the importance of this concept in his own aesthetic
philosophy: 'Mythology in general and any piece of mythological
literature in particular is not to be understood schematically or
allegorically, but symbolically. For the demand of absolute artistic
representation is: representation with complete indifference, so
that the universal is wholly the particular, and the particular at
the same time wholly the universal, and does not simply mean
it.'[49]

Coleridge's definition of symbol is similar. The symbol 'partakes
of the Reality which it renders intelligible; and while it enunciates
the whole, abides itself as a living part in that Unity, of which it is
the representative' (*LS: SM* 30).[50] The parallels with his Logos
theme are evident. For him, the symbol both mirrors and par-
ticipates in the nature of the divine Word, the Logos, the
mediator between God and man; there is a consubstantiality in
the symbol which echoes the divine *homoousios*.[51] The symbol,

[47] See Modiano, *Coleridge and the Concept of Nature*, 66–7; Barth, *The
Symbolic Imagination*, 7.

[48] *The Maxims and Reflections of Goethe*, tr. Bailey Saunders (London, 1893),
102, § 2022.

[49] F. W. J. Schelling, *Philosophie der Kunst* (1802; WW V, 411); see Gadamer,
Truth and Method, 69, 507.

[50] See also *BL* i. 156.

[51] Coleridge was fully aware of the debates in the early Church councils
concerning the nature of the Father–Son relationship. He appears to have thought
that a pre-Christian model, that of Philo, concerning this distinction-in-unity
would have overcome the difficulty between the Nicaeans, who insisted on
'homoousios' (of the same substance), and those who emphasized 'homoiousios'
(of like substance) (see *TT* i. 34–5 and n. *s*; *CL* iv. 850). For a fuller account of
Coleridge's views, see his annotation on an endleaf of Heinrich Steffen's *Ueber
die Idee der Universitäten* (Berlin, 1809). Coleridge searches for a formula or

unlike the allegory which merely *points* to a unity of appearance and ideality, *is* an inward unity of the objective reality of the universal idea and the subjective apperception of that reality expressed in a particular form.

Coleridge's early writings had represented nature itself as a language symbolic of the divine (*LPR* 339 n.);[52] this representation had sometimes an almost pantheistic emphasis, in common with Wordsworth. Later, after 1805, his theory of symbol became closely interwoven with his Christian faith, and particularly with the Logos idea. In April 1805 the progress of this development is evident:

> In looking at objects of Nature while I am thinking, as at yonder moon dim-glimmering thro' the dewy window-pane, I seem rather to be seeking, as it were *asking*, a symbolical language for something within me that already and forever exists, than observing any thing new. Even when that latter is the case, yet still I have always an obscure feeling as if that new phænomenon were the dim Awaking of a forgotten or hidden Truth of my inner Nature / It is still interesting as a Word, a Symbol! It is Λόγος, the Creator! ⟨and the Evolver!⟩. (*CN* ii, § 2546)

From this time on, Coleridge sees the whole of creation as a 'prophetic Symbol!' (N 50, fo. 45), a symbolic witness to what will be, to ultimate redemption through the regeneration by Christ (N 47, fos. 17^v–19) which is the true destiny of the human person. His exploration of the symbols of Scripture takes up, perhaps deliberately, an Augustinian theme. He noted that the New Testament uses symbols of the 'vegetative life', such as the 'Seed of Christ ... the Root—the Branches' to express 'the incidents States and functions of our spiritual Being, while those from insects and animals are with few exceptions applied ... to [man's] evil passions and appetites' (N 47, fo. 17). Among the 'exceptions' are the symbols of the ant and bee which are used with regard to 'the prudential obligations, to the exercises of the Understanding as the potentiated Adaptive Faculty'.[53]

---

phrase somewhere between 'sameness' and 'likeness'; this subject has significance for his theory of symbol.

[52] See also *SM: LS* 70 and n.

[53] Coleridge may perhaps be referring to the ant in Proverbs 6: 6–8; 30: 25, which is given as an edifying example in an exhortation to improved behaviour. This would come under his definition of 'prudential'. See also the reference to the bee in Isaiah 7: 18; here the bee is used as a symbol of impending threat due to

Coleridge gave, as an example of the symbols of redemption in nature, that of the growth and development of coral. 'The whole work of Redemption in the *Redeemed* which is the same as or consists in Regeneration, is a Process of spiritual Transsubstantiation—a daily Eucharist and I know of no more beautiful Symbol in inferior Life than the Coralline Zoolithe with its' root of rock and stem of Stone, softening as it rises into flesh and finally blossoming into animal Life & the Functions of Life' (N 47, fo. 17^v).

The Symbol as Revelation

Like that of St Augustine, Coleridge's theory of symbol asserts the inner spiritual meaning of Scripture to be perfectly reconcilable with its 'outer' historical truth.[54] Both understood Adam to be the symbolic representative of man; of the universal in the individual; and neither questioned his historical status as the first man.[55] Coleridge, like Augustine, emphasized that it is the *spiritual* meaning which is to be sought behind the 'letter', or the literal, historical facts of the matter. The role of the symbols and signs in Scripture is to express the truth of ideas. A symbol, he argued, is that through which the reconciliation of spiritual truth and the facts of experience and of history may be communicated and brought to birth in human consciousness: 'An IDEA, in the *highest* sense of that word, cannot be conveyed but by a *symbol*; and except in geometry, all symbols of necessity involve an apparent contradiction' (*BL* i. 156). An *apparent*

the recalcitrance of the people of God. Although these might, by some effort of imagination, be seen to conform to examples of 'prudential obligations', it is not clear how Coleridge connects the ant and the bee 'to the exercises of the Understanding as the potentiated Adaptive Faculty'.

[54] For a recent survey of the spiritual meaning of Scripture in Augustine, see *Œuvres de Saint Augustin, Les Confessions*, xiii. 12. 13; note: 'L'Interprétation de l'écriture', ed. M. Skutela, notes by A. Solignac, Bibliothèque Augustinienne, xiv (Paris, 1962), 622–9. In the *Confessions*, Augustine describes the light mentioned in Genesis 1: 3 as referring to the 'spiritual creation'; here is an example of the reconciliation of the literal description of physical creation which Augustine accepted as the story of Genesis, with the 'spiritual' meaning of Scripture; *Confessions*, xiii. 3.

[55] See Augustine's *De Genesi contra Manichaeos*, ii. 1; see also *De Trinitate*, xii. 12. 17–19, and Coleridge's N 41, fos. 7–7^v. See also J. A. Stuart, 'The Augustinian "Cause of Action" in Coleridge's *Rime of the Ancient Mariner*', *Harvard Theological Review*, 60 (1967), 180 n.

contradiction (such as the symbol's reconciliation of universal and particular reality) is the necessary result of the limitations of the finite mind. Augustine linked the symbol to the consequences of the Fall. Because man has fallen, truth is now no longer translucent to him but can only be seen as if through a cloud or veil. The symbol presents spiritual truth through the fallen medium of sensual objects. A necessary consequence of this is the 'contradiction' to which Coleridge referred; an act of faith is required in order that the reality in which the symbol participates may be glimpsed. This is not an act of faith in opposition to reason, but the very birth of reason itself.[56]

The reconciliation between universal and particular which the symbol both effects and reveals is the basis of Coleridge's insistence that the difference between symbol and allegory is of vital importance to theology, particularly to Scriptural exegesis. He believed the failure of his contemporaries to comprehend the nature of the symbol had disastrous consequences for the pursuit of truth: 'It is among the miseries of the present age that it recognizes no medium between *Literal* and *Metaphorical*' and that it 'confounds SYMBOLS with ALLEGORIES' (*SM: LS* 30). Coleridge rejected the allegorical interpretation of the Bible, insisting that '[t]here is, believe me, a wide difference between *symbolical* and *allegorical*' (*AR* 310 n.). He points to the Eucharist as an archetypal symbol: 'If I say that the flesh and blood (corpus noumenon) of the Incarnate Word are power and life, I say likewise that this mysterious power and life are *verily* and *actually* the flesh and blood of Christ' (ibid.). He scorns attempts to transform a difficult passage of Scripture into something more

---

[56] Paul de Man writes of Coleridge's treatment of the symbol: 'The material substantiality dissolves and becomes a mere reflection of a more original unity that does not exist in the material world. . . . In truth, the spiritualization of the symbol has been carried so far that the moment of material existence by which it was originally defined has now become altogether unimportant' (*Blindness and Insight*, 192). In this, de Man fails, I believe, to recognize the logocentricity of Coleridge's symbol theory: the symbol reflects the polarity or opposition of which the Logos, 'alterity', is the principle, that is, it is both universal *and* individual, both spiritual *and* material. This is not a matter of contradiction, nor of material reality lost in spiritualization, but, in Coleridge's view, of the symbol's reflection of, and participation in, the *two* natures of ideal Humanity, revealed in particular form in Christ, the God-Man who is also the creative Word (John 1). Coleridge's emphasis on the incarnation of the Logos in human history does not allow him to devalue material, historical reality.

easily acceptable; this is the aim of those who 'moralize' it, and turn it into a 'hyperbolical metaphor'.

As 'always itself a part of that, of the whole of which it is the representative', the symbol, according to Coleridge's theory, acts as a positive mediation between the world of spirit and that of individual and finite being. This is reflected in, for example, his *Ancient Mariner*; here, creatures such as the albatross and water snakes represent, to the journeying soul, complex universal ontological and spiritual realities in individual forms. Here he echoes an Augustinian emphasis on the importance of our encounter with outward symbols. The recognition of these becomes, through an act of faith, the inner light of revelation. Only through the inner light of the Logos (Reason) can the symbol reveal the full truth of the universal in which it participates, that of a reality beyond mere sign or representation:

> we may in a sound and good sense say that reason is the ray, the projected disk or image, from the Sun of Righteousness, an echo from the Eternal Word—*the light that lighteth every man that cometh into the world*; and that when the will placeth itself in a right line with the reason, there ariseth the spirit through which the will of God floweth into and actuates the will of man, so that it willeth the things of God, and the understanding is enlivened, and thenceforward useth the materials supplied to it by the senses symbolically, that is, with an insight into the true substance thereof. (*CM* iii. 723)

Thus, through the mediation of the Logos, the greatest of all symbols, human reason becomes the spiritual power by which the whole personality is regenerated and enlightened.

Coleridge suggested that the more closely a symbol shares in the reality of what it represents, the more difficult it is to understand (*CM* i. 687–8). This same sense of the effort required in mind and will for the mediation of symbol to be fruitful is present in Augustine's writings. He too had seen the whole creation as a symbolic language which tells of its Creator, and believed that the transcendent mystery of God is never fully revealed. The encounter with the Word can only take place in response to man's questioning; to his active longing for, and searching out of, truth.[57]

---

[57] In the *Confessions*, Augustine describes the questioning of earth, sea, air, and of the heavens in the search for God. Each one questioned points beyond

Augustine had linked the search for self-knowledge with the inner witness which recognizes symbols of divine truth. Coleridge himself made this connection; symbols are mere empty figures of speech unless they are encountered by a 'Being seeking to be self-conscious' (*CN* ii, § 3026). He follows Augustine, too, in linking the function of memory to the symbolic nature of words, objects, and numbers. Augustine held that both sense impressions and mental conceptions recall to mind and order what is in some mysterious sense already present in the memory, though hidden in its deep recesses: 'In [the cloisters of my memory] are the sky, the earth, and the sea, ready at my summons, together with everything that I have ever perceived in them by my senses, except the things which I have forgotten. In it I meet myself as well. I remember myself and what I have done, when and where I did it, and the state of my mind at the time.'[58] Coleridge expressed this same sense of outer things revealing themselves as symbols of inner truth by recalling what seems to be already present at an unconscious level: 'I have always an obscure feeling as if that new phænomenon were the dim Awaking of a forgotten or hidden Truth of my inner Nature' (*CN* ii, § 2546).

The Symbol of Selfhood

Like Augustine, Coleridge believed that the human individual constantly craves a completeness which is felt to be lacking. Each

---

itself. Augustine replies: ' "Since you are not my God, tell me about him. Tell me something of my God." Clear and loud they answered, "God is he who made us". I asked these questions simply by gazing at these things, and their beauty was all the answer they gave' (*Confessions*, x. 6). It is, insists Augustine, the 'inner' witness which hears and judges of the witness of outer things: 'The inner part of man knows these things through the agency of the outer part. I, the inner man, know these things; I, the soul, know them through the senses of my body. I asked the whole mass of the universe about my God, and it replied, "I am not God. God is he who made me" ' (ibid.). The activity of the human mind in this encounter is essential: 'The animals, both great and small, are aware of [the universe], but they cannot inquire into its meaning because they are not guided by reason, which can sift the evidence relayed to them by their senses.' Augustine emphasizes that this applies also to some human individuals, but not to all: 'to the man who merely looks it says nothing, while to the other it gives an answer. It would be nearer the truth to say that it gives an answer to all, but it is only understood by those who compare the message it gives them through their senses with the truth that is in themselves' (ibid.).

[58] Ibid. x. 8.

individual longs for the 'both–and' which is his true self; and the fulfilment of this craving is to be found in love. The beloved becomes a symbol of that perfect completeness and whole-ness which is unity with God in the divine Humanity of Christ. Coleridge expressed the creativity of the symbol as a transform-ing power of encounter and relationship:

The best, the truly lovely, in each & all is God. Therefore the truly Beloved is the symbol of God to whomever it is truly beloved by!—but it may become perfect & maintained lovely by the function of the two. / The Lover worships in his Beloved that final consummation ⟨of itself which is⟩ produced in his own soul by the action of the Soul of the Beloved upon it, and that final perfection of the Soul of the Beloved, ⟨which is in part⟩ the consequence of the reaction of his (so ammeliorated & re-generated) Soul upon the Soul of his Beloved / till each contemplates the soul of the other as involving his own, both in its givings and its receivings, and thus still keeping alive its *outness*, its *self-oblivion* united with *Self-warmth*, & still approximates to God! Where shall I find an image for this sublime Symbol ⟨which ever⟩ involving the presence of Deity, yet tends towards it ever! (*CN* ii, § 2540)

Coleridge regarded marriage as itself a symbol of the love union between God and Man through Christ. Like all symbols, however, it becomes actual, creative, and mediative only through the faith of those who recognize and participate in its reality: 'the actualizing Faith being supposed to exist in the Receivers, it is an outward Sign, co-essential with that which it signifies, or a living Part of that, the whole of which it represents. Marriage, there-fore, in the Christian sense (Ephesians v. 22–33) as symbolical of the union of the soul with Christ the Mediator, and with God through Christ, is perfectly a *sacramental* ordinance' (*AR* 49).

The Fall of Adam was, for Coleridge, a symbol of the loss of self, the alienation of will from reason to which man had succumbed. This alienation of self from self (the consequence of the separation of self from Other-self[59]) is entered and overcome by the 'second, but spiritual, Adam', Christ (*LR* iv. 2). As the Symbol beyond all symbols, as the Word who is himself God and with God, he is the antidote to man's fallen state.[60]

Coleridge asserted the necessity for the human individual to

---

[59] See below, Ch. 4.3.
[60] 'Jesus was both the Christ and the Symbol of Christ' (*CM* i. 821).

find his individuality as a universal principle; to recognize that his selfhood was held in common with others, and thus fulfil his own humanity (N 44, fos. 64ᵛ–65). This is made possible through Christ, the particular individual in whom is contained universal humanity. In connection with this necessity for a symbol through which Man as universal divine principle and man as individual are reconciled, Coleridge emphasized (in the 'Opus Maximum' notes) the dependence of all self-consciousness on a *representative* of the self:

what that representative shall be is by no means unalterably fixed in human nature by nature itself; but on the contrary varies with the growth bodily, moral and individual of each individual . . . the body becomes our *Self* when the reflections on our sensations desires & objects have been habitually appropriated to it in too great a proportion but this is not a necessity of our nature. Even in this life of imperfection there is a state possible in which a man might truly say my self loves A or B freely constituting the object i.e. the representative or objective Self (as distinguished from the primary originative Self) in whatever it wills to love, commands what it wills, & wills what it commands. Without this power indeed the commandment 'that we should love our neighbour as our Self and God more than either' would be a mockery. The difference between Self love and a Self that loves consists in this that the objects of the former are *given* to it according to the law of the senses and organization while the latter (a Self that loves freely) determines the objects according to a higher law. (OM iii, fos. 49–51)

Here the influence of Augustine is clear, not only in the borrowed phrase,[61] but in the contemplation of the association of a proper self-love with a self that loves, and loves because it loves God. Augustine expressed this simply: 'You were there before my eyes, but I had deserted even my own self. I could not find myself, much less find you.'[62]

The Mystery of the Symbol

Together with his concept of the symbol as overcoming a dualism between the concrete particular and spiritual reality, thus reconciling the historical and the ideal, Coleridge consistently upheld

---

[61] 'Give me the grace to do as you command, and command me to do what you will!' (*Confessions*, x. 29).
[62] Ibid. v. 2.

its mysterious nature. The symbol transcends reason, but is not in conflict with it. He had strong views on mysteries and declared that they are of two kinds: legitimate and illegitimate.[63] In a notebook entry of 1809 he wrote: 'to understand a thing is to see what the conditions of it were, & causes' (*CN* iii, § 3559). This applies only to the phenomenal world. To look for conditions and causes for that which is supernatural or of the spirit is obviously a nonsense. Thus, from the Christian point of view, although the symbol is the medium which conveys the truths of Reason, through an ontological participation in these truths it also participates in ultimate mystery.

Coleridge's concept of symbol owes much to the Hermetic tradition on which the symbolism of the alchemists also drew.[64] Alchemical symbols showed the real connection of living, causative power between spiritual realities and their earthly counterparts; here again the relationship is not one of representation only, but of participation.[65] We are reminded of Coleridge's insistence that the symbol is 'an actual and essential part of that, the whole of which it represents' (*LS: SM* 79). In recent years, H.-G. Gadamer has made use of this principle in hermeneutical theory and similarly asserted that the power of the symbol lies in its actual presence, not in merely pointing beyond itself.[66]

---

[63] Coleridge derogates the 'ULTRAFIDIANISM' of those who delight, like Sir Thomas Browne, 'to believe a thing not only above but contrary to Reason' (*AR* 199).

[64] Qualities of spiritual reality were believed by the alchemists to be found in gems, metals, plants, animals, colours, and sounds and often associated with the positions and particular powers of the planets under whose influence they came into being. The phenomena of the natural world symbolized the power of unseen spiritual forces (see e.g. N. Powell, *Alchemy: The Ancient Science* (London, 1976)).

[65] Ralph Coffman has listed books in Coleridge's library on alchemy and on Egyptian mythology containing Coleridge's marginalia (e.g. R. Fludd, *Philosophia Moysaica* (Gouda, 1638); G. Pereira, *Antoniana Margarita* (Medina del Campo, 1554); and the writings of Iamblichus, *De Mysteriis Aegyptiorum, Chaldaeorum, Assyriorum* (Geneva, 1607); see R. Coffman, *Coleridge's Library* (Boston, 1987)). Coleridge would also have gleaned much information from Tenneman's *Geschichte der Philosophie*, and from T. Stanley's *History of Philosophy*, both of which contain detailed chapters on alchemy. Coleridge found in Egyptian religious symbols an expression of the nature and function of Logos (see 'On the Prometheus of Aeschylus', *LR* ii. 342–3). He may have developed this theme from a reading of Plutarch; in the latter's *On Isis and Osiris*, for example, the Logos figure appears in the guise of the Egyptian God Osiris. See n. 87 below.

[66] Gadamer, *Truth and Method*, 65.

Some of the most ancient and significant symbols of alchemy frequently appear in Coleridge's writings; the sun, for example (associated with the process of turning base metals into gold, and with excellence, beauty, supreme power, light, and perfection), is used by him as a symbol of Christ, the Logos, not only in the sense of the light of reason, as in Christian Platonist traditions, but in the sense of a living, dynamic, and transforming power.[67]

Coleridge recognized that the sixteenth-century German mystic Jacob Böhme had preserved the element of mystery and had interwoven the symbols of alchemy with those of Christian theology. The importance of the connection between language and alchemical secrets, processes, and rituals was already well established. Paracelsus (1493–1541) himself had written in a strange mixture of German, Latin, and words that he coined himself. He had given the name *al-kohl* to spirits of wine (strangely, it was the Arabic word for black eye-paint), and the word 'spagyric' for his own kind of alchemy, which was concerned with healing. Coleridge was similarly fascinated by the coining of new words; he too, as we have seen, insisted on a true relation between words and things and, particularly, powers. The mysterious spirituality not only of words but of the idea of 'Word' itself was recognized as an indispensable part of alchemical processes. It is a most important symbol in Böhme's writings and one from which Coleridge derived much insight. Böhme's use of 'Word' is often related to his understanding of the Fourth Gospel. In the *Threefold Life of Man* (1620), which Coleridge read and annotated, there is evidence that, for Böhme, as for Coleridge, the Fourth Gospel was pre-eminent:

John, the Evangelist writeth very well, also deeply and clearly, that in the beginning was the Word, and the Word was God, and all things were made by it: for the Word revealeth the Deity, and generateth the Angelicall World [which is] a Principle in it selfe: which is to be understood as followeth.

---

[67] It is interesting to note that the *tetractys* appears to have had an important place in the symbolism of alchemy. See Powell, *Alchemy*, 106–11. Powell has shown that this symbol played a large part in the symbols of the 'Twelve Keys' propounded by the alchemist Basil Valentine (a mysterious figure whose history and true name are unknown). It is associated with sacredness, power, and polarity (see the Tenth Key).

The first Eternal Will is God the Father, and it is, to generate his Sonne, viz. his Word; not out of anything else but out of himselfe.[68]

Böhme had explored the symbolism of the divine Word in a rich variety of ways: as creative power, as the Will, as the Creator, as the 'second Word' who is 'the Sonne, and the brightness of the Father'; as the relation between the meaning of the Word and 'the forming of words'; as the Incarnation of the Word in Man and as 'How the soule formeth the Word'. Coleridge described the representation as *more* than metaphor. It was a transforming and illuminating influence in the mind of man (*CM* i. 568).

The Idea of the Word, he asserted, is a purer reality of mind and soul than any mathematical concept. Plato and Pythagoras attempted to express reality by using the purest form of human reasoning: that of number, harmony, proportion, and figure as symbols which are to be recognized as the actual constituent forms of all finite and particular reality while yet being universal a priori truths. 'Word', for Coleridge, is a still more powerful and adequate expression of the highest form of reality and fulfils all the functions of symbol. In human discourse and relationship it is the medium of encounter between the speaker (or writer) and the hearer (or reader), the medium through which minds meet. It is 'begotten' through an act of will, and its reception depends upon another such act. In the fulfilment of its nature and role it relies on a common experience of language, a common principle of humanity. Coleridge accepted Christ as the divine Word, as the supreme spiritual and ontological realization of all these qualities of mediation, transformation, and relationship. The importance which he attached to Word as symbol is evident from the following parenthetic note:

(And God said = uttered = went forth in—the Word—(Moses) God, the Word (*Ο Λογος προς τον θεον, και θεου*) (St John) went forth from God.—*εις αφισταμενους* (to the apostates) *απο του θειου εξιτητεον εκ του θεου**). But that which goeth forth yet so as in its essence to remain, is a Word. Therefore and for other kindred reasons is the Intelligibile et patrem et se ipsum communicans, the communicative and communicable

⁶⁸ J. Böhme, 'Three-fold Life of Man', in *The Works of Jacob Behmen*, tr. J. Sparrow, ed. G. Ward and T. Langcake, 4 vols. (London, 1764–81), ii, §§ 60–1: 'The Forms of Nature'.

Intelligence designated the Word, with a wonderful adequacy greater, I deem, than that of any other Symbol.[69]

[* The Logos with God, and God . . . There had to be a going forth from God to the apostates (i.e. to those who fell away) from the divine.]

One of the most interesting symbols employed by Böhme is that of 'Salitter' (saltpetre or potassium nitrate), also an important agent in the alchemists' work. An editorial note in the first volume of the Coleridge *Marginalia* explains, 'Böhme uses the term symbolically to mean the substratum of the "Divine Powers", the forces that constitute the universe, both spiritual and material' (*CM* i. 569 n.). Coleridge's development of this symbol accorded with his emphasis on the relationship between the world of spirit (of intelligences or 'principles') and the material world of the senses. It is clear that he saw Böhme's 'Salitter' as a symbol of the divine 'principle of BEING', which he elsewhere[70] proclaimed to be the Logos:

Salitter is *Salnitter* in the original German, i.e. Sal Nitrum—i.e. the chrystallized or fixed Principle of Nitre—a better symbol could scarcely have been chosen to represent the basis, ground, or principle of BEING as distinguished from the causes of *Existing*—. Salnitter may be literally translated with relation to our present chemical nomenclature Carbonazot, the Sal = Carbon, or principle of Fixity & Coherence, by attraction, and the Nitre or Nitter = Nitrogene (or azote) by Repulsion. (*CM* i. 572–3)

Coleridge proceeded to draw a connection between Böhme's 'Salitter' and 'Mercurius' as symbols of the powers of Ideas which have their being in the Logos, the 'adequate Idea of the divine beings' in whom 'are contained all possible Ideas *eminenter*'. Here he linked the secret symbolism of alchemy, in which mercury represents spirit, fusibility, and volatility, with what might be described as a Christian Platonist view of creation through the Logos. To Coleridge, mercury represented the 'Messenger', the idea of the transmission and communication, the go-between dynamic of sound and light as creative and productive forces. He translated Böhme's 'Salnitter' into the old Paracelsian com-

---

[69] BL MS Egerton 2801, fo. 119. Here again we see the link which Coleridge made between the Christian doctrine of redemption through the 'Condescension' of the Logos and the redemptive nature of language, especially of symbols.

[70] See below, Ch. 3.2.

bination which is the ground of all material substances: salt, sulphur, and mercury (he represents salt by carbon and sulphur by 'Nitrogene'). In Böhme's symbolism of 'Word', of 'Sun' and 'Son', of 'Salitter' and 'Mercurius', Coleridge recognized, however mysteriously presented, that 'translucence of the Eternal through and in the Temporal' (*SM: LS* 30) which has its source in the divine Logos.

He was impressed by Emanuel Swedenborg's (1688–1772) symbolism, though critical of aspects of the latter's religious views, which seemed to him fantastical and unsound. His close study of Swedenborg began after 1820, at a time when his own concept of symbol in the context of religious truth was already well developed. In a notebook entry Coleridge commented on what he saw as Swedenborg's errors; but then he continued: 'considered as Product humanity, I scarcely know an uninspired Writer from whom so large a sum of important Truths and impressive Symbols of Truth could be collected as from this so-called Madman & Visionary' (*CN* iii, § 3474). Prominent in Swedenborg's writings too is a representation of the Son of God through the symbol of the Sun. Coleridge explored this theme in a notebook entry of 1828:

Lastly, meditate on the Sun, Dynamically considered, the Sun is co-extensive with & expanded as it were over the whole area filled by his influence—but yet his *Phasis*, his selfness self-manifested, is the central Orb. Even so in the center or focal place of the all-present son of God the *Son of Man* (i.e. the Son of God revealed in the Divine Humanity) sits enthroned.

Whatever I may think of the way in which Swedenborg has filled up and dramatized this Idea, the Idea itself meets my full concurrence— namely, that our Divines have laboured so effectually to remove every sensible form from our notion of Heaven as to leave no form at all—and nothing for Hope to lay hold of but a few general terms, Joy, Felicity, Bliss & the like. (N 36, fos. 64^v–65).

The 'sensible form' transformed by the inner vision which can recognize it as symbol is itself the medium through which the divine Spirit and Word is encountered.

Logos and Tetractys

Coleridge took up St Paul's description of Christ himself, in his Incarnation, entering the world of symbol, in which his divinity, whether manifested in action or word, is veiled in flesh (*AR* 309–10). Many of Christ's words will be 'hard sayings' for us: in him spirit and flesh are reconciled, but for us the contradiction is still present. The man Jesus 'was both the Christ and the great symbol of Christ' (*CM* i. 821). The distinction between unveiled reality and the representational function of symbol sheds light on Coleridge's definition of the apparent contradictions which are inherent in symbolic expression. It also makes clearer his acceptance of some apparent dichotomies, such as that of the Logos as both coequal and subordinate to God the Father, a paradox which he would have found expressed, for example, in the work of Philo and Origen.[71] Coleridge suggests that, as one with the Father and present eternally with him, the Son is coequal. Under the condition of his going forth as the Word, however, he represents the whole, the universal, as revealed in the particular forms of the finite world. Similarly, the universal Logos is symbolized by the historical individual Jesus Christ, and the Logos in Christ is symbolized in the nature of man. There is, in all Coleridge's representations of these relationships, both a genuine unity and the distinction and subordination of particularity. The 'circumference' which delineates the forms of Ideal reality becomes a new centre, that of the symbol which expresses and represents it in particular form; the 'circles' of universal and particular reality are thus constantly interlinked. In the two natures of Christ, Coleridge argued, are contained both the reality of the historical individual and the universal principle of divine humanity; as the Logos, he is the universal in which all individuals are contained (N 44, fos. 62^v–66).

One of the most important descriptions of the eternal Logos in Coleridge's work is the 'Idea of Man'.[72] Since 'an IDEA, in the *highest* sense of that word, cannot be conveyed but by a *symbol*' (*BL* i. 156), the Incarnate Christ is, then, both Idea and Symbol; or, more accurately he is himself the Exemplar of symbol.[73] He is both the ideal reality of humanity, and the medium through

---

[71] See below, Ch. 4.1.

[72] See below, Ch. 4.1.

[73] Karl Rahner has, in more recent times, richly developed this idea of the Logos as the '*Realsymbol*' of the Father; as 'the inward symbol which remains distinct from what is symbolized' *Theological Investigations*, tr. K. Smith (London, 1966), iv. 236. He defines the symbol as 'the representation which allows the other "to be there"' (p. 225), and claims that 'the theology of the Logos is strictly a theology of the symbol, and indeed a supreme form of it' (p. 235).

which that reality is communicated; he is thus, in fact and idea, the true 'self' in self-consciousness, the birth of reason.[74] Reflecting this archetype, man participates in the mediating activity of symbol; in himself he symbolizes the divine nature. With Augustine, Coleridge saw the human individual as a triunity: 'There exists in the human being, at least in man fully developed, no mean symbol of Tri-unity, in Reason, Religion, and the Will. For each of the three, though a distinct agency, implies and demands the other two, and loses its own nature at the moment that from distinction it passes into division or separation' (*LS: SM* 62).

He admired and often made use of the concepts of the symbolic nature and function of number which had been explored by Pythagoras and Plato. The Greek *logos* principle, as expressed in the Platonic Ideas and in Pythagorean philosophy, is eternal form and spiritual reality; it is also the active principle within the material universe and thus dynamic and causative. Coleridge made use, as we have seen,[75] of the figure of the *tetractys* (sacred to Pythagoras and adopted by Plato). For him, it became a symbol of true Being (Logos), that which underlies all derivative reality. Here too the element of mystery remains. The origins and history of the significance of the *tetractys* to the Greeks are now (and were by Coleridge's own time) difficult to reconstruct or identify with confidence. Much of his own development of the theme was based on the comprehensive treatment given to it in Ralph Cudworth's *True Intellectual System of the Universe*.[76]

Coleridge also knew Henry More's exploration, in *Conjectura Cabbalistica* (1653),[77] of the relationship between the Pythagorean *tetractys* and the sacred numbers and letters of the Jewish cabbala in its elaboration of the Genesis creation myth. Coleridge's deep interest in the ancient Jewish writings, in the Torah and the cabbala, is evident in his frequent notebook references to them.[78]

---

[74] See below, e.g. Chs. 3.2 and 4.3.

[75] See above, Intro., n. 33.

[76] Ralph Cudworth, *The True Intellectual System of the Universe* (1678), 2nd edn., 2 vols. (London, 1743), I. i. 4. 375 ff.

[77] More, *Conjectura Cabbalistica*, app.: 'The Defence of the Philosophick Cabbala', 154 ff. Coleridge makes reference to a section of this work; 'The Moral Cabbala', in NQ, fo. 57.

[78] The relationship between being, word, idea, and number is as close in the Hebrew tradition as in the philosophy of Pythagoras and Plato. The numerical significance attached to every Hebrew letter and combination of letters deter-

He would probably have found discussed in Henry More's works, some of which he annotated, the association of the *tetractys* and the *tetragrammaton* (the sacred name of God consisting in the four Hebrew consonants). Cudworth too mentions the belief of many scholars that the Pythagorean *tetractys* (used as a form of sacred oath) was derived from the *tetragrammaton* (or tetragram). More, however, was adamant that the *tetractys* would not have been an object of worship, but a symbol expressing the nature of God, who alone may be worshipped. He quoted what he described as 'the rabbinical saying "He is his name and his name is He"', emphasizing that when the name of God is mentioned in this context, it is not merely a solecism but expresses the truth that 'when the name Jehovah is applied to any person . . . it is not in scripture an idle name, but that thing itself is understood by it: as, where the angel of the covenant and the leader of the Israelites is called Jehovah, it implies that Jehovah himself was the person understood, and that it was in reality Christ or the soul of the Messiah combined with the eternal Logos'.[79]

According to More, the *tetractys* is 'only the repository of the Tetragrammaton, as also of other mysteries, of which it may be the appropriate symbol'. Whatever the correct interpretation of the relation between the *tetractys*, the tetragram, and God himself, Coleridge was familiar with the debate and probably with the further development of these symbols by Philo and the Fathers.[80]

mines the hidden and holy as well as the manifest meanings of words. It is interesting to speculate on the possible connection of Coleridge's reference in 'Kubla Khan' to 'Alph, the sacred river' with the first and primal Hebrew letter, *aleph*, the first of 'Elohim', the source of all things; especially since Coleridge himself commented on this letter in the context of a discussion of numerical symbols: 'The Aleph, say the Rabbinical Philologists, is no Letter; but that in and with which all Letters are or become (*CL* v. 99). For the Jews, the other most holy form of the name of God, the sacred Name which may not be spoken and which must never be erased if written, has within it numbers and possible permutations of number relationships which represent the source of all being and time.

[79] Coleridge may have also known the Latin edition of Cudworth's *True Intellectual System* (1743), which includes Mosheim's notes to the text. Mosheim quotes this passage from Henry More (*Conjectura Cabbalistica*, II. i. 4, § 20 n.). He refers to the speculations of those such as Henry More who understood the *tetractys* to be related to the tetragram, and to have been used to signify the Name of God.

[80] Coleridge probably drew, from Philo and from the early Christian Fathers, the association of the *tetractys* with the Jehovah-Word, which the latter identified

In 1805 Coleridge's letters from Malta were sealed with a signet ring bearing the imprint of the triangle. His interest, and the sacred significance which he henceforth gave to it, suggest that this seal is a representation of the *tetractys* symbol. He was beginning to find himself convinced of the divinity of Christ and of the triunity of God, and the *tetractys* perhaps powerfully symbolized this development in his own thought. Later, he referred critically to the 'failure of the Fathers from Justin Martyr to Augustine' to hold on to the truth of the *tetractys*, substituting for it the less adequate *trias* (triad) (N 52, fo. 16ᵛ). This criticism centred around Coleridge's fear of a distortion which threatened the doctrine of the Trinity (the fundamental, relational reality). This distortion resulted in the failure to distinguish the Absolute Will, as Identity and Abysmal Power, from the Ipseity–Alterity–Community of God as self-realized. As we have seen, the *tetractys*, unlike the *trias*, involves *four* terms: 'It cannot... be denied that in changing the *formula* of the *Tetractys* into the *Trias*, by merging the *Prothesis* in the *Thesis*, the Identity in the Ipseity, the Christian Fathers subjected their exposition to many inconveniences' (*NED* ii. 195).

To Gregory Nazianzus' (329–89) assertion that 'We may, as I conceive, preserve [the doctrine of] one God, by referring both

as the Logos, the Creator God: 'The incorporeal world is set off and separated from the visible one by the mediating Logos as by a veil. But may it not be that this Logos is the tetrad through which the corporeal solid comes into being?' (*Quaestiones et Solutiones in Exodum*, ii. 94). Here is the Greek concept of the *tetractys* as the numerical reality of the solid. Hierocles, as quoted in Cudworth's *True Intellectual System*, developed the same idea: 'there is nothing in the whole world, which doth not depend upon the Tetractys, as its root and principle. For the Tetrad is, as we have already said, the maker of all things; the intelligible god, the cause of the heavenly and sensible God [that is, of the animated world of heaven]' (i. i. 4. 375). In Pythagorean philosophy, the *tetractys* is a triadic figure, constituted from a ground of four through the relations and proportions constituted within the numerical series $1:2$, $2:3$, $3:4$ (the principle on which the universe itself is ordered and which is, for example, the mysterious form of the musical harmonic series itself). An intriguing feature of this figure is that it consists of, and exists only in, the numerical proportions, relationships, and oppositions of the Decad, representing the fullness, and totality, of the dynamic operation of the Logos as the Idea through which all that is comes into being. The *tetractys* is the symbol through which human reason can participate in the divine mystery of life and being. The tetragram begins with the letter *yod*, which for the Hebrews is associated with the number ten, and is also the first letter of the name Yeshua, or Jesus.

the son and Holy Ghost to one cause',[81] Coleridge responded: 'Another instance of the inconvenience of the Trias compared with the Tetractys' (*NED* ii. 196). These criticisms suggest that he was aware of the interest of the Church Fathers not only in the Hebrew tetragram but in the *tetractys* itself.[82] In the *trias*, there is no 'prothesis' distinguished from thesis. This, he believed, would be to omit one of the most crucial factors in understanding the divine nature. In a triad, the synthesis holds the only position of identity, but Coleridge wished to emphasize the priority of 'prothesis'—not as the result, but rather as the antecedent *ground*, of the interdependence of thesis and antithesis in the representation of all kinds of reality (the priority, that is, in terms of human logic and the necessary succession of finite thought).

From the sacred *tetractys*, the epitome of pure relationship and of the potential for dynamic opposition in unity, Coleridge derived the logical or 'noetic' Pentad. This he used as symbol of the distinction-in-unity of human thought and being; as such, unlike the purer *tetractys*, it contains a mediative term, the 'indifference', or 'mesothesis' between thesis and antithesis. The 'prothesis' of the *tetractys* is not to be identified with its synthesis. It is thus not liable to what Coleridge came to regard as the chief error in Schelling's philosophy, namely, that the Absolute is the identity of *identity* and distinction rather than of *unity* and distinction. Schelling's concept also suggested, to Coleridge, a *process* by which absolute identity was seen to be derived from synthesis; it implied that the Absolute required process in order to truly be what it is. This Coleridge finally rejected completely.[83] The Absolute 'Prothesis' is, on the contrary, prior to the distinction of thesis and antithesis and the Ground of both. It is also, paradoxically, to be understood as 'belonging' to both, a life and quality which they not only *are* but which they *have*, an existential power and agency.

The *tetractys*, as a numerical and figurative symbol symbolizing universal ideal reality, expresses causative, dynamic relation, form, and distinction-in-unity. Coleridge also used it to symbolize

---

[81] Gregory Nazianzus, *Oratione*, 29; see *NED* ii. 196.
[82] For references to the *tetractys*, see *Ex Origene: Selecta in Psalmos*; Psalmus, ii. 539 (Migne, 12. 1104B). See also Hippolytus' *Refutatio Omnium Haeresium*, 6. 34 (Migne, 16. 3246A) and Irenaeus, *Adversus Haereses*, 1. i. 1 (Migne, 7. 448A).
[83] See below, Chs. 2.2, 2.3, and 4.3.

both the Idea of God ('Idea' here in his special sense of primal reality in the form of communicable intelligence) and all the processes and relations of life and mind in the creation. Since the Logos is, for him, the Idea of God, the principle of relation and the Creator, the *tetractys* symbolizes the nature and function of the divine Word. As such it could provide, he believed, as a tool of human reason, the means to true knowledge: 'Never, never, can I too often assert . . . the great truth, that the Divine Tetractys is the Form and Regula Maxima of all Knowledge "the mystery in which are contained all treasure of Science"' (N 47, fo 10ᵛ).[84]

The *tetractys* powerfully expresses the principle of polarity. Coleridge also frequently employed the circle, and particularly the relation between centre and circumference, as a symbol of, for example, the distinction and yet the complete coequality and coeternity of Father and Son in the unity of Love (Spirit). The centre point of the circle becomes a symbol of the Logos who is begotten as 'position'—as the point from which all else may be drawn. According to this figurative language, God the Father may be represented as the Circumference. In one sense, the Point is that from which the Circumference may be drawn; in another, the Circumference is that through which the Centre is found. Thus the self-realization of God through relation is symbolized. Here, as so often, Coleridge draws on Greek thought. The ideal reality of the circle, as the perfection of mathematical form, was central to the thought of Pythagoras and Plato and was the basis of much Greek philosophical speculation and dialectic.[85] In Coleridge's scheme, it became, like the *tetractys*, a symbol of

---

[84] For Hegel's idea of the 'divine Triangle' as influenced by Franz von Baader's essay *Ueber das pythagoräische Quadrat in der Natur, oder die vier Weltgegenden* (n.p., 1798), see H. S. Harris, *Hegel's Development: Night Thoughts* (Jena, 1801–6; Oxford, 1983), 184: 'In Baader's essay the 3 domains of natural history (animal, vegetable, mineral) and the 3 types of matter (combustible, salty, earthy) are subordinated under 3 "basic forces" or "principles" (fire, water, earth). These elements would remain inert however, were it not for the 4th principle (air) which enlivens them. The relation of the 4 elements is symbolically portrayed as a triangle with a point in the middle (representing air). This symbol (triangle with a point) Baader calls the *Quaternius* or Pythagorean Square.' Harris also mentions Böhme's influence in this context; and Coleridge makes use of the 'triangle with a point' in his annotations of Böhme (*CM* i. 649).

[85] It had, for example, a prominent place in Plato's cosmology (*Timaeus*, 36c ff.).

the nature and quality of the *Idem et Alter* reality of the Trinity, realized only through the begetting of 'alterity', that is, through Logos. At the same time, like the *tetractys*, this symbol always involves a relation with the finite, created world. Coleridge outlined his conception of the relationship between the symbol of the Circle and the Symbol of the Logos in his annotations on Böhme's works:

As the Sun is . . . the manifested Convergence of all the Astral powers, subsisting from them, yet re-acting as that which is the Condition of *all* being a Whole: so the Son is the omnipresent Center of that infinite Circle, whose only Circumference is in its own Self-comprehension, the eternal Act of which for ever constitutes that Center. The immanent energy of the divine Consciousness is, and is the cause of, the co-eternal Filiation of the Logos, the essential Symbol of the Deity, the substantial, infinite, sole adequate, Idea, in God, of God; in and by whom the Father, thus *necessarily* self-manifested, doth *freely* in the ineffable over-flowing of Goodness create, and in proportion to the containing power, manifest himself to, all Creatures. (*CM* i. 564)

The Prophetic Symbol

Coleridge's later thought increasingly explores prophecy as an important function of symbol. Christ, as the 'Jehovah-Word' of the Old Testament, was the Word of prophetic utterance. Here too we find the Logos portrayed as the Archetypal Symbol. Coleridge's association of prophecy and symbolism was encouraged by his reading of Creuzer's discussion of the meaning of σύμβολον ('symbol') in ancient Greek philosophy and religion. His notes suggest that he found in Greek religion, as much as in that of ancient Egypt, an apprehension of

the peculiar force of the Symbol, as omening the presence of the Divine, the sense of the inexplicable, or aboriginal—. That which unexpectedly, from the depths of Nature, started upon the Eye as Prediction or Warning, was Συμβολον, in the wider sense—& then, by philosophic Precision, that which was itself supposed to be one with, or a living part of, or having its constituent principle from, the higher somewhat, the whole of which it represented. Thus those Statues, Images, or Signs of a God, in which having been magically constellated to the influence of the same God the God himself had a virtual & efficient Presence, were *Symbolic*. (*CN* iv, §4831)

He seems to have believed that the archetypal reality of Logos was foreshadowed in the nature and function of the early Greek and Egyptian symbols; in the divine Word, the 'virtual & efficient Presence' of God was most completely and perfectly revealed. He would also have found this theme of Logos as the εἰκών of God taken up by Philo.[86] Together with Coleridge's increasing preoccupation with the processes and powers of the redemptive Word as manifested in all life, thought, and experience, we find his emphasis on Christ as the Symbol beyond all symbols: 'the εικων, portrait, substantial Image, such as that in the Mirror would be, were it begotten and not merely reflected: were it representative adequately, and in toto, not of the surface alone—Hence the Cabbalists, and St Paul (Coloss.) appropriate the term 'Εικων' to the only begotten Word, the Filial Deity, all other Words being at their highest dignity *Symbols*' (*CN* iv, § 4831).[87]

So the divine Word is, for Coleridge, the transcendent source of all symbols and, at the same time, immanent within them as their reconciling power. The Logos is the life and power of mind, the ground of relationship, the revelation of prophetic utterance, the completion and presence of love in which all true symbols (as the manifestation of Ideas) participate; yet the Word can never be reduced to words, and the mystery of the true Symbol remains.

1.3. 'JEHOVAH-WORD', NAME OF GOD

'Religion is revelation, and revelation the only religion', wrote Coleridge (*NED* ii. 232). This statement is related to his assertion 'No Christ, no God': the Logos, the Son, is the Idea and revelation of God without which religion has no object, and no reality. He believed revelation through the Word to be the substance not only of religion, but, like F. H. Jacobi,[88] of reason

---

[86] Philo, *Legum Allegoriae*, iii. 96. Coleridge was well aware of Philo's use of this term (see *CL* iv. 632–3).

[87] Coleridge wrote these passages while reading G. F. Creuzer's *Symbolik und Mythologie der alten Völker*, 4 vols. (Leipzig, 1810–12); 2nd edn., 6 vols. (Leipzig, 1918–23). Creuzer's influence is strong on Coleridge's later development of the idea of religious symbols and the place of the Logos in these (see e.g. *CN* iv, § 4831).

[88] F. H. Jacobi, *Werke*, 6 vols. (Leipzig, 1816), iii, p. xxxiii: 'Alle menschliche Erkenntnis gehe aus von Offenbarung und Glauben' ('All human perception proceeds from Revelation and Faith').

itself: '[man] received his first human instruction, the means and conditions of his *actual* humanity (i.e. rationality) in the School of Revelation' (N 26, fo. 39). He maintained that the nature and identity of revelation, reason, and religion (and thus the truth of human nature and of the divine–human relationship) is most adequately expressed through the analogy of the Word. Not only reason, but the interdependence of history and prophecy,[89] Coleridge believed, must be understood in the light of revelation, through the Logos who is the Word and *Name* of God. The Logos is revealed in his creation, in external, objective reality; but the encounter with Logos as the Person of God takes place in the inner life of spirit. Coleridge was convinced that only through this inner revelation could the individual's understanding be raised to Reason and the truths of Ideas. It transformed individuals into persons.[90] The argument of the 'logosophic' system is interwoven, in a hermeneutical circle which Coleridge accepted as symbolic of *all* understanding, with that which sought to establish the unity of reason and revelation. They are mutually dependent. This is not to say that the argument is circular in a pernicious sense; rather that, on whichever track and at whichever point the journey is begun, the paths inevitably cross or merge at intervals.

The Analogy of the Word

Coleridge made much use of the Scholastics' doctrine of the analogy of being,[91] and declared 'Word' to be an especially fine example. Analogy, he claimed, is a valid tool of human reason.[92] We are justified in drawing analogies between the objects of our finite experience of phenomenal reality and those spiritual realities which by their very nature cannot be liable to explanation (causes and conditions, he argued, as the terms of explanation, are categories belonging only to phenomenal reality).

[89] See below.
[90] See below, Chs. 4.1 and 4.3.
[91] This aspect of Coleridge's thought has been explored by Boulger, *Coleridge as Religious Thinker*, 138.
[92] See Coleridge's notes on Immanuel Kant's *Die Religion innerhalb der Grenzen der blössen Vernunft etc.* (Königsberg, 1794), 297: 'there is another inferior sense of the word explanation, in which it is possible—namely, the co-classing of this Object of Faith with analogous Objects or Facts of Experience—and tho' this does not increase our insight, yet it enlarges our view, and facilitates our belief, our rational belief'.

He revered Origen, Jerome, and Augustine 'as the three great fathers in respect of theology' (*TT* i. 79 n.), and made frequent admiring reference to their work—particularly to that of the first and the last—in order to support or illustrate his own points of argument. All three had explored in depth the analogy between Logos and human speech, especially in connection with the Fourth Gospel. Those to whom he accorded the highest status 'in respect of rhetoric', that is, 'Basil, Gregory Nazianzen, and Chrysostom', had also given close attention to this analogy. Coleridge often wrote of the importance which he, and those whom he most admired, attached to the term 'Word': 'To me (why do I say to me?) to Bull, to Waterland, to Gregory Nanzianzen, Basil, Athanasius, Augustine, the terms Word and generation, have appeared admirably, yea, most awfully pregnant and appropriate' (*NED* ii. 136). He was familiar with an earlier emphasis on the peculiar appropriateness of 'Word' in the work of Philo and the Alexandrian Jews, in whom the Greek and Hebrew traditions of thought were joined. He claimed that: 'Philo names the Logos the only-begotten Son of God to distinguish the Word from a Thought', and that 'the very term, the Word, implies this distinction, and was chosen by the Jewish Platonists to express self-subsistence without self-origination' (*CM* ii. 458). Certainly Philo distinguished the Logos, existing as a generic unity, from God the One, the indivisible unity, wholly unqualified. The Logos is 'antecedent to all that has come into existence',[93] the 'eldest and most embracing of created things'. He emphasized the distinction between the *generated* self-subsistence of the Logos and the self-origination of the One God. Coleridge himself often echoes Philo's assertions that the Logos had been revealed in various forms (such as God's Angel) in the Old Testament. Philo believed the Father–Son relationship to be often misconceived and the distinction of persons neglected: 'For just as those who are unable to see the sun itself see the gleam of the parhelion and take it for the sun, and take the halo round the moon for that luminary itself, so some regard the image of God, his angel, the Logos, as his very self.'[94] Although they share the same designation of being, ὤν, they exist differently.

The above passage and others of a similar tone suggest, how-

---

[93] *Migratione Abrahami*, 6.   [94] *De Somniis*, i. 239.

ever, that Coleridge's empathetic response to much of Philo's insight into the nature of Logos allowed him to project the idea of consubstantiality as the latter's theme without adequate justification. Following John Whitaker (*The Origins of Arianism Disclosed*[95]), he maintained that Philo's use of the term 'Word' was one of the models which influenced the thought of the New Testament writers: 'Surely, there must have been an intellectual propriety in the terms, *Logos*, Word, *Begotten before all creation*,—an adequate idea or *icon*, or the Evangelists and Apostolic penmen would not have adopted them. They did not invent the terms; but took them and used them as they were taken and applied by Philo and both the Greek and Oriental sages' (*CM* iii. 524). St John, Coleridge declared, would have used these terms in the 'known and received sense' and this was 'the strongest extrinsic argument against the Arians, Socinians, and Unitarians'; against all those groups which he consistently and frequently attacked on the grounds that they failed to uphold the coequal distinction-in-unity of the Trinity and Christ's nature as God and Man.

The distinction between Word and thought, like that between word and mere sound, was important to Coleridge; here again the emphasis is Augustinian, as is his own exposition of the importance of the analogy of the Word.[96] Both Augustine and

[95] John Whitaker makes the relation of Philo's thought to that of the Church Fathers a central theme of *The Origins of Arianism Disclosed*; this, no doubt, prompted Coleridge to take up the idea.

[96] Coleridge was probably familiar with Augustine's exegesis of the Prologue to the Fourth Gospel. In *In Joannis Evangelium Tractatus*, Augustine re-emphasizes that the Word was 'in the beginning with God', and that the second person of the Trinity is neither subordinate to nor created by God. Augustine offered an analogy through which the paradox could be understood that the Son of God, who exists as a distinct Person (the Creator who, in unity with the Spirit, becomes the life within all Creation and the light and life of man), is yet eternally *one with* the Father. The analogy is that of word and Word: 'With thyself, O man, a work in thy heart is a different thing from sound; but the word that is with thee, in order to pass to me, requires sound for a vehicle as it were. It takes to itself sound, mounts it as a vehicle, runs through the air, comes to me and yet does not leave thee. But the sound, in order to come to me, left thee and yet did not stay with me. Now has the word that was in thy heart also passed away with the passing sound? Thou didst speak thy thought; and, that the thought which was hid with thee might come to me, thou didst sound syllables; the sound of the syllables conveyed thy thought to my ear; through my ear thy thought descended into my heart, the intermediate sound flew away; but that word which took to itself sound was with thee before thou didst sound it, and is with me, because thou didst

the tradition of Christian Platonism influenced his assertion of the identity of the Word (that which is with God and yet goes forth to create, to reveal and to mediate) with the Stoic and Neoplatonic concept of Reason.[97]

Reason and Revelation

Coleridge, like many of his contemporaries, sought to confirm, not least to his own satisfaction, that reason and revelation were reconcilable.[98] Much of the so-called 'Higher Criticism' in Germany seemed to him to place too much emphasis on the correspondence of Scripture with human understanding, and too little on the transcendent nature of its spiritual truth. On the other hand, he was quite clear that the Bible must (and could only) be defended on grounds of reason and not by appeal to an authority which had not been tested. His avowed aim in undertaking a systematic study of the Bible in 1827 was 'to give an insight into the rationality of the Scriptures' (N 37, fo. 40).

Repeatedly, Coleridge asserted that true religion must imply

---

sound it, without quitting thee. Consider this, thou nice weigher of sounds, whoever thou be. Thou despisest the Word of God, thou who comprehendest not the word of man' (*Lectures or Tractates on the Gospel according to St John*, xxxvii. 4, tr. John Gibb and James Innes, in *Nicene and Post-Nicene Fathers of the Christian Church*, ed. Philip Schaff (New York, 1888), vii). In this same context, Augustine makes clear that it is not syllables and sounds which form the basis of this analogy, but rather the communication, in words, of the presence and the mind of the speaker. The Word can no more be separated from the divine Speaker than the brightness of the sun from the sun itself: 'See God; see His Word inhering to the Word speaking, that the Speaker speaks not by syllables, but this his speaking is a shining out in the brightness of Wisdom' (xx. 13). The Word has its source 'in the heart' of the speaker and thus remains with him when it is spoken (i. 8–9). Coleridge himself often develops the analogy of Word and word in similar ways. See below, n. 97.

[97] See e.g. his description of the Logos as: 'that which goeth forth yet so as in its essence to remain is a Word. Therefore and for no other kindred reason is the Intelligibile et patrem et se ipsum Communicans, the communicative and communicable Intelligence designated the Word' (BL MS Egerton 2801, fo. 119).

[98] Abraham Tucker's *The Light of Nature Pursued* (7 vols.; London, 1768–78) was published under the name of Edward Search. The work is concerned to show the reconcilability of reason and revelation. Many of Tucker's statements contain interesting parallels with Coleridge's views, e.g. 'the knowledge of religion and morality arises from the knowledge of ourselves' (vol. i, p. xxix); 'without accuracy of language it is impossible to convey a chain of close reasoning' (vol. i, p. xl). Tucker, like Coleridge after him, insists that, in any philosophical investigation, we must begin with human nature (vol. i, pp. xlv–xlvi).

revelation. He claimed in the 'Opus Maximum' that: 'The object of this work consists in the assertion—first: of religion as implying revelation, or that the words *revealed religion* is [*sic*] a pleonasm or definitio per idem' ('the definition of itself', a tautology) (OM iii, fo. 85). He linked the necessity of revelation in religion with God's self-realization through an interdependence of relationship (*NED* ii. 232), suggesting that the necessity of revelation as the ground of religion would be made clear in any 'battle fairly fought out' between Christian belief and those of 'Spinoza, or a Bhuddist, or a Burmese Gymnosophy': 'Then I am fully persuaded, would the truth appear in full evidence, that no Christ, no God,—and conversely, if the Father, then the Son. I can never too often repeat, that revealed religion is a pleonasm. Religion is revelation, and revelation the only religion' (ibid.). Coleridge affirmed Luther's view of the truth and moral necessity of revelation (OM iii, fos. 87–9), and he too saw this necessity as established by the nature of humanity's 'disease', that is, the evil ground existing in the fallen will.[99] He was increasingly oppressed by a sense of his own state of sin, and this awareness prompted him to affirm that 'I receive with full and grateful faith the assurance of revelation, that the Word, which is from all eternity with God, and is God, assumed our human nature in order to redeem me, and all mankind from this our connate corruption' ('Confessio Fidei', in *LR* i. 392). He believed that the Word revealed both the possibility of redemption, light, hope, and wholeness, and the *need* for such redemption.

All reason, according to Coleridge, has its origin in revelation. In this he agreed with Jacobi's assertion: 'All human knowledge proceeds from revelation and faith.'[100] Yet there are indications that his agreement with Jacobi was not complete. In his analysis of Jacobi's rejection of Spinoza's philosophy, he referred to the former as one who, 'slighting or rejecting all supernatural evidences of an historical and outward nature finds the only sure ground of all religious convictions in inward revelation, in an instinctive Fore-tokening of the Conscience and in Faith as a *sentiment*'.[101] Coleridge himself was adamant that the first step of faith, like that of reason, involves an *act* of will. He insisted that

[99] See below, Ch. 2.1.
[100] Jacobi, *Werke*, vol. iii, p. xxxiii; see n. 88 above.
[101] BL MS Egerton 2801, fo. 8.

reason and revelation must be understood as having the same source:

when we affirm of any moral or religious truth that it is susceptible of rational or philosophical demonstration we are so far from implying that the knowledge of its truth had its primary origin in the unaided efforts of human reason that we regard the present existence & actual exercise of such a power as the result of a revelation which had by enlightening the mind roused, *discipline*[*d*], and invigorated all its faculties and appealed to experience and history for the confirmation of the fact. Whether we direct our historical researches to Egypt, to India, or to the earliest scientific schools of Greece there where the sciences are we find either claims to a revealed religion or traditions of the same: and in the religions themselves for which the claims are made[,] the farther back we are enabled to trace its [*sic*] existence, the more simple do its creed & forms become, the more clearly do they discover themselves to be the reliques of a religion having every claim to the character of revelation that internal evidence and congruity with the philosophic idea of God, and the nature & needs of man can supply. (OM iii, fo. 20)

Coleridge declared that the facts which 'constitute the history of revelation' show it 'awaking the reason to the knowledge & possession of its powers' (ibid. 21). A notebook entry records his view that 'the first Act of Human Reason consisted in the receiving of a Revealed Law' and that man 'received his first human instruction, the means and conditions of his *actual* humanity (i.e. rationality) in the School of Revelation' (N 26, fo. 39):

in the *first* Man, even as in all his descendants 'born of woman', the knowledge of the *Legislator* and the conviction of his Right to be obeyed must have been antecedent to the sense and conviction of the rightfulness of the *Law*, and the *Conditio sine qua non* of the latter. And in this case Religion must have been the Basis of Morality, and Morality of sciental Insight: In other words, the Light from God (i.e. God's revelation of his Being and attributes generally, and of his Will relatively to Man) must have been introductory to the Light of Reason in the Conscience, and the Light of Reason in the Conscience to the Light of Reason in the Understanding. (N 26, fo. 40ᵛ)

Coleridge concluded that revelation is antecedent to reason, that a moral awakening must precede a rational awakening: 'Observe, This is the corner-stone of *my* system, ethical, metaphysical and theological—the priority, namely, both in dignity and order of generation of the Conscience to the Consciousness in Man.' He drew a connection between this dependence of reason on conscience, and the dependence of the 'I am' (the birth of language, self-consciousness, and reason) on the experience of a 'Thou': 'No I without a Thou: no Thou without a Law from *Him*, to whom I and Thou stand in the same relation. Distinct Selfknowledge begins with the sense of Duty toward my Neighbor; and Duty felt *to*, and claimed from, my Equal supposes & implies the Right of a Third, superior to both because imposing it on both' (N 26, fo. 41).

The Logos as both the 'inner' Light of Reason and the 'outer' Light of objective truth is the ground of Coleridge's declaration: 'The principle has ever been that Reason is *subjective* Revelation, Revelation objective *Reason*. . . . I must deduce the objective from the subjective Revelation or it is no longer a revelation for me, but a beastly fear and superstition' (*CL* vi. 895). The truth of the Christian religion, he argued, depended on this identification of reason and revelation. His letter to J. H. Green emphasized this point: 'If I lose my faith in Reason, as the perpetual Revelation, I lose my faith altogether.' He insisted that

our business is not to *derive* Authority from the *mythoi* of the Jews & the first Jew-Christians (i.e. the O. and N. Testament) but to *give* it to them—never to assume their stories as facts, any more than you would Quack Doctor's affidavits on oath before the Lord Mayor—and verily in point of old Bailey Evidence this is a flattering representation of the Paleyian Evidence—but by *science* to confirm the *Facit*, kindly offered to beginners in Arithmetic. (*CL* vi. 895)

Following the tradition of Christian Platonism, Coleridge maintained that the distinction-in-unity of reason and revelation provided the basis for a reconciliation of philosophy and religion. This became one of the most important elements in his attempt to overcome the fragmentation and alienation of human experience and thought. For this, he especially valued the thought of John Scotus Eriugena, who 'dared avow, that Faith was Fealty to Reason, and that any articles of faith that were not Ideas of Reason were jargon for Traitors to conjure with, and that Religion was but Philosophy contemplated principally in its influences on the Will' (N 35, fo. 23).

The Logos Encounter: Inner and Outer Word

Reason, unlike the understanding, Coleridge insisted, involves the whole personality; will, faith, conscience, and feeling. His emphasis on the rationality of religion was not meant to suggest that religion is merely a matter of intellectual conviction. Divine Reason is manifested in the divine Person;[102] thus revelation involves the encounter of *persons*. The Logos reveals God as loving and willing. He is 'will in the form of reason' (*LR* iv. 2), both source and mediator of Life and Love. In the letters later published as *Confessions of an Inquiring Spirit*, Coleridge explored the revelation of Scripture as encounter. The Bible bears witness to 'the Word that is light for every man, and life for as many as give heed to it' (*CIS* 10). In Scripture, he declared, 'I have met every where more or less copious sources of truth, and power, and purifying impulses . . . I have . . . found words for my inmost thoughts, songs for my joy, utterances for my hidden griefs, and pleadings for my shame and my feebleness. . . . In short whatever *finds* me, bears witness for itself that it has proceeded from a Holy Spirit' (ibid.).

In a note scrawled on the back of an invitation card to his philosophical lectures[103] Coleridge wrote of the impossibility of defining this sensation of being 'found' by the Word, because all definition is synthetic and our sensations are, on the contrary, *simple*. He described sensation as 'an act of the Self, or Natura duplex [second nature], in its primary Potency', and linked this to the statement that 'All Science derives its reality from immediate, or intuitive Knowledge.' On this ground he could affirm that the direct intuition or sensation, that which 'found' the reader of the Scripture, need not be set against rationality, but rather was its ground. This was consistent with the condition of all knowledge which could be claimed to correspond to reality, that it was derived from experience. Coleridge, like Kant, never rejected the insights of empirical philosophy. Indeed, experience, and the *sensation* of being 'found' by the Word, were the basis of his claim to know its truth.

In emphasizing the element of the Logos or Christ encounter in revelation, he echoed a theme which had interested thinkers as

---

[102] See below, Ch. 4.2.   [103] VCL S MS 5, card 9.

historically distant as Origen and Luther. Origen had asserted that creation bears the image of the Logos in the rationality, the purpose and meaning of created things. His exegesis of Scripture had pointed to three stages of the revelation of the Word of God. First, the teaching of Christ as Word is the universal content of the Old and New Testaments. The second and supreme mode of revelation is the Incarnation, and the third is Christ revealed to us in the present, the Logos disclosing himself to the soul.[104] Coleridge himself envisaged a great scheme of redemption, realized in stages, in each of which there is a distinct revelation of Logos. He concluded from his study of the Bible that the whole of the varied content of the Old Testament witnesses to the revelation of the Word and prophesies the redemption, the hope of man: 'In the Bible History all is *prospective* & for that reason the Past is never forgotten, but ever more presented anew, in every sense *re*-presented in each immediate experience and every anticipation recalled as the Ground & pre-declaration of the Hope' (N 43, fo. 17ᵛ).

He maintained that all the various parts and traditions which make up the Old Testament were, in total, a unique revelation of the divine Word; the 'Sethian, Noetic, Patriarchal, Mosaic, Prophetic and Messianic'[105] are one and the same revelation. Like Origen, he held that the degree of inspiration of the prophets and law-writers is dependent upon the depth of their personal encounter with the Word, the Son of God (*CM* i. 438).[106] As for the second stage in Origen's exposition, the incarnation of the Logos in the God-Man Jesus Christ: of this Coleridge, after the short interlude of his Unitarian sympathies, was convinced. He believed with Origen, that, in present revelation to the individual believer, *encounter* is crucial. He echoed both Origen and Augustine in emphasizing the importance of the individual's receptivity to the Word. He too asserted the futility of words without the necessary correspondence of reason (the truth of

---

[104] See K. J. Torjeson, *Hermeneutical Procedure and Theological Method in Origen's Exegesis* (Berlin, 1986), 109.

[105] Coleridge lists here the historical epochs or stages of revelation: 'Sethian' refers to the earliest period, following the birth of Adam's son; 'Noetic', to the period following the repopulation of the earth by the descendants of Noah. The age of the Patriarchs is that of Abraham, Isaac, and Jacob.

[106] Torjeson has outlined this aspect of Origen's thought; op. cit. 119.

Ideas) present in the speaker or the hearer: 'Without the *Idea*
present to the mind of the Speaker or Hearer what can *Words* be,
but articulated sound, vox et præterea nihil?' (N 35, fo. 43).

Despite his admiration of, and great affection for, Luther,
Coleridge suggested that the latter over-emphasized the infal-
libility of Scripture where he 'every where identifies the living
Word of God with the written word, and rages against Bullinger
who contended that the latter is the word of God only as far as
and for whom it is the vehicle of the former' (*CM* iii. 762–3).
Elsewhere Coleridge outlined what he took to be the dangers of
this position and of 'the obstacles which this assumption of an
infallible and perfect totality in every position of a canonical
book places in the road of rational conviction. To me the very
imperfection and still adhering prejudices of the first disciples of
our Lord furnish some of the strongest, the most convincing
proofs of the Truth' (N 41, fo. 22). He described himself as
following in the footsteps of Luther and the Reformers in their
continual assertion that the proof of the Christian revelation was
based not on the miracles recorded in the New Testament but on
'the truth & necessity of the revelation' (OM iii, fos. 85–7).
He agreed with Luther's theology of existential encounter, con-
firming that what a man *is* depends on the extent to which he
'hears' and affirms, by faith, the word of affirmation spoken to
him.[107]

Luther, remaining faithful to the Fourth Gospel, had, so
Coleridge believed, expressed the spiritual truth and necessity of
the revelation in both its 'inner' and 'outer' forms. St John
and Luther had represented perfectly what many of the Church
Fathers had only obscurely set out, that 'the Idea, God, contains
distinct ideas of the Father, of the Son, and of the Spirit; yet such
that being distinct they are at the same time inseparable, and
after a determinate and immutable Order' (N 35, fo. 45). Few
had remained true to this revelation. Some had suggested, for
example (Eusebius was, Coleridge claimed, one such), that the
Logos was 'before all time', implying that there was another time
outside time; in other words, their thinking was not wholly
emancipated from dependence on the images and conceptions of

---

[107] G. Ebeling makes this point about Luther's idea of encounter; see *Luther:
An Introduction to his Thought*, tr. R. A. Wilson (London, 1970), 74.

the understanding and the senses. In contrast, Luther, following the Fourth Gospel writer, had emphasized the *inner* life and light and the *inner* revelation of Person to persons through Love.

Coleridge often returned to this important distinction between 'inner' and 'outer' revelation. He consciously echoed the Stoic distinction between *logos prophorikos*, uttered speech, and *logos endiathetos*, unuttered speech or thought, a distinction later developed by Philo, and woven into Christian thought by St Augustine. Philo had described the potential in man for the development from 'outer' speech (represented allegorically by Aaron, the first High priest, brother to Moses) to 'the unlettered thought', which alone is capable of being pure logos, '*hieros logos*', the proper understanding of Scripture revealed by Moses.[108] Augustine explicitly devalued the external word, which is dependent upon the vagaries and particularities of different tongues (*lingua*), and contrasted it with the inner word, which is independent of any such phenomenal associations, and is the mirror and the image of the divine Word.[109] Coleridge too remarked "*Αλλο μεν το ρημα, αλλο ο λογος*" ('the spoken word is one thing, the Word another') (*CN* iv, § 5338), and emphasized the distinction between the Word and 'the written *ρηματα*, or Scriptures'.[110]

---

[108] *Quis Rerum Divinarum Heres sit*, 185; *Quod Deterius Potiori Insidiari Solet*, 39–40; *De Migratione Abrahami*, 81–4.

[109] See above, Ch. 1.1.

[110] See also *CM* iii. 521. In the work of H.-G. Gadamer a similar preoccupation is to be found with the relationship between human speech and thought, particularly as it was expressed in the theology of the Word from the Fathers to the present day. He has found it important in the context of connections drawn between Trinitarian theology and hermeneutical theory: 'The mystery of the Trinity is mirrored in the miracle of language insofar as the word that is true, because it says what the object is, is nothing by itself and does not seek to be anything: nihil de suo habens, sed totum de illa scientia de qua nascitur. It has its being in its revealing. Exactly the same thing is true of the mystery of the Trinity. Here also the important thing is not the earthly appearance of the redeemer as such, but rather his complete divinity, his consubstantiality with God. To grasp the independent personal existence of Christ within the sameness of being is the task of theology. Here the analogy of the mental word, the verbum intellectus is helpful. This is more than a mere image, for the human relationship between thought and speech corresponds, despite its imperfections, to the divine relationship of the Trinity. The inner mental word is as consubstantial with thought as is God the Son with God the Father' (*Truth and Method*, 381). Gadamer had suggested that Aquinas combines St John and Aristotle: the doctrine of the 'inner word' which he continues from Augustine is, for him, 'the obvious premise for his

He asserted the interdependence of the 'outer' and 'inner' word, of thought and word, of self-consciousness with the root of language itself, the first word 'spoken' to oneself, represented by εἰμί, or *sum*. Of all these, the exemplar is the divine Word. The Logos is, in a sense, God speaking himself *to* himself, the one Word in which the whole totality of his Thought is at once formed and 'uttered' as Being and Revelation. Yet the Logos, as the divine Principle of humanity, also 'speaks' to, and in, man; this is the mediating and redemptive act. Logos, in unity with Spirit, communicates, in the revelation of the objective truths of reason and experience, in the forms and processes of thought and in the inner revelation, the light of conscience: '*To* the mind in and through the *mind*, the *Book*, and the outward *Creation*: in all three the Spirit works and speaks to us' (*CM* i. 674). To the following passage in Luther's *Table Talk*:[111] 'The ancient Fathers said: Distingue tempora, et concordabis Scripturas; distinguish the times; then may we easily reconcile the Scriptures together,' Coleridge responded: 'Yea! and not only so, but we shall reconcile truths, that seem to repeal this or that passage of Scripture, with the Scriptures. For Christ is with his Church even to the end' (*CM* iii. 745). His desire to show the identity of Reason and revelation remained, as we shall see, a constant stimulus to his thought.

The Revelation of History and Prophecy

The idea of a progressive revelation gained ground throughout the nineteenth century. It was to become, after Coleridge's time, one of the most prominent and controversial elements in the articles contributed by seven leading liberal churchmen in *Essays and Reviews* (1860) and an important part of the work of J. H.

---

investigation of the connection between forma and verbum' (p. 382), and in St Thomas 'the object, when conceived by the intellect, is at the same time ordered towards being made known'. The inner word is, in being thought through to the end, spoken to oneself. The word, in being formed, *is* the act of knowledge itself; in Scholastic thought the 'word is simultaneous with this (*formatio*) of the intellect' (p. 383). Coleridge's view was 'that to the scholastic philosophy the Reformation is attributable, far more than to the revival of classical literature' (*PL* 316).

[111] Luther, *Table Talk*, ix. 205.

Newman.[112] Coleridge's close study of G. E. Lessing's (1729–81) work had made him familiar with the theme of *Erziehung des Menschengeschlects* (1780). Here, Lessing had identified education with revelation: 'What education is to the individual man, revelation is to the whole human race. . . . Education is revelation coming to the individual man; and revelation is education which has come, and is still coming, to the human race.'[113] The extent of the revelation depends, Lessing claimed, on the level of maturity in terms of moral perceptions and the capability, for example, of abstract reasoning, of the human race as represented in a particular period or culture. The *outer* revelation of the progress of reason and knowledge in mankind as a whole must coincide, at any given time, with the *inner* light of truth and reason, which the education of the individual provides. The inner and outer revelations will be interdependent.

Coleridge agreed that progress in human learning and knowledge would make possible a progressive revelation of God. For example, he proposed a lectureship which should be concerned, for five days a week, with a 'Textual Exposition' of the Scriptures, verse by verse, in the original languages, and with a complete commentary 'excluding all dogmatic theology and purely grammatical, logical, geographical, historical, phyto- & zoo-logical elucidation'. This might be prepared for the use of candidates for Holy Orders. He suggested that it would be necessary and right for 'the Professor to make such additions, correction, or other improvements as successive Research & increasing Lights of the Age might supply' (N 44, fos. 21ᵛ–22). On this basis of belief in an evolving reason and a progressive revelation, it became clear that 'The vehement Belief of the Devil & his numberless Army of Rebel Angels was Heroism in Luther—a pitiful Anility in Mr Wilberforce' (N 44, fo. 49).

---

[112] C. R. Sanders has explored the influence of Coleridge on such as Frederick Temple, James Martineau, J. C. Hare, F. J. A. Hort, and F. D. Maurice (*Coleridge and the Broad Church Movement*, 265 ff.). Sanders shows that J. H. Newman too, despite believing that Coleridge 'indulged a liberty of speculation which no Christian can tolerate', recognized him as 'a very original thinker' who 'installed a higher philosophy into inquiring minds than they had hitherto been accustomed to accept' (*Apologia pro Vita Sua* (London, 1891), 97; Sanders, *Coleridge and the Broad Church Movement*, 31 n.).

[113] H. Chadwick, *Lessing's Theological Writings* (London, 1956), 82 ff.

Coleridge always emphasized the integration and interdependence of historical facts and the ideas of reason. According to him, 'the Factors of Revealed Religion, [are] Fact and Idea' (*CM* ii. 482). This relation between fact and idea provides the framework for his support for a polarity of revelation, inner and outer. He insisted that the Scriptures are 'in addition to Reason, Understanding, Learning and Experience both inward and historical';[114] the historical, outward revelation through the Christian Church is an essential part of the whole:

The everlasting Truths, the ever-present redemptive presence and mediation of the WORD who became Man, yea, σαρξ εγενετο*—O! how do they soften, raise, fill the soul! But what should I have known of these glad Tidings, what should I have been—if indeed I should have at all been—had not a Christian Church been established? If Christianity had not been made a *fact* of History? (*CM* i. 446)

[* 'became flesh']

An *inner* revelation, Coleridge agreed with Jacobi and Schleiermacher, is crucial to the life and salvation of the individual, but this is inseparably linked, like the two polar extremities of one line, to the outward, factual, historical revelation. Commenting on the work of the early 'Historians' of the Old Testament, Coleridge concluded: 'to consider . . . the knowle[d]ge of *facts* for their own sake . . . or for mere purposes of exact chronology, & to present succession without vacua, is a refinement of modern times'. The proper purpose of history is one with the purpose of revelation: 'In the ancient [historian] the Moral purpose was ever predominant / and History differed from Poesy in the *materials* rather than in the *forms* of putting them together.—His Jewels were all precious Stones—i.e. *real* facts—not factitious diamonds &c—but in the *Setting* he was determined by the Object, he had in view' (*CM* i. 446).

Coleridge's view of the relation between prophecy and history is consistent with the importance which he attaches to revelation as the integration of fact and idea:

To prophecy is to unroll and draw out the involved consequences, be it of a state of things, or of an action or series of actions, or of a truth—&

---

[114] See Coleridge's annotations of Swedenborg's *True Christian Religion*, tr. T. Hartley, 2 vols. (London, 1819), vol. i, p. viii.

on this the moral governance of rational finite creatures depends, that they are Beings born and qualified to look afore and after—and the latter for the sake of the former. Individuals who devote their time to the acquisition of a minute knowledge of the Past for its' own sake, we call Antiquarians . . . not historians: and their attachment to this study a foible, or maggot. Homo est historicus ut esset propheticus;* to exhortation, to edification and to comfort.[115] (N 41, fos. 17ᵛ–18)

[* 'a man is a historian inasmuch as he might be a prophet']

He asserted that every 'successive' scheme of organization (Coleridge contrasted 'simultaneous' organization—for example, in animals—with 'successive, as in one of Handel's or Mozart's Overtures'), including that of 'the great scheme of Revelation', is made up in every integral part of both prophecy and history, 'save the last or consummating Fact, which will be only History, and the initial which can only be prophecy'. The Word may be recognized in prophetic revelation of all that is to come (for example, in the Old Testament), in the whole redemptive scheme of the creation (here the Word is revealed in the symbolic 'language' of the natural world), and in the witness of the facts of history to the economy of Providence. In the beginning was the Word, and the Word was then, Coleridge believed, a great Prophetic voice calling all into being and to a future hope. At the completion of the 'great scheme of redemption', Christ, the Logos, will be seen as the consummation of History (*CL* vi. 684).[116]

The Name of God

Coleridge believed that both history and prophecy—the witness of the past and the witness to the future—proclaim the Idea of God; and that this Ideal reality is the archetype of 'Name' and 'Word'. His notebook entries, particularly those from 1827 on, show his growing conviction of the importance of recognizing the Logos as the *Name* of God. Again, Philo may have been the dominant influence here.[117] Coleridge clearly defines the term 'name': 'The Name of a thing, in the original sense of the word,

---

[115] See also *CL* vi. 684–5, 689.
[116] See also *CL* vi. 677, 583.
[117] Coleridge would have found this aspect of Philo's work discussed by John Whitaker; see *The Origins of Arianism Disclosed*, 77.

Name (*Nomen*, Νουμενον, το *intelligibile*, *id quod intelligitur*) expresses that which is *understood* in an appearance, that which we place (or make to *stand*) *under* it, as the condition of its real existence' (*AR* 221). This passage is one of many which have a Kantian tone. Coleridge greatly admired Kant's development of the noumenon/phenomenon distinction, and took it further; but he rejected the total unknowability of Kant's noumenon, declaring that it may be understood objectively or subjectively. In the former case it must be recognized as the 'true Numen' (the Light of Reason) from which no appearance or phenomenon can be separated; in the latter case, subjectively, in the revelation to the mind and heart of man, it is the transforming power and presence of the Name of God: 'the Νουμενον, that which is to be *understood*, that which contemplated *Objectively*, and as one with the φαινομενον, is the true *Numen*, and which taken subjectively, and distinctly, is the *Nomen*, or Noun, and Nominator—the Noumenon, I say, is the Logos, the WORD. The Phaenomenon, or visual and literal Apprehension, is ρημα—a fluxion' (*CL* v. 325–6).

Coleridge's connection between 'name' and 'person' is consistent with his belief that Christ (incarnate Logos) is the 'Person' of the Father, who is the source of *personëity*:[118]

Name [means] that by which any thing is understood. Hence Name and Person are equivalents when the former is used respecting a Spirit; and the latter employed in its' *primary* sense, = id, *per* quod *sonat* aliquis,* and *not* as identical with the I AM, dem *Ich*, *Word* that which uttereth the will, purpose &c of a Spirit. Christ is therefore with equal propriety called, the *Name*, the *Person*, and the *Word*—of God. (N 42, fo. 36^v–37)

[* 'that through which anyone makes sounds']

He believed that the Fourth Gospel revealed Christ to be, not merely etymologically but ontologically, the Name of God. He commented on John 12: 20: '*Important*. Here our Lord expressly calls himself [?by] the Father's *Name*. I have long believed our

---

[118] 'Personëity': Coleridge's term for the living energy of the distinction-in-unity of reason, will, and love, which is what might rather be called 'personhood', suggesting a state of being, than 'personality', which might be understood as character or quality.

Lord to be intended in a majority of the passages in which the *name* of God is spoken of in the O.T. but I had not noticed this confirmation' (N 36, fo. 62ᵛ). A little later he took up this idea again: 'Progressively does the view explained in this book of Christ as the Jehovah-Word, the Jehovah-name, the Jehova *Person* εξηγησις [exegesis] perfect itself in the harmony of scripture!' (N 36, fo. 65ᵛ).

Coleridge often identified *nomen* and *numen*; that is, he identified the name, 'which expresses that which is *understood* in an appearance', with the '*numen*', the intelligible presence, the spirit, will, and power of that thing. Again, the inspiration is the Fourth Gospel. He commented on John 3: 18: 'Observe too the full proof afforded by the text of the true gospel import of "The *Name*" nomen = *numen*' (N 47, fo. 33). It is clear, Coleridge argued, that Christ is the identification of the *nomen* and the *numen* of God. As such, he is not merely Reason, the Greek Logos, but Being and Power; he is indeed, the living Jehovah of the Old Testament. According to Coleridge, Christ is rightly called 'the *Name*, the *Person*, and the *Word*—of God'. There was, however, more than representation and revelation involved. He continued: 'But as Logos, or the supreme living Reason, *is* the Supreme *Being* (for Reason *is* Being, and all true Being is Reason)—hence he is likewise the Jehova, or Ja-/[sic] and it would be much more accordant with the meaning of the original instead of "the Word of Jehova" to render it, "the Jehova-Word"' (N 42, fo. 37). In the same notebook, the point is later re-emphasized: 'I know few points in Scripture, which it more concerns a Christian to bear in mind than that Christ as the Logos θεανθρωπος was the Jehovah of the Old Testament' (N 42, fo. 61).

To Coleridge, the evidence that Christ is the *Word* and *Name* of God constantly referred to throughout the Old Testament was overwhelming:

Can [the Jews] deny that their ancient Masters of the Law gave to the expected Shiloh the titles of, *The Word*, and the *Name*? or that Name as applied to the Deity signifies always his Numen, his Going-forth, his representative Presence? And that it is the same with the Angel, or Messenger, of his Presence? And have not the Gentiles been made to know that the *Name* of the Holy Will, the absolute superessential Good, the Causa Sui, who from eternity to eternity affirmeth, ɪ ᴀᴍ, is *The*

Lord? We have one God, the Father, and one Lord even Christ—and that *the Lord* alone is mediator between God and Man?[119] (N 36, fo. 37)

In his notes on Waterland's *A Vindication of Christ's Divinity* (*NED* ii. 189),[120] Coleridge criticized the latter for failing to recognize that Jehovah is Christ; that ὁ ὤν, which Waterland rightly interprets as *Jehovah*, 'St John everywhere and St Paul no less, makes the peculiar name of the Son'. This view of Christ as the 'Jehovah-Word' Coleridge would have found endorsed in his reading of Emanuel Swedenborg's *True Christian Religion* (1819).[121] Swedenborg also asserted: 'That Jehovah signifies I AM, and TO BE (Sum, et Esse) is well known.' This same correlation of Logos with the Jehovah, which expresses both the 'I AM' and the 'He is' of the divine Father–Son relationship, was important to Coleridge's understanding of the divine Name (*C & S* 182). It was associated in his thought with the name of God in Exodus 3: 14: 'I AM THAT I AM' (*TT* i. 423 and n.).

He believed this to be a mysterious truth of the highest order. As the Name of God, the Logos not only represents, reveals, and communicates but *is* God:

The hidden God, the unutterable in his own superessential absoluteness—Jehovah is his *Name*,—the *Name* uttered from eternity, the Word that declareth representeth and is God, the Jehovah *Person*. In this transcendent absolutely unique Mystery, which in the still and stedfast extacy of Adoration the Eye of the Spirit may contemplate, but which not the Tongue of Angels nor the Language of Heaven can explain, the profoundest and most pregnant Truths, when we attempt in vain to convey them in human words, or only by failing succeed, will sound as *Truisms*,—even such as in the wise men of this world may excite a laugh or a sneer.—Yet a most vital Truth it is, that Jehovah's *Name* IS Jehova! *Hallowed be thy Name!* (N 36, fo. 22ᵛ)

As in all Coleridge's later work, what was important to him here was not only the belief that the personality of a living God is made known in the Logos, but the conviction that the Logos is the divine humanity; that whatever is true of Christ as Word is potentially true of the human individual, the family, the nation,

---

[119] See above, Intro., n. 55.

[120] D. Waterland, *A Vindication of Christ's Divinity: Being a Defence of Some Queries Relating to Dr Clarke's Scheme of the Holy Trinity, etc.*, 2nd edn. (Cambridge, 1719).

[121] See *True Christian Religion*, i. 38–43, 493.

and of universal humanity. His concentration on the theme of the Name of God was linked to a great desire and hope for himself and for humanity as a whole, a hope in which he was often discouraged, but in which he persevered all his life. Since Christ is from all eternity, the Name of God all who come to him, Coleridge believed, may be called by his Name; they may become his Sons and Daughters, transformed into his likeness. Sometimes this is expressed in philosophical language; at other times the language is purely that of orthodox Christianity: 'Thou art the King of Glory, O Christ! The Hosts of Heaven acknowledge thee, the Fullness of the Father! Blessed be thy name. Thy words were found and I eat them: and thy Word has been to me the joy and rejoicing of mine heart: for I am called by thy Name O Lord God of Hosts!—Amen! Amen!' (N 36, fo. 38ᵛ).

Coleridge sees human individuals called by the Name of God as the catalysts through which the redemption of the whole created world takes place. The theme may have been taken from his reading of John Scotus Eriugena. Humanity is the point at which the natural and the spiritual meet and within which nature and spirit may be reconciled. When humanity participates in Logos, that is, in its own realization in a divine, universal Humanity paradoxically incarnate in the *individual*, the God-Man—then all the forms of the natural world, having reached their consummation in man, are included in his redemption. Through Adam's naming of the creatures in Genesis, he participates in the deep significance of the naming act. This involves the recognition of appearance (phenomenon) as the manifestation of a higher reality (noumenon) which is to be understood by, and underlies, that appearance (*CL* v. 325–6). He also participates in bringing order out of chaos. The forms which belong to the Logos as 'forma formans' are mirrored in human reason (*logos*) and the act of naming bears witness to this correspondence, in the divine Reason, of thought and thing, of noumena and phenomena.

The Theology of the Word

We have seen that Coleridge recognized and absorbed, like Philo centuries before, the significance of the symbolism of 'Word' in both the Greek and Hebrew traditions. His thought echoes the reconciliation of *memra* and *logos* which is found in the Fourth

Gospel.[122] The creative Word reveals mercy and covenant and is also the archetype of all language, and of the act of naming. The divine Word is the transcendent reality containing the mystery of symbol, the source of reason and ideas, of form and distinction. The Logos is revealed as living Person, as the pattern of person-*hood* to those who 'hear' or encounter it and who are enabled to recognize their own life therein, the *actual* reality of what in them has been only a potential selfhood: 'if even through the words of a powerful and perspicuous author . . . I identify myself with the excellent writer, and his thoughts become my thoughts: what must not the blessing be to be thus identified first with the Filial Word, and then with the Father in and through Him?' (*CM* iii. 522–3).

[122] In the context of this investigation of Coleridge's fascination with the Name of God as used by Philo, John, and Paul (John Whitaker, in *The Origins of Arianism Disclosed*, 39–40, had discussed the close relation of 'Logos' and '*Memra*'), it is interesting to note a more recent resurgence of interest in this subject. As C. T. R. Hayward shows ('The Holy Name of the God of Moses and the Prologue of St John's Gospel', *New Testament Studies*, 25 (1979), 16–32) in the light of the complete text of the Palestinian Targum (contained in the *Codex Neofiti* of the Vatican Library discovered in 1956), the relationship between the *Memra* (utterance, Word) *of Yahweh* and St John's Logos has become clearer. *Memra* has been described as 'an exegetical term which stands for the Name revealed by God to Moses at the burning bush, the Name 'HYH, I AM / WILL BE THERE' (Hayward, 'The Holy Name of the God of Moses', 17). *Memra* signifies God's presence (ibid. 24; Hayward refers here to *Neofiti* to Gen. 26: 3, 28: 15, 31: 3; Exod. 4: 5 and 7) 'in past and future creation, history and redemption'. It is also God's mercy which creates and sustains the world. St John, it has been argued, probably knew of the significance of *Memra* and incorporated it in his Logos. St John's Gospel shows awareness of specifically Targumic traditions in, for example, the identification of Jesus with the true bread from heaven (6: 41–51) 'He is the Bread' (*Targum Neofiti*, Exod. 16: 15); and the symbolism of water. Coleridge's belief that there is an important connection between the divine Name of Exodus 3: 33–4 and the Prologue of St John is still shared today (M. D. Hooker, 'The Johannine Prologue and the Messianic Secret', *New Testament Studies*, 21 (1975), 40–58; quoted by Hayward, 'The Holy Name of the God of Moses', 27) and both associated with *Memra*. Coleridge's assertion that the Prologue is concerned with the exegesis of the divine Name (N 36, fo. 65 ff.; see also N 42, fo. 37) has been echoed in recent exegesis. The Name revealed to Moses was 'Christ under the veil of Moses' according to Coleridge. As C. T. R. Hayward writes, if the hypothesis that St John did use the *Memra* is accurate, 'The final revelation of his Name through Jesus would constitute Jesus as a new Moses in the eyes of St John' (Hayward, 'The Holy Name of the God of Moses', 28). Here then is what may have been an early influence on both the writer of the Fourth Gospel and on the work of Philo (*De Somniis*, i. 75), that of *Memra*. Coleridge may well have been familiar with Whitaker's discussion of this idea; see Whitaker, *The Origins of Arianism Disclosed*, 39–40.

Coleridge found that the act of creation itself, which he described as beginning in a polarization of Life and Light, could be expressed in terms of the analogy of the Word:

you are likewise to keep in mind with regard to the Power, *Light*, that the word in Gen. i. v. 3 does not mean visual Light or solar Light, which was not yet in existence; but that which is no less present in Sound, Odor and in whatever else *goes forth* to *declare*, like a word *spoken*; or remains on the surface (or *out*side) to *distinguish*, like a word *written*; and in both cases, makes the thing *out*ward, and *outers* (now spelt *utters*) its nature. P.S. Hence the Son of God is called indifferently The Light, that lighteth, and the Word.[123]

We shall see that his philosophy of nature was developed out of this theme of the Word as Light and Life.

This emphasis on the importance of the study of words and language for both theology and philosophy has become a central focus of twentieth-century thought. Linguistic analysis has taken on a new significance, and theology has had to re-examine the concept of revelation and of the nature and function of the divine Word in this context. The verification and falsification principles by which logical positivism sought to distinguish between meaningful language and 'nonsense' (that which did not impart information which could be tested empirically) are open to the criticism, as Coleridge would no doubt immediately have declared, that while attempting to show metaphysics as meaningless, they themselves are grounded in a metaphysic.[124] Among other theories grappling with this issue has been that which seeks the meaning of religious language in the way in which it is *used* (Wittgenstein, R. B. Braithwaite, Ian Ramsey), and that which attempts to find some way in which religious language, either through analogy or through symbol (Paul Tillich's theme), really communicates truth about God.[125] Naturalist and idealist theories of language still contribute their respective insights. The former

---

[123] BL MS Egerton 2801, fo. 143ᵛ.

[124] 'The fact is, the verification principle is a metaphysical proposition' (John Wisdom, *Philosophy and Psychoanalysis* (Oxford, 1953), 245).

[125] See e.g. L. Wittgenstein, *Philosophical Investigations*, tr. G. E. M. Anscombe, 3rd edn. (Oxford, 1972), 11, 93, 135–6; R. B. Braithwaite, *An Empiricist's View of the Nature of Religious Belief* (Cambridge, 1955), 9–20; I. Ramsey, *Religious Language* (London, 1957; 6th imp. 1982), 19, 47, 49; P. Tillich, *Dynamics of Faith* (New York, 1957), 45.

develop the theme that language has evolved naturally alongside human experience and the attempts to picture the outside world; the latter suggest that language *shapes* sense experience into a world; that it in some sense creates a world. Attention has been paid to the concept of language as *discourse*;[126] that is, as having an essential, interpersonal dimension. Martin Buber, for example, distinguished between the different extents to which the whole person is involved in what he or she says: 'The primary word "I–Thou" can only be spoken with the whole being; the primary word "I–It" can never be spoken with the whole being.'[127]

Coleridge's philosophy (or perhaps 'theosophy') of language appears to have foreshadowed many of these issues and developments. In one respect it differs significantly from most. Rather than exploring what religious language has in common with language in general, he sought to show that *all* language was fundamentally 'religious', participating in the divine Logos. As we have seen, both analogy and symbol play an important part. On the basis of his understanding of Logos as Word, he developed a theory of language which combined both naturalist *and* idealist insights, in other words, one in which the world of thought and the world of nature are seen as interacting and interdependent in concrete existence, reflecting the activity of the Logos as the divine Idea, the source of both nature and mind. He showed language as active in shaping the world of experience, but he also followed Vico and Herder in establishing the evolution of language as a reflection of the life and experience of a people or nation. Finally, to Coleridge *every* word which proceeds from persons in whom will and reason are united (that is, persons enlightened by the indwelling Logos) is itself both analogous to, and a symbol of, the divine Word. It is therefore, potentially, if never perfectly, creative, revelatory, and redemptive.

---

[126] As J. MacQuarrie points out, the Greeks had no word for language outside of '*discourse*', '*logos*'; *God-Talk* (London, 1967), 67.

[127] *I–Thou*, tr. R. Gregor Smith, 2nd edn. (Edinburgh, 1958), 3.

2

Logos: Light and Life of Nature

Meanwhile, until the world's structure is held together
by philosophy, she [nature] maintains its working through
hunger and through love.

(Schiller)

2.1. THE REDEMPTIVE SCHEME OF NATURE

The Fourth Gospel, following its affirmation of the pre-existence
of the Word, proclaims this Word as light and life (John 1: 4).
Coleridge saw this as the highest expression of those truths on
which he founded his philosophy of nature. The writings which
eventually formed *Hints towards the Formation of a more Com-
prehensive Theory of Life* all contain the germ of the Logos idea.
Nature, for him, was itself a revelatory 'language'. He became
convinced that the study of its laws, products, and processes was
a means not only by which this revelation might be received, but
by which human nature and human destiny might be understood.
The intensity of his interest was motivated by his search for a
unified system of knowledge, by an intense emotional response to
nature, and by an insatiable curiosity of intellect. In his earlier
writings, during the period of his close friendship with William
Wordsworth, his attitude to nature is one of wonder, awe, and
an almost pantheistic reverence.[1] Increasingly, however, as the
Logos became the central focus of his search for unity, he rejected
pantheism and proclaimed nature to be not *itself* divine, but
rather the working-out of a great scheme and history of recon-

---

[1] See the early collection of poems, e.g. 'The Eolian Harp': 'And what if all of
animated nature | Be but organic Harps diversly fram'd, | That tremble into
thought, as o'er them sweeps | Plastic and vast, one intellectual Breeze, | At once
the Soul of each, and God of all?'—and 'Frost at Midnight': 'The lovely shapes
and sounds intelligible | Of that eternal language, which thy God | Utters, who
from eternity doth teach | Himself in all, and all things in himself.'

ciliation and redemption. The creation, for example, became to him the loving response of God to the primal alienation and separation of a spiritual apostasy. He interpreted the Johannine Logos of 'light and life' as the Creator who transformed a chaos of non-being into a dynamic process of life expressed as power and product. His criticisms both of the 'mechanico-corpuscular' philosophy and of German idealism reflect what he saw as their failure to reconcile Kant's dichotomy of phenomenal and noumenal reality. His own 'dynamic system' was his response to this perceived failure.

Moral and Natural Philosophy Unified

In the early nineteenth century explanations of the origins of the natural world were increasingly polarized between the mechanistic view that life could be defined as an inherent power of organization within matter, and the idealist view that all being, and thus all life, had its source or origin in the act of self-conscious Mind. Both appeared to offer some kind of a unified approach in their own terms, yet only by excluding the other. Coleridge found both unsatisfactory. The former seemed to him to offer a circular argument: that phenomena could somehow be explained by phenomena and that life, manifested in organization, could, at the same time, be *defined* as organization. The latter, on the other hand, failed to admit the reality of matter and the physical world. His attitude to the work of Isaac Newton was ambivalent. He rejected the mechanistic, atomistic interpretations of matter which Newton had suggested; yet he found praiseworthy the latter's theory of gravity and his insistence that its explanation must ultimately be dependent upon the recognition of metaphysical reality, of God's free act. Coleridge attributed this part of Newton's thought to the earlier influence of Johannes Kepler (1571–1630), for whom his admiration was unbounded (*AR* 395).[2] He admired Kant's attempt to overcome the stalemate produced by both Cartesian idealism and Humean empiricism; yet in Kant's avowal that the noumena are unknowable, his solution, Coleridge believed, was flawed. He had divided reality

---

[2] See also *TT* i. 210–11.

by a dualistic system which left mind and being ultimately unreconciled.

Coleridge asserted life to be a process; more significantly, an *act*. No 'proof' may be offered regarding an original and originating act to which there are no witnesses; suggested explanations may only arise from the results and consequences of this act. He found only one explanation which was consistent both with reason and with experience; this he claimed to be a sufficient criterion of its truth.[3] His theory of life was based on a principle antecedent to, and independent of, organization, and he found support for this idea in the work of scientists such as John Hunter (1728–93). A member of the Royal College of Surgeons, and an eminent physiologist, Hunter was greatly admired by Coleridge for his confirmation of this principle:

The Hunterian idea of a life or vital principle, *'independent of the organization'* . . . demonstrates that John Hunter did not individualize, or make an hypostasis of the principles of life, as . . . a phænomenon . . . but that herein he philosophized in the spirit of the *purest* Newtonians, who in like manner refused to hypostasize the law of gravitation into an ether, which even if its existence were conceded, would need another gravitation for itself. The Hunterian position is a genuine philosophic IDEA, the negative test of which as of *all* Ideas is, that it is equidistant from an ens logicum (= an abstraction), and ens repræsentativum (= a generalization), and an ens phantasticum (= an imaginary *thing* or phænomenon). (*Friend*, i. 493–4 n.)

Coleridge aimed, like Hegel, to produce a system which reconciled the truths of empiricism and realism with those of idealism. He approved of Francis Bacon, 'the British Plato', as the 'experimental philosopher' (*PL* 223). Indeed, in Bacon's

---

[3] In adopting this epistemological ground, i.e. what is necessary as the condition of reason and experience must be postulated as true, Coleridge again follows Kant. See e.g. Kant's statement that what is necessary to the empirical employment of my reason, that is, a 'systematically complete unity', rests in turn on the necessary idea of a transcendent cause of the systematic unity of the universe. The first may be assumed, at least as an idea: 'I shall not only be entitled, but shall also be constrained, to realise this idea, that is, to posit for it a real object'; and Kant argues the same for the second (*Critique of Pure Reason*, A 677, B 705). We are then entitled to assume what is necessary to reason and to an intelligible universe—though only, says Kant, as regulative ideas. Coleridge uses this same argument, but goes further to claim that *ideas*, which bridge the gulf between the infinite and the finite, subject and object, are not only regulative but *constitutive* of reality, and that they are their own evidence. See below, Ch. 3.3.

work, Coleridge believed he found the stirrings of a reconciliation
between ideas and empirical facts. Such a reconciliation was the
necessary basis of science (*Friend*, i. 488–93). The exploration of
Coleridge's *Theory of Life* given below avoids analysis of its
philosophical status or of his belief that ideal reality was con-
stitutive of physical law. We will explore his idea of the ultimate
homogeneity of mind and nature in more detail below. He does
not neglect to provide grounds for this unity and attempts a
philosophical defence of the correspondence between ideas and
finite reality.[4]

While Coleridge sought a unified system through which the
knowledge obtained by the various disciplines would be found to
be compatible and mutually supportive, he was, at the same time,
aware of the dangers inherent in using the conclusions of one
branch of knowledge as the starting-point or as the underlying
axioms of another. He insisted, for example, that the disciplines
of theology and of natural science should be kept separate, and
that each should seek its own ends without being conformed to
the other in any way. He was opposed, too, to the natural
theology of his day, which was based on the evidence of the
senses and neglected the exploration of the *processes* of self-
conscious mind, of conscience and feeling (*AR* 400). There are,
he wrote,

two ways in which a History of Nature may be given. The first begins
with the Highest, the true first and absolute Cause, and ultimate Ground
of all. . . . The other on the contrary begins from the lowest; and takes
as its first grounds the most general characters and properties of the
Objects that surround us, with the active powers inferred from the Facts
or known by immediate Consciousness. In other words, it begins with
Nature—and whether that Term be [understood] only as the name of the
Active Powers collectively, and construed as *One* in the Calculus of
Science for the facility of Reasoning and the convenience of expression
or whether something more than a merely verbal or logical Unity should
seem to be required by the facts, under whatever form of thought it may
be conceivable—in either case a Nature is the first and indispensable
Postulate of Natural History in this second Form, with which exclusively

[4] See below, Ch. 3.2. With the development of relativity theory and of quantum
physics the role of mind (notably the mind of the scientist-observer) as in some
way constitutive of the world which it observes is recognized as crucial in all
physical science.

the Naturalist and Physiologist, simply as such, are concerned. (N 56, fos. 11^v–12^v)

The first method of setting out a 'History of Nature', Coleridge stated, 'is a Branch of Theology'. It begins with a First Cause and with an acknowledgement of the reflection of this Absolute Will and Reason in the moral and intellectual nature of man. It traces natural history backwards, from its high point in human nature, and is 'completed and immutable'; that is, the very power of interpreting and telling the (hi)story witnesses to its completion in the emergence of moral and intellectual beings. He claimed, with regard to these two forms of the 'History of Nature', that it 'would be . . . unreasonable & presumptuous to judge the recorded facts of the one [theology] by the fluctuating influences of the other [natural science]'. He also maintained, however, that

to interpret the facts of the latter in accommodation to the declarations of the former is to twist and de[s]tort the Road of Science and its direction, and by interrupting its' progress to prevent it from reaching the higher ground from which both would be seen in perfect harmony. (N 56, fo. 14)

His conclusion was:

that Theology and Physics are best friends, when they keep at a respectful distance, and are likely to agree the sooner, the less they think of agreeing at all. The contrary Plan has in every instance caused a sort of intellectual Strabismus. While each is looking asquint at the Other, neither sees what lies strait before them.[5] (ibid.)

So the 'History of Nature' to which Coleridge turned his attention sporadically from *circa* 1816, was, according to his own definition '*Philosophy* only as it proposes for its objects to discover . . . how far the human Reason assisted by Observation and Experiment

---

[5] This appears somewhat inconsistent with Coleridge's claims for the progressive nature of revelation. In his defence, it must be said that he is here referring to what he believed that he (and Kant before him) had elsewhere demonstrated as necessary, that is, to the *Idea* of God, and of the doctrine of creation (though it must be admitted that his theory of ideas as *constitutive* of reality gives the assertion of necessity in this context a different and more dogmatic slant than that of Kant). It was not his aim here to describe the details of the *processes*; these belonged, he thought, to the second form of a 'History of Nature'—natural science. Nevertheless, he cannot be defended against the charge of advocating one procedure and practising another.

can solve the problem of Organic Forms, and the Riddle of Nature' (N 56, fo. 11ᵛ).

Apostasy and Anastasy

Coleridge's 'History of Nature' is based upon the theme of creation as the working-out of the first great scheme of redemption; and as the manifestation of originating powers of light and life—these representing the activity of the Logos, the Creator. Asked to define 'nature', he responded thus:

1. What is Nature? Multeity co-erced into Number and Rhythm 2. How? *Δια του ΛΟΓΟΥ, δια Λογων των μεν εν τω Λογω και εξ του Λογου**—by the WORD, and by every Word that proceedeth in and thro' the same. Call the Words Numbers numerant, Living Numbers; or Ideas; or Laws or Spirits; or ministrant Angels; if you please & when you please. The Terms are all equivalent . . .[6] (N 26, fo. 119ʳ⁻ᵛ)

[* 'through words which indeed are in the Word and out of the Word']

Nature, he claimed, is 'not a primary Existent but a secondary and resulting Unity'. It is, as 'the antithesis of God as the Supreme Being or Eternal Utterance . . . a unique Idea . . . on all accounts therefore it is a work of no common difficulty and delicacy to select the least inadequate, and most suggestive expressions'. Nature was 'multeity' and chaos reduced to order, number, and form by the Logos. The powers and processes of the physical creation were only fully understood as part of a unified system of nature and mind and in the light of this scheme of redemption.

Coleridge's primary interest was not in the forms themselves, but in the powers which produced them and which themselves, he believed, had their source in a higher reality of Idea and Law. Finding the term 'Nature' defined in William Nicholson's *Journal of Natural Philosophy, Chemistry and the Arts* as 'the wisdom of God in the creation of the world', he comments in a margin note:

---

[6] Coleridge appears here to draw together themes from Pythagoras' sacred and constitutive numbers (see *CM* i. 689–91), Plato's *ειδος*, and the angels which in the work of both Origen and Jacob Böhme are creative spiritual energies. Coleridge often combines these terms, e.g. 'the adequate *Idea* of the Supreme Mind, who calleth the Host of living Ideas his own, his Angeloi discurrentes [angels who run about]' (N Fo, fo. 6).

far better and more reverential, as well as more correspondent to the phenomena, would the following definitions of Nature be, me saltem judice.* The Law or Constructive Powers excited in Matter by the influence of God's Spirit and Logos. (*CM* iii. 943–4)

[* 'as it seems to me']

Coleridge's 'system', as much *theo*sophical as *philo*sophical, describes a twofold scheme of divine regeneration and restoration: an inner, moral redemption and an outer which precedes it and prepares for it, that is, the creation itself (N 50, fo. 45). There are, he claimed, 'three great Epochs': the generation of the Word from eternity, the *re*generation by Christ to eternity, and, between these two, the epoch of '*Formation* as the Bridge over the dire Chasm of apostacy', which is 'the Creation of the Universe from the Chaos' (N 50, fos. 44^v–45). He argued that the progress and the realization of the outer redemptive plan were to be found within the processes of the natural world. One stimulus of his interest in natural science in all forms, but particularly in what he called 'physiogony' (N 65, fos. 1^v–2) (his term for 'natural history') was his belief that the study of the natural world would provide greater insights for faith. It was necessarily true, he insisted, 'if Christianity a *world*-religion, be of God, that universal Physics but zoology especially must form a part of the magnificent System of Redemption & so St Paul indeed asserts. But if so, then must the Insight into the Faith increase with the growth & expansion of Science & Philosophy' (N 35, fo. 29).

The 'Condescension' of the distinguishing Word and the unifying power of Spirit imparts form to formless chaos. Coleridge was convinced that nature could not be taken as reality in any absolute sense: the '*really* real' must, of necessity, be *meta*physical. But he insisted that the forms and products of nature had varying degrees of reality; they were indwelt by the divine Will and Reason and thus participated in Being, '*o ωv*', the Logos. He rejected the thesis implicit in some idealist systems that the phenomena of nature are illusory appearances of an ideal reality. The definitions of nature which are found in his later writings are positive affirmations of the reality of the natural world, its forms, and processes, though he rejected the tendency to identify God and Nature which he found, for example, in

Schelling. He found attempts to revive the ancient theme of the emanation of the cosmos from a divine source equally unsatisfying; in this, freedom seemed to be swallowed up by necessity. In opposition to the 'Identity' system of the Germans, which he criticized on several counts (*CN* iv, § 4662), he proclaimed the advantages of his 'anastatic System', in which Creation is presented as the response of a holy, loving, and intelligent Will to the self-loss of a primal Fall brought about by a mysterious opposition and rebellion to this Will:

It is the chief merit of the anastatic System to have got rid of this Identity—except in that state in which it is at its' proper Home, namely, in the Chaos as the realm of contradictions. In our Absolute (i.e. the ineffable God-head) there is no Dualism, no antithesis, consequently *no* 'Identity' in the sense affixed to the term by the new *Decoraters* of Spinosism. We have the eternal Prothesis, and the co-eternal Thesis, εν δε πληρωματι[7] τω της αυτης τιθεται τα παντα οσα μεν οντως εστι.* (*CN* iv, § 4662)

[* 'in its fulness are posited all things that really exist']

For Coleridge, the Fourth Gospel was a matchless and supreme expression of the symbolic unity of life and light in the Logos, the Creator who is incarnate within the forms and processes of his creation. Commenting on the Prologue, he wrote: 'The divine Cycle cannot be more adequately expressed, from Light to Light thro' Life' (*CN* iv. § 4662). According to Coleridge's scheme, in the first act of creation (the loving response to apostasy) Christ, the Light of the world, self-sacrificially transformed that Light into a polarity of life and light from which all the forms and processes of nature came into being. Finally, as the inner light and life of the redeemed and realized human person, Christ draws the whole creation back to himself. Coleridge's religious language appears strange and even disquieting in the context of a history and philosophy of *nature*. It is easier to understand when recognized as interwoven with his theory of the symbol, that which both represents and participates in universal reality.

---

[7] Coleridge makes constant use, following a tradition of Patristic theology and of Christian Platonism, of the term 'pleroma' (fulness) in references to the Logos. This term is found in the Fourth Gospel, see e.g. John 1: 16: πληρωματος. Coleridge uses it to suggest the plurality which has its source in alterity, and to indicate the Logos as the source of all Ideas, of all the forms of reality.

The Idea of Life

Much of Coleridge's work between 1815 and 1818 was dedicated to a refutation of the mechanistic philosophy of nature and the attempt to replace it with a dynamic scheme which found the source and origin of life in a spiritual reality of divine Will. Both his *Theory of Life* and those parts of the 'Opus Maximum' and the notebooks which deal in concentrated fashion with the theme of nature were written during this time. He argued that, while the study of natural life is the study of organisms and of organization, organization itself cannot be the explanation of life but must depend upon life as precedent (*TL* 27).[8] What *precedes* the phenomenal explanation of life cannot itself *be* the merely phenomenal. It must be that through which the organization and co-inherence of phenomenal reality comes into being. In the early years of the nineteenth century, during his enthusiastic explorations of German philosophy, Coleridge was intrigued by (and often appreciative of) the studies of the *Naturphilosophen*, of Kant, Oken, and Steffens. Through their work, and particularly through that of Schelling, who emphasized the dynamic quality of will[9] and of the primary 'potencies' within nature, Coleridge

[8] See also OM i, fos. 8 ff.: Coleridge believed it was necessary to challenge the claims of the 'corpuscular philosophy' and to 'examine whether we may not be more successful in reversing the order of priority, namely whether in life we may not find the conditions of universal organisation and again in universal organisation the conditions and the solution of mechanism'.

[9] See F. W. J. Schelling, *Sämmtliche Werke*, ed. K. F. A. Schelling, 14 vols. (Stuttgart, 1857), vi. 417–20, 460. Although Schelling's work was increasingly criticized by Coleridge, the former's ideas were enormously influential in the development of the 'logosophic' scheme; for example, Coleridge would have found in Schelling's work *Philosophische Untersuchungen über das Wesen der menschlichen Freiheit etc.* (Landshut, 1809), an exposition of the Idea of God, the Logos, as the Other who is yet Self, and of the role of the Logos as the birth and realization of Reason begotten by Will. However, it is possible to see, in the following passage, emphases in Schelling's thought with which Coleridge was unhappy, such as the concept of Reason as the birth of 'Logic' (here there are close parallels with Hegel) from an 'irrational' longing in the Absolute: 'There is born in God himself an inward, imaginative response, corresponding to this longing, which is the first stirring of divine Being in its still dark depths. Through this response, God sees himself in his own image, since his imagination can have no other object than himself. . . . This image is the first in which God, viewed absolutely, is realized, though only in himself; it is in the beginning in God, and is the God-begotten God himself. This image is at one and the same time, reason—the logic of that longing,* [original footnote:* In the sense in which one finds a Logos in Logographs . . .] and the eternal Spirit which feels within it the Logos

found an alternative to the 'necessitarian' schemes of David Hartley and Joseph Priestley, and to mechanism, atomism, and materialism.

While affirming that the origin of life is act and power, Coleridge denied that nature was itself self-creating, or divine. The importance which he attached to the connection between Life and Will is expressed in a letter to Samuel Mence (12 January 1825):

I am aware of few subjects more calculated to awake a deep [and] at once practical and speculative interest in a philosophic mind than the analogies between organic (I might say, organific) Life and Will. The Facts both of Physiology and Pathology lead to one and the same conclusion—viz. that in some way or other the Will is the obscure *Radical* of the Vital Power. (*CL* v. 406)

His 'Dynamic System' was based upon the conviction that the original polarity which resulted in the productive power and energy within the forms of nature was that between God and Nature. Life and light were the first manifestations of Will and Reason in the finite world, gifts of the Logos as 'will in the form of reason', who had freely entered the chaos of non-being. The power of life within nature is communicated by the Spirit and the Word; from the polarities of energy and form which they introduce, the organization and phenomena of nature develop. Again, the language of theology, rich in symbols, is often interwoven with the language of physical science. Coleridge seemed to find this (to twentieth-century minds) odd juxtaposition the best way to convey primal realities of power and form and their source in 'personëity'. At times, the blend has more in common with Greek philosophy; for example, he described life in the following terms: 'the most comprehensive formula to which life is

and the everlasting longing. This is not the One itself, but is co-eternal with it. This longing seeks to give birth to God, i.e. the Unfathomable unity, but to this extent it has not yet the unity in its own self. Therefore, regarded in itself, it is also a will: but a will within which there is no understanding. . . . Out of this which is unreasonable, reason in the true sense is born' (*Philosophische Untersuchungen*; tr. James Gutmann as *Of Human Freedom* (Chicago, 1936), 35–6). Although this passage contains many similarities with Coleridge's own concept of Logos, the latter insists, in contrast to Schelling, on the formulation which he believes expresses the truth of the Christian Trinity. Not only is the Logos Will in the form of Reason, but God the Begetter is Reason in the form of Will: There is no irrational moment of longing in God, just as there is no succession.

reducible, would be that of the internal copula of bodies, or (if we may venture to borrow a phrase from the Platonic school) the *power* which discloses itself from within as a principle of *unity* in the *many*' (*TL* 41–2).

He indicated two main errors concerning the understanding of the life and organization of nature which he believed were prevalent in his own time. The first was that which saw life as the product of organization, 'whereas the organization is nothing but the consequence of life, nothing but the means by which and through which it displays itself. . . . The man, therefore, who states life to proceed from organization, acts as a mathematician would who should be mad enough to assert the centre was placed in the circumference' (*PL* 358). He believed the second error to be the idea that life is somehow introduced from without, in the form of soul, for example. One who maintained this 'would commit an equal fault in logic, namely he would make the centre out of the circumference'. Coleridge also insisted that life, which is common to animals and man, must not be confused with the *responsible* nature in man which distinguishes him from animals, that is, the soul, the will, conscience, and reason.

If life did not originate in material or phenomenal organization, neither was it to be identified only with ideal or spiritual reality. He argued that both spirit and matter were ultimately homogenous. Life is an Idea manifested in polarity. Just as, for the finite understanding, the truth of Ideas ('light') can only be expressed through polarities (which often appear as contradictions), so the life of nature is manifested out of the tensions of polarities. The Idea of life, like all spiritual truth, may not be regarded as an *explanation* of life, because, Coleridge reminded his readers, explanation refers to cause and effect; a model which is only valid in the treatment of phenomena. His alternative model of 'light and life' is the conclusion, he said, which, when empirical investigation has reached its limits, best fits both the structures of human thought and the totality of human experience. It is therefore compatible with the dictates of reason. Life, in Coleridge's scheme (like the 'light' of Reason), can only be its own evidence, since it is the Idea, the law of its own action. The analysis of the Understanding (that is, the cause and effect structures which logic imposes on the manifestations and phenomena) may be inevitable, but these cannot grasp the Idea and Law of Life, the source and form of the processes of mind. Indeed, the supposition of cause and effect within nature is itself misleading according to Coleridge. Criticizing de Luc's 'electrical fluid',[10] he found it regrettable that the former did not learn from Francis Bacon 'that the notion of cause and effect belongs to Logic—to the arrangement of *our* thought, and dare not be supposed in nature, or rather cannot be without a contradiction in terms'.

Coleridge claimed that the facts (in the physical world, the phenomena), philosophically understood, presupposed the Idea,[11] the spiritual reality and power which could be recognized in 'that most general form under which Life manifests itself to us', that is, in the two opposing principles of 'individuation' and 'connection' or 'attachment'. In November 1816 he wrote to James Gillman of the study of the living world, its forms, and processes, which he proposed to undertake as part of his projected 'Logosophia' or 'Opus Maximum': 'I propose to begin at once with Life; but with Life in its very first manifestations—demonstrating that there is no other possible definition of Life but *Individuality*' *(CL* iv. 690). His *Theory of Life* fulfils this intention:

By Life I everywhere mean the true Idea of Life, or that most general form under which Life manifests itself to us, which includes all its other forms. This I have stated to be the *tendency to individuation*, and the degrees or intensities of Life to consist in the progressive realization of this tendency . . . this tendency to individuate cannot be conceived without the opposite tendency to connect, even as the centrifugal power supposes the centripetal, or as the two opposite poles constitute each other, and are the constituent acts of one and the same power in the magnet. *(TL* 49)

Here Coleridge revealed the dynamic of his philosophy of nature: the idea of life manifests itself through a polarity of *individuation* and *attachment*. While his concept of polarity was by no means

---

[10] See *CM* iii. 948 for notes on J. A. de Luc, 'Analysis of the Galvanic Pole', pt. 2, Nicholson's *Journal of Natural Philosophy, Chemistry, and the Arts*, 26 (1810), 113–36. De Luc, a Swiss geologist and meteorologist, invented a form of hydrometer and published the first correct rules for measuring heights by the barometer. His work was important for its contribution of facts about heat and moisture.

[11] See below, Ch. 3.2.

original,[12] he gave it a new emphasis in the context of his belief in the creative Word.

We have seen that his philosophy of nature (both as power and as product) is interwoven with the revelation of the Logos in the Fourth Gospel, through the symbolism of 'light' and 'life'. He explored light as spiritual, intellectual, and physical reality, and as the medium between these worlds of spirit, mind, and nature. He traced the 'light' motif through a wide range of theological, literary, and scientific sources from the age of the Greek philosophers to his own time.[13] Here again, the originality of his theme lies in his compilation of connections, in the blend of symbolic expression with scientific investigation and philosophical analysis. The distinctions between 'light' used as a representation of physical reality and as a theological or symbolic term seem often to be deliberately blurred; this enabled him to suggest the homogeny of matter, mind, and spirit, which he believed could be demonstrated through the Logos principle.

He believed that the 'Light', the mysterious, manifesting energy, of the Word was operative in the processes of life itself. As such, it could equally appropriately be the subject of a physical or a metaphysical study; in fact, these two fields were found, on this basis, to be interrelated. He claimed that, if the search for knowledge was begun from the insights of physical science, these would lead inevitably to the inescapable conclusion that there was a higher form of reality, the source of the laws and powers of the physical universe; and that this Reality must be a *personal* unity of Will-and Reason. If, on the other hand, the search was begun from the postulates of theology, that is, from the necessary Idea of God, and from the recognition that the qualities and needs of human nature are beyond the scope of phenomenal explanation, this would point irresistibly to the witness of creation

---

[12] It is possible here only to make brief reference to the history of the polarity principle. As an indication of the sources on which Coleridge drew, this principle may be found in embryonic form in the philosophies of Heraclitus and of Plato, in the Hermetic and mystical traditions (such as that of Jacob Böhme), and in the theology of, for example, Nicholas of Cusa and Giordano Bruno. It is also a feature of the work of the German *Naturphilosophen*, such as Oken and Steffens, and is further developed in the work of Schelling (see also O. Barfield, *What Coleridge Thought* (London, 1972). 179–93).

[13] See below, Ch. 2.2.

as a great scheme of redemption, and lead to a recognition of the ultimate unity of fact and idea, life and mind.

The conclusions to which Coleridge's study of nature led him can only be understood when seen in the context of the 'logosophic' scheme. His search for a system to counteract the mechanistic philosophy which prevailed in Britain in his own time was the motivating factor, and the Logos remains the point from which all connections must be drawn. His interest was declared, and the axioms on which he based his search were admitted. His emphasis on the necessity of an act of will as the starting-point of all knowledge and on faith as an essential component of reason might give him, according to recent hermeneutical theory,[14] the basis for a defence against any accusation of 'bad faith' in his acceptance of a metaphysical ground for physics. His scientific interest was genuine and profound. His conclusions, though occasionally fantastic, nevertheless do not seem so extravagantly drawn in the light of continuing scientific preoccupations today with the search for a unified system and the sometimes unavoidably *meta*physical nature of, for example, quantum physics.

'Individuation' and 'Attachment'

Coleridge believed that 'individuation' and 'attachment' were the fundamental principles of finite life, and that each principle had its source in the power symbolized in the creative Word (Logos). Individuation was for him, as for the German *Naturphilosophen*, the efficient and formal cause of the refinement and perfection of nature, of the evolution of ever higher forms. He took up the

---

[14] See Intro., n. 47, above; H.-G. Gadamer, for example, has asserted the necessity of an acceptance of prejudice as a *starting-position* in the hermeneutical endeavour and in fact one of the fruitful aspects of the traditions of thought which mould our minds. Those prejudices are then subject to modification through the *encounter* with the 'text'; some are confirmed, some must be abandoned. Pure objectivity is not only impossible, but *undesirable*; our very prejudices and their historical nature are essential to the act of understanding (*Truth and Method*, 238). Coleridge sees will and faith in much the same light; his concept of faith as loyalty ('An Essay on Faith', in *LR* iv. 425–6) has something in common with Gadamer's view on the prejudices which make understanding possible. For Coleridge, like Jacobi, all knowledge inevitably contains the elements of faith and will; and since will is, for him, the condition and justification for the acceptance of metaphysics, he has no difficulty in accepting a metaphysical ground of physics and of all the natural sciences.

Aristotelian emphasis, which Scholastic theology had developed, on the movement from potential to actual, finding in individuation the explanation and confirmation of both the teleology and the dynamic agency of the living world.[15] His study and admiration of Duns Scotus (*PL* 280) perhaps confirmed the importance of the individuation principle in his own thought. It is likely that Scotus' conception of a principle which *contracts* nature into a singularity[16] also contributed to the importance which Coleridge came to attach, both in a metaphysical ontology and in his philosophy of nature, to *contraction*; to the 'intension' of the point, or centre, and to its opposite pole, 'dilation' or expansion to a circumference or sphere.

The cause of universality, according to Scotus, is to be found in the intellect (derived from the divine Reason). The principle of individuality, however, is to be found within 'this-ness' or 'haecceity',[17] which is neither matter nor form but the 'ultimate reality' of the being composed of these.[18] This ultimate reality must be understood as *act*, rather than formal principle.[19] Coleridge himself associated individuality with will and act, believing it to be 'the *Self* in every creature' (*CM* i. 629) which participates, however remotely, in the original creative act by which the Word manifested the ultimate truth of the divine 'I AM'. He insisted, however, that this only became *real* individuality (as opposed to foreshadowings and appearances of it) in animate forms.[20] Here we find confirmed the association which he wished to maintain between individuation and *act*. In 1801 Coleridge's notes show him to have been increasingly preoccupied with the subject of will in response to his reading of German philosophy, and particularly that of Kant (*CN* i, §§ 1704–5; 1710–17), which explored the internal relationship of self-consciousness between the individual as active subject and as known object. On the subject of the individual and the self, Coleridge wrote to Robert

---

[15] Thomism had adopted the view that individuation was a quality of *matter*, not of form. Coleridge, however, agreed with Duns Scotus.

[16] *Opus Oxoniense*, ii, *d*. 3, *q*. 6, n. 2, in *Duns Scoti Opera Omnia*, Vives edn. (Paris, 1891–5).

[17] Ibid. ii, *d*. 3, *q*. 5, nn. 1, 8, 12, and 13.

[18] Ibid. ii, *d*. 3, *q*. 6, n. 15.

[19] Coleridge's note on Tennemann's *Geschichte der Philosophie* shows him to have been familiar with this aspect of Scotus' work (viii. 765).

[20] See below.

Southey of his study of Duns Scotus and of his intention to 'set the poor old Gemman on his feet again' (*CL* ii. 746). In his notes on the sixteenth-century divine Richard Hooker (*LR* iii. 21), he contrasted what he suggested was the latter's inability to cope with Pythagorean concepts, with the 'high metaphysical genius' of Duns Scotus, of which he could 'think of no other instance . . . in an Englishman'.

The whole evolution of nature's forms can be seen, according to Coleridge, to bear witness to the power and process of individuation:

> From the first moment of the differential impulse—(the primæval chemical epoch of the Wernerian School)[21]—when Nature, by the tranquil deposition of crystals, prepared, as it were, the fulcrum of her after-efforts, from this, her first, and in part *irrevocable*, self-contraction, we find, in each ensuing production, more and more tendency to independent existence in the increasing multitude of strata, and in the relics of the lowest orders, first of vegetable and then of animal life. (*TL* 70)

The striving towards individuation, and the opposing tendency towards the attachment to generic, universal nature, is evident, he suggested, from the very beginning: 'In the polypi, corallines, etc, individuality is in its first dawn' (*TL* 72). Individuation becomes increasingly fulfilled as the 'ladder' of nature is ascended through the emergence of higher forms.

Coleridge's concept of nature might be seen to be consistent with that which A. O. Lovejoy has designated the 'Great Chain of Being';[22] the hierarchical, interlinked progression of plenitude and continuity of the physical world which was sketched in the philosophy of Plato and Aristotle and remained, in various forms, the predominant model of nature until the eighteenth century. Yet Coleridge clearly distinguished between the necessity (which accompanies the innate, a priori framework of time) of a concept of nature which incorporates succession, causation, and progression, and the *life* of nature itself. When looked at retrospectively, according to the logic of the Understanding, Nature is found as 'an infinite ascent of causes', and when '*pro*spectively as an interminable progression of effects' (ODI, fo. 7). The 'ladder'

---

[21]   Abraham Gottlieb Werner (1750–1817) was a German geologist and founded the 'Neptunist' school.

[22]   A. O. Lovejoy, *The Great Chain of Being* (Cambridge, Mass., *c.*1964).

or 'chain' theory of nature could be recognized as the mind's active structuring of the world through the processes of logical thought, and correspondence must be admitted, Coleridge argued, between the *forms* of thought and the products of nature.[23] Yet Reason revealed the organic unity of the whole, and the *metaphysic* of Will (the true source of the powers and processes of both mind and nature) could not be satisfactorily expressed in terms of cause and effect or by mechanistic models such as the 'ladder' theory.

In his *Theory of Life*, Coleridge outlined the stages of differentiation and progressive individuation within the forms of nature. Metals, having the most 'attachment', the least 'individuation', are a 'mere unity of powers'. Crystals, he maintained, are not only a unity of powers, but of parts, and as such are 'the simplest form of *totality*', of a whole which consists of, and contains, distinct parts. In the ascending scale of nature the geological strata follow, in which animal and vegetable life are to be found in residue. The next development is found in the simplest life-forms: 'In the lowest forms of the vegetable and animal world we perceive totality dawning into *individuation*.' He emphasized the gulf between the lowest animate and the highest inanimate forms. In the latter, individuality is

purely and merely phenomenal. Either *Schein**[*] as in dendritic[†] Stones & the like—or Erscheinung[‡] as in Chrystallization. It is never an *Individual* properly, tho' possibly Unique; but always a species—i.e. it has nothing but its' simple Existence that is not determined ab extra, according to some general Laws. (*CN* iv, § 4677)

[* 'apparent', 'merely phenomenal'
† stones classified as fossils, exhibiting patterns of minerals
‡ a stage slightly closer to individuation than the former]

Coleridge insisted that individuation was not to be confused with separation or fragmentation:

the principle of individuation [is] the bond or copula, which gives a real unity ... in contradistinction from the mere semblance or total

---

[23] In fact, Coleridge saw flaws in the 'chain' model, and preferred that of a ladder (implying an impetus within nature to rise ever higher rather than a static fixed order) or that of the circle: 'It has been before noticed that the progress of Nature is more truly represented by the ladder, than by the suspended chain, and that she expands as by concentric circles' (*TL* 70).

impression produced by an aggregate on the mind of the beholder and
even from that combination of parts which originates and has its whole
end and object in an external agent[,] a unity different in short from that
of a heap of corn or from a steam engine or other machine. (OM iii, fos.
48–9)

He emphasized that unity was not to be identified with mere
'attachment' or indistinction.[24] A unified whole *presupposes* the
distinction of parts. Individuation results in parts which interact
with the whole which they comprise and in which they are con-
tained. Life is that power of individuation and 'the power which
unites a given *all* into a *whole* that is presupposed by all its parts'
(*TL* 42). It is 'the principle of unity in *multeity*'. There is an
'inverse ratio' between 'the antithesis of generic nature and the
Principium Individui'. In the higher forms of life, as individuality
increases, so there is a gradual and proportionate detachment
from the 'amassive' tendency within nature. However, life itself
presupposes the presence and power of the principle of indivi-
duation to some degree: 'even in the lowest order of bonâ fide
Animals the Princ. Indiv. must be presumed, tho' as existing in
an immanifestable minimum'.[25]

True and False Principles of Individuation

Coleridge interwove his theory of individuation with a theology
of *anastasis*. The ground of Nature, the opposite pole to the
supreme Being, 'whose name is Chaos & Hades, dimly appre-
hensible by predicating of the same Subject innumerable Multeity
by defect of Number and Unity of Indistinction by defect of
the Unific. This is indeed the *ground* of matter, materia im-
materiata.'[26] He saw the principle of individuality as divine and

---

[24] In seeing individuation not as separation but as distinction, and in denying
that unity is mere sameness or identity, Coleridge disagrees with Schelling's
identity philosophy. The first 'potency' etc. of individuation is *not*, as Schelling
has it, the irrational will; this is rather the cause of *separation* than of the
possibility of fruitful relationship—e.g. in polarity.

[25] BL MS Egerton 2801, fo. 48.

[26] But Coleridge criticized Oken's view concerning what Coleridge called the
'dark mosaic fire', the ground of nature. He believed that Oken, and other
Naturphilosophen, confused this with the phenomenal fire, as an element. Anno-
tations on the flyleaf of Oken's *Lehrbuch der Naturphilosophie* (Jena, 1809–11),
i, nn. dated 6 July 1830.

indestructible. It was inseparably linked to the idea of distinction, which he everywhere associated with Logos: 'As the Unity is absolute, so is the *Distinctness*. . . . The force of the term, Logos, is the Distinctive Power' (N 36, fo. 64). Yet the mystery of the apostatic Fall itself consisted in the separation (rather than distinction) of individuality by rebellious act. An 'eternal possibility' of opposing will mysteriously strove to become actual in its own right, independent of the divine unity and the universality of the divine Idea (Logos). The attempt of what is actual only as 'eternal possibility' to become *independently* actual necessarily resulted in self-contradiction and in non-being. The fallen will was then deprived of actuality in that it had no possibility of self-realization. It remained a dreadful potentiality of evil and chaos; but the Logos, the true principle of individuality, the redeeming Word of God, was spoken in and to this dark chaos. This was the beginning of the creation, the process of transformation and actualization in the gradual emergence of the individual forms of nature. What was mere fragmented, alienated '*multëity*' became imbued with power and form. Here again, the influence of the Logos theology of the early Greek Fathers is evident. Coleridge set out this process of the Fall and Redemption of Individuality in detail in a notebook entry of 1826:

The primary Powers [of Nature] are the potential Individualities, Individuality being the indestructible Consequent of the Absolute Will essentially causative of Reality-/This Princ. Indiv. that must have been as an eternal *Possibility*, but latent in the Idea and *willing* itself one with its' Divine Form, and offering the Hallelujah Sacrifice of its' Idiocentricity to the universal Center, ought never to have become Actual.—The apostatic Act, accursed, did take place—and the instant Birth was the *Lie* Essential, the dark Mystery of Self-contradiction . . . the primæval Inversion. In the impossible attempt to actualize the Potential, the Actual was potenzialised—i.e. existed only as a *possibility*.— The Offspring or Phænomen[on] of this Apostacy was the Chaos—when in the infinity of love and mercy the Redemptive Word had reduced this Multeity to Number, the Princ. Indiv. became Atoms, i.e. Self centers; but as all these fallen Spirits were *objectively* one and the same Spirit of Evil, and only *subjectively* i.e. in the evil imagination, several, there resulted—first, a Unity of Omnëity, secondly, an infinite series of Unities included in the first, according to the Classes, Kinds, Species consequent on the Forms, which the Divine Spirit & Word by co-ercive polarization had rendered it possible for them to strive after, or compelled them into by their own Counter-striving (as Pigs by struggling against the man are made to enter into a Ferry-boat).[27] (N 26, fo. 120^{r-v})

Such language was not likely to commend itself to those trained according to the Newtonian model of quantities, mathematical measurement, and atomic proportions; but Coleridge was imitating, however unconsciously, the language of German *Naturphilosophie*, such as that of Schelling. This often drew on mystical and alchemical traditions for its symbols and qualitative descriptions. Nature has a tendency, Coleridge maintained, to supersede itself, and this leads to ever more complex forms in which the individuality principle is increasingly manifested. Finally, the evolution of nature is completed in man, the microcosm in whom all the previous stages and forms are contained, but to whom the Word imparts mind: 'The Logos added *mind* to the Princ. Indiv, in the last produced animal, & this made it *Man!*' (N 26, fo. 119). In man, the individuality principle is found in its highest form, when, that is, it is detached from nature and realized in personality.[28] Coleridge suggested that individuality could not sustain itself, but must be attached either to the ground of nature (in the sense of that 'otherness' of non-being which remains as an evil potential), or to God:

If there be anyone conclusion of my investigations coercive on my faith it is that the Principle of Individuality (which of all creatures known to us is in the highest relative energy in Man) cannot remain without a supporting or a sustaining Power—It must [be] in vital consociation either with a supporting *Nature* ab infra, or a Sustaining Divinity a supra—it must obey the attraction either of the terrestrial or of the celestial Magnet . . . only by the attraction of the Celestial Magnet can man maintain even his mobility in the nature to which he is bound / move *on* it instead of sinking *into* it. (N 35, fos. 39^v–40)

---

[27] I have quoted this note at length because it clearly conveys the significance in Coleridge's system of the action and 'Condescension' of the Logos, and the introduction of polarity by Spirit and Word in the Creation process. It shows the contrast which he drew between the mass of mere 'multëity' and potentiality and the production of individual atoms as 'Self centers' through the introduction of number. It portrays the polarization process as resulting in a striving within the 'Unity of Omnëity' for distinctions, and the production of a series of distinct unities of class, kind, and species.

[28] See below, Ch. 4.2 and 4.3.

From Pythagorean philosophy to the poetry of Alexander Pope (*An Essay on Man*, 1733–4) in the eighteenth century, the concept of man as microcosm had been explored and developed both philosophically and theologically.[29] Coleridge's acceptance of the completion and perfection of nature in man is a variation on a long and well-established tradition within Christian thought. However, the deep respect which marked his attitude to certain thinkers frequently determined the particular emphasis or 'angle' of his use of a familiar concept. In the writings of John Scotus Eriugena, for example, Coleridge found a strong emphasis on this aspect of man as microcosm and on the divinity of the principle of individuality. Eriugena believed, as did Coleridge, that the redemption of the whole creation was included and fulfilled in man's redemption. He emphasized that individuality would be preserved in the reconciliation and union with God.[30] Despite Coleridge's comment that Eriugena appeared 'in some points to have come too near to pantheism' (*PL* 271) his admiration is evident and his own work reflects his agreement with the principle that the whole creation is to be redeemed through the redemption of humanity. Man is the salvation of the 'inferior creation'. Only in Man, restored to the divine Humanity, 'is the solution of their dark Enigma' (*CN* iv, § 4984).[31]

Gabriel Marcel, writing on the relationship between the work of Coleridge and that of Schelling, suggests that the former was unaware of the importance to Schelling of the individuation principle. Yet in marginal notes to Schelling's *Philosophische Schriften* (1809) Coleridge makes clear that he is unconvinced by the mere unsupported assertion of individuation as a dynamic principle. He sceptically challenged the foundations of Schelling's hypothesis of the principle of distinction and individuation, and questioned the basis of the latter's postulate of a principle of life which separated itself into multiple forms from the mysterious

---

[29] E. M. Tillyard explores this in *The Elizabethan World Picture* (London, 1943) and looks back to the influence of classical authors on the period. See e.g. his citation of Photius' *Life of Pythagoras* on this subject (p. 74).

[30] Coleridge's recognition of this aspect of Eriugena's work is evident (N 35, fo. 23); for his own views on the subject see e.g. N 26, fo. 44, N 36, fo. 64.

[31] Coleridge approved of Justin Martyr's view that it was necessary for essential life, or 'life by nature', to be united with human nature, in order to save it (see *NED* ii. 209–10).

'Ground' of existence.[32] Coleridge had criticized Spinoza's work on a similar point concerning the principle of individuality. In the latter's denial of a divine Will (or personality),

> he necessarily precluded either all alterity or all unity for in the idea of the Will only are these found as co-inherent. He chose to exclude the alterity but in so doing he necessarily excluded all intelligence in any conceivable sense of the word inasmuch as that necessarily implied an alterity of subject & object . . . [he] denied intelligence inasmuch as he made its essence to consist in its limits but as these limits were utterly alien to the substance and as the substance contained alone all reality the limits were not real and it would be vain to seek for any distinction.[33]

Individuality must be the result of the possibility of distinction and the limits of form; the gift of the Logos as 'Will = Reason'.[34] Spinoza's system was defective because it failed to recognize the Divine distinction-in-unity.

The Logos, in Coleridge's system, is not only the 'Self in every creature', the 'Principium Individuum', but also 'alterity', the principle of polarity. Through these two elements, he constantly strove to demonstrate the ultimate unity of physics and metaphysics. We shall see that his polarity theme is as detailed and as logocentric as his concept of individuation in nature. This concept of polarity was, in many respects, borrowed from the nature philosophy of such as Schelling, Oken, and Steffens; but Coleridge wove it more closely into the Christian framework of apostasy, and anastasy. Polarity was part of the process of the whole scheme of redemption, acceptance of which, he was determined to show, was compatible with all areas of the human and physical sciences.

---

[32] 'We will grant for a while', wrote Coleridge, 'that the Principle evolved or lifted up from this mysterious *Ground* of Existence, which *is* and yet does not exist, is separate (geschieden) from God: yet how is it separate from the Ground itself? How is it individuated? Already the material phaenomen of Partibility seems to have stolen in.—And at last I cannot see what advantage in reason this Representation, this form of Symbol, has over the old more reverential Distinction of the Divine Will relatively to the End, from the same Will relatively to the means' (Coleridge's notes on Schelling's *Philosophische Schriften* (Landshut, 1809), 438).

[33] BL MS Egerton 2801, fo. 13ᵛ.

[34] 'Christ as the filial Godhead, the *ο ΩΝ εν τω κολπου* [*sic*] *του πατρος*, [who is in the bosom of the father], is essentially & from everlasting was Will = Reason' (N 44, fo. 62ᵛ).

2.2. POLARITY

As we have seen, Coleridge denied that the origin of life could be anything other than *meta*physical; and he believed it could never, for this reason, be adequately explored or expressed through the language of cause and effect, or of Newtonian science. For him, the language and symbolism of Christianity proved best fitted for the task. He took, as the foundation of his philosophy of nature, the concept of an apostatic Will, self-separated from the Holy Will, which was realized in Being, Intellect, and Love. From this separation, he argued, resulted the original polarity between God and Hades or Chaos, the ground of Nature.[35] He took up a theme developed by Patristic theology (by, for example, Augustine and Origen), that of the divine Word which entered Chaos in love and grace, transforming it into the seed-bed of creation. According to Coleridge's interpretation, mere 'multëity' became, through the 'condescension' of Logos, the generative relations of polarity; life and being began with the first polarization of Light.[36] In this first act of creation, Chaos became the potentiated 'Mosaic Darkness'[37] and was transformed into degrees of becoming through the polarity induced by Spirit and Word. Coleridge saw this dynamic polarization repeated at every stage in the life of the natural world, and in the powers and forces through which it is produced.

The theme of opposition or polarity as a creative and dynamic principle has a long history. He recognized the important place which Heraclitus had given it, and hoped (as he wrote to C. A. Tulk) to expound the philosophy of 'Heraclitus redivivus' (*CL* iv. 775). Heraclitus' *logos* is the principle of becoming through opposition; as such, the life within both nature and mind.[38] Coleridge develops this emphasis on polarity in every aspect of

---

[35] I have capitalized 'Nature' where I am using it in Coleridge's sense of the ground and principle out of which life is drawn.

[36] BL MS Egerton 2801, fos. 143–4; see also *C & S* 175.

[37] Coleridge takes the term 'Mosaic Darkness' from what he takes to be Moses' account of the creation in Genesis, that is, from the term 'Tohu Bohu' in Genesis 1: 2. For a detailed account of the Logos connection which Coleridge sees between the Prologue of the Fourth Gospel and Genesis 1: 3, see *CN* iii, § 4418.

[38] See W. K. C. Guthrie, *A History of Greek Philosophy*, 6 vols. (Cambridge, 1967), i. 435.

his 'logosophic' system.[39] He claimed to have been familiar with the principle long before he had read Schelling's work (in which polarity is prominent) and to have developed his own particular form of it from his reading of 'Plato, and the Scholars of Ammonius, and in later time of Scotus (Joan, Erigena), Giordano Bruno, Behmen, and the much calumniated Spinoza' (*CL* iv. 775). He was familiar with Plato's treatment of polarity in the *Timaeus*, where 'sameness' and 'difference' are the constituent elements of the World Soul,[40] and in the *Sophist*, where Being contains the opposition of these two poles. Being and non-being are crucial polarities in Plato's metaphysics;[41] his tool of reason, the dialectic, may itself be seen as an expression of the polarity principle. Coleridge believed that Plato, like Heraclitus, had seen polarity as creative and dynamic and had understood that the higher reality of ideas can often only be expressed through apparent contradictions: '[Plato] leads you to see, that propositions involving in themselves contradictory conceptions, are nevertheless true; and which, therefore, must belong to a higher logic—that of ideas. They are contradictory only in the Aristotelian logic, which is the instrument of the understanding' (*TT* ii. 77).

Coleridge carefully distinguished between opposition and contradiction: 'Antagonist forces are necessarily of the same kind. It is an old rule of logic, that only concerning two subjects of the same kind can it properly be said that they are opposites. Inter res heterogeneas non datur oppositio, *i.e.* contraries cannot be opposites' (*C & S* 117). He uses the figurative symbols ⚹ and ⚹ to distinguish between contradiction and opposition, but denies that either can be applied to the relation between soul and body (N 44, fo. 56). It is not spirit and matter which are opposed, but rather God (as Being) and the ground of nature (as the tendency to non-being, to revert to formless chaos). He believed that Plotinus had been nearer than Plato to Christian doctrine in at

---

[39] We have seen that Coleridge believed the principle of polarity to reflect its source: the Logos as 'alterity', the realization of God as *Idem et Alter*.

[40] *Timaeus*, 35a–36b. Coleridge's familiarity with this work is clear (see e.g. *BL* i. 283).

[41] P. Seligman gives an analysis of this polarity in Plato (*Being and Not-Being: An Introduction to Plato's* Sophist (The Hague, 1974)). For Coleridge's knowledge of this aspect of Plato's thought, see *CM* i. 573 n.

least one respect, that of finding 'God as the real ground both of substance and form'; 'Plato, in the public writings at least, was a Dualist.'[42]

Coleridge represented the creation of matter as one of the first steps in the redemptive scheme; the product of a polarity of powers the origin of which is spiritual. This scheme, he admitted, had something in common with Plotinus' thought. The latter 'derived the phænomena of extension from the representative powers by means of spiritual intercommunion'.[43] Yet Coleridge rejected the emanation theory of Plotinus and the Neoplatonists as failing to provide an explanation of the *agency* behind the process (ODI, fos. 173–5). They offered no concept of will, no idea of creative act or intention from which a dynamic polarity might be deduced; Plotinus, for example, offered no equivalent to Coleridge's postulate of a polarity of Will.[44] The idea that all opposition proceeded by mysterious emanation from the One was simply inadequate.

Greek philosophy was not the only source for Coleridge's use of the polarity principle. Often the application of his theory had more in common with an Augustinian emphasis on moral, spiritual, and psychological polarities than with post-Heraclitean Greek thought. Augustine, in the *City of God*,[45] had modified the Greek concept of polarity, combining it with the Judaeo-Christian focus on God's goodness and creative power. Just as a poet uses antithesis and contrast to add to the beauty and to the communicative power of his poem, so, to enrich the beauty and richness of the world, God introduces thesis and antithesis. Coleridge, like Augustine, saw the introduction of polarity as a response of love to the original spiritual Fall. He greatly admired the treatment of this theme in the work of Nicholas of Cusa (1401–64) and of Giordano Bruno (1548–1600), both of whom developed the doctrine of Christ as the Providence in whom

---

[42] BL MS Egerton 2801, fo. 33.
[43] Ibid.
[44] See e.g. Plotinus' description of the soul's fall; *Enneads*, 4. 4. 4–5; and his discussion of Evil in the realm of Non-Being: 1. 8. 3 and 15; see also 2. 4. 16; 3. 6. 14. There is no concept anywhere here of an originating act of evil by an apostatic will.
[45] Augustine, *City of God*, xi. 18. For Coleridge's familiarity work, see e.g. *CN* iv, § 4611, fo. 45ᵛ.

all opposites are reconciled.[46] Coleridge had first encountered Bruno's work in April 1801 (*CM* i. 347),[47] and reacted to the polarity theory with great enthusiasm. Many admiring references demonstrate his agreement with Bruno that here was the creative and dynamic principle within all life. He found the interdependence of polarity and trichotomy[48] most powerfully expressed in the Pythagorean *tetractys* (*CM* i. 347–8).

In later notes, marginalia, and sketches for the 'Logosophia', Coleridge emphatically rejected the idea of polarity in the Absolute.[49] At the same time, he denied that God could be represented as Identity; this contained no possibility of creative agency. The model of triunity was that in which both unity and distinctions could be realized through the dynamic impetus of relations; it was the only adequate solution to the age-old problem of the One and the Many.

He became critical of the suggestions which he found in Bruno, Böhme, and Schelling of a potential polarity within the Identity of the Absolute. These failed to recognize the begotten Logos as alterity, as the 'Out-terance', the Word spoken out, yet remaining, the distinction (without separation) which makes unity possible. Here was the archetypal Principle of polarity. Both the antinomies of Reason which Kant had set out, and the polarities in which physical and moral life are manifested, reflect the nature and work of the Logos as Creator (N 41, fo. 10). Their dynamic opposition leads beyond themselves to a *tertium aliquid*.

---

[46] See Nicholas of Cusa, *De Docta Ignorantia*, iii. 12: 'Whence all diversities that become united take their unity from that very maximal union of the natures in Christ' (tr. G. Heron as *Of Learned Ignorance* (London, 1954), 170); and G. Bruno, *De la Causa, Principio et Uno* (London, 1584), iii. 83. See also D. W. Singer, *Bruno: His Life and Thought* (New York, 1950), 57, 84.

[47] See *CN* i, § 927.

[48] 'Trichotomy': A system of logic and reasoning which overcame the problems of dichotomy and involved a '*tertium aliquid*' as a higher principle emerging as the source and unity of all thesis and antithesis relations. Coleridge attributed this concept to Richard Baxter 'a century before' Kant (OM ii, fo. 38 n.).

[49] Perhaps this is the important inspiration that Coleridge reported to Henry Crabb Robinson he had found in Proclus and from which point he had begun the development of his philosophy (H. C. Robinson, *On Books and their Writers*, ed. Edith J. Morley, 3 vols. (London, 1938), i. 70 (3 May 1812)). Proclus declares 'as the Pythagoreans say, the One is prior to all oppositions' (*In Platonis Timaeum Commentaria*, 54D). Coleridge would, no doubt, have been familiar with Thomas Taylor's translation of Proclus (*The Commentaries of Proclus on the* Timaeus *of Plato* (1820)). The ὑπερούσιος (above-being) is a term also found in the writings of the Church Fathers (*CM* ii. 726).

Coleridge described 'the two forms in which all true being is comprehended[,] the Idem et Alter' (OM ii, fo. 269). The 'ipsëity' of the Father, the 'alterity' of the Son and the 'Community' of their relation (Spirit)—these were the ground of all distinction, the source and life of the processes and products of nature and of mind as manifested in the creation. Only in the begetting of the Logos were 'ipsëity' and 'alterity' realized in a unity of distinctions undiminished by the separateness of plurality. Of all the truths contained in the idea of the Trinity, that of distinction-in-unity, based on the relationship of Self and Other, was most fundamental to Coleridge's theory of life; it was on this principle that he based his concepts of a created order, of the homogeneity of ideal and real, and of the integration and interdependent relation of part and whole, whether in biology, chemistry, or physics.

Creation

The actions of the Word as Creator were, according to Coleridge, of three kinds: 'evocative', 'ingenerative', and 'potenziative', the last being the intermediate term between the first two: 'more than the first, less than the second' (N 37, fos. 45^v–46). There were four stages in the creation of life: first, the Word called forth those distinctions which were ultimately to become the 'self in every creature'; distinction emerges from indistinction. Next, 'multëity' is 'potenzialized', that is, prepared to receive the divine influence. Thirdly, there was the 'influx of the divine power' for growth and development, and lastly life was communicated through the 'ingenerative' act. The Logos—the principle of distinction—is thus also the medium of the *relationship* between distinctions. Coleridge represented the Logos as the 'Indifference', the 'Mesothesis', of all polarities, the point at or within which extremes meet. Without the Logos, there was only Identity or contradiction. True homogeneity, he insisted, necessarily requires distinction. The whole process of creation was dependent upon 'the mitigation of the self-contradictory one into the reciprocally opposing *two*'.[50] Almost always Coleridge provides a

---

[50] N 44, fo. 69: 'the divine & the natural—the Will of God, transcendently One, and the Will of Hades, essentially contradictory, and which cannot *be*,

correlation (explicit or implicit) between descriptions of the Word as the life and light of the natural world on the one hand, and as the archetypal Symbol of human language on the other. These parallels lie at the heart of his attempt to work out a unified system of thought. Here, the 'evocative', 'potenziative', and 'ingenerative' qualities of agency in the creation are suggestive of parallels with, for example, that quality of the symbol which reawakens a kind of hidden unconscious memory, with words as powers giving birth to self-consciousness and reason, and with the evolutionary progress of language as the 'growth and emanation of a People'.[51]

In the Creation, the act through which polarity was introduced into a kind of 'potentialized' darkness was followed by a 'constant interposition of the mesothesis'. The Word voluntarily interposed as mediator between God and the alienation of non-being, and also acted as '*mesothesis*' within the ground of nature itself, separating it into light and darkness.[52] At every stage of creation this process was repeated. The mediation of the Word was sustained and gradually life was drawn towards light. Regarded from 'below', on the other hand, from the point of view of the evolution of Nature from its beginnings, Coleridge argued that the process could be seen as the production, from a mere indistinction, of polarities which in turn generate a higher form of reality, ever more distinct and individual. This is then itself productive as one of yet another pair of opposites in the process of the redemptive scheme towards the emergence of mind.

Actual and Potential

Coleridge never lost touch with philosophy's unsolved and ancient problems; he drew widely, in his philosophy of nature as in other areas of his system, on traditions within Greek philosophy and classical theology and on German thought, though he remained

cannot manifest itself but by division, and the mitigation of the self-contradictory [one] into the reciprocally opposing *two*'.

[51] See above, Ch. 1.1.

[52] In Coleridge's 'Logical Pentad' (the finite expression of the sacred symbolism of the *tetractys* figure) mesothesis stands between thesis and antithesis, the 'Mid-position or the *Indifference* of the Two' (*C & S*, App. E, 233). In mesothesis both are contained in varying proportions and predominance, according to the point of perception.

critical of all previous 'solutions'. With Thomist Aristotelianism, for example, he agreed that God is pure Act. Non-being, by God's grace, remains purely potential; but in all the degrees of being of the physical world, there is something of both actuality and potentiality. The opposition of God and the chaos from which Nature is drawn is represented in all becoming. Coleridge insisted that the potential must not be identified with the *unreal*: '[W]hen the Real is *distinguished* into Actual and Potential, it is not meant to affirm that the Real is exclusively either Actual or Potential but . . . simply that these are its' Thesis and Antithesis —not precluding but on the contrary implying the mesothesis & syntheses' (N 43, fo. 47) (here Coleridge describes *finite* reality; degrees of being). He declared that the Absolute contains the potential only as the opposition of mere unrealized *possibility*, the realization of which is unthinkable (as 'outside' the ontological and intellectual reality of the Idea) until *after* the mysterious fall has occurred. On this basis, he disagrees with Schelling's analysis of Absolute Reality as the 'Indifference' of actual and potential. Only in contemplation of the moment between the primal Apostasy and the condescension of Spirit ('Breath-energy') could the Real be seen as both exclusively actual and exclusively potential, reality consisting, in that moment, of pure act and pure potentiality in *separation*, not unity (N 43, fos. 47–8). From this point on, the forms of the physical world always combine varying degrees of actuality and potentiality. It was Coleridge's assertion that God's self-comprehension as the One and Infinite must include 'a knowledge of the finite and whatever exists finitely in relation to each finite & as a knowledge belonging to, & under the condition of the finite' (ODI, fo. 61). He argued at some length that the potential must be understood as in some sense *real*, and suggested 'the necessity . . . of predicating both the actual & the potential of one & the same subject, namely that its being is actual as far as it is in the being of God & potential in relation to itself as particular existence'. He concluded that

whatever actually is, even for ourselves, is thus wholly & solely by the presence of the Deity to the mind & that sense itself as if it were an opake reason is possible only, by a communion with that life which is the light of man, which lighteth every man that cometh into the world, & without which the solar light would be a contradiction in thought, a powerless power, a light that is darkness. (ODI, fo. 63)

Coleridge's logosophic system claims an inseparability of potentiality and actuality in the forms of finite thought and being, implying a constant process of dynamic change and development. Despite his division of thinkers into Aristotelians and Platonists (*TT* i. 172–3), this aspect of his own work appears to build a bridge between the dynamic 'becoming' which is characteristic of Aristotelian (and later of Hegelian) thought and the transcendent Reality of Plato's Good.

He believed that the fundamental error of the *Naturphilosophen* was their failure to understand polarity as the result of a *positive* act of creation, the act of Logos as 'Will in the form of Reason'. Instead, they attributed polarity to the Absolute, which, on the contrary, he declared, must be understood as pure Act, *beyond* all Being and Mind (N 41, fo. 82^v). In this, their philosophy suggested a diminution of perfection in the Absolute (*CM* i. 627). Although contradiction is, according to Coleridge's theory, the result of a mysterious apostasy of will, it is transformed, by a sublime paradox, through the Condescension of Logos, into the process of polarity by which life and being are restored in *becoming*. Polarity was at the heart of the creative act which commenced the great scheme of redemption. It was the consequence, not of divine emanation through the manifestation of the physical and finite world, but of an act of Will. Coleridge described the fallen will as the *condition* of contradiction, but asserted that Will in the form of Reason (the Logos) is both the ideal and real Principle of this polarity, transforming self-contradiction into self-realization through the introduction of 'otherness' and relationship.

Schelling's polarity of 'essence' and 'form', and Oken's of positive and negative (+ and −), were attempts to explain the relation between infinite and finite reality. Coleridge praised Schelling's development of the polarity principle, his exposition of magnetism, electricity, and galvanism, and his analysis of the concepts of length, breadth, and depth. He also admired Schelling's attack on the 'mechanic' and 'corpuscular' philosophy; but he dismissed the latter's polarity theory as 'Behmenism . . . reduced at last to a mere Pantheism', and 'Plotinised Spinozism' (*CL* iv. 883). The errors common, in his view, to Böhme, Plotinus, and Spinoza (the failure to recognize an opposing will as the ground of nature, and the suggestion of polarity within an

Absolute Identity) were incorporated into Schelling's scheme. The result was a view of Nature as ' "gemina Natura quae fit et facit, creat et creatur", of which the Deity itself is but an Outbirth';[53] Schelling's Nature was thus self-creating and necessary to the perfection of the Deity.[54]

In admitting the interconnectedness of all life, Coleridge was in partial agreement with the pantheists: 'Thinkest thou that thou canst understand the nature of the Soul without an insight into the soul of Nature?—So, or something tantamount, says Plato. From earliest manhood the Power of this sentiment worked in me as a presentiment before I had any distinct conviction of its truth. . . . The older I am and the more I know, the stronger does this Feeling become.'[55] He insisted that, without the Trinity, the distinction between Creator and creature was lost, as indeed were ultimately *all* distinctions in any other than an illusory sense. In the 'Opus Maximum', he had described the role of the Logos as

the two forms in which all true being is comprehended[,] the Idem et Alter . . . in this other all others are included . . . in this first substantial & intelligible distinction (= $o\ \Lambda o\gamma o\varsigma$) all other distinctions . . . are included. (OM ii, fos. 269–71)

He shared many of the interests, the enthusiasms and hypotheses of the *Naturphilosophen*, yet his response to them was often critical and fault-finding. He believed that he had outclassed them in scientific method, in the consistency of his thought, and the validity of his conclusions.[56] Yet, like them, he himself acknowledged a progressive development in the forms of life. Life, he concluded, had so far been defined only by its effects, whereas it is 'the law of action' which science must seek to

[53] This phrase is drawn from the work of John Scotus Eriugena (see Coleridge's attribution of 'et fit et facit et creat et creatur' to Eriugena (*CN* ii, § 1382) and Giordano Bruno (*Friend*, i. 115–17, 146, 471; ii. 80), from which it is clear that the phrase *'gemina natura'* is from the latter). The translation here is 'Twin Nature who is made and makes, creates and is created'.

[54] At this point, in 1818, Coleridge was 'carefully re-perusing the first part of Schelling's *Einleitung zu seinem Entwurf eines Systems der Natur-philosophie . . .* I seem to see clearly the rotten parts and the vacua of his foundation' (*CL* iv. 873).

[55] BL MS Egerton 2801, fo. 47.

[56] See e.g. Coleridge's annotations on the front flyleaf of Oken's *Lehrbuch der Naturgeschichte* (Jena, 1813) where he compares Oken's scheme unfavourably with his own.

announce: 'Life itself is not a *thing*—a self-subsistent *hypostasis*—but an *act* and *process*' (*TL* 94). It is clear that German thought profoundly influenced his development of the concept of polarity in the forces and forms of nature; yet his understanding of the reality and role of the divine Word is the source of important disagreements with his German contemporaries.

Spirit and Word

Coleridge's notes in the period 1817–18 show the intensity of his interest in theories concerning the origin and processes of life. He constantly attempts to show how new developments in the physical sciences might support and confirm the truths revealed in Christian symbolism and how these developments require a new, non-mechanistic philosophy of nature. He describes life in terms of the co-operation of Spirit and Word in the act of creation, and in the polarities through which life evolves. This is the unity of Life and Love: 'The whole system of Nature—is it or is it not a striving actuated & rendered possible by the divine Love, (the Spirit & the Word) after a re-union? Is it not the constant tendency of this *nature* to *supersede* herself?' (N 35, fo. 30). The first two elements of the '3-fold polarity' by which he explained the creation and evolution of the natural world in the 'Opus Maximum' notes are developed around this interaction of Spirit and Word. The first polarity was 'that of the Creaturely and the divine Will': the very existence of a 'creaturely' will implied an act of grace by which it was released from the evil will which could only exist potentially. The second is 'the Indistinction and the Multeity in the creature itself which having been actualised by the Spirit and the Word constitute it existentially i.e. are both the Creature and its properties as a Being'.

Coleridge's theory postulates existence as dependent upon the polarity within unity (constituting the organism as a whole) which has distinct 'properties' of being. This unity he thereafter consistently represented as Word acting through and in *Spirit*; *distinction*, on the other hand, he expressed as Spirit included in the influence of *Word*. He adopted a theologically orthodox view, that the Spirit proceeds from the Father *and* the Son. His description of the action of Spirit and Word expressed what was for him a vital truth of the idea of Trinity,[57]—distinction-in-unity—which could be introduced into the separated finite only as polarity. The act of creation is accomplished through a polarization which transforms indistinction into unity (the peculiar quality of the Spirit of Love and Community); and 'multëity' into individuality (the peculiar quality of the 'Word', who is distinction, 'alterity') through an evolutionary process.

The a priori conditions of all experience and of all reason (identified by Kant as time and space) correspond, according to Coleridge, to ideal realities which he represents symbolically as constituted by the activity of the Spirit and Word: 'REASON is the Identity, or Co-inherence, of Unity and Distinctity. Unity without Distinctity = SPACE: Distinctity without Unity = TIME' (*C & S* 118 n.). These two interact and share a common source in a higher ideal power. Many of Coleridge's notes on this subject suggest that he was familiar with Philo's rendering of the Stoic principle 'Time is a measured space'.[58] For example, he describes the polarity of Space and Time as creating a fruitful struggle, a 'war & love embrace' (OM i. fo. 81), out of which emerges a new polarity of 'attraction' as 'Time, Limit, Form, Negation', and of 'repulsion' as '+ Space, Area, Substance, Positum' (*CM* i. 563). Coleridge's researches into the subjects of time and space (these were stimulated by his reading of Kant's first *Critique*), together with his knowledge of the debate between Leibniz and Newton over the nature of time, led him to the conviction that he had found (and corrected) the flaw in materialism: 'If I do not greatly delude myself, I have not only completely extricated the notions of Time and Space; but have overthrown the doctrine of Association, as taught by Hartley, and with it all the irreligious metaphysics of modern Infidels—especially, the doctrine of Necessity' (*CL* ii. 706).

He believed he could show that time and space, which Kant had suggested were the a priori conditions of experience and knowledge, were *one* sense. He could thereby begin 'to solve the process of Life & Consciousness' (ibid.). This relationship of time

---

[57] The idea of *perichoresis* seems to be in Coleridge's mind here. *Perichoresis* he elsewhere calls 'an ineffable cycle of Will, Being, Intelligence, & communicative Life, Love and Action' (ODI, fos. 6–7).

[58] Philo, *De Opificio Mundi*, vii. 26.

and space is explored in detail in his later writings.[59] He admired the theory of H. Steffens, in this connection, and agreed that 'Space = the form by which the Infinite is taken up into the Finite—Time = the form by which the Finite is taken up into the Infinite' (OM i, fo. 79) (though Coleridge rejected the association of 'Infinite' with 'Magnitude' or 'Exceedingness'). He maintained that 'in the generation of a line[,] that which supplies the fluency is space and . . . the fluent is Time. . . . Space is that which gives the continuity to the point and Time that which superinduces the point on the continuity, the synthesis of both being Motion' (ibid.). Steffens failed to recognize, according to Coleridge, that, while his view was accurate in terms of geometry and the realm of the ideal, it could not simply be transferred on to the real, physical world, nor could this be seen as a kind of self-activating life. Steffens had failed to provide any indication of *agency*. He had made time actual and space 'a mere term for the power implied in the act' (OM i, fo. 80). Coleridge insisted that space must first have been 'actualized', and then must 'react as co-agent with Time at once its spouse and its antagonist' (ibid.).[60] His description of the Spirit and the Word as the Agents of time and space, energy and form, extension and motion, may be seen as expressing the relationship of the metaphysical and the physical through Christian symbolism; but it must be borne in mind that for him symbols are a part of the reality which they express. He maintained that mystery remains at the heart of the origins of life; his language attempts to bridge the gulf between this mystery and empirically based developments in the physical sciences.

The interaction of Spirit and Word must '*account* for the *position* of the phenomena' (*CN* iii, § 4483). Coleridge believed that all the powers and forces within the physical universe were derived from a series of polarities which began with this polarity of time and space, of 'unity' (Spirit) and 'distinctity (Word). He set out the equation that 'Time × Space = Motion. Attraction ×

---

[59] See e.g. OM i, fos. 78–82.

[60] Coleridge greatly admired Bishop Berkeley; the latter's suggestion that time and space are not absolute (as Newton held) but ideal and therefore relative realities may have influenced Coleridge's own view. See Bishop George Berkeley, *Philosophical Commentaries*, transcribed by A. A. Luce (London, 1944), notebook B: 'Time a sensation, therefore onely in ye mind' (fo. 104, § 13); 'Extension a sensation, therefore not without the mind' (fo. 105, § 18).

Repulsion = Gravity as Depth.—These are ideal relations. The ideal = real, or rather the Ideal = Real, World rises out of chaos (= Indistinction) or begins, with the creation of Light' (*CL* iv. 771). Matter itself, for example, is the '*tertium aliquid*' of the forces of attraction and repulsion, which themselves are created by the polarity of 'centripetal and centrifugal' belonging to the powers of gravity and light.

According to this system, the polarity principle produces ever greater degrees of individuality in the evolutionary process (*CL* iv. 574). The evolution of nature consists in a series of polarities which constantly produce a *tertium aliquid* and so lead to the realization of yet higher forms. Coleridge's *Theory of Life* and his 'Opus Maximum' notes set out in great and complex detail (in which metaphysics and symbolism mingle with scientific theory) the interaction of Spirit and Word as seen in the processes of nature. His belief in the ultimate correspondence of facts with the necessary ideas of Reason,[61] allowed him to express elements of physical science in terms of Christian theology, a mixture which appears somewhat fantastic today. Indeed, he was convinced that only in these terms could a full and adequate account of the relationships within the physical world be given; for him this meant one which went beyond mere appearances, and was consistent with reason, experience, and faith.

From the polarization of spiritual Light into the opposition of Light and 'Mosaic Darkness', the forces, elements, and forms of the physical world, according to Coleridge, evolved. His later notes show a determination to reconcile the language of Genesis with the language of science, through his theory of symbol. In the 'Opus Maximum', for example, four stages of creation are outlined. The first stage was 'mere potentiality' or 'chaos'. The second, 'the same actualized' as Aether: 'Darkness as the positive ✗ and possible basis of Light: Materia prima: Indistinction in actu'. This he links to Genesis 1: 2, 'the face of the waters' (OM i, fos. 64–5). The third stage was 'Verbum lucificum: Lux = > ∴ the Multeity actualized but in union with the already actualized indistinction i.e. Continuity. . . . Offspring, Matter of Light'. Coleridge's notes are often too abbreviated here to be

---

[61] For Coleridge's attempted reconciliation of fact and idea, see e.g. *CN* iv, §5299: 'Religion is: Ideas contemplated as Facts.' See also *CM* ii. 482.

clear, but he suggests that the Word created a polarity of *continuity* (already 'actualized' indistinction; that is, unity) with 'actualized' *multëity*, or distinction; this produced 'Matter of Light'. 'Darkness' (the 'agglomerative' power, or gravitation) and 'light' (the power of distinction, outwardness, and manifestation) interacted and the whole process of polar relations and dynamic production was under way.

Increasingly, as he developed a system which might avoid the dangers of an irreconcilable dualism on the one hand, and of pantheism on the other, Coleridge extended his concept of Spirit–Word interaction as the basis of evolution through polarity. He stressed that, in every polarity of powers, each pole contains something of the other and that both have their source in a higher unity in which, nevertheless, the distinctions remain as fundamental. This concept of the unity-of-distinctions led him to conclude that attraction-and-repulsion, contraction-and-dilation, are each two forces of *one* power.[62] The Spirit–Word polarity is reflected in all the powers, forces, and products of the natural world. In all the processes of life, either unity (containing distinction) may predominate, or distinction (within unity), but once 'Chaos' is breached and contradiction transformed into polarity, all is within the sphere of influence of the creative Word.

Coleridge declared that the unity which the Spirit 'actuates' could not be one of indistinction (unity and indistinction being incompatible terms); rather, 'in the succeeding & alternate moment the Multeity must be actuated by the Logos so as to be Multeity with distinction or Multeity realized into the semblance of distinction' (OM i, fo. 53). So distinction-in-unity is the fundamental characteristic of all creation. The full realization of distinction (as individuality) and of unity (as community of love) is possible only in humanity. But from the very first stages of the creation, the Spirit 'potenzializes' and the Word 'actualizes' this potentiality. This, Coleridge declared, was the origination of motion in space (OM i, fo. 50) and from this developed both position and locality, produced from 'the two-fold act of the Logos in the Spirit following that of the Spirit as Going forth and

---

[62] This concept of the two forces of one power is echoed in his theology. In another context, he suggests that, in the Old Testament, 'under the Law . . . the Word (the Logos, the Son of God) was included in the Spirit' and that 'since the Incarnation, vice versa—the Wisdom in the Living Word' (N 37, fo. 44ᵛ).

preparing for the Logos' (OM i, fo. 53). As for the 'cohesion' necessary to the formation of body, or matter, this resulted from the 'outness' produced from two 'entelechies' which could not fill the same space, themselves the commencement of the tendency to individuation and the tendency to attachment.[63] This twofold activity within matter denied the axioms of mechanistic philosophy. Elsewhere, we have seen, Coleridge described this activity as 'The Law, or Constructive Powers, excited in Matter by the influence of God's Spirit and Logos' (*CM* iii. 944).[64]

Significantly, Coleridge admitted no possibility of the triumph of the apostatic will in this great drama of creation: resistance to the influence of the Spirit only assisted the influence of the Word and vice versa. He described

the ineffable distinction in the transcendent unity of the Spirit and the Word, and the correspondent Distinctness-in-unity of their influence, the first offerings of which[,] as we have seen[,] are the actualizations of the Indistinction and Multeity, which[,] so actualized[,] and in all the after degrees of their potenziation[,] are the real *poles* in the omni creato. Hence it is evident, that there is no possibility of resisting either influence but by assisting the other[.] it [the Creaturely Will] cannot resist the Word but by subjecting the principle of Multeity to that of Indistinction and thereby allying itself . . . with the influence of the spirit or the divine principle of communion and so vice versâ.[65] (OM i, fo. 67)

Coleridge saw a constant struggle within the finite world of thought and being between, on the one hand, the tendency to indistinction and chaos, and, on the other, the tendency towards a reality and actuality of distinction (individuality) in unity (community). He described the tension between indifference and difference as the truth from which all things spring. It is a struggle which is transformed and turned against itself by the activity of Word and Spirit, so that, whichever tendency predominates in the conflict, it must always be assisting the divine process. Like the *Naturphilosophen* (especially Oken and Steffens), and like

---

[63] For more on the action of the Spirit and the Word as manifested in the principles of 'individuation' and 'attachment' see e.g. *CN* iii, § 4483: 'The divine Influence is absolutely necessary to *account* for the *position* of the phænomena—and for this the presence of the Agents, as the Spirit, and as the Logos (εναρθωσις θεια) [divine articulation]'; see ibid., § 4418, fo. 14.

[64] See also Ch. 2.1 nn. 8 and 12.

[65] See also Coleridge's MSS, BL Add. MS 34225, fo. 153.

Schiller and Goethe, he sometimes used the figure of the spiral to signify the processes of the natural world—those 'of circular return [?fused] with the idea of linear progress'.[66] These processes involve polarities and relationships which cannot be understood in terms of a mere linear progression; many of Coleridge's diagrams and examples are connected with or drawn from the interaction of the line and the sphere. We have seen that the circle represents the Word in the Spirit of love, unity, community, the 'globose'; and the line represents direction, time, motion, and figure, Spirit manifested in the Form of the Word.[67] In the pure forms of mathematics, he found the principle of form and 'distinctivity' (Logos) best represented by the point and the line; that of unity and community (Spirit) by that of the circle and the sphere. Their interaction can be represented by the spiral as the expression of the evolution of life through dynamic polarities.

The Logos-Polarity of Light

I have suggested that the symbol of Light as representative of the Logos was a constant theme in Coleridge's writings. Christ is described by him, for example, as the Light above Being: θειοτατον το προσωπον του φωτος υπερουσιον ('most divine countenance of the Light above Being') (*CN* iii, § 4489). The Logos is the en*light*enment of reason, and the light of life (power, agency, and energy); Light is the source and the instrument of the creation. All realization (he writes in 1819) is 'separation without destruction of unity'; the Logos creates through the introduction of the process and principle of polarity, beginning with the polarization of Light:[68] the 'very act, the true superinducent of Distinction and

---

[66] See Beer, *Coleridge's Poetic Intelligence*, 6–7, 9, 56–7; and Heather Jackson, ' "Turning and Turning": Coleridge on Our Knowledge of the External World', *PMLA* 101 (1986), 850.

[67] Coleridge's exposition of the processes of creation as a divine *perichoresis* (the Will of the Father manifested in the interacting Spirit and Word) was not original. In Eriugena, for example, the idea of the spiral within the creation is also to be found and here it is specifically linked with spirit. In *De Divisione Naturae*, as Heather Jackson has shown ('Turning and Turning', 852), Eriugena quotes Ecclesiastes 1: 6, 'gyrans, gyrando vadit Spiritus' ('turning and turning the wind rushes on') (*De Divisione Naturae*, 127). Coleridge's originality lies in his detailed working-out of the idea in a scheme which combines the scientific theories of his own time with concepts of classical theology.

[68] See above, n. 36.

therein of Actuality et vice versa' (OM i, fo. 49). Coleridge insisted that to speak of the Light *of* Nature was a mistake: 'There is, there can be no Light *of* Nature. There may be a Light *in* or *upon* it; but this is the Light, that shineth down into the Darkness—i.e. in Nature; and the Darkness comprehendeth it not' (*CM* ii. 298). His view had changed since the early years, and he could no longer agree with Duncan Forbes's claim in 'Thoughts concerning Religion, Natural and Revealed',[69] that (in Coleridge's summary) 'by the Light of Nature, as contra-distinguished from all Revelation, Man could have learnt any of the moral attributes of God' (*CM* ii. 787).

Coleridge admired Jacob Böhme's recognition that 'not Heat but Light is the Heart of Nature' (*CM* i. 623), but emphasized that this Light was the product of the redemptive act—it was not self-created or self-evolved. In his symbolic representation (the symbol's reconciliation of Idea and fact is significant here), the Logos entered the darkness of Chaos, of 'Hades', transforming it into a Darkness containing a hidden Light. This Darkness became the ground of Nature, an opposition to God, but one which (as all true opposition), contained a common Principle, in this case the Light of the Logos.

The 'Mosaic Darkness' is

the container and withholder . . . out of which light, that is, the *lux lucifica*,* as distinguished from *lumen seu lux phaenomenalis*,[†] was produced;—say, rather, that which, producing itself into light as the one pole or antagonist power, remained in the other pole as darkness, that is gravity, or the principle of mass, or wholeness without distinction of parts.[70] (*LR* ii. 339)

[*'light-making light'
[†]'radiance of phenomenal light' or 'light as it appears in nature']

---

[69] Duncan Forbes (1685–1747), 'Thoughts concerning Religion', in *Works* (Edinburgh, 1755), i. 1–2.
[70] Here and elsewhere (see *CM* i. 624; *SM: LS* 95) Coleridge echoed ancient distinctions concerning the nature and function of light which can be found in the work of Plato, of the Neoplatonists, and in the phases of creation as described in Genesis, that is, the progression from God as the source, to the manifested creative energy of light, or 'light-making light', to the phenomenal light of the sun. Augustine himself employed similar distinctions (see e.g. *De Genesi ad Litteram*, i. 3. 7). Coleridge was familiar with this work (e.g. BL MS Egerton 2801, fo. 141). That he may have been directly influenced by Augustine here is suggested by the proximity to this of another notebook entry (BL MS Egerton

Here, thought Coleridge, was the Light shining in the darkness which the Fourth Gospel describes. At the beginning of the Creation, light, he maintained, existed in a diffused state; that is, life and light were one and the same 'NEITHER existing *formally*, yet BOTH *eminenter*' (*C & S* 175). From the third day of creation, light 'was polarized into outward and inward': the 'inward' remained in the darkness as gravity, mass, wholeness; the 'outward' became the phenomenal light of the sun. This was the basis of his claim that Light must be seen as a bipolar Power and not merely a polar force (*CM* i. 624). The dynamic forces of creation had come into being out of the polarity of light and gravity. Light, he wrote, is 'centrifugal', the outward, manifesting, power which is 'extroitive', 'peripheric', and 'distinctive'. Gravity is the 'centripetal' power, the 'agglomerative' and 'amassive', 'tending towards the centre'. It is 'introactive', the power of 'hiding'.

Coleridge made a distinction between the 'light' energy which is always to some degree present within the life of Nature as a whole, even in inanimate forms, and that which is manifested in animate creatures. He suggested that, in the former, light, as potenzializing power, is absorbed and then manifested in the *multëity* and in 'the increase of specific gravity in the aggregate'. The gravitational pole is established in an intensity of amassive power. In contrast, '*in Life* Light must be the Entelechie, the central Point, that takes up, & is not taken up—The Word is *Light*—in it is *Life*—and this Life is the Light of man. . . . The divine Cycle cannot be more adequately expressed, from Light to Light thro' Life' (*CN* iv, § 4677). The Light which has created life brings 'light' (mind, intellect) out of that life; in man, the microcosm, this synthesis of life and light is restored to unity with its spiritual source. The Light of the Logos, finally, is that through which the enlightening and 'ensouling' of man takes place, and through which true self-consciousness develops (*AR* 244 n.).[71] For Coleridge, the one source from which both the objective light of life within the creation and the subjective light of Reason

---

2801, fos. 143^v–144), where Coleridge writes of his intention to 'copy Moses and call the Distinctive Power *Light*, and the agglomerative or *amassive* Power, *Darkness*—n.b. the *power* of Darkness, that is *Opacity*, or what causes *opaqueness*; *not* Darkness considered as the mere absence of Light'. See also ODI, fo. 31.

[71] See below, Chs. 3.3 and 4.3.

proceed guarantees, on the one hand, the intelligibility of nature, and, on the other, the objectivity of the forms and processes of mind.

We have seen that he was deeply inspired by Jacob Böhme's symbolic studies of Light. There is a strong resemblance between passages from Böhme's 'The Three Principles of the Divine Essence' and the mystical language of 'Kubla Khan'. Coleridge's marginalia provide evidence of his attention to the following extract from the 'Three Principles':

> Thus now henceforth the Fire-flash is the Father of the Light, and the Light shines in him, and is now the only Cause of the moving Birth, and of the Birth of the Love. That which in the Beginning was the aking Source, is now SUL, or the Oil of the lovely pleasant Fountain, which presses through all the Fountains, so that from hence the Light is kindled.[72] (*CM* i. 637)

The similarity between the language of Coleridge's poem and the above passage is striking, particularly in the light of his letter to Ludwig Tieck (July 1817). Here he stated that there were certain ideas concerning light and sound which 'before my visit to Germany in September, 1798, I had adopted (probably from Behmen's 'Aurora', which I had *conjured over* at School)' (*CL* iv. 751).[73] The 'mighty fountain', the 'flashing eyes', the play of light and mystery in 'Kubla Khan' appeared to Coleridge, if his report is to be believed, in a dream. A notebook entry of 1810 asserts that 'J. Boehmen's mind may be well illustrated from Dreams—there is meaning, important meaning, in both; both the exponents are almost accidental' (*CN* iii, § 3692). In the margin note mentioned above Coleridge developed Böhme's theme: 'Light issued forth out of the Depth, and the Depth becometh Gravity: and the Gravity submitteth, openeth, *utt*(out)*ereth* itself to receive the Light, and so giveth it a resting place of fixity, and the Gravity under the dominion of the Light becometh Color: and the Light in love entereth into and yielding itself to the Gravity becometh Sound' (*CM* i. 637).

During the years 1817–18, Coleridge often returned to the

---

[72] J. Böhme, 'The Three Principles of the Divine Essence', in *Works*, i. ii. 18. 12.

[73] Coleridge's spelling of the German mystic's name varies considerably; e.g. from Behmen to Boehme.

theme of the relationship of light, colour, and sound.[74] He had assimilated the polarity theories of the German *Naturphilosophen* such as Oken and Steffens; and, in annotations of Oken's work, described the latter's theory as 'the ancient doctrine of Light and Shadow on the grand principle of Polarity'.[75] He was familiar, too, with the rival theories of light and colour in his own time, with the corpuscular theory of Newton, and with Goethe's *Farbenlehre*.[76] His development of the idea of a correspondence between light and sound makes clearer that other correspondence which he intended to show between Light and Word, the revelation of the divine Logos. Both demonstrate the quality of distinction without separation; both relations are fundamental to all revelation, communication, and declaration,[77] and thus to intelligibility itself. Here again can be seen the influence of the Logos, the Word which is 'spoken out' in the Creation and yet remains from eternity with God.

2.3. LIGHT, LIFE, AND LOVE

We have seen that Coleridge made much use of the theories of the *Naturphilosophen*, though he was not uncritical of their

---

[74] Coleridge often explores the analogy of the Word as representing both the communication of sound (e.g. in speech) and that of vision (e.g. in art, architecture, and the forms of nature). Here again the Logos is the 'communicating and communicative intellect' (see e.g. NQ, fo. 15^v; *CN* iii, § 4397).

[75] Annotations on L. Oken, *Erste Ideen zur Theorie des Lichts etc.* (Jena, 1808), 40 in *CM* iii. 1018.

[76] Coleridge was familiar with the rival theories of light and colour in his own time, with the corpuscular theory of Newton, and with Goethe's *Farbenlehre* (Tübingen, 1810), as evidenced by the above quotation from his notes on Böhme. (see also letter to L. Tieck, July 1817: *CL* iv. 750). There are passages in Goethe's work with which Coleridge's own forms of expression and his understanding of a polarity of colour have much in common, for example, the following extract taken from *Farbenlehre*: 'When the distinction of yellow and blue is duly comprehended, and especially the augmentation into red, by means of which the opposite qualities tend towards each other and become united in a third; then, certainly, an especially mysterious interpretation will suggest itself . . . when we find the two separate principles producing green on the one hand and red in their intenser state, we can hardly refrain from thinking in the first case on the earthly, in the last on the heavenly generation of the Elohim' (tr. C. L. Eastlake as *Theory of Colours* (London, 1840), 'Allegorical, Symbolical, Mystical Application of Colour', 350, § 919).

[77] BL MS Egerton 2801, fos. 143–4.

work and was well enough versed in empirical method to know when metaphysical speculation was in conflict with scientific respectability (as his critical margin notes show). He, like Kant, repudiates all metaphysical claims which overstep the bounds of reason. What may, for example, in his notes on Böhme, be seen as the heights of mystical speculation, is, in fact, often less fantastical when seen in the light of his incorporation of the symbolic imagination into the very structures of reason itself. There is no doubt that his concept of nature as a symbolic language encouraged him to find parallels and connections between the evolutionary processes of thought and language and the life processes of the physical world. Sometimes these connections are extravagantly drawn. What is at times difficult to discern is how far his use of mystical or religious language to describe the powers and processes of nature is intended as symbolic or analogous (this he could defend), and how far it leaps beyond symbolism and analogy into the area of unbounded fantasy.

Coleridge rejected those idealist theories of nature in which phenomena were deprived of reality or in which the Idea of nature was itself seen as absolute. His whole 'system', on the other hand, was directed towards the overthrowing of the 'corpuscular' or 'mechanical' philosophy, which identified life with the organization of phenomena. Kant's unresolved dualism, the separation of noumena and phenomena, was no more acceptable. Coleridge complained that Kant, having begun with what he admitted to be merely appearances, proceeded, quite unjustifiably, to treat as *real* everything that followed from those appearances. If nature was intelligible in any sense, it must have been intelligibly generated; and if nature and mind shared a common source, they must be essentially homogeneous. If, on the other hand, nature began with phenomena, and was merely the manifestation of appearances rather than the product of an underlying reality of idea and law corresponding to and discoverable by reason, we would be left, Coleridge admitted, with an irreconcilable dichotomy (*CN* iii, § 4449). He himself was convinced that the origins of the physical must be *meta*physical and intelligible. In the 'logosophic' system, we have seen, the life of nature is part of the great redemptive scheme. As the creation of divine Will it reveals an inner directional and purposive principle (Logos). Divine Will and 'alterity' (the source and condition of plurality) are interdependent.[78] The dynamic agency within all life is, in consequence, grounded in the relationship of 'this-ness' and 'otherness', which, Coleridge argued, is attributable only to an act of intelligent Will. Life (both as the manifestation of plurality in nature's products, *natura naturata*, and as the powers and energies of nature, *natura naturans*) has its source in will and relationship. Its reality cannot, therefore, be defined in causal and quantitative terms:

> Our reason convinces us that the quantities of things, taken abstractedly as quantity, exist only in the relations they bear to the percipient; in plainer words, they exist only in our minds, *ut quorum esse est percipi*. For if the definite quantities have a ground and therefore a reality, in the eternal world, and independent of the mind that perceives them, this ground is *ipso facto* a quality. (*TL* 38–9)

[*'as things of which to be is to be perceived']

The naturalist, Coleridge admitted, has at first to assume both nature and time as given, 'jam demonstrata' ('already proved'). Yet these are not phenomena or quantities, but represent qualities and relationships. The naturalist must begin

> with Nature as the potential Will with the minimum of Actuality, and this too derivative, and climbs upward conscious that at every grade of ascent he [the naturalist] is meeting the descending Power, the Principle of all Actuality, and in a less and less obscure form, the higher he ascends in the History of Nature which consists of three main Sections I. from the Birth of Light and Gravity to detached Organisation = Physica/. From det. Org. with the indifference of inward and outward Light = vegetable Life, to the polar bi-partition of Light into Light ✳ Life, the Genesis of the Centro-peripherical system, and the commencement of animal Life. Physiozoical. 3. From the Protozoa to the Creation of Man. In this the first Act in the great Drama of Redemption is completed. (N 37, fos. 43ᵛ–44)

Coleridge's later notes and letters constantly emphasize relationship as the ground of idea and law, of phenomenal and noumenal reality:

---

[78] Coleridge criticized Spinoza for failing to recognize this point (BL MS Egerton 2801, fo. 13–13ᵛ).

The Alphabet of Physics no less than of Metaphysics, of Physiology no less than of Psychology is an alphabet of *Relations*, in which N is N only because M is M and O, O. The *reality* of all alike is . . . the *Identity* of [Alpha and Omega], which can become an object of *Consciousness* or *Thought*, even as all the powers of the material world can become objects of *Perception*, only as two Poles or Counterpoints of the same Line. (*CL* iv. 688–9)

In Philo, whom Coleridge frequently cited in support of his own Logos doctrine, the notion of Logos both as separator[79] and as bond and mediator of opposites in the work of creation[80] is seminal. Coleridge became increasingly hostile to idealist theories of a polarity which is somehow self-inducing and self-reconciling. He rejected the concept of nature as the origin of its own evolutionary self-perfection, and denied that the world was the manifestation of divine self-realization: only a positive and essential unity could be that. He rejected Oken's concept of the 'One and All' which was to become a common feature in German idealist philosophies of nature (N 26, fo. 27),[81] insisting that the Logos 'awakens the Duplicity in the identity' (*CN* iv, § 4843). The life and forms of nature are drawn from the ground of non-being, of 'contradiction', by the Logos who transforms this barren chaos into fruitful polarity: 'it is evident that every approach toward actualization must depend on . . . transmuting the contradiction a⚹b into an Opposition a⚹b and that even this is impossible but by a superinduction ab extra (i.e. in this case a supra) of an actualizing Energy the Ground of which is absolutely *good*' (N 43, fo. 8^{r-v}).

We have seen that in his 'History of Nature', and his *Theory of Life*, Coleridge constantly blends doctrines of Patristic and classical theology, of Christian mysticism and Greek philosophy, with the terminology of *Naturphilosophie*. In theological terms, he, like Origen,[82] describes nature as drawn towards an ever higher goal, to a restored unity and perfection; but it is drawn

---

[79] Philos, *Quis Rerum Divinarum Heres Sit*, 130.

[80] Philo, *De Plantatione*, 8–9 and 10. Coleridge would have found this aspect of Philo's work discussed by Whitaker (*The Origins of Arianism Disclosed*, 74, 90).

[81] H. S. Harris explores the theory of ἐν καὶ πᾶν developed by Hegel, Hölderlin, and others out of Spinoza's philosophy (*Hegel's Development: Toward the Sunlight, 1770–1810* (Oxford, 1972), 97 ff.).

[82] See App. B, below.

from a bare identity of non-being in which neither distinction nor unity is found. It was legitimate, Coleridge allowed, to refer to the 'Idea' of nature, but only when speaking of nature as redeemed and perfected in humanity (*CN* iv, §4648, fo. 14). Nature is 'the Servant and Delegate of the informing Word' (N 26, fo. 30ᵛ). The relationships of the forces and products of the natural world, like those of mind, have their source in the Will–Reason–Love relationships of divine *perichoresis*. Coleridge's later writings repeatedly emphasized this unity of Life and Love:

to have seen that Life = Love must be presumed as one of the eternal, in nihil aliud resolubilium Distinctitatum in Unitate Divina,* was an opening out of the Circle of Contemplations for which I have daily occasion to lift up my heart in awe & thankfulness to the Father of Lights. (N 47, fo. 13)

[* 'resoluble into nothing else, in the Divine Unity']

He regarded the greatest obstacle to the right understanding of Scripture as 'the want of insight into the nature of Life, what it is and what it is not'. The Idea of life must be distinguished from the 'Life of Nature', even though the latter is dependent upon the former. Life in the Idea is revealed, he wrote, in 'the distinctive essence and character of the Holy Spirit. Here Life is *Love*— communicative, outpouring love. *Ergo*, the terrestrial or the Life of Nature ever the shadow and opposite of the Divine is appropriative, absorbing *appetence*' (*AP* 305–6).

Coleridge's Models and Methods

It may, with some justification, be argued that the vast scope of Coleridge's metaphysical speculations precludes serious consideration of his theories as contributions to scientific theory. To the extent that his hypotheses are largely not only unverifiable but also unfalsifiable, this is undeniable. His dynamic philosophy of nature, is, as has been shown, based on the primacy of interacting relationships the source of which is a primary *Idem et Alter*, only comprehensible as the product of Will. He began with an ontology drawn from a perceived reconcilability of philosophy and theology, and grounded his theory of nature in a metaphysic. He boldly claimed that the fact that all knowledge began with what must first be assumed, and with an act of faith in its favour, made reasonable such assumptions as those from which his investigations started, such as that phenomena may not be explained by phenomena, or that will is an undeniable fact of experience, inexplicable because explanation depends upon causal relationship. All science, he maintained, anticipating hermeneutical theories of the twentieth century, begins from an a priori position, from some assumed basis of truth, a 'leap of faith'. Whether it is only the rudiments of language or of basic arithmetic, even the earliest steps towards knowledge are 'received' before they are later critically examined. The assumed basis of truth is an act of faith, conscious or unconscious, an act of will as much in the scientist as in the religious believer (OM iii, fo. 1). This claim exemplifies Coleridge's anticipation of issues (such as that concerning the stalemate of objectivism versus relativism) the importance of which was not generally recognized in scientific circles until a much later date.

Confidence in the absolute and infallible objectivity of correctly established scientific knowledge has been shaken in the twentieth century. Quantum theory has confirmed the importance of the creative role of the observer, and shown that law-based systems relying on quantifiable data (the foundations of the seventeenth-century scientific revolution) are necessarily and inextricably bound up with the vagaries of human subjectivity. Coleridge recognized that if human reason in its highest form can be shown to correspond to, and be interdependent in some way with, being itself, with the forms of reality of the external world, then this inevitability of subjectivity may be welcomed and accepted. The Cartesian dichotomy of the separation of subject and object is then overcome and, with it, what has become known as the objectivist–relativist conflict. For Coleridge, the Logos principle overcomes the dichotomy between subjective faith and objective truth, reconciling fact and idea, external reality with mind.[83] The symbols of Word, Light, Life, Reason, communicate a wealth of meaning and association, and offer an 'alchemical' transformation of perception and relation, revealing the Logos as the principle of unity.

In the twentieth century scientists have explored beyond the phenomena to the relationships and interactions of, for example,

---

[83] See below, Ch. 3.2.

relativity theory, quantum mechanics, and 'chaos' theory. Some of these developments have much more in common with Coleridge's emphasis on the dynamic relationships which underlie both the physical world and the world of mind than with the Newtonian model. It is interesting today to note the optimism of some non-mechanistic, evolutionary concepts in physics and cosmology. For example, Paul Davies[84] has suggested a Teilhardian movement towards unity and complexity through what seem to be patterns of co-operation and relationships of interdependence throughout the physical universe, at both microcosmic and macrocosmic levels. The physicist Stephen Hawking has described the continuing search for a unified theory among scientists, and how this appears to be centring around a quantum theory of gravity in which the understanding of interactions of light and gravity (in connection, for example, with 'black holes') plays an important part.[85] We have already seen the importance which Coleridge attached to the primary powers of gravity and light. Stephen Hawking's descriptions of the explosive polarity of particles and anti-particles is, no doubt, very remote from Coleridge's concept of polarity; again, however, the importance of the polarity principle seems to have been confirmed as fundamental to physical reality. We have also seen Coleridge's concept of an interplay, a dynamic, generative polarity, of time and space. Each pole interacts with and modifies the other in such intimate connection (he uses the imagery of the relationship of lovers, of parents, of husband and wife, and, paradoxically, of antagonists) that the fourth dimension of Einstein's space-time, which was to become the future basis of astrophysics, is easily, with the aid of hindsight, brought to mind.

Coleridge's blend of theological language with the concepts of physical science appears extravagant and odd today, yet perhaps less so than when the mechanistic Newtonian view was dominant in his own time. In the late twentieth century, for example, atoms and molecules are viewed by many scientists in an almost Coleridgean light, as *models* and representations of reality useful in terms of the relationships which they express, and not in any mechanistic sense. Rather than the mechanistic model of

---

[84] Paul Davies, *The Cosmic Blueprint* (London, 1987), 110, 190.
[85] Stephen Hawking, *A Brief History of Time* (London, 1988), 155–6.

atomism, Coleridge chose organic models of powers, forces, and relationships which he represented in the ancient Christian symbolism of Chaos, Light and Darkness, Spirit and Word. Since all reality, he believed, is ultimately a unity of will (productive act) and reason (form and law), it can be expressed only through the language of a reformed metaphysics in which symbols—those of religion, of mathematics (his theories are often expressed in geometrical figures and numerical relationships), and of the poetic imagination—have a new importance: 'True natural philosophy is comprized in the study of the science and language of *symbols*' (*LS: SM* 79).

It is only with extreme caution that parallels may be drawn between thinkers so widely separated by history, culture, and scientific knowledge and practice. Yet Coleridge would have had few qualms about such comparisons. He himself drew together strands of thought from the earliest articulations of theology and philosophy, tracing what he believed to be their movement (at times their distortion, at others their evolution and progress) through the history of thought to his own time. He was, at the same time, willing to 'prophesy' concerning the future processes and products of human reason in, for example, the physical sciences. Owen Barfield's suggestion[86] that Coleridge's friendship with Humphry Davy may have contributed to the development of field theory does not seem improbable (Faraday was to remain in close contact with Davy throughout his formative years as a scientist). It must be admitted, however, that Davy knew something of the developments in German *Naturphilosophie* and may have been more directly influenced by the emphasis on polarity. Davy lost favour with Coleridge in the latter's later years; he himself probably found Coleridge's metaphysics irritating and his motivation suspect.

Coleridge devoted much time and energy to the development of his philosophy of nature in the last twenty years of his life. He attended lectures at medical schools, immersed himself in the learned journals, corresponded and conversed at length with those engaged in scientific controversies and debates. The surgeon J. H. Green supported and encouraged him on an almost daily basis. Behind all this activity the 'logosophic' motif is a constant

---

[86] Barfield, *What Coleridge Thought*, 138.

presence. Coleridge believed the study of nature should be rigorously pursued because, while theology and philosophy could show the Logos as the revelation of divine humanity and the unifying principle of Reason and Will, the natural sciences, in a unified system, would reveal the Light and Life of the Logos to be no less that of the natural world. The Creation was the 'first Act of Redemption', and study of the physical sciences would reveal to humanity its own relation both to nature and to God.

3

Logos: Divine Reason

Reason, which is, as it were, the light and lamp of life.

(Cicero)

3.1. REASON AND UNDERSTANDING

The Fourth Gospel declares that the life of which the Λόγος is the source is also the 'light of men'. Coleridge himself took up this identification of light and Λόγος;[1] for him, the 'light of men' was Reason, the 'communicative Intelligence'. His development of this theme owes much to Philo;[2] it also has much in common with traditions of Stoic, Platonic, and Gnostic philosophy,[3] but with important differences. The most significant of these was Coleridge's belief that Reason (identified by the early Fathers of the Church with the second Person of the Christian Trinity, God the Son) is, at least in some senses, subordinate to the divine Will (God the Father).[4] His philosophy, despite its emphasis on

---

[1] To maintain some consistency in my use of the terms throughout this section I have not transliterated Λόγος or Νοῦς, whatever the context or sense in which they are used.

[2] Whitaker quotes Philo's description of the divine Logos as 'the *most ancient* of the universe of intellectuals, the nearest (there being no boundary of distinction between them) to the only one who is fixed without falsehood' (*The Origins of Arianism Disclosed*, 89; *Philonis Judaei omnia quae extant opera* (Paris, 1640), 465. Whitaker also states that 'Philo . . . esteems a *Word* to be the external image of *Reason*, and considers *Reason* as the internal *Word* of the *Mind*' (*The Origins of Arianism Disclosed*, 51).

[3] It must be said that, despite similarities on the point of divine Reason, Coleridge had little sympathy with the Gnostic tradition on the whole; it failed, in his opinion, to recognize the significance of history in the Christian religion (*CM* ii. 482). In Coleridge's opinion, the 'common and characteristic error' of the Gnostics was 'the divulsion of Christianity from all *previous* history, and then from *all* history, so as to leave it a pure speculative Edifice.'

[4] The Logos is, in Coleridge's view, both subordinate *and* equal (see N 49, fos. 3ᵛ–4; *CL* iv. 686; see also below, Ch. 4.2).

Reason, cannot, owing to the primacy which he attributes to Will, be adequately categorized as idealist or rationalist.

The Crucial Philosophical Distinction

Coleridge's distinction between Understanding and Reason is at the heart of his 'logosophic' system. It represents the distinction between, on the one hand, human intellect as the product of evolution, the agency of which is the immanence of the Λόγος within the powers and life processes of the creation; and, on the other, the enlightening and 'ensouling' power of Reason, super-induced in self-conscious mind, revealing the truth of ideas. Through this revelation, Coleridge argued, individuals become persons. The Reason/Understanding distinction was, on this account, of great importance to philosophy and to its relationship with religion. Both Reason and Understanding have a twofold sense; 'theoretic or intellective, and moral or practical'. The theoretic Understanding he defined as 'The power of generalizing the motives of the Sense, and of judging of the objective *reality* of all Appearances by their reducibility to a genus or class. Hence it is the faculty of *mediate* Truths, or knowledges obtained *discursively*. Hence in our elder writers *Discourse* means the *Understanding*' (*SM: LS* 60 n.). The practical Understanding, Coleridge continued, 'is substantially the same faculty as the intelligent *Instinct* in the Dog, Beaver, Elephant, Ant, &c and becomes Human *Understanding* by its co-existence in one and the same Subject with the Reason and the Free Will. Hence Shakespear calls the U. "Discourse of Reason".' Reason, in contrast, is in its theoretical form 'the contemplation of *immediate* truths—or the *immediate* recognition of the Necessary and the Universal in negative and positive positions'; and in its practical sense 'the power of determining the Will by Ideas, as *Ultimate* Ends'. Coleridge, however, defined Reason 'in the highest sense of the term' as 'the focal point of the Theoric and Practical . . . as both in One, [it] is the Source of Ideas'. He represented divine Reason by both Λόγος and Νοῦς, according to emphasis and context; but he also used the terms to distinguish human Understanding from Reason.

The distinction between a higher and lower mental faculty and a higher and lower form of knowledge can be traced, in various forms, through the whole history of philosophical and theological discourse;[5] Coleridge himself claimed that there was 'the frequent occurrence of this distinction in the Jewish and Christian Scriptures . . . the importance attached to it must have struck the most superficial reader' (OM ii, fo. 184). In the eighteenth century Wolff had described *Verstand*, the Understanding, as 'the faculty of distinctly representing the possible', as 'the faculty of seeing into the connection of truths'.[6] This aspect of Reason as the power of inference and connection, central to the thought of Kant and Jacobi, is perhaps the most significant characteristic of Coleridge's version of the distinction. Kant's idea of Reason involves a transcendental element, that unconditioned unity which makes possible the unity of experience and understanding.[7] Coleridge echoed this definition. He distinguished between

the Systematic Unity, which the Understanding made intelligential by the *Light* of Reason ⟨strives after⟩ and the Identity in all Alterity or absolute Unity, peculiar to Reason in its own Sphere, to Reason as opposed to Understanding and distinct from even the Light of Reason in the Understanding. Perhaps, *Union* or Totality would be more appropriate to the Systematizing Tendency of the Understanding; while Unity might be reserved for the higher Gift, Reason as the Source and Seat of Ideas or Spiritual Verities. (*CN* iv, § 5373)

Jacobi's influence on Coleridge's concept of the distinction between Reason and Understanding was at least as great as that

---

[5] R. Wellek lists those who employed the Reason/Understanding distinction (*Immanuel Kant in England 1793–1838* (Princeton, NJ, 1931)). Wellek points out that Coleridge is indebted not only to Kant for his use of this distinction: 'Harrington, Hooker, Bacon, Hobbes, Jacobi and Hemsterhuis are mentioned in one essay of the *Friend* as drawing analogous distinctions' (p. 103). He shows that Coleridge also ascribed it to Jeremy Taylor and Archbishop Leighton, and to John Smith (the Cambridge Platonist), and that, in any case, it is a development of an older distinction expressed in different forms by Plato, Aristotle, and Aquinas. For Augustine's use of *sapientia* and *scientia* see *De Trinitate*, xii. 14. 22, and xii. 7. 12. Aquinas makes a similar distinction in *Summa Theologica*, i. 79. 9c. Eriugena's *contemplativus animus* and *theoreticus animus* pertain to *sapientia* and *scientia* respectively; see *De Divisione Naturae*, 98. Wallace, in notes to his edition of Hegel's *Logic*, gives an analysis of the history of the Reason/Understanding distinction, especially in the work of Wolff, Kant, and Goethe; see e.g. Hegel's *Logic*, pt. 1 of *Encyclopedia of the Philosophical Sciences* (1830), tr. W. Wallace (Oxford, 1975), 310–11.

[6] C. von Wolff, *Vernünftige Gedanken von Gott. etc.* (Halle, 1751), §§ 277, 368, as quoted in trans. by Wallace, pt. 1 of *Encyclopedia of the Philosophical Sciences* (1830), tr. W. Wallace (Oxford, 1975), 310.

[7] Kant, *Critique of Pure Reason*, 'Transcendental Deduction (A)', A 107–8.

of Kant. Jacobi, in his early writings, asserted the superiority of feeling and faith over both *Verstand* and *Vernunft*, as forms of the speculative intellect. Later, he identified faith with *Vernunft*, which he then acknowledged as the capacity for immediate intuition of the real and the true, a 'sense of the supersensible'. He made the point that 'Nobody has ever spoken of an animal *Vernunft*: a mere animal *Verstand* however we all know and speak of.'[8] This is the same distinction as that made by Coleridge (for example, in his 'Essay on Faith') between the 'mind of the flesh' (*LR* iv. 433)—further evolution of animal intelligence— and Reason, which is of another order altogether.

The Understanding maintains the forms and distinctions of what Coleridge described as 'syllogistic' logic (*TT* i. 201), but it remains confined within its own rules; Reason, on the other hand, as Goethe puts it 'takes delight in developing'.[9] It is the dynamic power which can produce a *tertium aliquid* from the connections and relationships which it finds. Coleridge here drew on a theological tradition as much as on the development of the German distinction. *Intellectus* as opposed to *ratio*, according to Nicholas of Cusa, is that which is able to grasp the truth of the 'coincidence of opposites'.[10] *Ratio* is concerned with 'either–or', with the incompatibility and exclusion of opposites. Coleridge's assertion that the Understanding can only grasp Ideas in terms of contradictions[11] refers to the forms and distinctions of the human λόγος, the limitations of 'fallen' language.[12] Reason, however, is the source and the medium of those Ideas, and of the dynamic oppositions which they engender in consciousness. Reason is '*immediate*' as opposed to the mediate concepts and images of the understanding (*CN* iv, § 5377), and includes (Coleridge agreed with Jacobi) the faculties of faith and feeling as immediate intuitions of truth. It is never in conflict with but transcends the merely speculative forms of intellect. Reason is 'the power by which we become possessed of principles' (*Friend*, i. 77).

---

[8] Jacobi, *Werke*, iii. 8.

[9] Goethe, *Sprüche in Prosa*, ed. G. von Loeper (Berlin, 1870), § 896: 'Die Vernunft . . . erfreut sich am Entwickeln.'

[10] For Coleridge's appreciation of Nicholas of Cusa, see Barfield, *What Coleridge Thought*, 179–93.

[11] See below, Ch. 3.3.

[12] See above, Ch. 1.1.

Even in his early writings Coleridge was convinced that Reason and revelation could not be in conflict. A note written in 1796 proclaims: 'Reason the Sun—Revelation the comet which feeds it' (*CN* i, § 88). The Word, divine revelation, is the Idea of God, Truth, and Reason. Coleridge found the concept of the *Λόγος* as Word and Reason emphasized in Bishop Bull's *Defensio Fidei Nicaenae* (1685),[13] an important source of material from the Patristic writers for his *Λόγος* theme. The revelation of the Word *is* Reason; it involves the whole personality including all the deductive and speculative faculties of the Understanding, but transforms them through an interpersonal encounter or communication.[14] Both Reason and revelation may be described as what 'finds' us in the depths of our being. The Understanding alone is not equipped to judge the truth, which surpasses logic, deduction, analysis, and the merely phenomenal evidence of the senses. The speculative intellect, relying on the analytical tool of the understanding, 'can lead us to a general affirmation of the supreme reality of an absolute being', but it can take us no further, wrote Coleridge in a paragraph which in 1818 he instructed his friends he wished to be added to the text of the *Friend*: 'It is utterly incapable of communicating insight or conviction concerning the existence of the world as different from Deity' (i. 522 n). It can prepare the way for the enlightenment of revelation through Reason, but can do no more.

Νοῦς *and* Λόγος

In the period before his first visit to Germany in 1798, Coleridge's concept of *Λόγος* combines the Stoic idea of a universal, all-pervading rational Principle or Act with the

---

[13] George Bull (1634–1710), whose *Defensio Fidei Nicaenae* (1685) Coleridge greatly admired, quotes Tertullian (*Adversus Praxeam*, v): 'The word itself . . . is in a certain way a second [person] within thee, through whom in thinking thou speakest, and through whom in thinking thou speakest. The word itself is another [than thyself] . . . How much more fully then is this carried on in God, of whom thou also art counted as the image and likeness?' (*Defensio Fidei Nicaenae*, iii. 10. 7; tr. anon., 3 vols. (Oxford, 1852), ii. 522).

[14] Coleridge's thought echoes that of the Cambridge Platonists perhaps more in this than in any other aspect: that he too strove to show Reason as the power by which the whole personality was fulfilled and united in its search for truth, and that Reason and revelation were not only compatible but interdependent.

Neoplatonic tradition in which Νοῦς is a mysterious emanation of the One. In a letter to Thomas Poole of 1796 (*CL* i. 195) he expressed appreciation of Lardner's Unitarian view of Λόγος as an attribute of the One God. At this stage he saw the structure and processes of human mind as reflecting divine Reason. Following his joyful conviction of the truth of the Trinity (*c*.1805), he remained in close agreement with Schelling's concept of the unity of consciousness, divine and human. Coleridge's later distinction between the 'mind of the flesh' on the one hand, and, on the other, the Reason which is characteristic of *persons*, had not yet fully emerged. By 1806 the Reason/Understanding distinction was established as a basic and fundamental tenet of his philosophy; this is clear from a letter responding to Thomas Clarkson's question concerning 'the difference between the Reason, and the Understanding (νους και επιστημη: Vernunft, und Verstand)' (*CL* ii. 1193). Notes and letters written in 1805 suggest that Coleridge had, by this time, finally accepted a Trinitarian understanding of Λόγος;[15] the fact that they precede this emphasis on the importance of the Reason/Understanding distinction by only one year seems an unlikely coincidence. He now believed Reason to be not a divine attribute, but the divine *Person*, both transcendent and incarnate. Reason was distinct from the highest forms of evolved intelligence of which it was the source. Far more than mere mental activity, it was the communication of *persons*.

From the early years of the nineteenth century, and contemporaneously with his reading of German philosophy, Coleridge became increasingly convinced that the 'mechanico-corpuscular' theories of life and mind, which he believed to be the offspring of exclusively empiricist philosophies such as those of Locke and Hume, had demonstrated their own inadequacy. By ignoring the distinction between phenomenal and noumenal reality, and by failing to understand the nature of self-consciousness and the relationship of the knowing subject to its object, they had confused Reason with Understanding and ideas with images. The fundamental principle underlying Coleridge's view of Reason is the conviction that Ideas are the true reality not only of mind, but of nature. While this clearly echoes Neoplatonic and idealist

---

[15] See e.g. *CN*, § ii. 2448, and Intro., above.

traditions, his use of the term 'idea' is not always conformed to these.

Following Origen's blend of Philonic and Platonic thought, Coleridge too held that it is in God's Idea of himself—the Idea of Ideas—that all reality has its source and its being: 'God's Thoughts are all consummately adequate Ideas, which are all incomparably more *real* than what we call *Things*. God is the sole self-comprehending Being, i.e. he has an Idea of himself, and that Idea is consummately adequate, & superlatively real—or as great men have said in the throes and strivings of deep and holy meditation, not only substantial or essential, but super-substantial, super-essential' (*CL* ii. 1195). The above quotation might suggest that he belongs exclusively within the tradition of idealist–rationalist philosophy; but the common ground which he shares with F. H. Jacobi makes such a view untenable. Both asserted an ultimate primacy of Will over both Being and Reason. Conscience, and the truth of revelation as *experienced*, were thus the indispensable foundation of all knowledge. Jacobi and Coleridge concurred that the supreme I AM is a personal and living God revealed as the unity of Will and Reason; humanity potentially reflects the divine in the qualities of personality and the will–reason unity. Their emphasis on a psychological foundation of will as the ground of reason gives their thought a markedly different emphasis from idealist and rationalist epistemologies.

Neither Jacobi nor Coleridge despised the Understanding, the faculty of perception, of intuition and deduction. Both respected the claims of empirically derived knowledge. Jacobi's philosophy had much in common with the *Gefühlsphilosophie* of Hamann and Herder, valuing direct and immediate intuitions (both physical and psychological) above detached and rational deductions. Coleridge agreed with Jacobi, however, that experience is more than mere sensibility, because the consciousness which is necessary to experience is *active* and one with life and being.

Like Jacobi and Hegel, he saw the abstract universal as an empty concept. It must be completed through its relation to the concrete, the individual, and the particular. The Understanding perceives universal and particular as mutually exclusive opposites, but Reason reveals supreme Reality as the unity of particularity and universality. This relation is perfectly expressed in the Christian Trinity, as is the ultimate ontological unity of intellect with will and love; thus, Coleridge believed, Christianity provided a means, consistent with reason, of solving the dichotomies which philosophy had left unresolved. Philosophy without religion was incomplete and unable to bridge the gaps of dualism or to overcome the undifferentiated 'all is one' of monism to find a basis for the reality of distinctions. It was incapable of the final step of recognition that Reason must include faith and conscience and be grounded in will. Through a further exploration of the Christian doctrine of Trinity, and of its epistemological and ontological implications, Coleridge wished to restore the ground of philosophy which Hume appeared to have cut away and which Kant, despite all his great and valuable achievement, left divided between phenomena and noumena. He boldly asserted 'not only the perfect rationality of the Doctrine of the Trinity but that it is Reason itself, & supposed in whatever else is called rational' (OM ii, fo. 148). He also claimed (in agreement with his contemporary Hegel, but independently of him) that the reconciliation of universal and particular (found in the faculty of the imagination, and characteristic of Reason) is achieved through Λόγος. A mediation is required within experience and thought; not simply the mediation between sinful mankind and transcendent God, but psychologically, between the human will and reason, and rationally, in reconciling the subject/object dichotomy, which is the root of philosophy's self-alienation. Jacobi and Coleridge were agreed that 'Sensuous Evidence itself was a species of Faith and Revelation' (*CM* iii. 640). The coherence and unity by which sense perception becomes experience itself requires an act of faith and can reveal nothing to the human mind without it.

Coleridge, in the Preface of his *Aids to Reflection*, boldly ascribed to Christianity 'the PERFECTION of human intelligence' (*AR*, p. x). He claimed that revealed religion redeemed the empirical understanding from the tyranny of the senses, so that it could be seen as properly concerned with means rather than ends and as such fulfil its necessary function. He described the Understanding as 'the power of selecting and adapting means to medial ends, or what is the same to immediate or proximate purposes' (N 42, fo. 3^v). As means, the senses on which the empirical understanding is based are essential to the natural development of human consciousness, the potential for which is itself implanted by the Creator (Λόγος). Human Understanding is derived from the coexistence in man of the intelligent instinct of the higher animals with self-consciousness, the reflection of the Self-knowing-Self of the Trinity. In this all humanity, to some degree, bears the image of the Λόγος.

The faculty of the speculative intelligence is, for Coleridge, the point of 'indifference', the meeting-point, between the world of spirit and that of nature. It has evolved through the life of nature, and is not yet reunited with what is, in reality, its spiritual origin in Reason. He saw this human λόγος, with its faculty of analysis, articulation, and logical connection, as reflecting the activity of the Λόγος who communicates order, distinction, form, and relation. But he firmly maintained that unless the Understanding itself undergoes a redemption, being transformed through will, faith, and conscience towards the light of Reason (Λόγος), it cannot find the means by which to overcome the dichotomies which it experiences in thought and being, philosophical no less than moral. Communicated by love and grace, the enlightenment of Reason is received only through a responsive act of will and faith. The life of Reason is dynamic, not static, relational rather than analytic.[16] Inclusive of faith and conscience, it is the power by which individuals become persons. Reason was (as Coleridge knew it to have been for Plato) inseparable from virtue and

---

[16] This point has relevance, I believe, to the Deconstructionist critique of Coleridge by Paul de Man. De Man suggests (correctly) that Coleridge's theory rests on will and that therefore it has implications which are not explicitly involved in what critics usually understand by 'theory'; rather, in the end, it leads to 'a discontinuous world of reflective irony and ambiguity' (*Blindness and Insight*, 28). Again, I think de Man has failed (see above, Ch. 1.2 n. 56) to give sufficient weight to Coleridge's emphasis on the difference between Reason and Understanding; and to see that Coleridge's 'system' is 'dynamic' and based on a *unity* of reason and will. Coleridge could not accept the incompatibility of theory and voluntarism. For him, theory is indispensable, as is the faculty of the means and categories of human discourse (the Understanding); his system involves, and is dependent upon, the theoretical processes of the Understanding. But its aim is to provide 'materials' to stimulate will, conscience, and reflection, and to establish a unifying principle through which a harmony of all knowledges may be achieved, through interrelation rather than a coherence of dogmatic or structural detail. All truth must be reduced to the forms of the Understanding (*AR* 224 n.); but the theoretical forms of the speculative intellect are not to be reified despite their indispensability. Coleridge insisted that 'Kant has shown, that the Intellect is not the whole of Human Being, nor the only Organ of Truth' (*CM* iii. 641). Coleridge admitted that the speculative intellect must always be subject to Reason, which involves will, faith, and conscience. Nevertheless, Reason in its highest form (i.e. the divine Logos) is the 'focal point of the Theoric and the Practical' *SM*: *LS* 60 n.

moral responsibility. Any epistemological solutions must have a sound psychological basis which recognized that Reason involved the whole personality. Christianity recognized in the Λόγος the revelation not only of divine Reason, but of Will (the Father) and Love (the Spirit); the very being and the acts of the Λόγος are always to be seen in the context of this unity.

Coleridge's history of the derivation and variety of meanings attributable to the term Λόγος, in his *Logic*, demonstrates the importance which it held for him both philosophically and theologically.[17] He was well aware of the distinction made by Platonists and Gnostics between Νοῦς and Λόγος. He was emphatic in correction of Fleury, for example, that Νοῦς represents the pure Reason and Λόγος 'the intelligential Imagination, or Reason manifesting itself in *forms*'.[18] In a note of 1827 (N 35, fo. 42ᵛ), written contemporaneously with his reading of Claude Fleury's *Ecclesiastical History* (1727–8), he remarked that Eusebius (of Nicodemia, a pro-Arian member of the Council of Nicaea) failed to note the distinction of the Greek concepts of Λόγος and Νοῦς as the difference between the Understanding and the Reason. Λόγος represents to the Greeks the formative, distinguishing, and manifesting Agent of the Supreme Mind.

In a margin note on Böhme, Coleridge linked *Vernunft*, *Verstand*, and the unifying operations of mind to the distinct parts of human personality and intelligence and, again, to the relationships of the Trinity (*CM* i. 654). *Vernunft*, which he identified with the Soul, is the ground of thought, reflection, and perception; as such it represents God the Father. The Son is represented by *Verstand*, self-knowledge, the Light shining in the soul which gives knowledge of power and life and is the means of the individual's self-definition and self-development. Mind,

---

[17] Coleridge shows his philosophical interest in the term 'logos' in his *Logic*: he refers, for example, to 'A higher sense of the term "logos", in which it signifies the reason as including the understanding' (*Logic*, ed. J. R. de J. Jackson, *The Collected Works of Samuel Taylor Coleridge*, Bollingen Series, xiii (Princeton, NJ, 1980), 169); and to 'the etymological history of the Word (Logos) etc.' (ibid. 282). He describes 'the sense of the term as expressing the ground or faculty by which men are enabled to connect words conclusively'.

[18] For more on Coleridge's distinction between Νοῦς and Λόγος, see also his correction of Thomas Taylor's translation of Νοῦς as 'Intellect' in the former's annotations of *The Philosophical and Mathematical Commentaries of Proclus etc. and A Translation from the Greek of Proclus's Theological Elements* (London, 1792), i. 127: 'Νοῦς . . . in English ought to be translated "pure Reason".'

as the unity of the faculties, is represented as the Community of the Holy Ghost. When Coleridge, in *Aids to Reflection* (*AR* 249), identified λόγος with the Understanding as the faculty of means, of discourse, and of logic, he drew on the insights of the Greek tradition and of Philo's writings, interpreting the Λόγος as the faculty of distinction and limitation. He attempted to reconcile these attributes with Trinitarian theology. God may be represented in thought as the pure Reason, Νοῦς. The Λόγος, with God and God, is the archetype of the mediating activity by which human intelligence itself brings order out of a chaos of perceptions, framing the necessary conditions of experience in the forms and structures of human language, of analytical logic and the deductions of mathematics. Here Coleridge's concept of the human λόγος seems very like the 'antecedent unity' which belongs to Kant's noumenal reality and which is an a priori framework for all experience.[19] Λόγος, unlike Νοῦς, has connotations of plurality and of communication[20] which are also mirrored in the human λόγος.

We have already traced Coleridge's concept of the role of the divine Λόγος as the Creator of space and time, the necessary conditions of the finite world. He believed nature to be permeated with the Λόγος activity, so that 'The language of nature is a subordinate *Logos*, that was in the beginning, and was with the thing it represented, and was the thing it represented' (*LR* ii. 50–1). The λόγος of the human understanding participates in this activity within the finite limits of its own nature. Yet he maintained that it had no power to raise itself beyond its static function of intellect to the Νοῦς, the 'Intuitive Reason, the Source of Ideas and ABSOLUTE Truths, and the Principle of the Necessary and the Universal in our Affirmations and Conclusions' (*AR* 249 n).

Coleridge used the Greek terms Νοῦς and Λόγος to elucidate the distinction, in the human mind, between Reason and Understanding. Here, Λόγος is associated with the forms and distinctions

---

[19] Kant, *Critique of Pure Reason*, 'The Transcendental Deduction (A)', A 107–8.

[20] See Origen, *Commentaria in Evangelium Joannis*, i. 23, and *Contra Celsum*, iii. 34. Logos, for Origen, 'possesses both the unity of God and the multiplicity of the world' (see A. Tripolitis, *Origen: A Critical Reading* (New York, c.1985), 128–9).

of the logical faculty as distinct from *Νοῦς*, the relational and dynamic truth of ideas which are their own evidence, conforming to the needs and experience of the whole personality. The *Λόγος* of the Fourth Gospel, however, is not only the source of all those functions and qualities contained in the varied expressions of the Greek *λόγος*, but is identified by Coleridge with the Neoplatonic *Νοῦς*, the realization of God's self-knowledge.

In his identification of *Λόγος* and *Νοῦς* as the second Person of the Trinity, Coleridge follows John Scotus Eriugena. The latter attempted to reconcile the Neoplatonic doctrine of the One as somehow beyond thought and knowledge with the Christian doctrine of God's absolute knowledge of himself, by making the divine *Λόγος*, in whom are contained the distinctions of the pleroma of Ideas, the first 'theophany' of God, by and through which God's self-knowledge is realized. His concept of the Christian *Λόγος* thus, as Frederick Copleston has shown,[21] corresponds to the Neoplatonic *Νοῦς*. Yet Coleridge believes Eriugena's treatment of the subject to be too close to an emanation theory which leads to pantheism. Coleridge himself appears to make use of a similar relation between *Νοῦς* and *Λόγος*; but his argument for the *Λόγος* 'alterity' as begotten in God's self-realizing Act of Will ('Will in the form of Reason'), and his emphasis on the primal polarity of Wills due to the spiritual apostasy, make consistent his insistence on a positive free act of creation through and in the *Λόγος*. It also emphasizes the radical 'otherness' of God and Nature. Here again the *Λόγος* of the Fourth Gospel remains the source of inspiration, a dynamic Light and Life which, through 'alterity' and personhood, surpasses the Greek *Νοῦς*.

Coleridge saw the incarnate Christ as the reconciliation of *Νοῦς* and *Λόγος*, of transcendent pure Reason with the immanent manifestation and communication of Ideas in the finite creation. He easily identified the *Νοῦς* of the Pythagoreans and of Anaxagoras with 'the *Logos* or *Word* of Philo and St John' (*PL* 175). The Word is subordinate to the One[22] in that he is begotten by the

---

[21] F. Copleston, *History of Philosophy*, 9 vols., ii (London, 1959), 134.

[22] Philo subordinated the Logos to the Supreme God (*De Opificio Mundi*, 16). Origen did the same in *De Principiis*, i. 2. 13, where he distinguished between God the Father as *autoagathon* or *agathotes* ('Good itself', or 'goodness') and Christ as merely *agathos* ('good').

Father, yet he is coequal and eternal with him: 'the communicating and communicated Logos', who, in the Greek sense, is the agent of the One, *is* also that One expressed in Triunity. *Λόγος*, Coleridge believed, is a superb figurative expression of the Son of God as Creator, as Revealer, as Incarnate Word and Mediator. *Νοῦς*, on the other hand, expresses the unity of the Son with (and yet his distinctness from) the Father as the source of universal and Absolute Truth. 'Ideas', writes Coleridge, 'are their own evidence' (*SM: LS* 32). The *Λόγος* is the Idea of Ideas; the only adequate Idea of God. Like all Ideas, he is his own witness: Reason revealed *through* Reason to *be* Reason.

Coleridge's concept of Reason is recognizably a synthesis of classical theology, Greek philosophy, and Kantian 'trichotomy'. He respected the grounds of Kant's denial that any dogmatic statements could be made by human reason and of his claim that noumenal reality was beyond our reach. However, the gap between noumenal and phenomenal, between *Νοῦς* and *Λόγος*, *must* be bridged if human thought and experience were not to remain hopelessly fragmented. Kant had suggested that the antinomies of human reason were inevitable, but ultimately only generative of concepts, not realities; Coleridge believed that these antinomies were the result of the necessary polarities of thought through which the truth of ideas was expressed, and that they led inexorably to the necessity for faith and for an act of will which in turn revealed the reconciliation achieved by *Λόγος*. True to his conclusion that it was reasonable to assume whatever was required in order to account for the necessary conditions of thought and being, Coleridge believed he had found in the Christian *Λόγος* a solution which met the needs of humanity because it was found in the very Principle of Humanity, that of Personhood. To this solution, Reason, conscience, faith, and experience all bore witness.

3.2. LOGOS: UNIFYING PRINCIPLE

Coleridge, in common with most philosophers after Hume, recognized that the pursuit of objectively true knowledge of external reality was ultimately hopeless unless the structure and processes of the human mind could be shown to correspond in some way to that reality. Truth must either be given up in favour of a relativism and subjectivism which offers the best alternative for making sense of the world, or such a correspondence must be established. His 'system' was grounded in his apprehension of this dilemma. He struggled against both the 'mechanico-corpuscular' philosophy of Hartley and Priestley (of which he had once approved), and against subjective idealism (that of Fichte, for example) on this basis. Mechanistic and materialist philosophy spurned any concept of ultimate reality behind the phenomenal; subjective idealism reduced all external reality to mere appearance. Neither provided any means of reconciling the inner life of mind with experience of an outer world. Without such a reconciliation, Coleridge believed, both the philosophical and the theological enterprise must be null and void. Kant's philosophy seemed to him to have come closest to resolving the dichotomy; yet, finally, it had failed and left the gap unbridged. One of the most important tasks which Coleridge set himself was to establish an 'ideal Realism' (the terms, but not the concept, followed Schelling's pattern) as a philosophical ground for the correspondence of the subjective reality of mind and the objective reality of the external world. In brief, his conclusion was that there must be some kind of mediatory channel between consciousness and external objective being, and that such a mediation can be shown to exist in and through the idea, the symbol, and the agency of Logos. He believed that he could show the Idea of the Logos to be not only the means through which the finite intellect could grasp this unity but (as the Idea of ideas) actively constitutive of it.

The Greek Heritage

Of the thinkers whom Coleridge most admired, many, from the time of Pythagoras and Heraclitus to that of his own contemporaries Fichte and Schelling, had sought to provide a unifying principle of thought and being. The attempt to show the identity of the laws and structures of mind and the laws and powers of nature had become a feature of German *Naturphilosophie* in the early nineteenth century. Coleridge, like many of the German philosophers,[23] drew inspiration from the Greeks, especially from Heraclitus, Pythagoras, Plato, and from the Neoplatonists Plotinus, Proclus, and Porphyry. We have seen aspects of his mature philosophy that reflected Heraclitus' *logos* principle. The *logos*, Heraclitus had claimed, is both the everlasting communication of truth *and* the truth itself. He made no distinction in kind between the *logos* as the dynamic principle of reason within the human mind and the *logos* which operates within the laws and powers of nature. This idea has a fundamental importance in Coleridge's own system.

His 'Logosophia' was to be 'no other than the system of Pythagoras and Plato revived and purified from impure mixtures' (*BL* i. 263). Pythagoras, for example, is depicted in the *Philosophical Lectures* as believing

that those unknown somethings, powers or whatever you may call them, that manifest themselves in the intellect of man, or what in the language of the old philosophy, would be called the intelligible world, as numbers, and the essential powers of numbers, these same manifest themselves to us and are the objects of our senses, I mean as creative and organizing powers: in short, that the very powers which in men reflect and contemplate, are in their essence the same as those powers which in nature produce the objects contemplated. (*PL* 114)

The rejection of Pythagoras' position by later thinkers was due, Coleridge concluded, to their failure to grasp reality in any form but that presented to us by the senses:

Therefore an image supporting something (which in itself is a contradiction, for an image always supposes a superficies and a something supported, and is asked for under the name of a substance) is construed into an agent when we can no longer boldly bring forward a thing for it; and this agent is contradistinguished from an act as if these oppositions of our human language and thoughts were really the true conditions and the very essence of our being. (*PL* 115)

In other words, the mind is taken to be a 'mould' or a passive recipient, instead of being recognized as itself active. According

---

[23] Kant, Schelling, Goethe, Schiller, Hölderlin, and Hegel, for example, all drew extensively on Greek thought, particularly in order to question and address fundamental issues of ontology and epistemology.

to Coleridge, Plato had drawn on the insights of Pythagoras when he 'argued that, as there was that power in the mind which thinks and images its thoughts, analogous to this was the power in nature which thought and imaged or embodied its thoughts, in consequence of which he resolved the ground of all things into the dynamic' (*PL* 187). Coleridge greatly admired the *Timaeus*, in which, he believed, Plato described a primary and personal act of Will as begetting the Ideas or Forms which are reflected in the forms and laws of the finite world.[24] Even Aristotle in order to avoid the atheism and destruction of morality which would have resulted, Coleridge argued, from the objects of the senses being regarded as the true realities of nature 'was obliged to admit that *in* this reality, but not as *distinct* from it, there existed, as he called it, an ENTELECHIE, that is, a power which contained in itself, as it were, a capability of producing all that should be derived from it independent of time' (*PL* 187). This confused notion, Coleridge declared, had led to compounded confusion in the minds of later philosophers as to whether Aristotle was a theist or an atheist, that is, as to whether he believed in a transcendent reality or whether the only reality was of nature as somehow both producer and product.

Coleridge's division of all mankind into Platonists or Aristotelians[25] reflects an antithetic which he found at the heart of all philosophy, that between an 'ideal Realism' (the roots of this he traced to Plato's proclamation of an ultimate dynamic reality beyond the world of the senses) and materialism (of which Aristotle was the founder, having implied that nature was itself the highest goal of reason). A note probably written in 1810 (*PL* 53)[26] makes clear Coleridge's vision of the whole history of philosophy as preoccupied with asserting either an absolute Reality of being

---

[24] For Coleridge's study of the *Timaeus*, see *BL* i. 233. He described Plato's ideas as 'mysterious powers, living, seminal, formative, and exempt from time' (*BL* i. 97). Coleridge was aware of the dualism in Plato's philosophy, and saw a hiatus between the dynamic Ideas, and the 'copies' of these in the energies of nature (see BL MS Egerton 2801, fo. 33); but he believed that Plato had recognized the divine 'Personëity', the 'I am', as the source of all things.

[25] 'The one considers reason a quality, or attribute; the other considers it a power' (*TT* i. 173).

[26] A transcribed note from Coleridge's marginal notes on Tennemann, *Geschichte der Philosophie*, viii. 130.

which is one with mind[27] or the merely regulatory function of knowledge and the relativity of appearances (in Kantian philosophy). He insisted that one question was fundamental to philosophy: whether consciousness is only the passive recipient of sense impressions, at best ordering and regulating and thus providing the framework of experience; or whether it is a dynamic, creative power and Ideas living, substantial realities (*LS: SM* 114). His own conclusion is given in his notes 'On the Divine Ideas':

An Idea is not simply knowledge or perception as distinguished from the thing perceived: it is a realizing knowledge, a knowledge causative of its own reality; in it is Life, & the life is the light of men. And it is this which the eldest Sages of all nations have struggled to express in the various terms of Self-subsistent Light, living Light φως νοερον και νοητον[,] a Light at once intelligent and intelligible, and the communicative medium. (ODI, fos. 31–3)[28]

Heraclitus, Pythagoras, and Plato had, at the dawn of the Western intellectual tradition, ascribed all forms of thought and being to a transcendent principle in which mind and being were identified. Of these, Heraclitus' sense of a transcendent *logos* which was at the same time immanent, one in nature and in mind, most clearly influenced Coleridge's Logos theme. The identification of self-conscious Mind and Being in Aristotle has a different basis and is one which Coleridge ultimately rejected as the root of pantheism. This difference was the focus of the disparity between Hegel's view of the Logos and Coleridge's own.[29] In Aristotle's *Primum Mobile*, Intelligence contemplates its own Being; knower and known, subject and object are identified. This divine Intelligence is identified with the life of the cosmos; it is not a transcendent personal and creative Will. Coleridge accused Aristotle of neglecting the primary importance of the creative and constitutive nature of mind; of recognizing only acts *of*

---

[27] Coleridge mentioned Spinoza in this context, and in a note written in 1818 he included Oken, Schelling, and Hegel with Spinoza as 'doctors of the Absolute' (*CN* iii, § 4445).

[28] Here again, Coleridge's theory of Ideas is clearly linked to his thought on Word and Symbol (see above, Ch. 1.2).

[29] See pt. 2 of my article 'Logic and Logos', *Heythrop Journal*, 32 (1991), 192–215.

Reason, and failing (unlike Pythagoras and Plato) to recognize Reason itself as *Act*.

At a later stage, in the Neoplatonist tradition, Plotinus and Porphyry had developed the idea of self-conscious mind as the meeting-point of thought and being, suggesting that subjective Mind produces itself as objective Being. What we regard as the corporeal world, they declared, is the manifestation of the same Reality the nature of which is most adequately revealed in the world of self-conscious mind. Coleridge had much sympathy with this concept of self-consciousness as the reconciliation of thought and being which had been the ground of idealist philosophy from Descartes on. He admired those versions of it which were developed in German idealism, notably by Kant, Fichte, and Schelling, yet was never entirely satisfied with them.

He consciously followed Plato and the Neoplatonists in placing the One, the Good, *beyond* Being (ODI, fos. 157 ff.) and rejected Aristotle's claim that the One was identical with Being, the distinction being only in concept or definition. Coleridge maintained that the order of thought which places an efficient Good (an Act, a Will) before Being, although it involves a succession of concepts not attributable to eternal reality, corresponds to the distinctions necessary to *any* possible idea of God, and to the primacy of Will. He berated the Neoplatonists for their divine hierarchies (ODI, fos. 181–3)[30] and Plotinus for his failure to demonstrate how and why the second hypostasis of Mind might be derived from or related to an idea of the One which appears to be non-efficient, non-creative. Yet Coleridge's position was very similar to that of the Renaissance thinker Pico della Mirandola (1463–94), whose work he had studied and admired, and who had followed the Neoplatonists in identifying the realm of Forms and Intellect with Being.[31] Coleridge's answer to what he considered to be flaws in both Aristotelian and Neoplatonic philosophy was to assert the primacy of Will over

---

[30] See ODI, fos. 157, 161, 181. Coleridge shows that the idea of the Good is the first Principle of Plato. Although its representation is, in his opinion, flawed, Coleridge notes that the Good is also the first hypostasis of Plotinus, and Being is the second (see *CM* ii. 726).

[31] For Coleridge's interest in Pico della Mirandola's work, see e.g. *CN* i, §§ 374 and n., 1068 and n. Pico suggests that God is *above* Being, Form, and Intellect in one sense, in another these are seen to be a unity with him (*De Ente et Uno*, tr. V. M. Hamm as *Of Being and Unity* (Milwaukee, 1943), v).

both Mind and Being. He saw this not as a retreat into volun-
taristic and mystical presupposition, but as a necessary hypothesis
of reason, requiring for its realization only the fideistic leap which
was inevitable in every act of perception and through which the
hypothesis would be confirmed and found to fulfil the demands of
intellect and experience.

The Logos Reconciler

Coleridge almost always mixed admiration with criticism. While
he drew extensively on past thinkers' attempts to reconcile being
and thought, he found all these, to a greater or lesser degree,
flawed. The corrective principle which he believed he had estab-
lished was the idea of the Logos as Reconciler. He admired the
efforts of seventeenth-century thinkers such as Bacon, Descartes,
and Spinoza to establish the correspondence of ideas with external
reality. Of all these, it was 'the true Baconic philosophy' of which
he was most enthusiastically appreciative; for this consisted 'in a
profound meditation on those laws which the pure reason in man
reveals to him, with the confident anticipation and faith that to
this will be found to correspond certain laws in nature' (*PL* 333).
Bacon had shown the distinction between the 'ideas of the mind'[32]
and the 'idols': 'namely that the former are manifested by their
adequacy to those ideas in nature which in and through them are
contemplated'. The latter are the results of the application of the
understanding (as opposed to reason) to truths which are beyond
its limitations.

Descartes had established an identity of thinking and being,
but at the cost, Coleridge believed, of a separation of ideal
from concrete, material reality. He admitted that Descartes had
produced valuable insights concerning the distinction between
'two sorts of thoughts'; that is, between the workings of self-
consciousness as the mind tracing its own operations, and the
external ideas impressed upon the mind as passive. However,
Descartes 'was the first man who made nature utterly lifeless and
godless, considered it as the subject of merely mechanical laws'
(*PL* 376–7). Coleridge accused him of failing to recognize the
fundamental truth that, while being and self-consciousness are

---

[32] See below, Ch. 3.3.

identical for us and the ground of all our knowledge, both must themselves be grounded in an act of will. This, Coleridge remarked in his criticisms of Spinoza,[33] must imply 'alterity', that is, the Logos principle. As it was, in Descartes's philosophy, nature and concrete being were divorced from mind, and the truth of Ideas was, as a result, distorted.

Descartes, claimed Coleridge, had to depend on so-called 'material ideas' for any kind of explanation of the correspondence of mind with external reality. The brain was supposed, through its own inherent structures, to select for itself and to receive only those impressions which would convey true and accurate correspondence. The origin of these ideas was then to be found in the organization itself. As a consequence, the correspondence of external reality with the inner reality of thought depended on some kind of largely inexplicable mechanism of communication within the structure of the brain. Coleridge, in contrast, asserted that both phenomenal reality and the reality of consciousness are grounded in a philosophy of *act* and *will*. The powers working within nature and those within mind are therefore homogenous.

He greatly admired Spinoza's attempt to demonstrate the ultimate unity of all things and repudiated Jacobi's charge that Spinoza's Absolute was a merely abstract category (*CM* iii. 79–80). It was clear to him that Spinoza rejected any identification of God and the physical world: he 'disavows the identity of God and Nature, the confusion of the Universe with its great Author, as a grievous and fearful Superstition'.[34] Spinoza too had asserted that the laws of nature and mind are identical. His philosophy strongly impressed and influenced both Coleridge and Hegel,[35] though both finally rejected it. The latter found the first of Spinoza's 'Definitions' of the *Causa Sui*—'that of which the essence invokes the existence, or that whose nature cannot be conceived except as existing'—unremarkable: 'To say that God is Substance, the only Substance, and that, as Substance is *Causa Sui*, God therefore exists necessarily, is merely stating that God is that of which the

---

[33] BL MS Egerton 2801, fo. 13.

[34] BL MS Egerton 2801, fo. 10.

[35] See App. C, below, for an analysis of the parallels between the logocentric systems of Hegel and Coleridge.

notion and the being are inseparable.'[36] Coleridge's criticism was of a different kind:

the true Vice of the whole system is that it begins with a *definition* at all, as a foundation. The definition ought to be the conclusion, wherever the subject is not confined to the mind's own operations, & quoad rem externam* merely hypothetical. . . . Allow him to *begin* with any notion, no matter what, that expresses more than the mind's own agency & laws of action, and the same consequence would follow:—i.e. to begin with it as an ontological axiom.[37]

[* 'as regards an external thing']

Coleridge himself asserted of Ideas that they are their own evidence; that their being is a reality necessary to—inseparable from—thought itself. This definition accorded with the mind's own operations and was therefore not only plausible but, he suggested, undeniable. This view seems in sympathy with Spinoza's exposition of 'adequate ideas'.[38] Yet Coleridge develops this theme in a different direction in his frequent allusions to the Logos as the 'adequate Idea'. Despite his defence of Spinoza, he rejected the grounds on which the latter's philosophy was based: 'Spinozism consists in the exclusion of intelligence and consciousness from Deity—therefore it is Atheism' (*CM* i. 114). Spinoza's Absolute, as infinite thought which is identical with substance and not with the idea of will, is, wrote Coleridge, 'a centreless/pointless thing'. His system lacked the essential reality of the Logos, that is, of the infinite in the form of the finite, the 'measure of the measureless'. The very concepts of being and of mind depended upon the acceptance of the Ideas of both unity and 'alterity'. Coleridge argued that all Being must be grounded in an act: an act presupposes a will, and will must have an object. Since God self-realized (*Causa Sui*) is his own object, ultimate unity necessarily includes 'alterity'. The principle of distinction in unity is essential to both Being and Mind.

Coleridge believed that Spinoza's failure to recognize the primacy of will, and of 'alterity' within unity,[39] necessarily im-

[36] *Hegel's Logic*, 110.

[37] VCL S MS F2.11, notebook.

[38] For Spinoza's analysis of 'adequate ideas' see the unfinished text 'On the Importance of the Understanding' (in *Ethics*, tr. R. H. M. Elwes, Hafner Library edn. (New York, 1949), 11–13); see also *Ethics*, ii, d. iv.

[39] BL MS Egerton 2801, fo. 13.

plied denial of the reality of intelligence, despite the witness borne to this reality by the fact of Spinoza's own speculations. For the same reason, his system could not explain change nor consistently allow for modification of any sort since it presented no effective agent. Spinoza, in contrast to Descartes, had demanded that we 'remove any concept of self-individuality because it only depends on other correlatives I, Thou, it etc';[40] but Coleridge argued that to put self aside in the contemplation of being is simply impossible. In the act of setting aside the conditions of the empirical self, either we arrive at a self which is *not* merely empirical, or we are merely giving the empirical self another name. He accepted the necessity of Kant's antecedent unity of selfhood as the condition for all thought and experience, believing that Kant and German idealism had taken a crucially important step in proposing self-consciousness as the corrective to Spinoza's system. The later idealists had also indicated a means of overcoming the dichotomies of Cartesian dualism in proposing the self as active and participatory in regulating (if not creating) the world which it knows. Coleridge found the philosophies of Kant, Fichte, Schelling, and Hegel flawed in many respects,[41] but he agreed that, through the recognition of the active role of self-conscious Mind, both universal and individual, philosophy might once more find solid ground on which to build.

The *Gefühlsphilosophie* of J. G. Hamann (1730–88) and F. H. Jacobi offered an alternative ground for unity, that of feeling, faith, and conscience. Coleridge, despite his agreement with many of Jacobi's views, did not find there an altogether adequate philosophical reconciliation of the outward experience of concrete being with the inner world of thought and reason. He recognized, nevertheless, that the immediacy of feeling, the inspiration of the mystics, the involvement of the heart and of the moral impulse, must be an essential part of the relationship between mind and being. He himself longed for a reconciliation of rationality and feeling,[42] believing that this was to be found within Christianity in which the divine Reason (Logos) was revealed to be also the divine *Person*, incarnate within nature, mind, and history.

On these grounds, Coleridge criticized Kant's concept of the

---

[40] Ibid., fos. 11 ff.   [41] See e.g. below, Chs. 3.2, 3.3, and 4.3.
[42] BL MS Egerton 2801, fo. 101.

self. It was inadequate psychologically[43] and grounded too much, on the one hand (the phenomenal aspect), on the merely empirical self and, on the other (the noumenal factor), on the assumption of a 'perfect synonymousness' between reason and the will. Fichte had achieved a significant step forward: 'by commencing with an *act*, instead of a *thing* or substance, Fichte assuredly gave the first mortal blow to Spinozism, as taught by Spinoza himself; and supplied the *idea* of a system truly metaphysical and of a *metaphysique* truly systematic (i.e. having its spring & principle within itself)' (*BL* i. 158). Yet Coleridge was already critical, at the time of writing the *Biographia Literaria*, of Fichte's failure to find any reality beyond the act of self-consciousness. Fichte's 'Self' merely related to a negation, the 'Not-Self'. Here again external reality was sacrificed to 'a heavy mass of mere *notions* and psychological acts of arbitrary reflection . . . his theory degenerated into a crude "egoismus"' (ibid.).

Logocentric Unity

Despite his admiration for these German philosophers, Coleridge believed they had failed to find an adequate unifying principle for the laws of nature and mind. Schelling's system too was flawed;[44] it introduced a false polarity of 'ideality' and 'reality' into the idea of God. 'From the beginning,' wrote Coleridge, annotating the *Denkmal*,[45] 'I avoid the false opposition of Real & Ideal which embarrasses Schelling; Idea with me is contradistinguished only from conception, notion, construction, impression, sensation.'

---

[43] See below, Chs. 3.4 and 4.3.

[44] Coleridge proclaimed many of Schelling's ideas to be a new formulation of well-established positions from the whole history of philosophy. He recognized that, for example, the importance of the polarity principle, of 'individuation', of the potencies manifested in the being of mind and nature, of a chaos reduced by the Word to order and form, all these (seminal elements of Coleridge's own system) are to be found in the work of, for example, John Scotus Eriugena, Giordano Bruno, Jakob Böhme, Richard Baxter, and Spinoza, and may be traced back to Plotinus, Proclus, and Porphyry. Coleridge often draws attention to this; e.g. to Schelling's adoption of potencies from Aristotle (*CN* iii. § 4449), and to the latter's borrowings from Böhme without acknowledgement (see Coleridge's marginal notes to Schelling's *Philosophische Schriften*, 442).

[45] F. W. J. Schelling, *Denkmal der Schrift von den göttlichen Dingen etc.* (Tübingen, 1812).

He attempted to establish the ultimate homogeneity of nature and mind through his own version of 'ideal Realism'. The difference between his concept of the Logos-unity of Reason and Will, and Schelling's philosophy (blind Will becomes self-consciousness through its manifestation in the evolution of the physical world) is clearly developed:

1. Absolute Prothesis
Will, absolutely and essentially causative of Reality
Therefore
2. Absolute Thesis of its own Reality. Mens-*Pater*
But the absolute will self-realised is still absolutely causative of Reality. It has all reality in itself; but it must likewise have all reality in another— that is, all eternal Relations are included in all reality—and here there can be no difference but of relation—an
3. Absolute Antithesis,
but the absolute of Mens is *Idea* absolute adequatum Deus Filius. But where Alterity exists without difference of Attribute, the Father beholdeth himself in the only-begotten Son & the Son acknowledgeth the Father in himself, an *act* of absolute unity is given—proceeding from the Father into the Son, from the Son into the Father . . .
περιχώρησις [*perichoresis*], processio intercircularis
4. Absolute Synthesis. Love
Deus Spiritus.[46]

The 'ipsëity . . . alterity' relationship is born out of an act of will which Coleridge pronounced the only possible source of all reality; of all the relations and processes of being and thought. The finite world emerges from the 'fallen' chaos of non-being, through the agency of Logos and Sophia, in dynamic polarities of light and life. The concept of Logos as both Intermediary and Creator is to be found in the work of both Philo and Plotinus; Philo draws his emphasis on the co-agency of Logos with the feminine principle, Sophia, from the Wisdom literature of the Hebrew Scriptures.[47] Coleridge's own 'logosophic' system sets

---

[46] Coleridge's marginal notes to the *Denkmal*, i. back flyleaf. Here again Coleridge introduced the concept of *perichoresis*.

[47] E. R. Goodenough has explored the relation drawn by Philo between Logos and Sophia; 'Philo speaks of the Highest Divine Logos who is the source of Sophia . . .'; 'that is, the Logos can be represented as derived from Sophia or Sophia as a derivative from the Logos' (*By Light, Light* (New Haven, Conn., 1935), 22–3). Philo develops the theme found, for example, in Wisdom 11: 1. This emphasis clearly influenced Coleridge's work.

out how, through the communication and 'condescension' of the Logos as the Idea, the Being (ὁ ὤν) of God, nature becomes mind and the human *logos* (as language, thought, communication, imagination) is realized. He declared that 'the Λογος which is generated by the mind is distinct, tho' not divisible, from the propagation and *actuation* of the Λογος into Reality' (*CM* i. 583). The Logos is the mediator between the one and the many, for 'Alterity leads to Plurality' (*CL* v. 99).

The Logos, then, is Coleridge's final solution to the search for a unifying principle. In his early writings, Being, Reason, and Truth are *attributes* of God (*CN* ii, §§ 2444–5); but an important feature of his later thought is 'the Identity of Reason & Being, and of both with the Eternal *Word*, the only-begotten Son and *Person*' (N 47, fos. 23ᵛ–24). He admitted that he found it difficult to avoid the inclination to think of truth and reason as mere attributes of pure Being:

After more than 20 years conviction, and more than 10 years earnest discipline of my mind and watchfulness and striving to mature my conviction into a habit of feeling, to combine the Light with a *Life*, and a sense of objectivity, I find it the most difficult of all the labors of Faith to disenthral my spirit from the tendency to think of Truth, Reason, Wisdom as accidents, properties of this or that Being . . . to raise it into a more satisfying contemplation of Truth, as *Being*, as = Ο αληθης.* (N 35, fos. 45ᵛ–46)

[* 'The true'—in person]

This passage illustrates the intensity of Coleridge's conviction that the contemplation of Truth *as* Being is essential to a philosophical apprehension of the idea of God, and, indeed, to philosophy itself. He repeatedly emphasized this point: 'Reason *is* Being, and all true Being is Reason' (N 42, fo. 37); 'Observe that *Reason* is not the Property of this or that Being or Class of Beings—No—Reason *is* Being: & Reason alone is true & Absolute Being' (N 59, fo. 1ᵛ). This conclusion is closely connected with his insistence that philosophical systems should not give primacy to Being. He criticized the Germans for failing to recognize this, and praised Plato for his avoidance of this error. The exponents of natural theology in his own time had, he thought, been seduced by it:

our Divines had adopted the foundations of their Faith (which they call Natural Religion) from Paganism—they begin with *The Being—O Ωω*— the necessary legitimate consequence of which is Pantheism, with Polytheism (i.e. the hypothesis of higher *Natures, οι θεοι**) as its' utterance or exoteric Half. (*CL* vi. 537)

[* 'the gods']

St John, said Coleridge, 'would have taught them a deeper philosophy, and the only one compatible with a *Moral* religion—'. The Idea of the Christian Trinity had, in his opinion, to be understood as St John presented it, in the following order '1. *θεος*. 2. *ο ων, ο μονογενης*. 3. *ο πατηρ*' ('1. God. 2. Being, the one self-generated. 3. The Father'). In the necessary order of thought 'under the intrusive form of *Time*, the Father is a reflex from the Son'.[48] Prior to Being (which is identified with the second person of the Trinity, God the Son) there is the 'Absolute, or Causa sui . . . essentially unutterable, deeper than all Idea'. This is the difference between a philosophy of 'It is', which begins with Being, and one grounded on 'I AM' which begins with an act of will, of self-realization.[49]

Coleridge criticized Schelling for failing to understand this point: 'Schelling overlooked the I AM in the Absolute—and then confounded the *Absolute* with *Nature*—identified Earth, yea Hell, with Heaven. He terrestrialized the celestial by the abortive attempt to celestialize the Terrestrial' (*CM* i. 138). This was the inevitable consequence of a philosophy that began either with Being, or, like that of Schelling and Oken, with an *irrational* will or mere spontaneous energy. Coleridge saw as inadequate a theory in which will was merely the necessity of self-realization through temporal succession, the source of becoming rather than of Being. This concept was barren in comparison with the idea of Will as personal, 'holy', an eternal unity. Just as the act of self-consciousness is (as Descartes, Kant, and Fichte had demonstrated with varying degrees of success, in his opinion) the only possible starting-point for human reason and knowledge, so, Coleridge insisted, the absolute, the I AM, is the only possible intelligible source of Being and Reason.

---

[48] See also ODI, fos. 6–7: 'an ineffable cycle of Being, Intelligence, & communicative Life, Love and Action'.
[49] McFarland, *Coleridge and the Pantheist Tradition*, 55–61.

His argument is clearly set out in note form in 1815 (*CN* iii, § 4265): 'Know essentially a verb active. If we know, there must be a somewhat known by us, KNOWLEDGE WITHOUT A CORRESPONDENT ⟨Reality⟩ is no KNOWLEDGE. In other words, TRUTH AND BEING ARE CORRELATIVES.' On this basis, Coleridge argued that if knowledge is not an endless Cycle of 'Interfusion of all particular Positions', without reality (and therefore not knowledge), there must be some Point of Reality on which all else depends. This ultimate Principle must be 'itself self-established, independent, known by its own Light, unconditional'. It must, as Absolute, involve 'the identity of its *Being*, and its being *Known* to be. Therefore, the ABSOLUTE **GROUND** OF **KNOWLEDGE** MUST *be* A **PRINCIPLE** *in which* BEING AND THOUGHT COINCIDE, EACH INVOLVING AND PRESUPPOSING the other.' Coleridge asserted that since all *Things* are dependent for their being and reality on something else ('An infinite Thing is a contradiction, equivalent to an indefinite Definite'), this Absolute Principle of Reality 'cannot be a Thing or Object'. Nor can it be found in a Subject, as opposed to an Object: all subjects require an object, and vice versa. As it can, then, be 'neither in Object or Subject, taken separately . . . it must be found in that which is neither Subject nor Object, but the identity of Both.—Such a Principle is the SUM or I AM, essentially: and its description is a definition of Self-consciousness, abstracting all degree.'

Coleridge makes the following distinction between divine self-realization and human self-consciousness: the possible response of the finite human being to the question of how he came to be might be: 'I am because God is' or 'I am because I am in God'; but in the Absolute 'the Principle of Being and of Self-knowledge coincide . . . I am because I affirm myself to be: I affirm myself to be, because I am—.' All other truths, Coleridge argued, are mediate, and are dependent upon 'this sole immediate Truth'. Any suggestion of a different, unconditional truth would involve the implication that it could be known without knowledge, an absurdity: 'All Truths therefore are but deduction from, or rather parts of the History of Self-Consciousness.' Coleridge insisted that the Absolute can only be thought through the necessary *structure* of thought, that is, in the subject–object relation. It is in itself a perfect Identity of subject and object, but it becomes Other, or Object to itself by a free act of Will, in self-consciousness. His conclusion is that 'All Modes of Knowle[d]ge are Parts of the Process, by which the Will becoming an Object for itself becomes *the* SUBJECT, and in this creation of the material of Thought & Intelligence is self-revealed as Intelligence' (*CN* iii, § 4265).

Being and Idea

Coleridge argued that the first Principle or Absolute is Will: 'A Will only can be Self-Conscious, and Self-consciousness is the primary Act of a Will in and in order to Self-manifestation.' The Absolute Will, as we have seen, is 'the ground and source of all being and as such is *super*-essential i.e. no-being' (N Fo, fo. 1). The Logos is Being, '*o ωv*'(N Fo, fo. 39), Truth and Reason, God's Idea of Himself, begotten through an act of Will. This was constantly reaffirmed by Coleridge in his later writings (particularly from 1820).[50] '*One*', he wrote to Hartley in 1820, 'could not manifest itself or be wittingly distinguished as One, but by the co-existence of an *Other* . . . A could not be affirmed to be A but by the perception that it is *not* B; and . . . this again implies the perception that B *is* as well as A' (*CL* v. 97). The point is, that 'we can become conscious of *Being* only by means of Existence', but when we *are* once aware of existence, we are forced to realize that Being is prior (in thought) to Existence. We have to see in order to realize that we have eyes; once seeing, we realize its impossibility had not the eyes first been there. So it is, claimed Coleridge, with the relations of Being and Existence as represented in the language of Christian symbolism, of a triune personal Godhead. The Son is Being manifested, communicated, and intelligible. When he is known, it becomes at the same time clear that he does not have the source of his Being within himself. Yet Coleridge described 'the co-eternal Logos, in and by which God is manifest to himself, & without which, we may dare affirm, God would not *be*—in the same sense as we might say, that a circle would not be without a centre & circumference' (*CM* i. 679).

This is the basis of his affirmation of the Logos as the Being of God. Being includes all relations which, in order of thought, are

---

[50] See *CL* vi. 632, 850; N Fo, fo. 39.

inexplicable unless first grounded in Act. It can only be any kind of an object for knowledge through its identity with the Principle or Idea 'I AM'; and it includes within itself the quality of 'having' (that is, it *has* itself as the object of self-consciousness, it *has* relationship, it *has* the power of self-manifestation and self-knowledge). Any philosophy which failed to recognize this was, in Coleridge's opinion, building on a false foundation. To begin with a principle of Absolute Being is an error akin to that made by the Understanding when it views the natural world as beginning with phenomena, instead of showing how the existence of phenomena may be demonstrated intelligibly (*CN* iii, § 4449). Being must be found to be one with Truth and Reason, and dependent upon the act of Self-realization and Self-consciousness. The relation of Mind and Being as the foundation for the reconciliation of thought and experience is set out by Coleridge in terms of the identity of the divine Idea and Being:

Mens infinita, vere ens, non potest non habere ideam sui omnino adequatam—
    Idea *adequata in totum* est ipsa vere ens. Deus est mens infinita, cui ergo adest idea sui omnino adequata et ipsa vere ens.* (*CL* iv. 632)

[* 'Infinite mind, truly being, cannot *not* have an entirely adequate idea of itself. An idea *adequate in every respect* is itself truly being. God is infinite mind, to whom therefore is present an entirely adequate idea of himself and itself truly being.']

Coleridge's view of the Logos as Being and Idea, the manifest Self of the Mind of God, is, then, a central theme in his modification of the philosophies of self-consciousness. Since the Logos is the archetype of the unity of Being and Thought in 'I AM', objectivity and concreteness, rather than being found in the self-manifestation of the Absolute in external finite reality, already exist in the distinction-in-unity of the Trinity. Hence Coleridge's description of Logos as '*deitas objectivà*', God as not only subjective Act, but as objective Reality (*LR* iii. 2). He ascribed to the Logos the whole 'Plenitude of Being', not, however, as a static perfection, but as Being which is the realization of Will in Reason. Neither Being nor Mind are, in this sense, Absolute. The Absolute Principle, as we shall see,[51] is Will; it is this which

---

[51] See below, Ch. 3.4.

most distinguishes Coleridge's philosophy from that of Hegel, with which otherwise it has much in common.[52] Both Hegel and Coleridge assert the reality of a supreme Idea which is the archetype of mind and being, and which is manifested in concrete and historical humanity. Yet, ultimately, Coleridge's search for synthetic unity is grounded in *Will*; not in an absolute primacy of Mind, but in 'personëity' and relationship. His 'system' therefore is not contained within the forms of rational thought, however comprehensively interpreted, and in this it differs markedly from the systems of Spinoza or Hegel, while sharing many of their philosophical insights.

Coleridge's inclusion of will, faith, and conscience as essential elements not only of religion but of philosophy itself does not conform to the usual understanding of the criteria and formal structure of a philosophical system. It points beyond the completion of the circle of logic to a more open and dynamic *spiral*[53] of thought which is existentially and relationally self-transforming, thought which paradoxically both reflects and creates the world, thus mirroring the activity of the divine Logos. Here again we find an explanation of Coleridge's enthusiasm for the analogy of the Word as a superb means of communicating this unifying principle of mind and being. Words are, for him, living, transformative, both formal and evolutionary. He saw human language as both the vehicle of ideas and, in some sense, creative of the world which it represents. In this it reflected the activity of the divine Logos, who is the Symbol, Communication, and Substance of the unity of subjective with objective, external reality. Constantly, Coleridge sought to show a common thread of agreement concerning this unity in the work of those past and contemporary thinkers whom he most admired. He attempted to demonstrate that this agreement centred around either early foreshadowings or direct expositions of the Idea of Logos, whether these were expressed in symbolism, or in the philosophical, psychological, or scientific language of his contemporaries. The 'Logosophia' would show, he hoped, that what was missing or incomplete in the efforts of thinkers from Heraclitus to Schelling was remedied and perfected by and in the Idea of Logos.

---

[52] See below, App. C.   [53] See above, Ch. 2.2.

3.3. IDEA AND LAW

The strength of Coleridge's conviction that ideas are living realities, the proper ground of philosophy and of the reconciliation between philosophy and religion, is evident in the following passage, written *circa* 1825–6:

Let me by all the labors of my life have answered but one end, if I shall have only succeeded in establishing the diversity of Reason and Understanding, and the distinction between the *Light* of Reason in the Understanding, viz. the absolute Principles presumed in all Logic and the conditions under which alone we draw universal and necessary Conclusions from contingent and particular facts, and the Reason itself, as the Source and birth-place of IDEAS, and ⟨therefore⟩ in its conversion to the Will the power of *Ultimate* Ends, of which Ideas only can be the Subjects; and if I shall have thus taught ... as many as have in themselves the conditions of learning the true import and legitimate use of the term, Idea, and directed the nobler and loftier minds of the rising generation to the incalculable *Value* of Ideas (and therefore of Philosophy which is but another name for the manifestation and application of Ideas) in *all* departments of knowledge, not merely technical and mechanic, and their indispensable presence in the Sciences that have a worth as well as a *Value* to the Naturalist no less than to the Theologian, to the Statesman no less than to the Moralist ... I shall have deserved the Character which the fervid Regard of my friend, Irving, has claimed for me, and fulfilled the high Calling, which he invokes me to believe myself to have received.[54] (*CN* iv, § 5293).

His emphasis on the importance of Ideas as living realities makes the description of his philosophical system as a purified form of 'the system of Pythagoras and Plato' (*BL* i. 263) particularly appropriate. The Idea, he wrote, 'is itself but a particular Form of the Absolute' (*CN* iv, §5294). Many of his definitions of Idea closely follow both Plato's concept of Idea or ideal Form (εἶδος)—the true dynamic substance and reality of thought and being; and Pythagoras' theory of Number, which, Coleridge believed, had been an attempt to raise the mind to the truth of

---

[54] Coleridge's relations with Edward Irving (1792–1834) were variable. Coleridge expected much from the latter, having heard him preach at the Chapel at Hatton Garden, but he was concerned at what he considered an excessive mysticism and tendency to fanaticism in some of Irving's work, such as the latter's extravagant interpretations of Daniel and Revelations. See *C & S* 141 n. 1.

Ideas by overcoming the common patterns of association within language (OM ii, fo. 209). Coleridge's Ideas are a unity of distinctions within divine Mind. They are universal, having their being within the One; yet they are distinct forms of this universal Truth. He described them as 'God's *ideas* of finite things, *the finite things* which originate in him but acquire separate existence'.[55] To the question, what is a divine Idea, he responded:

I know of no other answer than that a divine Idea is the Omnipresence or Omnipotence represented intelligentially in some one of the possible forms which are the plenitude of the divine Intelligence, the Logos or substantial adequate Idea of the Supreme Mind: and that as such the Ideas are necessarily immutable inasmuch as they are One with the co-Eternal Act, by which the absolute Will self-realised begets its Idea as the other Self—Or more comprehensively since the divine ideas are one with the eternal act by which the absolute Will is causative of its own reality & of whatever is necessarily begotten or proceeding out of that reality. (ODI, fos. 29–31)

Coleridge, in common, he believed, with Plato and some of those whom he called the 'Platonic Fathers',[56] identified the Logos as the Idea of God, containing and communicating the whole 'pleroma' of divine Ideas as the Forms of universal Truth. He described the Logos as 'God's *infinite idea of Himself an infinite thing eternally conceived*'.[57] It is hard to know what he means by an ideal 'thing' in this context. The term is perhaps employed in order to suggest the limitation and particularity of form and distinction. The relation between God's Idea of Himself in the Logos, and the 'pleroma' of the divine Ideas is expressed as follows: 'The Logos—or coeternal idea—feeling himself infinitely representative of God & infinitely happy in contemplation of himself as the absolutely infinite & perfect likeness of God was impelled by *infinite Love* to multiply finite images of Deity each happy in contemplating itself & the images around it —as being representative of Deity.'[58] This passage shows that the term 'idea'

[55] BL MS Egerton 2801, fo. 113.

[56] See *CN* iii, § 3814, and ii, §§ 2445, 2448. The idealism of the Neoplatonists influenced both Patristic (Clement of Alexandria, Origen, Augustine) and medieval theology (Eriugena). The Logos of the Fourth Gospel was often identified as the Idea of God, containing and communicating the whole pleroma of divine Ideas as the Forms of universal truth.

[57] BL MS Egerton 2801, fo. 113.   [58] Ibid.

must not be understood merely in terms of the rational intellect; Coleridge here included within it not merely cognitive, but affective, states such as 'feeling' and 'love'. His interpretation of this doctrine of classical Logos theology can thus be seen to go beyond the familiar tradition of Christian Platonism. By combining it with the insights of German idealism, and by advocating the primacy of Will, he developed a more dynamic theosophy of ideas than the blend of Platonism and Cartesianism which he had found in his early studies of, for example, Ralph Cudworth's *True Intellectual System* (1678).[59]

Logos: 'Idea of Ideas'

Plato had postulated an 'Idea of ideas'; ultimate truth which is one with the Good. Aristotle had identified the 'Thought of thought' of the *Primum Mobile*.[60] Coleridge's 'Idea of ideas' is, like that of Origen, the Son of God, the Logos of the Fourth Gospel. Notebook entries in which he expounded the nature of Reason as the truth of Ideas also contain frequent references to St John and to the 'life' and 'light' of Christ,[61] or to St Paul, whom he believed to have shown the identity of Idea and Law in Christ, the necessary relationship between moral being and the truth of Ideas (*C & S* 47). The New Testament Epistles, in Coleridge's view, disclose that 'St Paul's Christ (as the Logos) the eternal *Yea* (Cor. 2.1.) is the fontal Idea' (*Friend*, ii. 76 n 4.). Here, as so often, he easily interpreted Scripture in the light of his own scheme. In the Old Testament Scriptures, he suggested, the Idea is represented as Vision, and this is the meaning of the statement 'Where no Vision is, the people perisheth'(*C & S* 58).[62] This Vision was the presence of the divine Word to the mind and heart of God's people. Ideas should be understood in this sense. They must not be identified with concepts, mental pictures, sense impressions, or logical constructs; rather they are both the life of the mind itself and its 'light', the revelation of Reason communicated through interpersonal encounter and

---

[59] Coleridge had begun to read the second edition of Cudworth's *True Intellectual System of the Universe* (1743), as early as 1795; see *CN* i, § 200 n.

[60] See Plato's *Republic*, 508e, and Aristotle's *Metaphysics*, 1074^{b}35. For Origen's concept of the Logos as the 'Idea of ideas' see *Contra Celsum*, vi. 64.

[61] BL MS Egerton 2801, fo. 81^v.

[62] 'Where no Vision is, the people perisheth', a variation on Proverbs 29: 18.

exceeding the grasp of intellect alone. Indeed, the perfection of intellect itself, for Coleridge, depends upon moral and spiritual development in will, faith, conscience, and love.

He adopted a theme from Philo's thought which had been further developed in classical theology: that of God self-realized as Being in his Idea (of himself), the Other who is yet Self, the only begotten Son (Logos).[63] As Being, we have seen, he not only *is* but *has* Absolute Will, Reason, and Love. The divine Reason is communicated to human mind through the revelation of Ideas; the supreme revelation is that of the Idea of ideas, Logos. Revealer and revealed truth are therefore one and the same. Coleridge described Reason as 'a Participation of *Ideas*: & strictly speaking, it is no Faculty, but a Presence, an Identification of Being & Having' (*CM* i. 682). He had found this truth dimly reflected in Descartes's *cogito ergo sum* and in Fichte's 'I', but we have noted his dissatisfaction with their conclusions, and his aim to provide a more adequate ground of the truth of ideas, a transcendent principle (Logos) incarnate in mind and nature.

Coleridge used the term 'Ideas' in several distinct but connected senses. He refers, we have seen, to God's Idea of himself as Logos, the perfection of 'I AM', Reality, Being, and Truth; but any divine Idea within the pleroma of Logos, since it is a *particular* Form, as opposed to the perfect universal Absolute, is only 'real' 'inasmuch as it is one with that Will, which, as we see in its definition is verily Idem et Alter'. In this sense, the Idea is the symbol reversed. Whereas the symbol reveals the universal in the particular, the Idea is a *particular* form within the universal, the Absolute. He agreed with Lessing (*Erziehung der Menschengeschlechts*) that God's unity cannot exclude plurality, as distinction in unity. Lessing asks:

Must not God at least have the most perfect conception of himself, i.e. a conception which contains everything which is in him? But would everything be contained in him which is in him, if it contained merely a conception, merely the possibility even of his necessary reality? I think not. Consequently either God can have no perfect conception of himself at all, or this perfect conception is just as necessarily real (i.e. actually existent) as he himself is.[64]

---

[63] For Philo's influence here, see e.g. *TT* i. 34–5, *CL* iv. 850.

[64] G. E. Lessing, *Erziehung des Menschengeschlechts* (Berlin, 1780); tr. Henry Chadwick as *The Education of the Human Race* (London, 1956), 94.

Coleridge's argument, perhaps influenced by his reading of Lessing, is similar; he believed that it confirmed in philosophical terms the heart of the Prologue to the Fourth Gospel. God's Idea is 'a realizing knowledge, a knowledge causative of its own reality; in it is life and the life is the light of men'. The Idea is one with the self-realizing act of the divine Will, and God *is* in and by his knowledge of himself. Reality is all in him, not in abstract, but in *spiritual* form (ODI, fos. 29–31).

To say that God knows the Universal only, without knowing at the same time whatever is contained in the universal, whether as arising out of himself, or out of the relations which the involved realities must form & represent to each other, would be if possible more absurd than to attribute to a man perfect insight into a genus with an entire ignorance of its species. (ODI, fo. 35)

In the context of human thought, Coleridge argued, the Trinity is the Idea which is the ground and source of all Reason:

The Trinity is indeed the primary Idea, out of which all other Ideas are evolved—or as the Apostle says, it is the Mystery (which is but another word for Idea) in which are hidden all the Treasures of knowledge—But for this very case it is the example & representative of all Ideas—it is the common Attribute of all, that the Absolute exists in the plenitude of its eternal Forms, entire in each and indivisibly one in all. (*CN* iv, § 5294)

According to Coleridge, an Idea may be communicated immediately to the human mind as a kind of instinct, or it may be a clear and distinct Cartesian form, such as a geometrical idea. Ideas, he insisted, are not the merely rational, but are the living powers of the imagination, of all revelation and inspiration. Since their origin is will, they are not merely tools of the intellect:

The Idea may exist in a clear, distinct, definite form, as that of a circle in the Mind of an accurate Geometrician; or it may be a mere instinct, a vague appetency towards something which the Mind incessantly hunts for, but cannot find, like a name which escapes our recollection, or the impulse which fills the young Poet's eye with tears, he knows not why. In the infancy of the Human Mind all our ideas are instincts; and Language is happily contrived to lead us from the imperfect to the full and finished form: the boy knows that his hoop is round, and this, in after years, helps to teach him, that in a circle, all the lines drawn from the centre to the circumference are equal. It will be seen, in the sequel, that this distinction between the instinctive approach towards the Idea, and the Idea itself, is of high importance in Methodizing Art and Science.[65]

It was Coleridge's contention that the reconciliation of heart and head has its origin in the Logos as the supreme Idea. While the imagination of the poet or artist may first be a kind of instinctual inspiration in which the whole person is involved in a response of feeling, the work of the philosopher, scientist, or theologian is to distinguish between this feeling response and the Idea itself, to reconcile the subjectivity of Idea with its objectivity as Law.

The Identity of Idea and Law

Coleridge believed the empiricist philosophies of his own time were content, having presented the finite as self-subsistent, to trace the connections between phenomena; this was the basis of the 'mechanical philosophy'. This tracing of connections, he noted with obvious sarcasm, 'is called *accounting for things*'. Yet once the finite and infinite have been separated:

> there lies a chasm between them, which no Industry can fill up, no Imagination over-bridge. Here the Ideas intervene, as the Reconcilers: for herein is it an Idea, that it presents to the mind the Particular in the Universal, and is itself but a particular Form of the Absolute. Hence is the mind raised above the Concrete, and refuses to receive as Axioms of Necessary Being, or Criteria of Truth and Reality, the positions generalized from the imperfections and negations of the Concrete which does not exist there, because it exists *here*, which exists only partially in this point of space because it exists partially in another, but totally no where, and no when. (*CN* iv, § 5294)

Coleridge was convinced that the true meaning of the term 'idea' had, by his own time, been largely lost to British philosophy, which was doomed to degenerate as a consequence; for the true definition of philosophy is 'the Science of IDEAS in contra-distinction from CONCEPTIONS' (*CM* ii. 500) and this distinction was no longer observed.[66] As early as 1800 he complained of the

---

[65] Coleridge, *A Treatise on Method*, 4.

[66] Coleridge believed that, at the time of the Glorious Revolution, the 'Mechanico-corpuscular Theory' had begun to flourish, and its effect could be seen 'in the remarkable contrast between the acceptance of the word, Idea, *before* the Restoration, and the *present* use of the same word. *Before* 1660 the mag-

common failure to distinguish between 'idea' and 'image' (*CN* i, §634), and frequently blamed the influence of John Locke's philosophy for this. In 1804 he extended his criticism to Berkeley (*CN* i, §1842), arguing that it was no less a mistake to confuse Ideas with conceptions. The latter, according to Coleridge, rely on the evidence of the senses for their material and on the necessity of time-and-space-framed perceptions. He emphasized the distinction thus:

As Space to Places, so are Ideas to definite Conceptions (= Begriffen), As Places to the Forms and Bodies contained therein, so is a Conception to the Intuitions & Images.—Nothing ως εμοι γε δοκει,* can be closer or more quadrated than these two analogies—especially the latter.[67]

[* 'as it seems to me, at least']

Within the speculative intellect, conceptions have their place, but only within the wider context of the truth of Ideas. Referring to his *Logic*, intended as part of the 'Logosophia', Coleridge asserted that this distinction between Ideas and concepts was a part of Plato's own philosophy: 'the whole Doctrine of Ideas, sensu Platonico [in the Platonic sense], as different from notions, conception, and whatever else the Understanding forms on the Data delivered by the Senses or acquired by reflection on it's own processes' (*CL* v. 275). In the *Parmenides*, Plato had rejected the notion that *eidos* might be comprehended as concept.[68] Coleridge insisted on the impossibility of forming a conception of an Idea (*CN* iv, §5294). An Idea is not an abstract representation of an object in thought, on the contrary: 'By an idea, I mean (in this

nificent *Son of Cosmo* was wont to discourse with FICINO, POLITIAN and the princely MIRANDULA on the IDEAS of Will, God, Freedom.' Philip Sydney, and Spenser, wrote Coleridge, had written on the 'IDEA of the Beautiful', and 'the younger ALGERNON—Soldier, Patriot, and Statesman–with HARRINGTON, MILTON, and NEVIL on the *IDEA of the STATE*'. In stark contrast, '*Dr* HOLOFERNES, in a lecture on metaphysics, delivered at one of the Mechanic's Institutions, explodes all *ideas* but those of sensation; and his friend, DEPUTY COSTARD, has no *idea* of a better flavored haunch of venison, than he dined off at the London Tavern last week' (*C & S*, 65–6).

[67] BL MS Egerton 2801, fo. 79.
[68] Plato, *Parmenides*, 132b f. 'The *eide* remain *onta* (things that are), they are not *nöemata* (thoughts) in the soul' (see Seligman, *Being and Not-Being*, 2; Seligman quotes from J. Stenzel's *Plato's Method of Dialectic*, tr. and ed. D. J. Allen (New York, 1964), 57).

instance) that conception of a thing, which is not abstracted from any particular state, form, or mode, in which the thing may happen to exist at this or at that time; nor yet generalised from any number or succession of such forms or modes; but which is given by the knowledge of its ultimate aim' (*C & S* 17). Concepts may be regulative, but Ideas are *constitutive*. 'An Idea is not simply knowledge or perception as distinguished from the thing perceived: it is a realizing knowledge, a knowledge causative of its own reality; in it is Life, & the life is the light of men' (ODI, fo. 3). Once again Coleridge identified the source of the constitutive power of Ideas—the 'Idea of Ideas'—with the creative Word, through his interpretation of the Fourth Gospel; and again the inspiration for his attempted integration of epistemology, etymology, and a philosophy of language is clear.

This aspect of the constitutive power of Ideas is, in fact, central to his whole system: 'whether ideas are regulative only, according to Aristotle and Kant; or likewise constitutive, and one with the power and life of Nature according to Plato and Plotinus is the highest *problem* of philosophy, and not part of its nomenclature' (*SM: LS* 114). Kant's failure to resolve the dichotomy of phenomena and noumena was the consequence, so Coleridge believed, of failing to recognize Ideas as constitutive. Kant, in his opinion, had not seen that the active principle of will is as much the 'parent' of Ideas as the speculative reason:

Kant's πρωτοψευδος,* the derivation of *Ideas* from the speculative Reason *entirely*, for the *behoof* indeed of the practical Reason and Active Principle, but not by *means* thereof, or in conjunction therewith: which latter is nevertheless the true and platonic theory of Ideas. Kant supposed the Ideas to be the *Oscillations* of the same Imagination, which working determinately produces the Mathematical Intuitions, line, circle etc.—a sort of total impression made by successive constructions, each denied or negatived as soon as made—and yet the constructive power still beginning anew—Whereas according to the true platonic view, the Reason and Will are the Parents . . . and the Idea itself the transcendent Analogon of the Imagination or die spirituelle Anschauung—spiritual Intuition.[69]

[* 'fundamental error']

---

[69] Notes on Tennemann's *Geschichte der Philosophie*, vi. 45, written on back flyleaves.

Thus Coleridge's view presents a strong contrast to that of Kant:

an Idea . . . must unite in itself the Speculative and the Practical, an identity of Subject and Object, which does not (as the merely speculative Faculty does) require an object out of itself, but has its own Being for its' Object.[70]

He maintained that Idea and Law are (respectively) the subjective and the objective forms of reality: 'a law and an idea are correlative terms and differ only as object and subject, as being and truth'.[71] Idea and Law each have their source in unity of Will and Reason: 'there being indeed no other difference between Law & Idea than that, Will (or Power) & Intelligence being the constituents of both, in the [*idea* we contemplate the Will or power in the form of intelligence; and in the] *law* we contemplate the intelligence in the form of Will or power' (ODI, fo. 33).

In the *Friend*, he argued that philosophy was 'bipolar', concerned with, at the one pole, 'the science of intellect' (as in the work of Plato), and at the other with the 'material pole, as the science of nature' (the area of Francis Bacon's work). It should not surprise us 'that Plato so often calls ideas LIVING LAWS, in which the mind has its whole true being and permanence; or that Bacon, vice versa, names the laws of nature, *ideas*; and represents what we have . . . called *facts of science* and *central phenomena*, as signatures, impressions, and symbols of ideas' (*Friend*, i. 492). His system was grounded in the judgement that 'Idea and Law are the Subjective and Objective Poles of the same Magnet—i.e. of the same living and energizing Reason. What is an Idea in the Subject, i.e. in the Mind, is a Law in the Object, i.e. in Nature' (ibid. 497 n.). No understanding of nature is possible without the attempt to universalize the many and various manifestations of a phenomenon under an efficient law which 'in a thousand different forms is evermore one and the same; entire in each, yet comprehending all, and incapable of being abstracted or generalized from any number of phænomena, because it is itself presupposed in each and all as their common ground and condition' (*Friend*, i. 467). The 'common ground and condition' of the forms of nature is Law; this, in the world of mind, is Idea.

Indeed, Ideas, Coleridge argued, are the objective Laws in

---

[70] BL MS Egerton 2801, fo. 82.
[71] *Friend*, i. 467: 'Essays on the Principles of Method'; and *AR* 171 n.

nature; they are also the true forms, the objective a priori being, of mind. Here he seems to have drawn on Kant's categories.[72] Thus Ideas are 'in the world of the intellect not as a result of sensation or unsubstantial product of volition' (OM i, fo. 20). Conversely, just as Ideas are also the active powers of mind as subject, as laws they are the active, dynamic, 'subjective' powers in nature 'acting in the world of the senses yet not as an object of sense' (ibid.). In Ideas, the opposition of the 'inner' life of mind and the 'outer' life of nature is reconciled: 'In the Soul [the idea] must exist as a nature[,] in Nature as a Soul.' According to Coleridge's theory, 'where it is not contemplated as Idea it presents itself as Law[,] where not as Law ever as Idea of that which cannot be conceived of in the subjective other than as objective or in the objective otherwise that as subjective'; he gave as an example the geometrical idea of the circle.[73] In *Aids to Reflection* he described the Idea as itself the 'mesothesis', or point of indifference of the subjectively real (as thesis) and the objectively real (as antithesis), both these having their source in the Absolutely Real (the 'Prothesis') (*AR* 170–1).

Logocentric Idealism

We see that Ideas, for Coleridge, are the ground of human reason, they are 'the living Truths, that may be re-excited but cannot be expressed by words, the Transcendents that give the Objectivity to all Objects, the Form to all Images, yet are themselves untranslatable into any Image, unrepresentable by any particular Object' (N 52, fo. 5ᵛ). It is 'the common character, the criterion and diagnostic of Ideas, that they are *expressible* only by two positions the one of which affirms what the other denies—

---

[72] For Kant's development of the subjective–objective reconciliation through the categories of human reason, see e.g. *Critique of Pure Reason*, A 77–83, 96–114; B 102–9.

[73] See OM i, fos. 20 ff. Coleridge explains that the physical points which constitute a circle and are called parts 'by anticipation' must in one sense pre-exist relatively to the circle. But on the other hand, 'as parts of that circle, namely as mental phenomena, they presupposed the circle, deriving the very principle of their constituence, by which they first became Parts of that particular character, from the Idea = Circle'. He shows that both mechanistic and organic principles are necessary in understanding the relation of parts to the whole, and insists that this relation shows the Idea to be 'both in the mind and in nature equally objective' (OM ii, fo. 246 n.).

the discursive faculty confessing, as it were, the transcendence and alien nature of the Truth strives by words to *suggest* what no words can indeed *express*' (N 34, fo. 12ᵛ).

The truth of Ideas, revealed to the senses only as contradictions, is found in clearest form in the supreme paradox of the God-Man, the incarnate Logos. This is beyond the understanding and impossible to grasp without a steady hold on the truth of Ideas (*CN* iv, § 5292).

Ideas, Coleridge argued, have their roots beyond the speculative intelligence, in the mystery of 'personëity'.[74] This root is deeper than all intelligence and cannot be comprehended, only contemplated. Thus he concluded that 'in Prayer alone can the reality of the Idea be found'. Only in the Idea is the paradox resolved in which man is recognized both as free agent, and yet, at the same time, acted upon and thus causally determined. Through Ideas, the solution is found to the apparent contradiction of man as '[conquering] for himself what is yet bestowed upon him of free grace'. It is a matter, again, of revelation as encounter, the Word heard and acted upon; of self-reflection which reveals the distinction between a ·'phantom self'[75] and a Self the truth of which is with God. Revelation leads to the choice for this true Self.

While the Idea could not be expressed in the linear, 'either–or', sequential forms of the Understanding or through 'syllogistic logic', except as contradiction, it might profitably be contemplated through the symbol of a circle. In a note written in 1826, Coleridge admitted that

the characteristic Formula of all *Spiritual* Verities or Ideas is an apparent *Circle*—i.e. a proposition which [if] predicated of Things or Conceptions, περι αισθητων, η περι λογων (εννοιων των λογικων)* would produce a vicious circle in Logic . . . an appearance of contradiction is the . . . necessary consequence of applying the Understanding to the immediate Truths of Reason, in other words, of the attempt to *conceive* what being simple & unique is essentially *inconceivable* . . . by admitting this circle in the first instance, and only by admitting it we avoid all future circles, and obtain a staple of a chain logical in all its Links (*CN* iv, § 5377).

[* 'of percepts, or of *logoi* (logical conceptions)']

---

[74] See below, Ch. 4.2.
[75] See below, Ch. 4.3.

The Idea could only be correctly understood as 'Spiritual Act'. The formula was: 'A is the Cause of B, in so far as B is the Cause of A' (ibid.). Later in the same notebook Coleridge explored further the circle as symbol of the Idea: 'A Point expanding or repeating itself in all directions, yet abiding entire in itself designates the Idea', and 'The Divine Power is a Sphere, whose *Center* is *everywhere* and its circumference *nowhere*' (*CN* iv, § 5406). That the Idea 'is a Truth bearing in itself the insight of its' own necessity' (N 50, fo. 34ᵛ) is again a 'circle' of reason. Freedom and necessity, polar opposites found as contradictions in the finite world, are one in Ideas: 'the Idea contains its necessity in its actual presence. The *so it must be* is involved in the *So it is*' (N 37, fo. 44ᵛ). In 1826 Coleridge reminded himself of the immense significance of an 'ideal Realism' which could show that the future hope of humanity lay in the reality of Ideas as the reconciliation of reason, faith, conscience, experience, and feeling: 'Mem: on the dignity and lofty Hope of the human Being on the hypothesis of *Ideas*—ταις γαρ ιδεαις ουσια αιδιος ενεστι, αρχας προμαθεστατας' ('for an eternal being resides in the ideas, the most providential principles') (*CN* iv, § 5296).

Coleridge's philosophy is idealist in so far as he regarded Ideas as their own evidence, 'as light is the only evidence of light' (ODI, fo. 93). An Idea 'implies the reality of that to which it corresponds as well as its own formal truth' (ODI, fo. 229). It is important here to bear in mind the distinction which he stressed between Idea and concept or image. He was, of course, not suggesting that any concept or thought necessarily has some correspondent objective reality; but rather that Ideas are of a different kind altogether. They are 'knowledges immediate, yet real, and herein distinguished *in kind* from logical and mathematical truths, which express not realities, but only the necessary *forms* of conceiving and perceiving and are therefore named the *formal* or *abstract* sciences. Ideas, on the other hand, or the truths of philosophy, properly so called, correspond to substantial beings, to objects whose actual subsistence is *implied* in their idea, though only *by* the idea revealable' (*C & S* 47). There is here a Cartesian element, a hint of 'clear and distinct ideas'. The German Idealists had developed the 'I am' as one such Idea, and had gone further (for example, in the case of Fichte), suggesting that it constituted its own reality and was itself the reconciliation of subject and object, finite and infinite. Yet Coleridge did not recognize the Idea as a merely subjective reality. He asserted 'the reality of the existence of distinct beings in the plenitude of the Supreme Mind, whose essence is Will and whose actuality consists in their being one with the Will of God. That this is compatible with the perfect unity of the absolute Will we are assisted in conceiving by the analogy of the predominant thought or ideas in our own minds' (ODI, fo. 89). The language of this passage, like many others, reflects Coleridge's attempts to reconcile themes in Philo, Origen, and Neoplatonism with elements of idealist philosophy. He maintained that the 'I am' which Descartes recognized as the first step for philosophy is necessarily an a priori given, a revelation. As such, it involves a host of Ideas or spiritual realities without which it cannot stand. It involves the concept of the noumenal, and is dependent upon a transcendent 'I AM' in which it participates and which is mediated and communicated to it. It is only, he insisted, through an understanding of the 'I AM' as divine Idea, and of the ground of will and relationship which underlies it, that the human self can be truly discerned and human reason grasp the nature of the reality of ideas. His system is not a purely logical construction built, like Kant's, on the necessity of ideas and of the ideal relations on which reason depends; it goes further to develop a theory of Ideas which takes account of the importance of psychological and moral factors. Ideas, he argued, are constitutive of human personality (*C & S* 47 ff.): 'For try to conceive a *man* without the ideas of God, eternity, freedom, will, absolute truth, of the good, the true, the beautiful, the infinite. An *animal* endowed with a memory of appearances and of facts might remain. But the *man* will have vanished.' A mind which only recognized phenomenal appearance, the outward mechanisms of cause and effect, the relativisms of subjectivity, did not constitute a human person, merely an individual.

Despite his many criticisms of 'eclectic' or Neoplatonic philosophy,[76] Coleridge admired Plotinus' further development of Plato's theory of Ideas. Plato's Ideas, lacking any positive explanation, could only lead to an irreconcilable dualism. Plotinus provided a more adequate account of the mediation necessary

[76] See ODI, fos. 181–3; *CN* iii, § 3825; and *PL* 249–50, 265–6.

between Ideas as eternal spiritual and formal realities and the substance of the finite world. Coleridge believed this to be the 'Influence of Christianity in Plotinus: God as the real ground both of substance and form—while Plato, in the public writings at least, was a Dualist. In short, Plotinus derived the phænomena of extension from the representative powers, by means of spiritual intercommunion'.[77] Plotinus' Logos is an intermediary between the One and the world of the finite. 'While Plato names and assumes the reality of the Ideas, he gives little more than an explanation of what they are *not*'; Coleridge believed that Plotinus, on the other hand, gave 'a *clear* and *positive* exposition of *Ideas*'.[78] Coleridge's own concept of their constitutive and dynamic nature developed this theme of mediation and of the positivity of Ideas in a later margin note to Jacob Böhme's work:

Εκ Περισσω Θεοτητος.* In the Logos, or adequate Idea of the divine Beings, all Ideas possible according to Wisdom, and Goodness (which is truly all that can be meant by the words 'in the nature of Things': for nature is the Creature of God, and to be the One, the Good, the Wise, is God's nature) in the Son, I say, are contained all possible Ideas *eminenter*. But in him all are as one/ yet even as the divine act of Self-consciousness gave substantial Essence to his great Idea, even so all the included Ideas produced existing Images of themselves in the power and thro' the free goodness of Deity/ for it was better that they should be, than not be. But yet by *existence*, i.e. *stare extra*, they of necessity became *finite*, & therefore *inadequate*, Images of their Prototypes in the divine mind; and as finite derived their distinguishing ⟨& separate⟩ Natures from *not-Being*: as Plato has set forth almost inspiredly. Hence the Chasm infinitely infinite between Deity and the Creatur[e]. (*CM* i. 573)
[* 'Out of the Superabundance of Divinity']

Coleridge believed that Kant was far from 'the true platonic view' in reducing ideas to abstractions and speculations; and in extending 'the difference between logical and real verity beyond the demonstrative faculties into the Intuitive',[79] so that, as a result, ideas become merely regulative. Schelling, he agreed, was

[77] BL MS Egerton 2801, fo. 33.
[78] Notes on Tennemann, vi, written on back flyleaves.
[79] Notes on Tennemann, vi. 299, written on front flyleaf.

right to see the error here and to insist that 'what is affirmed to be intuitive, cannot be expected to be demonstrated: for the Truths are supposed to be those, de quibis alia monstrantur [from which others are shown]'. However, while Schelling may have better understood the nature of Ideas, his system was basically flawed. His Absolute was 'no Idea, but a pure Abstraction' involving an Identity which was yet an opposition of ideal and real, a fundamentally false position, Coleridge believed, on which to ground philosophy. The Idea 'must be opposed not to the *Real*, but to the *Phænomenal*' (*CN* iv, § 5295).

For Schelling, the restoration of the Idea as the synthesis of ideal and real, of finite and infinite, is achieved through human self-consciousness, and, more perfectly, through the reconciliation of conscious and unconscious in the work of creative genius. Coleridge, in contrast, maintained that this reconciliation was achieved, not in the self-consciousness of an unregenerate self, the 'mind of the flesh',[80] but in the source of all polarity, Logos, who, containing the mystery of the two natures, transforms contradiction into opposition. Schelling's original opposition, we have seen, is contained within the Absolute: Reason is realized through an *irrational* principle or 'moment' of self-defection in the Absolute and which he represents as true freedom,—even freedom from Self. This is the conclusion of his work *Philosophische Untersuchungen über das Wesen der menschlichen Freiheit* (1809).[81] Here the divine Will is separated (even if ultimately to be reunited) from the divine Reason, a hypothesis unacceptable to Coleridge. He accused Schelling of confusion and groundless abstractions projected as self-activating potencies. No adequate explanation was given of the original Fall of Ideas; no explanation of the power within these potencies nor of the separation of Will from Reason. Coleridge, on the other hand, argued that the original separation from God could only be grounded in the realization of a possibility which was itself eternal but which sought, in apostasy, to become self-actual and, so seeking, had no part in the divine Being.[82] The Unity of God as 'Wisdom,

---

[80] Coleridge writes in his 'Essay on Faith': 'when the understanding in its *synthesis* with the personal will, usurps the supremacy of the reason . . . it is then what St Paul calls the mind of the flesh' (*LR* iv. 433).

[81] *Of Human Freedom*, 33–6.

[82] See above, Ch. 2.1 and 2.2.

Holiness and Love' is uncompromised, he argued,[83] by the apostatic act, which was not the first stage in a self-realizing process of history, but, on the contrary, self-defeating. Further, this was the only explanation consistent with the experience and *fact* of evil.

Coleridge, unlike Schelling, believed that divine Ideas were never separated from their source, the Idea of God (Reason, Logos). Manifested as the instruments of creation in the laws and powers of nature, they are also the communication of light and life in the revelation of Reason to human consciousness. The presence of Ideas to the mind is the presence of Logos. For Coleridge, the 'aweful consequence' of the truth of Ideas, and of the Logos—the ideal reality of Substance and Subject—is that the mind's grasp of actuality is dependent upon the communication of Ideas and therefore on the divine presence:

whatever actually is, even for ourselves, is this wholly & solely by the presence of the Deity to the mind & that sense itself as if it were an opake reason is possible only by a communion with that life which is the light of men, which lighteth every man that cometh into the world, & without which the solar light would be a contradiction in thought, a powerless power, a light that is darkness—this idea, next to that of the Will, or rather with it, is the great master key, not only of all speculative science[,] physical as well as metaphysical. Without a clear apprehension of truth, and such as the mind can rest on with inward quiet, even the conception of the absolute Will as conveyed logically in the definition so often repeated, is neither safe nor worthy the name of an idea. (ODI, fo. 63)

Beyond Empiricism: Beyond Abstraction

The Coleridgean (as the Hegelian) 'Idea' is problematic as regards the ontological circles which are involved in any attempt to comprehend it. For example, Coleridge's point that the only appropriate formula to express the inherently circular relationships of mind, reason, truth, and being in the Idea is 'that *One* could not manifest itself or be wittingly distinguished as One, but by the co-existence of an *Other*' or that 'we know A by B: and B by A' (*CL* v. 97–8)[84] represents the kind of statement which was

---

[83] MS notes inserted between the leaves of Schelling's *Philosophische Schriften*; Coleridge comments on pp. 123–4.

[84] See also *CN* iv, § 5377, fos. 45–6.

condemned by many of his contemporaries and later critics. In Britain, where empiricism, mechanism, and materialism were becoming the pillars of the philosophical edifice, and where Kant's new form of 'transcendental' logic was still little known and even less welcomed, Coleridge's complexity of thought and expression appeared nonsense, a mere jumble of contradictions, abstractions, and illegitimately grounded religious dogma. Walter Pater, for example, rejected his attempt to reconcile the 'other-worldliness' of religion with a philosophical system centred on humanity. Pater scathingly dismissed parallels drawn between the external being of the natural world and the life and forms of the mind: 'the suspicion of a mind latent in nature, struggling for release and intercourse with the intellect of man through true ideas, has never ceased to haunt a certain class of minds'. This occurs, he asserted 'wherever a speculative instinct has been united with extreme inwardness of temperament, as in Jacob Böhme, there the old Greek conception, like some seed floating in the air, has taken root and sprung up anew'.[85]

Coleridge anticipated such criticism and was careful to claim the support of experience. The reality of ideas in the mind could not be denied; neither could the experience of present-moment choice as the experience of free will; nor the recognition, in the study of the physical forms of nature, that life was more than, and must indeed be presupposed in, organization. Even the existence of physical laws, such as that of gravitation, presupposed, he claimed, a reality beyond the merely phenomenal. Given the legitimacy (the necessity, he argued) of metaphysical speculation on this ground, certain questions must be central to human inquiry and could not be ignored. These were concerned with definitions of terms which '*include* all the difficulties which the human mind can propose for solution' (*BL* i. 235). These terms included 'body' and 'matter'; 'spirit or power'; 'nature'

---

[85] 'Coleridge's Writings', *Westminster Review*, 86 (1866), 119. Coleridge is again perhaps ahead of his time here. He might have found more sympathy had W. H. Walsh been a contemporary, since Coleridge's philosophical arguments often proceed by the establishment of what seem similar to Walsh's 'colligatory concepts'. Walsh uses these to repudiate the idea that philosophical or historical explanation must be of the same type as that employed in the thinking of physical scientists. 'Colligation' is the tracing of connections, of intimate 'inner' relations between ideas or events (*An Introduction to Philosophy of History*, 3rd edn. (London, 1976), 23).

(active or passive); 'mind'; 'subject and object' (*PL* 370–3); in *Biographia Literaria*, the list includes 'space, time, cause and effect, consciousness, perception, memory and habit' (*BL* i. 234). Any philosophy which, without further investigation, took all these for granted was, in Coleridge's opinion, not worthy of the name. It was necessary to discover whether these terms represented ideas which are merely regulative of experience or whether in some way ideas themselves were actually constitutive of it. He argued that ideas were indeed constitutive of both subjective and objective reality through the very polarities which they involved. Just as the polarities of ideas (as manifested in the forces within nature) are generative of a *tertium aliquid*, so the oppositions through which ideas are expressed in human thought generate self-consciousness (through the opposition of self and other), language, human discourse, and philosophy itself—the love of and pursuit of Reason (Logos).

Coleridge was adamant that not only is scepticism an untenable position, since 'the Idea contains its' necessity in its' actual presence' (N 37, fo. 44ᵛ), but so too is a dogmatism, which excludes all mystery, since the ideas of Reason must always be rooted in an eternal possibility which remains (*as* possibility) mysterious.[86] Where there is mystery, faith is involved; but this act of faith is consistent, he claimed, with reason and confirmed by the facts of experience.

Although the Coleridgean theory of Ideas agrees with Cartesian and idealist philosophy that self-consciousness is the birth of reason, Descartes's *cogito ergo sum* and the 'I' of German idealism are rejected as flawed because they failed to maintain the importance of the distinction between the divine Humanity (Logos) and finite human consciousness (logos). Coleridge admitted Descartes's postulate—the *cogito*—as true only of the transcendent Self, whose Being *is* indeed realized in the begetting of his Idea of himself, and in whom, as Idea, is contained all objective reality. It must be understood as only derivatively true of the human self, of the human indwelt by the Logos. German idealism, on the other hand, appeared to offer either a self whose ideas have no correspondent objective reality, no positivity of 'otherness',[87] or a self whose ideas can never attain to a knowledge of

---

[86] See above, Ch. 1.2.
[87] Coleridge criticizes Fichte on this ground (*BL* i. 158–9).

ultimate reality,[88] or again, a self whose ideas inexplicably pass through a separation from Reason in order to produce the forms of the external world, and whose self-realization is dependent on this alienation. This was a phantom self, dependent upon 'it is' rather than 'Thou art'.[89]

The issue of the nature and existence of the self was recognized long before Descartes as integral to any theory of Ideas and problematic for both philosophy and theology. Augustine, for example, had attempted to solve it by using doubt itself to establish the undeniable certainty of at least one truth: 'Si fallor, sum'.[90] For Coleridge, on the other hand, neither thinking nor doubting but *willing* is the ground on which existence is established; it is the source of the reality of Ideas. It demands a metaphysic, since it cannot be explained by those things which, in fact, proceed from it (i.e. phenomena). His concept of the primacy of will distinguishes his theory of Ideas from those within the Greek and Cartesian traditions, and, finally, from Hegelian idealism. As we turn now to Coleridge's theory of Will, we shall discover how it determines his idea of the Logos revealed in Christ 'as the filial Godhead' who 'is essentially & from everlasting was Will = Reason' (N 44, fos. 62^v–63). This Will–Reason unity is the basis of his 'dynamic system'. The *active* subject has become, after Kant, a commonplace of philosophical and scientific speculation, but it was Coleridge's bold—now almost shocking— submission that only in the reality of the Christian Logos as Principle and Person was this concept fully reconcilable with objective reality.

3.4. 'WILL IN A FORM OF REASON'

Coleridge's deep interest in the will is evident even in his early writings.[91] One of the most significant developments in the

---

[88] This is Kant's failure, according to Coleridge; he accuses the former of '*barren* Dualism' (*CM* iii. 291).

[89] For Coleridge's criticisms of Schelling on this score, see BL MS Egerton 2801, fo. 75; also *CN* iii, § 4449, and *CL* iv. 873–6.

[90] 'If I am in error, [then] I am [i.e. I exist].' (Augustine, *De libero arbitrio*, ii. 3. 7).

[91] For Coleridge's views on this point, see e.g. *CN* i. § 1826 (Jan. 1804) and *LPR* 107 and n., where he explores the difference between a moral and a physical evil.

'logosophic' system was his rejection of those explanations of will which proclaimed it to be the result of certain causal conditions.[92] From being himself a committed 'necessitarian' by his own admission (*CL* i. 213), he became instead an advocate of the metaphysical nature and origin of the will. He concluded, as we shall see, that will was properly synonymous with *free* will. Clearly, his moral philosophy and his psychological and religious thought were influenced by this development; of greater interest still is its effect on his exploration of the epistemological role of will (as choice, as self-determining power, and as act) in relation to Reason.

The process of this change in Coleridge's thinking can be traced in his notes, written following an intense study of Kant's philosophy in 1803–4. In January 1804 he wrote of his concern: 'my Hope of making out a radical distinction between... Volition & Free Will or Arbitrement, & the detection of the Sophistry of the Necessitarians / as having arisen from confounding the two' (*CN* i, § 1827). By 1804 he was convinced, following Fichte, that will, reason, and love have no determined origin: 'The Will = the Ego is the prime mover—& what is Reason?—And Love too—No! that too is no Creature of Pain & Pleasure' (*CN* ii, § 2058). In 1805 his full acceptance of Trinity, based on a final conviction that the Logos is God and one with God coeternally, followed his study of Kant's concept of the unity of God, as *der Wille*, with God as Logos, Reason.[93] His reading of Kant contributed to what he described as 'the most important of all the truths that have been vouchsafed to me!', the divine unity of Will and Reason in the Logos, 'the will, which is the reason,—Will in the form of Reason' (*CM* iii. 720). Elsewhere he makes the same point in language which attempts to reconcile philosophy with theology, describing the Logos (according, he wrote, to St John's example) as 'THE WORD relatively to the Eternal Mind, the Reason, the living self-subsistent Reason;

---

[92] David Hartley, for example, had suggested that the will was determined by physical factors (*Observations on Man*); for Coleridge's response see *BL* i. 110. See also Coleridge's description of Hartley's error concerning the will (*CN* iii, § 3587).

[93] Coleridge would have found this in his reading of Kant's *Grundlegung zur Metaphysik der Sitten*, 4th edn. (Riga, 1797), preface, 8 ff.

relatively to the Absolute Will & as its only adequate Exponent'.[94] Coleridge's theory of will shows the influence of many of the thinkers whom he most admired;[95] Milton is one such, as is shown by a reference to the individual will 'or the Will considered as the principle of personality and free-agency, and which under the sanction of Milton's authority we might venture to distinguish by the term *Arbitrement* "free in thine own arbitrement it lies" *Paradise Lost*'.[96] But there is no doubt that one of the chief influences was the work of Immanuel Kant, which, following his return from Germany in 1799, Coleridge began to study closely. This intensified his preoccupation with the relation between will and reason. He was unconvinced, however, by Kant's concept of the unity of will and practical reason:

> Der Wille, says Kant, ist nichts anderes, als practische Vernunft.[*] This I doubt / My will & *I* seem perfect Synonimes—whatever does not apply to the first, I refuse to the latter /—Any thing strictly of outward Force I refuse to acknowledge, as done *by* me / it is done *with* me. Now I do not feel this perfect synonimousness in Reason & the Wille. I am sure, Kant cannot make it out. Again & again, he is a wretched Psychologist.
>
> Yet it is, doubtless, a most abstruse Subject, In all inevitable Truths, e.g. that the two sides of a Δ are greater than the third, I feel my will active: I seem to *will* the Truth, as well as to perceive it. Think of this! (*CN* i, § 1717)
>
> [* 'The Will . . . is nothing other than practical Reason']

Coleridge adopted Kant's concept of the rational will: 'the spirit of a man, or the spiritual part of our being, is the intelligent Will: or (to speak less abstractly) it is the capability, with which the Father of Spirits hath endowed man of being determined to action by the *ultimate ends*, which the reason can present' (*C & S* 123). Although he came to agree with Kant that the Ideal Man is a perfect unity of reason and will, he believed reflection, experience, and conscience revealed finite humanity, in its state of self-alienation, to be incapable of realizing this unity from

---

[94] Coleridge's annotations on an endleaf of Heinrich Steffens, *Ueber die Idee der Universitäten* (Berlin, 1809).

[95] For example, Coleridge recognized that the nature and function of the will, and the issue concerning its freedom, are central themes for Augustine and Luther (N 26, fos. 12–16), for Jacob Böhme (*CM* i. 689–94), for William Law (*CN* iii, § 3354), and for F. H. Jacobi (*CM* iii. 75–6).

[96] OM ii. fo. 1.

within itself. We have seen his attempt to reconcile the language of *natural* philosophy with that of religion and the truth of Ideas: a redemptive act was necessary to free the will from its attachment to the ground of nature; thereby not only humanity, but the whole creation *through* humanity (as St Paul had taught), would be redeemed: 'as Man finds his redemption from the Captivity of his own Will in the Divine Humanity, so (we are assured by the Apostle) does the whole inferior Creation, which fell not willingly, seek, yea, yearn and groan (i.e. significantly, tho' inarticulately, utter its desire) for Redemption in the Human Animal' (*CN* iv, § 4984).[97] Coleridge makes a distinction of crucial importance to his system between the mysterious Absolute Will and Will realized as a unity with Reason in God.[98]

Absolute Will

Coleridge has been accused of distorting orthodox Trinitarianism by suggesting a fourth Principle in his idea of God.[99] This he expressed in the *tetractys* figure by placing *Absolute* Will as Prothesis (realized in and possessed by God as *self-realized* Will: thesis), God as begotten Idea and Being (God the Son: antithesis), and God as *Godhead*, that is, the Community of Love (the Spirit: Synthesis).[100] Yet he repeatedly emphasized that the Prothesis of Will is 'an Absolute Identity antecedent in order of Thought, to the unity of Personal Being . . . the ground and eternal Antecedent of all Being, even of its' own' (N 41, fo. 82ᵛ). Only in the necessary order of human thought (unable itself to comprehend what is by its nature beyond being and thought) can (and must) the Absolute be understood as *prior* to God self-realized in Trinity; it must never be identified with *Being*. The Absolute 'All-might' which is 'Super-Relative' (*CM* ii. 881) is a concept which draws on the mysterious Ground of Godhead expressed in Christian mysticism; in, for example, Böhme's writings; and in those of the Hermetic and cabbalistic traditions.

---

[97] Here Coleridge paraphrases St Paul, Rom. 8: 22.

[98] In his insistence that the Absolute is beyond being, Coleridge again echoes an element of John Scotus Eriugena's thought; the *Qui plus quam esse est*. See *De Divisione Naturae*, i. 25.

[99] Newsome, *Two Classes of Men*, appendix C, 109.

[100] *TT* i. 77; also *CM* ii. 880.

It is origin and power, realized only in and as the Triune God; Father, Son, and Spirit. Thus the first principle of Coleridge's 'logosophic' system is, paradoxically, *beyond* all system in that it is neither Reason nor Being, but Will: 'The Will, the absolute Will, is that which is essentially causative of reality, essentially & absolutely . . . boundless from without & from within. This is our first principle, this is the position contained in the postulate of the reality of Will at all' (ODI, fo. 21).

Coleridge admired the primacy which Böhme and Schelling (who had closely studied the latter's work) gave to the 'Almacht Gottes' (*CM* i. 636); to the mysterious, 'abysmal' Will which precedes Being in order of thought.[101] He insisted that the Absolute Will cannot be an object of conception (OM ii, fo. 26). It is not an effect; it does not have a cause. To suggest that it is an effect would be a contradiction in terms. If it were such, it would not be free but causally determined, and Coleridge insisted that, properly used, the term 'will' is synonymous with *free* will. We can have no concept of this Absolute Will, because 'it is an idea incapable of abstraction' and it 'is higher & deeper than Power'; because it is 'that which God eternally *is*; whereas of power, yea even of power infinite taken in itself & abstractedly we must say that God hath it & hath it in himself & of himself rather than that he *is* it' (ODI, fo. 109): 'We not only cannot think of it abstracted from Intelligence and Love as real—for this would apply equally to the idea of an unbounded power, but we cannot think of it at all, which cannot truly be said of the latter i.e. of power as power' (ODI, fos. 109–11). Coleridge claimed that 'an insight into its truth is not possible and we are perforce constrained to the only succedaneium, the sense of the necessary falsehood of the contrary' (ODI, fo. 21). He was aware of the danger inherent in any attempt to describe what was beyond definition; but suggested, somewhat ambiguously, that

there is in the causative Allmight of God . . . a somewhat that God did not realize in himself, for the real containeth both the actual & the potential, but in God as God by the necessity of his absolute perfection there is no potentiality. (ODI, fo. 67)

---

[101] Schelling too, as Coleridge would have known, emphasizes the primacy of Absolute Will (*Philosophische Untersuchungen*).

His distinction between Will as Prothesis and Will as Thesis echoed an earlier recognition of the distinction which he found

in the discussions of the Greek Fathers and (at a later period) of the Schoolmen, on the obscure and *abysmal* subject of the divine *A-seity*, and the distinction between the θελημα and βουλη, i.e. the absolute Will, as the universal *Ground of all* Being & the Election & purpose of God in the personal Idea, as the Father. (*AR* 330)[102]

Coleridge represented the distinctions within the unity of the Godhead in language which clearly reflects the influence of Philonic, Neoplatonic, and mystical traditions:

[The] Depth ⟨of⟩ the eternal Act, by which God affirmeth himself, as the alone *Causa Sui*. The Depth begetteth not, but in & together with, the Act of Self-realization—the Supreme Mind begetteth his substantial Idea, the primal Self (I AM) its other Self, and becometh God the Father, self-originant and self-subsistent even as the Logos or Supreme Idea is the co-eternal Son, self-subsistent but begotten by the Father. (*CM* i. 694)

This distinction between Will self-realized in the Trinity (as Being, Mind, and Love) and Absolute Will was, as we have seen, the root of Coleridge's disagreements with Schelling,[103] and of his repudiation of pantheism. It was also the basis of his acknowledgement of the possibility of positive evil and of its nature: 'For pure Evil what is it but Will that would manifest itself as Will, not in Being (Ετεροτης), not in Intelligence (therefore *form*less) not in Union or Communion, the contrary therefore of Life, even eternal Death' (*CN* iv, § 5076).

Absolute Will cannot be adequately expressed in such phrases as 'the ground of the divine existence'. It must be borne in mind, Coleridge advised, when reading the attempts of the mystics to express this truth, 'that the words are used *proleptice* or by anticipation i.e. the Will contemplated after we have beheld its self realization, as the necessary being, *ens entium*, or Supreme Mind'. The Will of God as God (distinct from the power of that Absolute Will which God *has*) is perfectly actual, complete, and realized in Intelligence and Love. Will and Reason must, he

---

[102] Aquinas made use of these terms: see his reference to Θέλησις and Βούλησις in *Summa Theologiae*, i. 83. 4.

[103] See above, e.g. Ch. 2.1 and n. 9.

argued, be understood not as attributes of God, but as God (*CM* ii. 882). Will is revealed to humankind in the form of Reason, that is, as the divine Logos.

The Necessity of Freedom

Coleridge's Logos idea reflects the non-arbitrary, non-contingent nature of the divine Will in its coeternal unity with Reason. In an exploration of the foreknowledge of God and the question of its compatibility with human freedom, he suggested that

The mistake lies in supposing contingency to be the necessary character of Will or *Free* Agency/for if so, God could not be *free*. Are or are not, all things simultaneously present to God—Is, or is not, his knowledge always equally certain? If so, and if God knows his own Will & yet that remains free, why should his certain knowledge of *our* will be incompatible with its freedom? Its' *presentness* to God is not affected by its finiteness or evil Nature. (*CN* iv, §5271)

Choice between equally possible alternatives was not, thought Coleridge, the highest expression of will, though characteristic of the human state. He declared God's Will to be both totally Free and totally Necessary (N Fo, fo. 8). God 'is the originator of the moral Law, but not per arbitrium (Willkühr) but because he is essentially wise and holy and good—rather Wisdom, Holiness and Love'.[104] He followed the line of Christian orthodoxy in his conviction of the impossibility of a division of Will in God (*CM* ii. 250), but argued that there are distinctions in the human will which must be recognized. In notes written in 1827 and 1829, he returned to his investigation of the subject of these distinctions: the potentiated will, *ad libitum*, although it is merely 'will-wantonness' or 'will-freak', is contrary to purely natural inclination and desire (*ad licitum*). It is the *condition* of man's choice between the rational Will and the mere sensuous desire, the yearning for gratification of the animal will, the will of nature. Yet the human individual, Coleridge declared, lacks the innocence of the animal; he becomes, should he choose the will of nature, not an animal, but a fiend. Drawing on the language of Scholastic

---

[104] Annotations on Schelling's *Philosophische Schriften* inserted between leaves. Coleridge comments on pp. 123–4.

theology and of Fichtean philosophy,[105] he argued that *der Willkür*, the condition of choice, which depends on a prior superinduction of self-conscious intellect (human mind being different not only in degree but in kind from animal intelligence), is also a pre-condition for either the *loss* of personality (in submission to nature) or its *fulfilment* (in submission to Reason) (OM ii, fo. 1). As such *der Willkür*,[106] *adlibition*, or 'will-wantonness' is the transformation of the aweful contradiction between the evil will of non-being and the divine Will, by the communicative act of the Logos, into a dynamic polarity which is the ground of self-realization.

This is not, however, the truly free will which is united with Reason. The faculty of arbitrary choice between alternatives which is indeed characteristic of man, beyond mere selection or volition, is only, according to Coleridge 'the Shadow and Phaenomen of Will, namely *Willkühr*, Choice' (N 59, fo. 8ᵛ); *Willkür* is to be distinguished from *Wille*. Both involve the presence of intellect, but the interplay of will and intellect in *Willkür* involves an arbitrary factor which is absent in the redeemed

---

[105] See n. 106 below.

[106] Coleridge's use of the term '*Willkür*' is close in most respects to that of Fichte and Kant. Both use it to mean a subject's self-determination of his or her actions through free choice. Kant suggests that *Willkür* is not entirely random—that it is not *indetermined*. That is, although not determined by an external cause, it is determined by the subject's own incentive according to an already accepted practical moral maxim (*Religion* (1794), i. 23–4). Occasionally, Fichte seems to follow K. L. Reinholt (*Briefe über die Kantische Philosophie*, 2 vols. (Leipzig, 1790–2)) in suggesting that *Willkür* is the capacity for carrying out isolated and arbitrary choices; Coleridge's own view seems mostly consistent with this. But at other times Fichte seems closer to Kant's definition of the term. That Coleridge is familiar with Fichte's discussion of the subject of will in this respect is clear from his annotations on the latter's *Versuch einer Kritik Aller Offenbarung* (Königsberg, 1793). The notes show that he does not always agree with Fichte. He thinks the latter has failed to realize, at one point, that 'compulsion is not the same as necessity, nor Choice (*Willkür*) the same as Freedom. On the contrary, Necessity and absolute Freedom are one. And of this Identity the assent of the mind to a mathematical demonstration is a Foretaste and Analalgon' (*Kritik Aller Offenbarung*, 14; see *CM* ii. 641–2 for these annotations—though the capitalization there given does not seem to correspond to the original). See also James Ellington's note on the term '*Willkür*' in his translation of Kant, *The Metaphysics of Morals* (New York, 1964), 11 and n. Ellington states that '"*Willkür*" is the broad generic term indicating that faculty of the soul which has the power to choose.' See also John Silber's introductory essay 'The Ethical Significance of Kant's Religion', in *Religion within the Limits of Reason Alone*, for a discussion of *Willkür* in Kant. See Schelling's use of this term in *Philosophische Schriften*, 174. This page also contains marginal notes by Coleridge, though not specifically on this subject.

will, the freedom of which is one with the necessity of Reason. Aquinas had described the will in relation to reason as *liberum arbitrium*, the power to judge freely.[107] Yet Coleridge's concept of the redeemed will is one which not only involves the presence of intellect, but is united by its own act with the source and life of Reason, the Logos, in faith, conscience, and the truth of Ideas.

We have seen that, in contrast to Kant, Coleridge was aware of the fragility in human nature of the 'practical reason', the will which is one with reason (*CN* i, § 1717). In December 1803 he was prepared to identify will as the essence of selfhood and was unconvinced by Kant's assertion of an inescapable identification of the human individual will with reason. The Logos is the communicative power of this unity: 'Reason, as one with the absolute will (*In the beginning was the Logos, and the Logos was with God, and the Logos was God*), and therefore for man the certain representative of the will of God, is above the will of man as an individual will' (*LR* iv. 433–4). Coleridge insisted that 'the identity or coinherence of the absolute will and the reason, is the peculiar character of God'.[108] The doctrine of the Trinity provides a paradox of reciprocal relationship 'Intelligence is the *form* of the personal Will, and Will the essential Ground of the Intelligence' (*CN* iv, § 5377). This is the basis of the apparent contradictions involved in the attempt to define 'Idea'. It is this which gives such importance to the distinction of the Reason and the Understanding, which reveals God Incarnate '& not only as *Light*, Reason, but as Will and Life'; this was the doctrine of St John and St Paul (N 37, fo. 40ᵛ).

Since the evidence of experience and the creative power of will is fundamental to the 'logosophic' system, Coleridge's philosophy cannot be adequately defined as rationalist or idealist. On the other hand, the primacy of absolute Will which he postulated is a unity of freedom with necessity, and thus in no sense arbitrary or capricious. The divine Will is *necessarily* conformed to the divine Reason by the very nature and essence of its own free self-realizing Act. On this basis, Coleridge agreed with the Scholastic philosophers that 'a will not intelligent is no Will' (*CM* i. 355). As a consequence, not only must the term 'will' involve a con-

---

[107] Aquinas, *De Veritate*, xxiv. 4 and 6.
[108] Coleridge, 'Essay on Faith', in *LR* iv. 427–8; see also N 37, fos. 29–30, and OM ii, fos. 2, 148.

comitant responsibility at least of intelligent choice, thus providing a moral ground; but all life and being, while originating in will, and therefore being ultimately mysterious,[109] also manifests Intelligence, which is inseparable from Will.[110] He believed that Reason, as opposed to mere Understanding, provided the basis for morality since it involved will and conscience. Greek philosophy had been marred, he claimed, following Socrates' failure to recognize that virtue has its foundation not in the intellect but in the will (*PL* 151). It is not by intellectual persuasion that a man comes, finally, to the spiritual truth of Ideas (expressed in the Christian Trinity), and hence to virtue, but through the active assent of will and through 'that religion which is innate in man only because it is felt by the very necessity of it' (ibid.).

Coleridge particularly admired Kant's restoration of the idea of the will as truly free only when it is truly rational; in this the latter was the 'great restorer of the Stoic Moral Philosophy' (OM iii. fo. 63). Yet Coleridge's unity of will and reason has an affective psychological dynamic which is absent from the philosophy of Kant; it involves the dynamic of Love, realized in the third Person of the Trinity, and of Community, which binds Will and Reason in unity.[111] In this context, his idea of will has much in common with that of Emanuel Swedenborg, in its emphasis on the interdependence of will and love. It was Swedenborg's assertion that: 'Love in its essence, is to will, and in its existence is to do. For what a man loves, this he wills; and what he wills from love, this he does.'[112] He represented love as fundamentally a unity with willing: 'In its essence, conjugal love is nothing else than the willing of two to be one, that is, their will that the two lives shall become one life',[113] and asserted the unity

---

[109] BL MS Egerton 2801, fo. 92.

[110] William Barrett, in *Irrational Man* (New York, 1962), describes Coleridge as a melancholy Romantic who anticipates existential anxiety and whose work is 'of less philosophical significance' than that of Wordsworth (pp. 126–7).

[111] See below, Ch. 4.4.

[112] E. Swedenborg, *Arcana Caelestia* (Heavenly Mysteries), 8 vols. (Amsterdam, 1749–56), ii. 797; tr. in *Emanuel Swedenborg: Essential Readings*, ed. M. Stanley (Wellingborough, 1988), 35. Stanley gives the Latin title to this work. It is common practice for some of Swedenborg's works to be best known by their Latin and some by their English titles.

[113] E. Swedenborg, *Conjugal Love* (*Delitiae Sapientiae de Amore Conjugali etc.*) (Amsterdam, 1768); tr. in *Emanuel Swedenborg: Essential Readings*, ed. Stanley, 215, 138.

of these in God with Wisdom.[114] Whereas Coleridge was uneasy regarding Kant's omission of love as central to the concept of Will, he was also at times disquieted by the mystical enthusiasm of Swedenborg, which appeared to give too little attention to the unity of Will with Reason, that Reason which is not only manifested in faith and conscience, but which is also the foundation of the speculative intellect and of the logical faculty.[115]

On the basis of the priority which he accorded to will, Coleridge agreed with Kant that the only thing good in itself without qualification or restriction is a good will.[116] He insisted too that all knowledge rests ultimately on a primary act of will: 'Intelligence or self-consciousness is impossible, except by and in a will' (*BL* i. 279–80). His conclusion was that: 'The self-conscious spirit therefore is a will; and freedom must be assumed as a ground of philosophy, and can never be deduced from it' (*BL* i. 280). However, his later work emphasizes that the direction of the will determines whether the 'mind of the flesh', the mere intellectual understanding, predominates, or whether mind has reached its fully human form and become subsumed within personality, enlightened by Reason.

'*Will* = *Reason*': A Theological Corrective

A proper understanding of the relationship of will and reason was, Coleridge argued, essential to theology and philosophy.

---

[114] See e.g. Swedenborg, *Divine Love and Wisdom*, from *Apocalypsis Explicata* (1763), 34, 39; extracted and tr. by Society of Gentlemen (Manchester, 1813); tr. in *Emanuel Swedenborg: Essential Readings*, ed. Stanley, 36.

[115] Coleridge's annotations of Swedenborg's *True Christian Religion* read as follows: 'Swedenborg says—From God the Lord Man received a Will, and thro' God's effective presence he receives the power to exert this Will. The other party, meaning the same thing, say—It is God that is within us both to will and to do as far as we will and do righteously.—Without the operations of the Spirit man would be as *spiritually* dead as a stock or stone.—Then (retorts Sw.) he would no longer be a Man' (ii. 8. 184). Coleridge notes that what are taken as flaws in Swedenborg's concept of the will are really 'little more than an inconvenient phraseology'. Swedenborg himself asserts that the two 'faculties of life', reason and will, must be united (i. 436, § 249).

[116] See Kant's *Foundations of the Metaphysic of Morals*, tr. Lewis White Beck (Indianapolis, 1959), § 1: 'Transition from the Common Rational Knowledge of Morals to the Philosophical' (9): 'Nothing in the world—indeed nothing even beyond the world—can possibly be conceived which could be called good without qualification except a *good will*.'

Together with the distinction between Reason and Under-standing, the origin of Reason in Will is a central 'pillar' of his logocentric system. Many of the errors which had distorted previous philosophical and theological systems could be at-tributed, he argued, to a misunderstanding of this relationship. They had thus only been able to satisfy the 'head' or the 'heart' and provided no means for the reconciliation of these which conformed to human nature and experience. The true nature of the will, and the distinctions which must be observed in any accurate representation of its manifestations in human thought and being, were essential, he believed, if will were not to be falsely assumed as either biologically determined or as a super-natural energy altogether independent of reason. Will was ultimately a meaningless term unless it meant *free* will. Thus it could not be explained according to the 'necessitarian', deter-minist view that he would once have accepted from David Hartley; nor could it involve the impossibility of willing the contrary of itself or of any other will. It has the same spiritual source as Reason. To assume its independence of Reason was, for Coleridge, to lay the foundations of religious 'enthusiasm' and of fanaticism.

This assertion of the ultimate primacy of Will was to be devel-oped in a different direction within the existentialist and nihilist philosophies of the nineteenth and twentieth centuries. The pessimism of Schopenhauer (1788–1860)[117] and the nihilistic tendencies in Nietzsche's philosophy (1844–1900) were grounded on the concept of will as power or energy, desire and choice. They repudiated any kind of idea of Will as other than contingent and in opposition to, or simply overriding and directing, Reason. These later concepts of will were far removed from Coleridge's view; he had already concluded that these qualities and faculties were insufficient for an adequate understanding of the nature of will. The *experience* of free (and therefore responsible) will could not, Coleridge argued, be denied. Neither could it be explained in terms of cause and effect. It was indissolubly linked to intellect and self-consciousness. Its nature was misunderstood when it

---

[117] Although Schopenhauer was a younger contemporary, Coleridge, strangely perhaps in view of the fact that *Die Welt als Wille und Vorstellung* was published in 1819, never mentions him.

was seen as conditioned by phenomenal factors, by appetite or natural inclination.

The theological failure, conversely, to recognize the divine Reason as begotten by Will led, he declared, to an over-emphasis on the forms of intellect as merely categorical, regulatory, and analytic. This was the error within 'natural' theology. It also attempted to deduce God as divine Intelligence from the phenomena of the world, rather than to *find* or encounter him in the relation of persons. It was too closely allied to mechanistic and materialist philosophy (*AR* 399). Coleridge argued that if, in the Idea of God, Will is denied, then the positivity of creation and the personality of a living God are lost in a Spinozistic Identity which, finally, by denying will and 'alterity', also denies intelligence and consciousness, leaving only a kind of 'centreless' infinite thought.[118]

He maintained that some Calvinists and Methodists ignored the demands of Reason in a blind adherence to what was supposed to be God's Will: a contradiction, because this can never be arbitrary nor can it ever be separated from Reason. This led to the danger of a fanatical 'enthusiasm' which denied the claims of the intellect and made it impossible to hold that Reason and revelation were in agreement. When the Calvinists refer to the will of God, wrote Coleridge: 'they mean nothing better than the capricious enslaved dependent Wantonnesses of *human* Choice— determinations pre-determined by the appetites or at best by the ignorance of the Agents and the narrow limits of their Agency' (*CN* iv, § 5270). Will which is not united with Reason becomes a thing of dreams, fancies, passions, and of the unrestrained desires of the natural man. Coleridge claimed that the solution to both errors (as indeed to all error) must be found in the Logos as 'the intelligential Will'. He declared that the enlightenment of the Hebrews in preparation for the coming of Christ was accomplished through the gift to them of true vision, which revealed that

the Supreme *Mind* was neither separably other from the Absolute Will (the Holy *One* that inhabiteth Eternity) on the one hand, nor yet indistinguishably the same with it on the other. . . . Will is per suam propriam ipsëitatem* living, and the Root, (or Profundity) & therefore

---

[118] *CM* i. 113–14 and 566; see BL MS Egerton 2801, fos. 13–14.

the *Source* of Life—and the Will reflecting itself in the Form of *Mind* must be reflected as Living Mind, the Living Word, the Word of Life. 'As the Father hath Life in himself, so giveth he to the Son to have Life in himself' and thus the sublime enunciation was completed by the εν αυτω (i.e. τω Λογω) ην η ζωη . . . (which, however, was a *mental* life, Life in the form of Mind ζωη λογοειδης as was manifested in its communication—και η ζωη ην το φως ανθρωπου).† (N 37, fos. 29ᵛ–30)

[* 'in its own selfness'
† 'in him (i.e. in the Word) was life . . . life in the form of Logos . . . and the life was the light of men']

This unity of Will and Reason was communicated by and in the Logos as Light and Life, not only in the physical being of the whole Creation but in the intellectual and moral being of humankind. Through this unifying Logos principle, Mind could be seen as a living creative, active power, and (conversely) Life became intelligible. The power of the human imagination mirrored this unity: without Reason, it was mere 'fancy'; without will, it was powerless to create. There was no basis, without this unity, for a unified system of knowledge, nor for a unity of experience, nor for a reconciliation between heart and head. Coleridge's longing for such a reconciliation was clearly expressed in the following passage:

We have hearts as well as Heads. We can will and act, as well as think, see and feel. Is there no communion between the intellectual and the moral? Are the distinctions of the Schools separates in Nature? Is there no Heart in the Head? No Head in the Heart? Is it not possible to find a *practical* Reason, a *Light* of Life, a focal power from the union or harmonious composition of all the Faculties?[119]

In Coleridge's opinion, 'the Spirit cannot be entire but by the union of the Will and the Reason, and to desire the Will of Reason is to desire the Will of God, of the Omnipotence who willeth, and lo! it is!' (N 44, fo. 69ᵛ). The redemption and fulfilment of human nature required the unifying of Will and Reason:

The more advanced in the Life spiritual, the more perfectly the Will of the Individual is self-subjected to the Divine Light and Word (Ο Λογος ο φωσφορος, η το φως το λογικον* John I. v. I. 4. 9) as the representative and exponent of the Absolute Will; the more habitually the understanding is

---

[119] BL MS Egerton 2801, fo. 101.

submitted to the Light of Reason shining therein, and this Light of Reason in the Understanding is itself subordinated to the Reason in the Conscience; the more does our individual consciousness partake of the stedfastness and identity of the personal Subsistence, which is the copula and Unity of all the acts and shapes of the mind, the less loose and detachable is the consciousness of the events and objects that make up the Man's Experience . . . from the Self-consciousness which is the essential and inalienable Form of his Personal Identity. (*CN* iv, § 5377)

[* 'the light-bringing Word, or the light of Reason']

We shall see that in identifying both the idea of person[120] and of nation (N 44, fo. 63) as a unity of Reason and Will, Coleridge extends the Kantian concept of 'practical reason'. This development is rooted in his idea of the Logos as the Person of God, the Idea of Man, divine Humanity. For him, the Christ of history, rather than the *logos* of Greek philosophy, meets the needs of human nature, existential, psychological, and emotional needs in addition to intellectual. His theory of the unity of Will and Reason attempted to combine the emphases of classical and Reformation theology with those developed in German philosophy. There is a tension in his work between the concepts of the responsible will, sin, and guilt, on the one hand, and, on the other, the more poetic and imaginative concept of will as potentiating and realizing, as the power and life in nature and mind. These sometimes sit oddly together in his logocentric theory, the former idea increasingly occupying his last years, the latter being rather the means by which he attempted to build a bridge between the years of his absorption in the wonder of an all-embracing nature and those in which he found nature to be the witness to an 'anastasic' scheme in which the Logos was the central focus.

If the eighteenth century has been called the Age of Reason, the nineteenth century, which produced Schopenhauer, Kierkegaard, and Nietzsche, might perhaps be entitled the Age of

---

[120] It is important to note that, for Coleridge, personality is the unity not of will and *intellect* (this is merely the condition of the human *individual*) but of will and Reason. Writing of the judgements of 'human law', for example, he declared that in this too 'inquiry is not made concerning the quantity of knowledge & the degree of intelligence, but whether the individual be a *person* or not, and this is determined by the presence of the Reason in reference to the Will, and of the Will in its bearings on the Reason' (OM ii, fo. 185).

Will.[121] Coleridge's work might, with justification, be claimed for either side. His emphasis on Reason is both consistent and insistent, and the forms of the Understanding, whether grammar, logic, or deductive argument, are set against the activity of 'fancy', and against a mysticism which ignores the claims of Reason. On the other hand, the Logos is *Will*-begotten, and Coleridge, unlike Hegel, never identified the real and the actual merely with the rational. While adopting much of Kant's concept of the rational will, he included the qualities of love and faith in his idea of the unity of will and reason. Thus while he agreed that logic has its roots in the Logos reality, neither the Kantian transcendental logic nor the Hegelian ontologic can be identified with Coleridge's idea of Logos. As we shall now see, for him the responsible will was the deciding factor in all areas of human thought and experience; it was the means of the realization of nations and states as *communities* (the term 'Community' representing the unity of the Spirit) and of individuals as *persons* (in the image of the Person of God, the Logos).

[121] I refer here, for example, to Kierkegaard's concept of the act and risk of faith: 'Faith, surely, implies an act of the will' (Kierkegaard, *Journals*, tr. Alexander Dru (London, 1938), i. A, § 10); also to Schopenhauer's concept of will (see e.g. *Die Welt als Wille und Vorstellung*), and to Nietzsche's idea of the 'will to power' (*Der Wille zur Macht* (1901)).

4

Logos: The Human Principle

Man is not order of nature, sack and sack, belly and members,
link in a chain, nor any ignominious baggage, but a stu-
pendous antagonism, a dragging together of the poles of the
universe.

(R. W. Emerson)

4.1. THE 'IDEA OF HUMANITY'

Coleridge's 'logosophic system' is centred around his search for
an essential humanity and its source; his exploration is both
theoretical and existential. Rejecting the materialist philosophies
which he believed had developed out of a false use of the term
'idea' in the philosophies of such as Locke and Hume, he never-
theless agreed with the shift of emphasis from the question *what*
to the question *how* man is. He studied Christian dogmatics, the
changing ethical, moral, psychological, and biological views on
human nature of the Western intellectual tradition; he searched
his own dreams, the experiments of the Mesmerists, the spon-
taneous behaviour of children, and the political manipulations of
statesmen.

Any claim to a system of knowledge or to the authority of
doctrine must, Coleridge believed, be supported by its sufficiency
to the needs and nature of humankind. He maintained this
premiss consistently from his early writings to the later notebooks.
His whole system is rooted in the reality of a divine Humanity
which he identifies with Logos. Every area of his later thought is
grounded in a *theanthropology*.[1] His political and social criticism,

---

[1] Coleridge frequently uses the Greek term 'theanthropos', and the related
'theanthropology', and 'theanthropism' (e.g. *BL* ii. 246 and n.). For example, 'the
necessity of *theanthropism* i.e. the sinking of the Logos into Man in order that
Man might rise into the Logos' (N 37, fo. 44). See also N 44, fos. 63–63ᵛ and 66.

his exploration of the natural sciences, his epistemology—all are developed in accordance with his view of the nature and destiny of mankind as revealed in the God-Man, the incarnate Christ. He had a deep sense that a quality essential to human reason—therefore to human nature as a whole—had been lost through the growing dominance of empiricism, through the identification of concepts and images with 'ideas', and through the spread of a mechanistic or 'mechanico-corpuscular' emphasis since the seventeenth century. This quality might be rediscovered through the realization that philosophy, particularly in Britain, had taken the wrong path: in throwing out the abstruse fancies of un-grounded metaphysics, it had rejected metaphysics *as a whole*; this had prevented any real understanding of human beings as *persons*. Christianity, he believed, offered the best means of reconciling the insights of the physical and moral sciences, and revealed the essential characteristics of an ideal Humanity in the person of Christ.

Coleridge's later notebook entries frequently refer to the puzzle of the term which Christ used of himself, 'Son of Man', and the importance of its exegesis (N 48, fo. 12^v). Increasingly, too, the distinction between 'individual' and 'person' became prominent in his later thought.[2] In 1830 he wrote that religion must be tested by its congruence to the whole personality: 'every theo-logical scheme must [?fail] which appeals only to some one or more of the Qualities & Faculties of Man,—The infallible Test of Gospel Faith is that it appeals to all the constituents of our present Humanity, & brings them all to an equilibrium—to a Beauty of Holiness' (N 48, fo. 30^v). In the 1795 *Lectures*, his agreement with Joseph Priestley's affirmation of the humanity of Jesus Christ strengthens this emphasis. Priestley, in his rendering of the Fourth Gospel,[3] concluded that St John had written as a conscious opponent of the Gnostics (*LPR* 196 n. 4), who denied Christ's humanity. Coleridge supported this view. At this point he believed that the claim of Christ's divinity devalued the reality of his example.[4]

---

[2] See below, Ch. 4.3.

[3] Joseph Priestley, *History of Early Opinions concerning Jesus Christ* (Birmingham, 1786), i. 67–8.

[4] For a comparison of Hegel and Coleridge on this point see pt. 2 of my article 'Logic and Logos: the Search for Unity in Hegel and Coleridge', 16–18.

There is a marked contrast between his understanding of the Logos of the Fourth Gospel as demonstrated in these lectures and his later position, the central focus of which was the two distinct, yet inseparable, natures of Christ. In 1795 he referred to the Logos by the neuter pronoun 'It'; but after his acceptance and acclamation of Jesus Christ as God Incarnate (*c.*1805), this would have been impossible. Thereafter he identified Christ with the Word of God, and proclaimed the reality of Logos as both 'He is' and 'I AM', both the universal, objective, and ideal reality of Humanity, and the ideal Self, the unity of Reason and Will, the principle of personality. In a note written in the early 1820s Coleridge boldly claimed (with, as he himself noted, Luther and Swedenborg) that 'as the fontal God can only be known in the Logos, so neither can the Logos be sought aright but in the divine Humanity' (*CN* iv, § 4671).

In his early lectures (1795), he was already committed to the belief that religion is to be tested by its relation to human nature and human need. What changed was not this commitment, but his understanding of human nature itself. In finding Christ to be the ideal of humanity, and 'the Self in every creature' (*CM* i. 629), he became convinced that only in a kind of encounter and identification with Christ could the full potential of human personality be realized. He had begun by seeing Jesus as a man inspired by the 'divine Intelligence' or Logos, a perfect model for mankind, not a divine but a truly *human* being. Although he became convinced of the divinity of Christ, by the end of his life he had returned (as his later notebook entries show) to a deep preoccupation with the 'Son of Man', with the humanity of Christ and its mysterious unity with his divinity: 'More & more I see the necessity of devoting my best powers, & prayers as the best means of power, to the enucleation of this latter title, Son of Man' (N 48, fo. 12ᵛ).

The Greek Archetype, and Philo's 'Heavenly Man'

Coleridge's idea of a perfect form or principle of humanity has much in common with the Platonist tradition. His use of concepts such as the 'Idea of Man', the 'Exemplar of Humanity' and the 'Archetypal Man' also owe much to his reading of Philo and of the Greek fathers in whose work these expressions are commonly used. In his 'theanthropology' the Greek influence, which emphasized the ideality of the archetype, is held in creative tension with the 'God-Man', the Jehovah of the Hebrews who progressively reveals himself as living God in Person. The Son of God is here the Son of *Man*, who enters human history, the universal in the form of the particular individual. This dual source of Coleridge's 'Idea of Man' is consistent with his own admission of the most profound influences on his thought: 'if there be any two subjects which have in the very depth of my Nature interested me, it has been Hebrew & Christian Theology, & the Theology of Plato' (*CL* ii. 866).

Coleridge's representation of the Logos as both Idea of God and the Idea of Man[5] owes much to Plato's Ideas or perfect realities of spirit and intellect. His notes on Robert Robinson's *Miscellaneous Works*[6] reveal his belief that Plato had somehow anticipated the Christian Trinity. Robinson, in Coleridge's view, could not comprehend Plato's metaphysics and had failed to grasp the spiritual truth of Reason and Ideas. As a result he reduced passages in the New Testament to anthropomorphism: 'In the New Testament God assumes the Human Nature (νουμενον [noumenon])—in paragraphs, like these, the author seems to turn God into man (φαινομενον [phænomenon])'.

However questionable Coleridge's belief in the agreement between Plato's thought and Christian doctrine, he clearly believed Plato's metaphysics to be compatible with the idea of a *living, personal* God. He claimed that both Plato (and Philo) 'deduced the necessity of a *Deus Alter et Idem*' from the idea of personality (*CL* iv. 632), which they recognized as essentially a metaphysical unity of distinctions. The text of 'On the Divine Ideas', which was intended to form a part of the 'Opus Maximum' or 'Logosophia', suggests that Plato, unlike those who followed him (notably Plotinus), recognized the Good as *active* and *efficient*. Coleridge uses the term 'personëity' to denote the source of personality, that will and purpose which he (and, he believed, Plato before him) recognized as the origin of distinction-in-unity.

---

[5] *CM* i. 573; N 26, fo. 27ᵛ; *CN* iv, § 4907; N 41, fo. 74ᵛ.
[6] Robinson, *Miscellaneous Works*, iii. 120 ff.; transcribed annotations (VCL BT 37).

The idea of the Logos, the Son, as the Person of God became the foundation of his 'theanthropology'.[7]

He pointed to a division in the world of philosophy between those systems founded on the postulate of 'It is' and those which began with 'I Am'. Plato, he proclaimed, was the founder of the latter type. As such, he was closer than any earlier Greek thinker to the Christian starting-point:

Plato was a prophetic Anomaly—all the prior Theologians of Greece (unless Heraclitus was an exception) were φυσιολογοι*—their first principle was—Εστι.†—the first of the Christian Scheme Ειμι.‡—The former deduced the Persons—the latter begins with and from the Personal, or rather the Personëity itself. (*CL* iv. 538)

[* 'physiologists', i.e. natural philosophers, physical scientists
† 'It is'
‡ 'I am']

It had been suggested, Coleridge noted, that

there is . . . universal agreement, within the controversies [concerning the relationship of the Logos of Philo, John and Paul], that the Logos prologue [of the Fourth Gospel] is better illumined by an understanding of the Logos idea in Philo than by any other non-New Testament writing; it is agreed that Philo is by far the largest available source for the idea contained in the word Logos.[8]

Coleridge himself found significant parallels between Philo's idea of the Logos and those aspects of the Johannine and Pauline writings which he himself most admired.[9] A notebook entry

---

[7] See below, Ch. 4.3.

[8] Samuel Sandmel, *Philo of Alexandria* (London, 1979), 155. See also D. T. Runia's remark that 'In Philo's theology the mediator *par excellence* is, of course, the Logos'; 'God and Man in Philo of Alexandria', *Journal of Theological Studies*, 39 (1988), 48–75. Philo maintained the distinction between an unqualified Absolute and the Logos as 'the eldest and most all-embracing of created things' (*Legum Allegoriae*, iii. 175). The Logos is the highest and first-created being under which all other beings, relations, and qualities are subsumed. Coleridge would have found this aspect of Philo's Logos mentioned in Whitaker's *The Origins of Arianism Disclosed* (e.g. 52–3).

[9] For example, Philo's descriptions of the Logos as the divine image (εἰκών) of God (i.e. God is here Archetype of Logos), and as himself the archetype of all other things, which are his images (*Legum Allegoriae*, iii. 96), are reflected in Paul's letter to the Colossians (1: 15–20). There Christ is described as 'the image of the invisible God, the first born of all creation; for in him all things were created, in heaven and in earth, visible and invisible. . . . In him all the fulness of

shows his recognition of an affinity between the thought of Philo and the writer of the Fourth Gospel, and his rejection of the suggestion that these had differed in their understanding and exposition of the Word of God (*CN* iv, § 5071). He clearly had the highest admiration for St John, and remarked of those who argued that the views of Philo and John on the Logos were different: 'if they mean that John differs from Philo, as the Truth and nothing but the Truth from the same Truth in connection with sundry impertinences, and without the complemental accessories—to this I fully agree' (ibid.).

One aspect of Philo's thought in particular seems likely to have contributed to Coleridge's idea of the divine humanity. Philo incorporated in his writings an aspect of Jewish tradition to be found in the non-canonical Jewish texts and in some parts of the Old Testament (this element was later rejected as inconsistent with monotheism) which propounds the view of a second God (or even more than two). This tradition always links *Yahweh* as second God or Highest Angel with human form. The book of Daniel, a subject of intense interest and study to Coleridge, draws on this tradition. Coleridge himself believed that the Angel referred to in certain parts of the Old Testament is to be identified with the Logos who is Christ, the Jehovah Word (*CM* ii. 429).[10] A heavenly being in human form revealed himself to Daniel as the angel of fire and bronze sent to him to reveal the future (Daniel 10: 1–14) and he saw a vision of a manlike figure going up to his throne to be given dominion, glory, and kingdom (Daniel 7: 14).

Philo also saw the Logos as the divine Man: 'God's Man, the Logos of the Eternal . . . the Man after his Image'.[11] He distinguished between the 'heavenly' and the 'earthly' man. The former is 'made after the image of God' and is 'altogether without corruptible and terrestrial substance'. The earthly man is 'moulded' out of the substance of the earth; he is 'a moulded work of the Artificer, but not his offspring'. His 'earth-like

God is pleased to dwell.' Coleridge emphasizes Philo's description of the Logos as the '*εικων Θεου*, *image of God*' (see *TT* ii. 291).

[10] See also *CM* ii. 728 and 743. Again, Coleridge would have found this aspect of Philo's thought emphasized by Whitaker (*The Origins of Arianism Disclosed*, 98).

[11] Philo, *De Confusione Linguarum*, 41 and 146; see also *TT* ii. 291.

mind . . . is corruptible, were not God to breathe into it a power of real life; when he does so, it does not any more undergo moulding, but becomes a soul, not an inefficient and imperfectly formed soul, but one endowed with mind and actually alive; for he says, "the man became a living soul" '.[12] Coleridge's polarities of Understanding and Reason; the 'mind of the flesh' and the mind enlightened by the truth of Ideas; true Self and 'the false and phantom I' (the latter merely empirically discerned)—all these have their roots in a distinction also to be found in Philo's thought between the true, ideal nature of man and the natural man.

Neoplatonic Inadequacies

Coleridge admired Philo's recognition of the reality of sin and evil; he believed this was lacking in the Platonist tradition. The 'Eclectic' philosophy (that which attempted to blend Platonism with a religious mysticism, for example, in Neoplatonism), in denying the positive nature of evil, failed to provide either an adequate psychology of human nature, or a sufficient ground for morality. It had failed to recognize that human nature is the mid-point between two opposing poles: Nature (being drawn always towards indistinction, the dark ground of chaos) and God. 'Eclectic' philosophers held consciousness to be the ground of intellect and being; Coleridge insisted, in contrast, that, *conscience* is the condition of personality and indeed of all knowledge. Accordingly, man must be defined primarily by will as the ground of conscience. In 1803 he stressed the 'connection between Consciousness & Conscience / the mutual Dependence of Virtue & the Understanding on each other' (*CN* i, §1763); in later years the emphasis had shifted and he insisted that conscience was the ground of consciousness (OM iii, fo. 110).

He believed that Plato had inadequately drawn the distinction between the Good as Will in unity with Being and Intelligence and a Good which seemed merely to be the equivalent of 'Useful' or 'Advantageous', '*Utile Sive Commodum*'. This failure had led to the later errors of Neoplatonist philosophers, concerning the nature of the Good:

[12] Philo, *Legum Allegoriae*, i. 29–32.

in [Plotinus'] works & in the books of the Alexandrine Philosophers without exception the term is a mere reverential epithet without any substance to which it may be attached; for what conception can we possibly affix to a Good, independent of being, intelligence and action, of a Good, quae nec *efficit*; nec *est*[?]* (ODI, fo. 173)

[* 'which neither acts; nor is']

Coleridge argued that theories of emanation which accompanied this weak and non-productive idea of the Good were thereby basically flawed. No ground either of unity or of energy was provided from which the second and third divine hypostases of Plotinus (indeed, the whole universe of thought and being) could possibly be shown to proceed. The most dangerous error of all, Coleridge believed, was the denial of the positive reality of evil, a direct consequence of the theory of emanation. While acknowledging what he took to be the errors of Manichaeism, he was adamant that moral evil is experienced as a positive reality within the finite world. The spiritual Fall was real. He made the following criticism of the Neoplatonic view:

It is self evident that, on this scheme Good & Evil are distinguished each from the other by no positive difference but by a mere difference in degree; [of] diversity [?or] difference of Kind there exists none nor can exist. Nor is this all: either the idea of guilt is absolutely denied, and with it therefore responsibility and all the religion of the world, its hopes & its emotions; or by a strange absurdity, the crime, the evil increases as the guilt diminishes, for it is clear that an evil, whether positive or negative, accompanied with energy & intellect, only not perfect[,] will ensure a greater condemnation in respect of merit or demerit than tenfold that mass with obscure light, an encumbered intellect & an energy in its last dying vibrations. It would be superfluous to add how wholly unexplained or rather in what utter opposition to this scheme is the fact, that [to] the noblest & most intellectual nature alone do we attribute guilt, or the possibility of guilt, or in what contrast the scheme stands with that old & widely diffused idea, which is found as the basis of all religions that are more than local superstitions, or traditions blended with allegory, the idea, I mean, of an Evil Spirit, inferior only to God in Power & Intelligence. (ODI, fos. 191–3)

The positive reality of evil was, in Coleridge's view, a fact of experience and of human history;[13] it must be acknowledged by

---

[13] Despite the many parallels between the work of Coleridge and the German idealist philosophers, there is significant disagreement between, for example,

any adequate anthropology and theology. He insisted that only the Judaeo-Christian tradition offered an adequate moral and psychological account of human nature, one which bore witness both to humanity's attachment to nature, and to the evidence in history and experience of the fact of the responsible will as the basis of personality. It was the vivid testimony of the Bible to this aspect of human nature which, he believed, gave it a unique claim to be 'the only adequate organ of humanity' (*CIS* 72).

Christ the God-Man: The Influence of the Fathers

Coleridge's idea of the divine Humanity owes much to classical theology, which he quite unashamedly interpreted as not only consistent with but vindicated by developments in Kantian and post-Kantian philosophy. His deep admiration for Origen (*TT* i. 84) is reflected in words and phrases which clearly echo the latter's. He shared Origen's emphasis on, for example, a primal spiritual apostasy, on the primacy of will and the moral impulse over the intelligential, and on the nature of the Logos as the Unity of Will and Reason.[14] Origen had taught a pre-existent union from eternity of 'soul' (usually characterized by him as below the realm of spirit and associated with the principle of humanity) with God. In Christ, the 'God-Man' (a term also frequently used by Coleridge) (N 42, fo. 61ᵛ), the only perfect form of soul—that which did not depart from God in the spiritual apostasy—still clings to God 'acting as a medium between God and the flesh':

it is therefore right that this soul, either because it was wholly in the Son of God, or because it received the Son of God wholly into itself, should itself be called, along with that flesh which it has taken, the Son of God and the power of God, Christ and the wisdom of God; and on the other hand that the Son of God, 'through whom all things were created', should be termed Jesus and the Son of Man.[15]

Coleridge and Hegel on this point; see below, App. C, and my article 'Logic and Logos', pt. 2. 207–11.

[14] It has been claimed that Origen's mystical thought centres on the relation between humankind and the Logos; P. A. Lieske, *Die Theologie des Logosmystik bei Origines* (Münster, 1938), 100 ff.

[15] Origen, *De Principiis*, ii. 6; Koetschau's text, tr. G. W. Butterworth, *On First Principles* (London, 1936), 111.

Coleridge too sees this perfect archetypal Soul as the divine principle and exemplar of humanity. It is the medium between God and the world of nature, 'a unity [which] must contain distinctnesses',[16] and, as such, the principle of self-consciousness and 'the Principle of the Differentiality of my Individuality' (N 26, fo. 118ᵛ).

The Logos as the Idea of Man is, we have seen, represented by Coleridge as Will in the form of Reason. Intellect divorced from the implications and consequences of will is therefore an insufficient criterion of human nature. Coleridge, like Origen, and following the emphasis of the Judaeo-Christian tradition, stressed the importance of the will, the reality of a spiritual evil, of apostasy, and of sin. Origen had insisted that evil of all kinds was related to the will; not however, to the Fall of Adam, but to the prior Fall of rational pre-existent souls from the original unity and harmony in which they were first created by God.[17] Coleridge found this concept of will and of sin helpful. He agreed with Origen's rejection of the idea of original sin as inherited from Adam and interpreted it thus:

Origen . . . plainly enough overthrows the phantom of hereditary guilt. . . . What then is it? It is an evil, and therefore seated in the will; common to all men, the beginning of which no man can determine in himself or in others. How comes this? It is a mystery, as the will itself. Deeds are in time and space, therefore have a beginning. Pure action, that is, the will, is a *noumenon*, and irreferable to time. Thus Origen calls it neither hereditary nor original, but universal sin. (*LR* iii. 312–13)

Coleridge wrote in his 'Confessio Fidei' (1816) 'I believe . . . that an evil ground existed in my will, previously to any given act, or assignable moment of time in my consciousness' (*LR* i. 392). His commitment to the reality of a moral and spiritual evil is as evident in his poetry (for example, in *The Rime of the Ancient Mariner*) as in his prose.

He took up another theme which had been part of the teaching of Origen: that the divine Humanity is revealed not only in his Incarnation in the flesh, but progressively through human

---

[16] BL MS Egerton 2801, fo. 81.
[17] Origen, *De Principiis*, i. 4: *On First Principles*, 41–3.

history.[18] The Old Testament bears witness to 'The *Word* of God, the God-Man, or Divine Humanity' (N 41, fo. 61): 'But it is so generally over-looked, or forgotten, (alas! I fear, that I ought not to have said, too generally not known) that the Divinity, the Filial Godhead was humanized before he was incarnate i.e. manifested himself *focally* (ut in foco) in an individual Man' (ibid.). Like Origen, Coleridge believed that, as the Logos is the image of the Father, so man is the image of the Logos, the intellectual Light. Origen had described an affinity between the mind and God, 'of whom the mind is an intellectual image'.[19] Here the emphasis is clearly Platonic:

Every mind which shares in intellectual light must undoubtedly be of one nature with every other mind which shares similarly in this light. If then the heavenly powers receive a share of intellectual light, that is, of the divine nature, in virtue of the fact that they share in wisdom and sanctification, and if the soul of man receives a share of the same light and wisdom, then these beings will be of one nature and one substance with each other.[20]

However, the realization of this universal mind is, according to Origen, 'in proportion to the perfection of our merits'.[21] The effort which Origen described as man's part in the progress towards the consummation of Reason and of his own ideality is also emphasized in, for example, Coleridge's *Aids to Reflection*. He too identified a need for reflection, for a search for true self-knowledge and the redirecting of mind from the exclusive operations of the Understanding to the inclusive personal truths of Reason. He also stressed the role of choice in man's destiny. If man follows his 'phantom self', the fleshly form of thing-ness, if he remains merely an object to himself, he becomes then not simply an unspiritual part of the natural world but a fiend (N 42, fos. 2–3). Self-realization is dependent (according to both Origen and Coleridge) on the individual's finding his true self in the Idea of Man, the Logos.

---

[18] See above, Ch. 1.3 and below, Ch. 4.4.
[19] Origen, *De Principiis*, i. 1: *On First Principles*, 13.
[20] Origen, *De Principiis*, iv. 4: *On First Principles*, 326.
[21] Origen, *De Principiis*, iii. 6: *On First Principles*, 246.

Trinity and Self-Knowledge: The Human Pattern

Coleridge consistently upheld the necessity of an adequate psychology to any philosophical system. Any claim to universal truth must be balanced by the particular experience of individuals, by empirical and historical research into human behaviour, and by the investigation of the interdependence of the various faculties, such as reason, will, appetite, and emotion. His many references (in both published and unpublished writings) to Augustine suggest his interest in the latter's psychological insights. His own writings often blend an interest in the life of the mind below consciousness (a preoccupation shared by many of his contemporaries[22]) with a Christian anthropology which owes much to Augustinian and Lutheran concepts.

His analysis of the relationship between will and reason, the self-determining potential within human nature, develops a theme found not only in the work of Origen and Augustine but in the whole Western theological tradition. It is on the subject of self-knowledge that Coleridge's thought most clearly resembles that of Augustine. The latter believed that man's nature mirrored, in the form of memory, understanding and will, the perfect Wisdom, self-knowledge, and love of divine Persons in the Trinity.[23] Coleridge, 1,300 years later, develops this idea, finding in man, 'at least in man fully developed, no mean symbol of Tri-unity' (*SM: LS* 62). This triunity is, according to him, 'reason, religion and the will' but the pattern of distinction in unity remains. The fulfilment of personality is dependent on the realization of all these through true self-knowledge (that is, through the recognition that the true Self is the objective (transcendent) and subjective (indwelling) Logos). Here again he echoed Augustine, who, following Plotinus,[24] had linked self-knowledge to knowledge of God: 'You were right before me: but I had moved away from myself, I could not find myself: how much less, then, could I find you.'[25]

---

[22] One example of the interest in psychological developments characteristic of this time is the intense speculation concerning 'animal magnetism' or hypnosis, in which Coleridge often enthusiastically joined. For his notes on Mesmer and others, see e.g. BL Add. MS 36532, fos. 11–16; and *CN* iv, §4512.

[23] *Augustine: The Trinity*, 464.

[24] Plotinus, *Enneads*, 5. 4.

[25] Augustine, *Confessions*, v. 2. 2.

The role of self-knowledge in human perfectibility was recognized as a crucially important issue by many of the thinkers whom Coleridge most admired. He was familiar with Nicholas of Cusa's rendering of the polarity principle (the '*coincidentia oppositorum*'), the reconciliation of opposites[26] through which the latter continually recommended the search for God as a process of self-discovery and self-realization. Nicholas of Cusa echoed the anthropology of Socrates and Augustine in his concentration on the interaction of self-consciousness and will, a concentration reflected in Coleridge's own thought. Cusa had also upheld the degree of freedom of the will which is implied by the element of choice.

O Lord, Thou sweetness most delectable, Thou hast left me free to be mine own self, if I desire. Hence, if I be not mine own self, Thou art not mine, for Thou dost make freewill needful, since Thou canst not be mine if I be not mine own. Since Thou hast thus left me free, Thou dost not constrain me, but Thou awaitest that I should choose to be mine own.[27]

This suggests that the human person comes to know God not through depersonalization, but, on the contrary, through self-realization. The importance of self-knowledge to the realization of the Idea of man was perhaps the most enduring contribution of Greek philosophy to the Christian tradition, where self-knowledge became identified with the knowledge of the divine Humanity. Those Greek thinkers whom Coleridge most admired, such as Heraclitus and Plato, had made self-knowledge the core of their philosophy.[28]

To Coleridge, this principle, and its ground in the will, remained paramount. He commented on his choice of motto for the *Friend*, which was taken from Zoroaster:

Seek thou the derivation of thy Soul (οχετον, canalis, aquaeductus*—a common and favorite metaphor of the orientalizing Platonists or rather Plotinus) whence and from what rank having fallen into slavery to the Body, to that rank, from which thou wert precipitated, Thou mayest

---

[26] Nicholas of Cusa, *De Docta Ignorantia*, i. 22: *Of Learned Ignorance*, 49.

[27] Nicholas of Cusa, *De Visione Dei*, tr. E. G. Salter as *The Vision of God* (London, 1928), 32.

[28] Heraclitus' method of seeking truth is revealed in the phrase 'I searched myself' (Guthrie, *A History of Greek Philosophy*, i. 101). See also Plato's *Alcibiades*, the command of Apollo 'know yourself', 129a.

re-ascend, uniting thy energy[†] with the Holy *Word* (Logos in the same
sense as in John I.1 = intelligential Energy, distinguishable (tho' not
separable even in thought) from the energic WILL).

[†] *or making it one work with* the holy Logos (*CL* iv. 884).

[* 'conduit, channel, aqueduct', all synonyms of the root meaning of
derivation]

In uniting his will, his own intelligential energy, with the Logos,
man attains true self-knowledge: 'that noblest Science, the Root
and vital sap of all others, the Science of Hëautognosy, or Self-
knowledge in respect of that Self, which (potentially at least) is
the same in all men' (N 56, fos. 10ᵛ–11).

Man, the Microcosm

Despite the influence of the arguably pessimistic and guilt-
inducing elements of Augustine's theology, and despite a firm
belief in moral and spiritual evil, Coleridge's view of the human
condition was fundamentally optimistic. This is evident in his
comments on John Scotus Eriugena, who in Coleridge's opinion
was to be praised because he 'dared avow . . . that Religion was
but Philosophy contemplated principally in its influences on the
Will' and had 'taught the final Redemption . . . of all men &
found no Hell but in the necessary consequences of the self-
retarded Return into Deity' (N 35, fo. 23). Eriugena saw man
himself as the microcosm of the creation and at the same time a
spiritual creature by free will and grace. Man is the apex of
Nature which will achieve redemption in him: 'God willed to
place man in the genus of the animals because he wished to
create every creature in him: he wished to make him in his image
and likeness, so that, just as the Primal Archetype transcends all
by the excellence of his essence, so his image should transcend all
created things in dignity and grace.'[29] Eriugena's is an optimistic
anthropology. Despite the perversion of the will, 'the Word of
God, the life and the light of men, does not cease to shine in our
nature which, examined and considered in itself, is found to be

---

[29] Quoted in J. O'Meara, *Eriugena* (Oxford, 1988), 124; tr. of Eriugena's
Periphyseon, iv.

a certain darkness without form; nor has that light wished to abandon it: it forms it, containing it through nature; it reforms it, deifying it through grace'.[30] Eriugena's optimism, like that of Coleridge, had been founded on the Fourth Gospel.[31] The Son of God became man, so that men could become sons of God: 'He who made a man from God makes gods of men'; and he is the Head of Humanity: 'the incarnate Word, our Lord Jesus Christ, received the plenitude of grace according to his humanity, since he is the head of the Church and the first-born of the universal creature, that is, of universal humanity, which is in him and through him cured and restored'.[32]

Coleridge's work in many respects echoed Eriugena's views concerning the relationship between man and nature and between man and his Ideal form in Christ. 'Man himself', he wrote in the *Theory of Life*, 'is a syllepsis; a compendium of Nature . . . the Microcosm!' In the Creation, the Logos, 'preceded by the pre-disposed Spirit' (N 41, fo. 74ᵛ), which moved over the formless void, brought 'Law, *Kosmos*' out of chaos. Coleridge asserted that 'the same process is repeated in the Microcosm of each individual *Soul*'. Blank potentiality is actualized into 'sentiency' and 'sensibility' and 'the Cosmos pours in' through the senses as a flood of impressions which are given order and form according to the law of the 'human logos', the human mind. Coleridge believed he had found a perfect analogy between 'the first days of the creative week' when 'Light existed only as Life, & because only as Life therefore as a dark Light;—a lifeless Life, even as now in the vegetable creation' and the microcosm of man, 'in the polar Division of the *Mind* into Soul & Spirit, Understanding and Reason' (N 41, fo. 75ᵛ). The vegetable life became animal life through the mediation of light (Coleridge pointed out that, between the appearance of the two in Genesis, light is given to creation in the sun, moon, and stars). In a parallel process, man's animal nature became rational and spiritual through the mediation of God manifested as the divine Humanity—as the 'light of men' to which the Fourth Gospel bears witness. Coleridge described

---

[30] John Scotus Eriugena, *Homily of John Scot*, quoted in O'Meara, *Eriugena*, 168.
[31] For the importance which Coleridge attached to the Fourth Gospel, see N 49, fo. 22, and above, Intro.
[32] O'Meara, *Eriugena*, 175.

this Light as 'indwelling & acting at the same time internally, in a form of Life as "the Spirit of Truth"'; so human redemption incorporates all previous stages of life and light within the physical world and all these reach completion in the restoration of human-kind to the Idea of Humanity revealed as the Person of God.

Eriugena's theme that men are begotten as Sons of God in the Idea of God, though they have fallen from this state, also recurs in Coleridge's work (ODI, fos. 81–3). Christ is the Head of the human race and the hope for humanity lies in this truth: 'the human race not by a bold metaphor, but in a sublime reality, approach to, & might become, one body whose Head is Christ (the Logos)' (*CL* ii. 1197). Coleridge too believed that the light of the Logos as Reason and Truth is never withdrawn, but that human individuals can, by their own choice, darken their minds and detach themselves from the true principle of their humanity.

The Restoration of Humanity

The theme of an Ideal Humanity which recurs in Western thought from Plato to Kant appears in the Fourth Gospel, in the Epistles of Paul, and in classical theology's affirmation of Christ as the divine Logos. It found further expression in the work of Martin Luther. Coleridge wrote of Luther's *Table Talk* that it was 'next to the Scriptures my main book of meditation, deep, seminative, pauline, beyond all other works in my possession, it *potenziates* both my Thoughts and my Will' (*CL* vi. 561). He annotated his copy of the work extensively between 1819 and 1829. From his first notes it is clear that he found in Luther a recognition and exegesis of the divine 'personëity' and of the contrast, on this ground, between the empirical self (which Kant was later to argue was the only knowable self), and the *person*, the mysterious ground of whom is will and conscience. Coleridge responded to Luther thus: 'I cannot meditate too often, too deeply, or too devotionally, on the personëity of God, and his personality in the Word, υιω τω μονογενει [the only begotten Son], and thence on the individuity of the responsible creature' (*CM* iii. 719–20).[33]

He admitted that he had, not intellectually, but in his 'common

---

[33] The word 'individuity' is coined by Coleridge to express the *dynamic quality*, rather than the outward form, of the individual.

habit of feeling', confused this true individuality in *personality* grounded on the responsible will with 'that complexus of visual images, cycles or customs of sensation, and fellow-travelling circumstances (as the ship to the mariner), which make up our empirical self' (*CM* iii. 720). From the revelation that the Logos was Will in the form of Reason, he could 'form a sufficient gleam of the possibility of the subsistence of the human soul in Jesus to the Eternal Word, and how it might perfect itself so as to merit glorification and abiding union with the Divinity'.

His notes on Luther's work are, interestingly, very similar in tone to Origen's work on the Soul of Christ.[34] His theme is that the 'alterity' of the Absolute, the Logos, '[laid] aside the Absolute, and by Union with the Creaturely become Affectible, and a Second, but Spiritual Adam, and so as afterwards to be partaker of the Absolute in the Absolute, even as the Absolute had partaken of passion ($\tau o \upsilon$ $\pi a \sigma \chi \varepsilon \iota \nu$) and infirmity in *it*—i.e. the fallen & finite Creature' (*CM* iii. 720). Luther had warned that there is no way to God but through the divine Humanity of Christ: 'take good heed in any case of high climbing cogitations to clamber up to heaven without this ladder, namely, the Lord Christ in his humanity'.[35] Coleridge supported Luther's view of the Humanity of the Logos: 'as the fontal God can only be known in the Logos, so neither can the Logos be sought aright but in the divine Humanity—this is the doctrine of Luther p. 17—as well as that of the Moravians & not less expressly tho' less fantastically than that of Em. Swedenborg' (*CN* iv, § 4671).[36] The ideal humanity is revealed in *history*. This is the unique revelation of the Christian religion: 'To know God as God ($\tau o \upsilon$ *Zηva*, the living God) we must assume his personality: otherwise what were it but an ether, a gravitation?—but to assume his personality, we must begin with his humanity, and this is impossible but in

---

[34] See e.g. Origen, *De Principiis*, iii. 6: *On First Principles*, 110–11.

[35] This passage is marked by annotations in Coleridge's copy of *Doctoris Martini Lutheri Colloquia Mensalia*; tr. Henry Bell as *Dr. Martin Luther's Divine Discourses at his Table, etc.* (London, 1652), i. 61; see *CM* iii. 729.

[36] Coleridge's reference to p. 17 is to Luther's text (see n. 35 above), the heading of which reads: 'That God is sought for and certainly found in his Word concerning Christ'. Luther continues: 'abstein from speculating and searching to know and to seek God the Lord, aswel what his Essence is, as also his Will, according to thine own sens, reason, and carnal cogitations: for without his Word, and his Son Christ, hee will not bee found'.

history; for man is an historical—not an eternal being. *Ergo*.
Christianity is of necessity historical and not philosophical only'
(*CM* iii. 729). God as personality is God in history—the incarnate Logos (*CL* vi. 677);[37] and Coleridge accepted Luther's
assertion of Christ's Humanity as alone acceptable to God.[38]

He found further support for his own idea of the divine Man in
whom the reality of personhood is confirmed in the work of
Emanuel Swedenborg.[39] He was in sympathy with 'Swedenborg's
sense of Redemption, the divinity of Christ, and the Tri-unity
as contained in, and connected with, the Manifestation of the
Divine Humanity'.[40] Swedenborg had stressed the danger of
attempting to comprehend the nature of God without recognizing
'that his form is the very Human Form';[41] he too claimed that:
'The Infinite Itself which stands above all the heavens and above
man's inmost being cannot be manifested except by means of the
Divine Human, which exists solely with the Lord.'[42]

The Platonist elements in Coleridge's theory of human nature
are often at odds with his more existential, psychological, and
historical understanding of the human condition. His notebooks
record a sense of personal crisis, of conflict, doubt, and need,
which appears inadequately answered by his emphasis on a trans-

[37] '[T]he God-Man, who as Jehova presented himself to mankind, and as
incarnate represented the perfected Man to the Father' (N 44, fo. 29).

[38] Coleridge's annotations show that he did not accept Luther's expositions
unequivocally, any more than those of the other writers whom he both criticized
and admired. For example, he did not share Luther's dedication to the Immaculate Conception. Instead he emphasized that the explanation of the phrases
'Son of God' and 'Son of Man' is to be found in St John's solution 'namely, the
eternal Filiation of the Word'.

[39] Swedenborg was suspicious of the term 'person' as applied to God: 'In the
spiritual world or in heaven, not persons but spiritual things are the subject of
reflection, for persons limit the idea, and concentrate it upon something finite'
(*Arcana Caelestia*, vii. xli. 5225, tr. anon. (London)). Coleridge recognized
Swedenborg's difficulty on this subject (see *CN* iv, § 5297). He too believed that
'the first step must be to get rid of that mischievous term *Person*—& to confine
the term to one & its true sense, viz. that in which Christ is alone the *Person* of
the Father' (N 49 , fo. 24ᵛ). He was not altogether consistent on this point, but
admitted that any other term is subject to the same difficulties; 'Person' could at
least properly be used of the Logos (see *NED* ii. 182 and *CL* v. 87–9).

[40] VCL S MS F2.1 (watermarked 1818),notes on Swedenborg, transcribed by
E. H. Coleridge. Coleridge appears to have made an especially close study of
Swedenborg's works around 1820 (see e.g. *CN* iv, §§ 4518, 4798–9, 4820).

[41] Swedenborg, *True Christian Religion*, 20: *Emanuel Swedenborg: Essential
Readings*, 39.

[42] Swedenborg, *Arcana Caelestia*, ii, § 1990.

cendent archetypal, ideal humanity. He admits to difficulty in understanding the nature of the Son of God who is also the Son of Man;[43] and while it is the former title which is often the focus of his expositions, his notebooks contain sudden halts in the flow of reasoned argument and an anguished appeal to the 'God who hears and answers prayer'. In this, his work seems to represent a wider unease which has continued to lie at the heart and the roots of Christianity and which suggests that the synthesis therein of the inheritance of Greek philosophy with that of Hebrew religion has often led to an uncomfortable tension.

4.2. PERSONËITY IN PERSON

More than once Coleridge stated his intention to write an important work on St John and St Paul.[44] Of the Epistles to the Ephesians, Colossians, and Galatians he wrote 'Had these Epistles with the Gospel of John been the only remains of the Apostolic Age, we should still be rich; and all the Books in the world could not repay the loss of Paul and John' (N 41, fo. 33). He thought Paul 'pre-eminent' in his exegesis of the Son of Man and of the mysterious mediation between 'the proper *human* life (the *principium individualitis* [sic] *in omnibus et singulis*), and 'the Idea containing all the Elect, the divine Humanity, in which the Father loveth Man' (ibid.). Paul, wrote Coleridge, gave the clearest exposition of the Son of Man as he who 'does actually bear our burthens, rejoice in our spiritual joy and sympathize in the spiritual groans and infirmities of the Redeemed'. John and Paul 'shine as a Double Star' in the exegesis of this 'the other Half of the precious Mystery' concerning Christ, 'that Christ came *to his own*, and that we become the children of God by adoption or assumption into the only-begotten Son of God' (ibid.). This idea of the divine Humanity Coleridge thought their most valuable contribution. In this context, John 'shines with a greater brightness because in the Gospel we have the words of the *Word* himself'.

---

[43] See N 39, fos. 20–1, N 37, fo. 18, *NED* ii. 346 for examples of Coleridge's difficulties over this issue.

[44] See the plans for the 'Logosophia' (e.g. *CN* iii, §§ 4266 and 4300; N 41, fos. 22 and 39ᵛ).

Coleridge consciously attempted to integrate the Johannine and Pauline writings with elements of Kantian and idealist philosophy; or rather, he found in the Scriptures the most adequate expression of the human condition, and attempted to use them as the basis of a critique of the philosophy of his own time. In Paul, he found materials through which to develop his own theory of human nature; his themes of law and grace, will and conscience, sin, death, and redemption. Paul asserted that humanity must understand itself in the light of both the first Adam and the second Adam who is Christ. He had shown that: 'What Adam was *quoad* Soul, Christ is *quoad* Spirit. The psychical Humanity was all in Adam, the spiritual Humanity all in Christ' (N 41, fo. 8). Human psychology—the relation between mind and body, between conscious and unconscious mind—must take into account, Coleridge argued, the experienced reality of moral evil. The distinction in classical theology between the Ideal Man in the realm of ultimate spiritual realities, and man as the apex of the natural world, owes as much to Paul as to the Platonic tradition. Coleridge noted Paul's emphasis on the detachment of redeemed man from nature and 'the flesh', on his transformation in Christ and his restoration to the human ideal. His comments on 2 Corinthians confirm this point:

St Paul taught & held that there was to be a redemption from the Body—as the lower part of the Coral consists of the same stuff with the Rock to which it is attached—so here. What the Calcareous Stem is to the Coral, the Body is to the Soul or Princ. Indiv.—This in the present life is to be continually loosening till finally it is transferred to a new ground—from that of Hades or Nature to Christ, the Ground and sustenance of the new Life.—What nature is to the natural man, in all its' particulars of Soil, Moisture, Air, Warmth, Light, magnetic attraction etc, that Christ is to the Souls of the Redeemed. (N 41, fo. 27)

In Paul, the Platonic and Stoic concept of Reason became that of Law, by which Coleridge understood Paul to mean 'the Law of Right Reason applied to the Will by the Conscience = the Individuum Subjectivum or *το Εγω*' (N 41, fo. 4–4^v). Coleridge himself attached the idea of *person* very firmly to that of conscience.[45] But Paul also, he believed, knew the antidote to the awe and dread which the Law inspired, because he had

---

[45] See below, Ch. 4.3.

proclaimed that 'the eternal Reason, the Word itself, became incarnate in Christ Jesus, to declare to Man that "my Father is greater than I"—that there is an Antecedent even to the Reason and that his Name is *Love*' (N 41, fo. 12). Here again, Coleridge introduced the aspect of interpersonal relationship as a means of reconciling the dichotomies which the Understanding was forced to admit.

His reverence for the Fourth Gospel pre-dates his close study of Paul's Epistles, which his notebooks[46] show to have been *circa* 1829. His 'theanthropology' was built on the foundation of the Gospel which he believed to be written by John and which, he claimed, showed God to be the Principle of 'personëity', and Christ to be God in Person. Both John and Paul taught Christ as the Principle of humanity, of personality; but, for Coleridge, John's great contribution was to show that this reality of Person had existed from eternity with the Father and was one with the divine Reason. The essentials of personality are will and life, and John had shown these to be manifested in the coeternal and coequal Logos. His purpose was 'to represent the Messias as the Regenerator and Redeemer of Man. Master this one truth: that it was the object of John to emancipate the idea of personëity from the phænomenal notion of Outline, and (generally) from the sensuous Definite in space and time, and you will meet with few difficulties in the fourth Gospel' (*CM* ii. 456).

Coleridge denied that the principle of personality (the essential ideal humanity) could be identified with bodily, phenomenal individuality. It was a transcendent, eternal principle, immanently revealed; therein lay the hope of humankind. The difficulty of reconciling personality with infinity had held him back, in his early manhood, from commitment to the Christian faith in a triune God. He had found, in the prologue to the Fourth Gospel—and confirmed in the work of those, such as Luther, whose work he most admired—a powerful witness to the 'personëity' of God. He believed immortality belonged to *persons*, rather than to rational souls. On the night of 23 December 1830 he recorded his hope that he might complete a commentary on St John's Gospel; this Gospel maintained in him a desire to live

---

[46] Notebooks 38–41 are all concerned with the study of Paul's epistles.

which, he claimed, he could not otherwise feel. He then sum-
marized what it was that he found to be of such great value:

How strongly throughout the divine Gospel & how beautifully in the first
nine verses, is the great idea confirmed of Christ, as the Base, Ground of
Antecedent Unity of our proper Humanity. The Ideal, therefore the
Actual, therefore the divine Man to whom all individuals Τεκνα θεου εξ
υιω τω μονογενει* [*sic*] as the Ideas to the Mind, as Branches to the Vine
the Logos to the Father = the absolute Idea—or as the Idea to Mind—
the Logos to mankind as the Mind to the Ideas. (N 49, fo. 21)

[* 'Children of god from the only begotten Son']

Here, as so often, Coleridge appears to read his own preoc-
cupations into the text he was studying; in this particular case, his
attempt to reconcile the antecedent unity which is the epistemo-
logical basis of Kantian philosophy with the Fourth Gospel is
clear.

He believed that John showed the importance 'for men of
Reason and Faith that they should distinguish the divine Humanity
of our Lord which was co-evil with the lucific Fiat—the "Let
there be Light!"—from his *Incarnation*' (N 48, fo. 26–26ᵛ). They
must distinguish the latter, in which he 'dwelt, a man among
men, in order to dwell in man, as the Spirit of Truth' from the
former truth, in which Christ can be seen as 'the Man in all
Nature'. Here again Coleridge's belief that the whole process of
what he called 'natural history' manifests a redemptive scheme is
evident. This process leads to the evolution of mind; to the
supernatural inspiration of self-consciousness; and, at last, to the
reunification of will and reason in human persons, the realization
of Logos, of 'Will + Reason' in finite humanity.

God in Person

The Fourth Gospel was the inspiration for the Light-theme to
which Coleridge frequently returned, following the example of
many of those with whom he felt an intellectual empathy, for
example, Augustine, Jacob Böhme, John Donne. He used the
imagery of Light to distinguish between Reason and Understand-
ing. Man 'contemplated as an intelligent creature' *is* the under-
standing mind, the highest point of nature, and the point at
which instinct has been superseded, enlightened by the sphere of

influence of a universal Light of Life. Here the only adequate terms are those of metaphysics and of symbol:

the understanding then *is* the Man whose rationality consists in the innate susceptibility of the Lumen & Luce—but the Reason is not the Man, but πρoς ανθρωπον,* which however, as far as he is a Spirit, might be named an *Attribute* of his Humanity by the virtue of the perpetual presence of the never-setting Light & Sun—. (N 47, fo. 23ᵛ)

[* 'with man', i.e. in the closest possible proximity without identity]

Coleridge believed that only the divine Humanity might properly be described as Reason, but that the potential for the light of Reason existed in every human individual and was awakened by faith and conscience. It is 'a necessity of the finite mind to distinguish the One Absolute Being into Person, the manifestative focal or central subsistence, and the *Sphere* in which he is everywhere present operatively. Hence Reason is the Sphere, the Light of the Son, the Light which the Son *is*—and this the Light, that lighteth every man that cometh into the World' (N 47, fos. 22ᵛ–23).

His theory of human nature is distinct from that strain in Greek philosophies which had claimed Reason to be the natural state and possession of all humankind. Man is 'susceptible' to the light, but his enlightenment is dependent upon the direction of the will. Reason, unlike the Understanding, is always concerned to pursue the proper ends of humanity, that is, the realization of persons in and through the second Adam (Christ). Reason is inseparable from act: it is not to be understood as merely theoretical analysis, speculation, or deduction, or as the forms of logic, but existentially—this is *practical* reason:

It is a *doing* of truth, a conversion or rather a completion of Light into *Life*, even that Life which is 'the Spirit of Truth'. And *the Light*—from this Text [John 3: 20–1] only the distinction of the practical Reason from the Understanding might be unanswerably deduced—He that doeth evil[,] so far from eschewing his understanding, idolizes it, as the faculty of selecting and adapting the *means* to his evil purposes. The Light, which *he* hates, is that which at once reveals and prescribes the ultimate *end*. (N 47, fos. 33ᵛ–34)

We have seen that, for Coleridge, the idea of person was both existentially and theoretically important. While he asserted that God is 'at once the absolute person and the ground of all personëity' (OM ii, fo. 189) he found the use of the term 'person' to refer to God problematic[47] (N 49, fos. 23ᵛ–4). Yet he believed one of the most fundamental doctrines of the Christian faith to be that of the 'personëity' ('by which term I mean the source of personality' (OM ii, fo. 243)) of God revealed in Christ as Person. 'The personality of the Creator, and the Creative Act of the Divine Person were the two fundamental Articles of the primaeval Faith' (N 26, fo. 41ᵛ). Having shown, as he believed, that God must be understood as the supreme unity of Will, Reason, and Love, Coleridge asserted, 'we have proved that the perfection of person is in God, and that Personëity[,] differing from personality only as rejecting all commixture of imperfection associated with the latter[,] is an essential constituent in the Idea of God' (OM ii, fo. 191). On these grounds, he insisted that the revelation of God to man was *moral* before it was intelligential or rational.

Both Coleridge's 'logosophic' theme and his attempt to overcome the difficulty of reconciling personality with infinity in the idea of God, hang on the assertion that 'the Logos, the only-begotten, *is* the *Person* of the Eternal Father' (N 48, fo. 7), and that 'In the Scripture-doctrine of the Trinity the Son alone is the *Person* (the exegesis) of the Godhead' (N 42, fo. 41).[48] Personality is distinction-in-unity and thus: 'the *personality* of the infinite Mind is an article of *faith*, not less dependent on a Revelation[,] or at least of a moral Assumption[,] than the doctrine of a trinity or *tri-personality* which indeed is the legitimate & necessary consequence of the former' (N 48, fos. 31ᵛ–32). The distinction of 'alterity' within God's self-comprehending Unity is now seen in a new light, as the basis of personality. 'God alone is a self-comprehending Spirit; and in this incommunicable *Adequate* Idea of himself (*Λογος*) his Personality is contained' (*CL* iv. 850). The

---

[47] See above, Ch. 4.1 n. 40. H. P. Wong has shown that 20th-cent. theology still has difficulties with the term 'person' as applied to the Son, the Logos (*Logos-Symbol in the Christology of Karl Rahner* (Rome, 1984), 210–16).

[48] 'In the most proper sense of the word, Person . . . the second Hypostasis of the Trinity is alone the *Person* of the Godhead—See John 1: 18—This the Scriptures far more worthily express by the words, the Name, the Glory, the Exegesis etc.' Here Coleridge is commenting on the Greek terms used in John 1: 18; that is, ἐξήγησις (N 50, fo. 28).

term 'person' should be reserved for Christ's 'exegesis' of this divine personality, in his revelation to and in human history. Concerning the Godhead,

the first step must be to get rid of that mischievous term, *Person*—& to confine the term to one & its' true sense, viz. that in which Christ is alone the *Person* of the Father—As many primary Functions, so many distinct Epiphanies of one and the same Person, El *Jah*, Elijah (or Elias) the Son of Man, and finally in the final fulfilment Son of God. (N 49, fos. 23ᵛ–4)

'Reason and *the* Will', wrote Coleridge, 'are the *co. efficients* of *actual* personality' (*CN* iv, § 5377); and the Logos, we have seen, is the 'intelligential Will', 'Will in the form of Reason'.

It is the nature of Christ, as God in *Person*, that forms the most powerful argument (so Coleridge argued) against Unitarians and 'Socinians'.[49] The unity of Will self-realizing its own Being, of self-knowledge in the Idea, in the love relationship of I–Thou—this he held to be the true definition of 'person'. Distinctions are as essential to the idea of 'person' as is unity; in the Godhead, both unity and distinction are eternal. God must be realized not only as Subject—'I'—but as Object—'Thou'. The Logos is the eternal distinction of 'alterity ... *Deitas objectiva*' (*Friend*, i. 316n.), the reality which, so Coleridge believed, is expressed in the Pythagorean *ratio*, and in Heraclitus' dynamic polarities.

Plato, Philo, and, later, Augustine had emphasized the distinct faculties within the overall unity of personality.[50] This concept of distinction-in-unity Coleridge believed to be essential to the idea of person, the primary characteristic. The only foundation for 'alterity' within unity must be will (thus he argued against Spinoza's philosophy[51]); this then is the ground of personality. Yet Will itself is a unity. There is only one Will: the Will of God which is freedom (all other wills are either entirely potential or

---

[49] Coleridge frequently repudiated the doctrines of the Socinians, the followers of the 16th-cent. Italian theologians Laelius and Socinus, who denied the divinity of Christ (see e.g. *CN* iv, §§ 4618 and 4620).

[50] Plato described these as reason, desire, and spirit (*Republic*, iv. 441); Philo observed 'that our soul is threefold, and has one part that is the seat of reason, another that is the seat of high spirit, and another that is the seat of desire' (*Legum Allegoriae*, i. 68–71); we have seen that Augustine found the image of the Trinity in man (*De Trinitate*, xv. 6. 10).

[51] See above, Ch. 3.2.

only partial, as only partially free). Distinctions are realized only in the Idea. Will then, in the form of Idea, or Reason, is

the essential meaning of *personality*, from the consideration of which Plato and Philo Judaeus deduced the necessity of a Deus alter et Idem—The notion of an Idea adequata, ergo vere ens,* as the contra-distinguishing attribute of the Supreme Being, whose thoughts are anterior to things and substantive thereof, i.e. *creative*. (*CL* iv. 632)

[* 'adequate Idea, therefore true being']

Coleridge's distinction between the 'personëity' of the Father and the *personality* of the Son is important in the context of his 'theanthropology', his idea of the relation between finite and ideal Humanity (in Christ). The Father is the source and origin of personality; the latter is begotten as ὁ ὤν, the Being and Person of the Father (*CN* iv, § 5297). Concentration on 'the so-called physical attributes' (*AR* 398–9), such as infinity, omnipresence, and immensity (in Coleridge's opinion only useful in emphasizing the contrast to any physical image), was the error of the Ancient Greeks and of Spinoza: 'Now that the *personëity* of God[,] the idea of God as the I AM, is presented more prominently in Scripture than the (so-called) physical attributes, is most true; and forms one of the distinctive characters of its superior worth and value' (*CIS* 168). He perceived the failure to recognize this as one of the greatest errors and sources of danger in the theology of his own time. It was the cause of the natural theology which he despised and of a loss of faith in the living, and personal, God (*AR* 398–9). Faith in Christ has little to do, he believed, with the evidences of natural theology:

to the general definition of Faith as the submission of the individual Will to, & consequent collapse with, the Universal Reason, the Christian Faith adds the spiritual reception of the Universal Reason, as *Life*, Person—and adores the Light, that lighteth every man that cometh into the World, as likewise the living self-subsistent *Word*, the only-begotten *Son* of the Eternal I AM, and the Visibility, the personal Exegesis of the Father—not the *To Ov** of Spinoza. (N 47, fo. 18)

[* 'What is', i.e. the 'It is' rather than the 'I am']

In the Christian faith, moral revelation takes precedence over the intellectual because God is revealed as Person; to discover his true self, man must find himself not merely as particular individual, but as person.

Unless the Logos is recognized to be *distinct*, self-subsistent, and not merely a personification, the doctrine of the Trinity is untenable. Coleridge's definition—echoing that of Schelling—of personality[52] as 'the union of a Self-subsistence with a Basis independent of it, so that both, mutually interpenetrated, are but one Being' (*CN* iv, § 4728) is consistent with his Trinitarian belief. He proclaimed 'the great purpose of the Doctrine of the Trinity, which is to vindicate & render intelligible the personality' (N 37, fo. 40). One of his main objections to Unitarianism and pantheism was that these failed to recognize God as Person. In his notes on Deuteronomy 12, he concluded that both idolatry and polytheism 'ensued in the apostacy from the primeval Faith in a Divine Person' (N 43, fo. 24). If God is not recognized as Person (that is, in the revelation of Christ), religion is separated from its true ground of will and from the 'ipsëity/alterity' relationship of the Triune God which—Coleridge was convinced—was the only possible ground of the I–Thou–He interdependence of personal relationship and, thereby, of self-realization.[53]

Son of God and Son of Man: The Historical Jesus

Coleridge, in his later notes, struggled to find a way of expressing the unity of the Jesus of history with the coeternal, coequal Logos, the Principle or Idea of the divine Humanity. His desire to emphasize the intelligibility of unity, and the reality of what Kant had called 'the architectonic interest of human reason',[54] compelled him to the search. He continued to seek a means of reconciling the transcendent truths of Reason with the historical development of human nature, with psychology and the polarities of his 'ideal Realism'. He believed that only in the figure of Christ, the incarnation of Logos, was such reconciliation to be found. On this basis, he interpreted Christian doctrine in a manner which was likely to fulfil his hopes and confirm his expectations.

From his reading of Kant, he would have been familiar with the latter's understanding of this unity of the two natures as

---

[52] See Schelling, *Of Human Freedom*, 46–7, 74.

[53] 'Personëity itself, the unity of Reason & Life in absolute oneness exclusive of contradiction' (N 53, fo. 21); see below, Ch. 4.3.

[54] Kant, *Critique of Pure Reason*, A 105–30, B 130–45.

a holy mystery.[55] Coleridge himself claimed that a full understanding of 'personality' was dependent upon the revelation of this mystery. Christ, was not only the universal Man in whose being and acts all men participate, but the particular human being in whom the universal Logos was revealed. Christ both took the form of man in the contingency of human history, and revealed what was, through the grace of God, the ideal destiny of humanity. In him, not only is God revealed to man, but man is acceptable to God.

After his reversion to orthodox Christianity, Coleridge constantly upheld the two natures of Christ, as set out in the Nicene Creed, against Unitarians, Arians, Sabellians, Socinians, and Arminians. Yet this Creed did not satisfy him as a sufficiently positive or adequate expression of the reality of the God-Man. In a note on John 9: 38 he concluded: 'The Nicene Form of the Trinity is valuable as precluding dangerous error in the conception of this Mystery; but not so good for a positive apprehension of the Truth—This verse is one of many proofs' (N 36, fo. 60ᵛ). The verse revealed not only the 'being of one substance' but the positive unity of the distinct Father and Son, the '*positive* Unity of God (Unity with Plenitude)' (*CL* v. 134).[56]

Coleridge, despite the value which he attached to the Nicene formulation, declared the teaching of John and Paul to be superior to all the later creeds. The truths expressed here, however, were in danger of being lost:

But alas! instead of John and Paul, or even of the Nicene Council, or της εκτεθεισης παρα του εν καλχηδονι Συνοδου πιστεως*, we are taught to monstrify our conception of this most fundamental truth by the heretical Pseudo-athanasian Creed, which in the very paroxysm of his Anti-arian Fervour the good Athanasius would have been foremost in anathematizing. (N 43, fo. 26)

[* 'of the creed set out at the Council of Chalcedon']

He believed that the Nicene Creed avoided the inherent dangers of the Athanasian which 'must either be interpreted laxly under

---

[55] Kant refers to 'holy mysteries' which are beyond the grasp of intellect, and describes the idea of the Son of God, 'the archetype of humanity' as one such (*Religion within the Limits of Reason Alone*, 129–38).

[56] 'Only a positive & essential Unity, an I AM, can be the Adequate Idea or Alterity (Deus alter et Idem) of the Absolute Will' (N 26, fo. 27ᵛ).

the superior authority of the Nicene Creed, or it could not be cleared of a very dangerous approach to Tritheism in its omission of the Subordination of the Son to the Father, not as Man merely, but as the Eternal Logos' (*CL* iv. 686). The so-called Apostle's Creed Coleridge believed to have been 'consequent on the Conversion of the Gentiles, and intended as a form of instruction for pagan Catchumens preparatory to Baptism' (*CM* i. 236).[57] In the first clause of both the Nicene and the Apostle's Creed he found a difficulty which he expressed in a comment on Richard Baxter's support for the latter: 'How could John or Paul have sanctioned the *first* clause of the Creed, who both expressly attribute the making of the Heaven & Earth to the Son?' (ibid.).

The question of the subordination of the Son to the Father had important implications for Coleridge's Logos theme. He argued that the divine Humanity is immanent in the finite world, and this immanence reflects his subordination; yet, in a sublime paradox, the Logos remains transcendent in equality with the Father. Humanity in its ideal form unifies, in itself, the worlds of nature and of spirit; thereby nature is drawn to its fulfilment in the Idea. This, together with the two natures of the God-Man, is the basis of Coleridge's understanding of humanity's ideal nature and destiny.

He concluded from his study of John 5: 17–19 that equality did not preclude subordination; the apparent contradiction was inevitable in the attempt at intellectual understanding of spiritual truth.[58]

Being, the Supreme-Being in whom is essentially whatever truly *is*—the Being is the eternal repetition of the Absolute Will which repeating it reveals. . . . From this & a concurring text we may likewise learn the true import of the term 'equal', and that it does not preclude *subordination*. He made himself *equal with* God in affirming himself to be the *Son* of God—not equal *to* God: for 'My Father is greater than I.—Why callest thou me *Good*? There is none good save only the Father'. The *Good*, the Holy Will, is the *Ground* of the Co-eternal Truth—which is good as being the *Form* of the Good—good derivatively. (N 49, fo. 3–3ᵛ)[59]

He criticized Fichte for failing to realize that Christ 'does not assert his *identity* in Fichte's sense of the Word—i.e. that the

---

[57] See also *CM* i. 312, 345, and *CN* iii, § 3880.
[58] See above, Ch. 3.3.   [59] See also *CL* iv. 686.

Father and he were the *same* Self or Person—but his union with the Father—and throughout attributes a distinct personality to himself—"My Father & I will come; and *we* will dwell in you".[60] Again, the relationship of distinction-in-unity is emphasized as the key to the mystery of the relationship of the Son to the Father.

The unity in Christ of Son of God with Son of Man became an object of intense speculation to Coleridge (N 48, fo. 12ᵛ). Notebooks written in the last decade of his life contain many examples of his preoccupation with the subject. The following extract is typical:

The Son of God became the Son of Man, but tho' whatever we may say of the latter we may rightly affirm of the former; the converse would carry us into strange errors—Remember it is the *Son of Man*, to whom the expressions of the Psalmist refer. The Son of God is the Great Being, the *Lord* most high who spake by the Prophets of the Son of Man, the Son of David—who will dare assert that the Gospel represents *Jesus* as omniscient in his personal consciousness as Jesus?—Jesus knew that the Son of God was the *true* and proper Ground of his Being which was to him what our Reason is to us, in this one respect. But I cannot write safely on this subject without writing largely. (N 37, fo. 18ᵛ)

Coleridge found in John 13: 32

a most momentous [verse] according to the view, I have been permitted to take, of the relation of Jesus to the Son of Man and of the Son of Man to the Son of God, the only-begotten co-eternal Word,—the distinction of these yet the perfect unity—not less but rather far more perfect than that of the Reason & the Understanding in one & the same Person, in every Man. So only could *Jesus* be greatly exalted. (N 48, fo. 42)

He drew an analogy between the understanding as within and subsumed under the Reason (of which it forms an essential part) and the spiritual development in the man, Jesus, towards the fullness of the Logos: 'Is it not observable, that as the End of the Dispensation in the flesh approached, our Lord's human insight

---

[60] Coleridge summarized what he took to be Fichte's view that Jesus 'totally rejects and disclaims an individuality in himself'; and accused Fichte of depriving Jesus of subsistence: 'consequently Jesus = 0 was not = God; but God *appeared* as Jesus, i.e. put on a phantom Body—in what sense could Christ even in his eternal Character be styled the Son of God, or speak of God as his Father?' (*CM* ii. 598).

into the great Objects of his Mission became clearer & more steady?—and that in the same proportion his "I" was raised up into the Logos?' (N 48, fo. 43). This question, unusually bold for its time, is consistent with Coleridge's belief that Jesus 'mapped out the course' for every human individual.

In order to fully comprehend the New Testament account of Jesus, it was necessary to understand the sense in which Jesus *became* the Logos: 'we should not exclusively think of Christ as the Logos united to human nature, but likewise as a perfect man united to the Logos. This distinction is most important in order to conceive, much more, appropriately to *feel*, the conduct and exertions of Jesus' (*TT* ii. 100 n.). This was to be the pattern for every person: self-realization through identification with the Logos: 'the possibility and the necessity of *theanthropism* i.e. the sinking of the Logos into Man in order that Man might rise into the Logos, & with the Logos ascend into the Glory of the Father' (N 37, fo. 44). Coleridge clearly summarizes his understanding of the Logos, Christ, as the reality of both universal and particular humanity in the following note appended to a later edition of the *Friend*.[61]

Christ, the Logos, Deitas *objectiva*, centred Humanity (always pre-existing in the Pleroma) in his *Life*, and so became the *Light* = Reason, of Mankind. This eternal (i.e. timeless) act he *manifested* in time—σαρξ εγενετο*—& dwelt among men, an individual Man, in order that he might dwell *in* all his Elect, as the Root of the divine Humanity in time.

[* 'was made flesh': John 1: 14]

Christ, he declared, remains the Root of the growth from in-dividual to *person*, from natural to ideal man.[62]

In the last decade of his life, Coleridge became increasingly interested in the subject of the suffering Christ, 'Deus patiens'.[63] Whether this was a consequence of his own increasing ill health and his continuing sense of unworthiness, or of a growing sense of the universality of human anguish, is not clear; notes written at the time suggest that both factors contributed. At the same time, many notes and letters refer to 'the God who *hears* and *answers*

---

[61] H. N. Coleridge suggested this was added in 1825 (*Friend*, i. 316 n. 1).

[62] It is important to remember that Coleridge does not accept the opposition of ideal and real; 'ideal Realism' is the basis of his system.

[63] See N 50, fos. 30 and 41–41ᵛ; also *CM* iii. 536.

prayer'.[64] The emphasis on the humanity of Christ which had characterized his early work was now renewed, but with an altered tone, to assert the identification of Christ with the inescapable condition of humanity, that of suffering. There are implications that Coleridge wished to include the experience of suffering as a quality essential to personality, particularly of suffering on behalf of another. At times, this gives his later writings a somewhat oppressive quality; the effort of maintaining faith and hope against the weight of experience is often apparent.

4.3. 'THEANTHROPOLOGY'

Coleridge's idea of person, as it emerges through his later writings, reflects his attempt to counter the mechanistic models of human nature which had prevailed in the eighteenth century and were still strong in the nineteenth. Eighteenth-century attempts to formulate a 'science of man'[65] had emulated, in terms of moral theory, Newton's achievements in the physical sciences. David Hume's empirical and naturalist exploration of human nature had denied the very concept of any metaphysical unity of selfhood. Kant, in attempting to answer Hume, had offered the concept of a 'unity of apperception',[66] showing the distinction between the empirical self and the self as that unity without which no experience was possible. Coleridge valued this aspect of Kant's work highly, yet his inspiration was not entirely derived from this source; many of his explorations of the idea of the self pre-date his close study of Kant (in 1803).

As a young man he had found the 'associationist' psychology

---

[64] See e.g. NQ, fo. 13; N 54, fo. 16; *CL* vi. 890.

[65] Alexander Pope wrote in the prefatory 'Design' of his *Essay on Man* (1733–4): 'The Science of Human Nature is, like all other sciences, reduced to a *few clear points.*' David Hume, in the *Enquiry concerning Human Understanding* (1748), calls moral philosophy 'the science of human nature' and suggests that philosophy may 'discover, at least in some degree, the secret springs and principles, by which the human mind is actuated in its operations' (*Enquiry*, ed. from 1777 edn. L. A. Selby-Bigge, 3rd edn. (Oxford, 1975), 5, 14).

[66] See Kant's description of 'transcendental apperception', or the 'transcendental ground of the unity of consciousness', or again, of 'synthetic unity' (*Critique of Pure Reason*, A 105–30, B 130–45).

of David Hartley seductive.[67] Later developments, such as Mesmerism, raised questions which Coleridge found increasingly fascinating and important, concerning the relation between will, reason, dream-state, and personality. The more he became convinced of the primacy of *will* in human personality, the more he insisted that all theories of human nature which were based on the merely phenomenal were inadequate. On this ground too, he attacked, for example, in the 'Opus Maximum' (iii, fos. 116ff.), those moral philosophies which were based on self-interest; whether to the exclusion of all genuine altruism (as, for example, in Hobbes's philosophy) or in a modified, apparently more benevolent form (in the work of David Hume). They were based, he argued, on an inadequate understanding of the nature of *persons*. Increasingly, he believed that his particular interweaving of philosophy and Christianity, centred on the Logos, offered both an epistemological and moral ground which confirmed the witness of his reason and his experience.

Coleridge's theory of personality is inseparable from the development of his theory of the Logos as the divine Humanity; that is, from his 'theanthropology', the framework of the 'logosophic' system. Although he was convinced of the existence of a Supreme Being, in his early manhood Coleridge had been able to find no intellectual justification for believing that intelligence and will could be attributed to this Being: 'my head was with Spinoza, though my whole heart remained with Paul and John' (*BL* i. 201). In the *Biographia Literaria*, he implied that he later found in Kant's *Critique of Pure Reason* (1781) confirmation of a dawning conviction that at least no intelligent argument could be directed *against* 'a holy and intelligent first cause'.

Kant's Influence

Coleridge adopted much of Kant's theory of personality, including the emphasis on the rational will, and on the absolute moral worth of each person as always an end in him/herself and never merely a means to an end. He agreed with Kant that the rational will (that good will directed towards Reason) is the essence of

---

[67] David Hartley (*Observations on Man*) gave a mechanistic explanation of the products of mind, memory, emotion, and reason as the result of atomistic nervous vibrations.

what it is to be human. 'Practical Reason', he wrote, 'is the *nature* or *essence* of a Person.'[68] He appeared sympathetic to Kant's assertion that, while mysterious and incapable of conclusive explanation because of the element of freedom, the rational will is not 'supernatural' in the sense of being separate from the essential nature of humanity. Human nature, that is, participates, through the capacity for Ideas, and the potential for personality, in the Idea of Man in whom Reason is the form of the divine Will. The whole principle of humanity, fulfilled in personality, consists in the unity of will and reason: 'the power of loving God, of willing good as good . . . the Kantean avers to be supersensual indeed, but not super-natural, but in the original and essence of human nature, and forming its ground and awful characteristic. Hence he calls it die *Menschheit*—the principle of Humanity' (*LR* iv. 359). Yet, Coleridge insisted, this is a truth of Reason, and, as such, it cannot be wholly grasped by the intellect alone; Kantian philosophy 'declares it a principle most mysterious' (ibid.).

The important point is Kant's admonition: 'Act so that you treat humanity, whether in your own person or in that of another, always as an end and never as a means only';[69] this Coleridge made the foundation of his political and social criticism (*C & S* 15). The distinction between 'person' and 'thing' must always be maintained: 'all social law & justice being grounded on this principle, that a person can never, but by his own fault, become a thing, or, without grievous wrong, be treated as such'. Coleridge echoed Kant in insisting that 'a thing may be used altogether and merely as the *means* to an end; but the person must always be included in the *end*: his interest must form a part of the object, a *means* to which, he, by consent, *i.e.* by his own act, makes himself' (ibid.). His concept of person, however, diverged from Kant's on psychological grounds. Unlike the latter, he did not separate rationality from feeling, desire, and inclination.

Kant had argued that self-love not only cannot provide the objective, a priori foundation of a universal moral law, but that its influence is excluded from this law which 'we impose on

---

[68] VCL S MS 9; notes written on the back of invitation cards to Coleridge's 1812 lectures on literature. See OM iii, fos. 63 ff., for Coleridge on Kant's concept of the Good Will.

[69] Kant, *The Foundations of the Metaphysic of Morals*, 47.

ourselves and yet recognize as necessary in itself. As a law, we
are subject to it without consulting self-love.'[70] He insisted that
'an act from duty wholly excludes the influence of inclination'.[71]
Self-love and feeling cannot provide any objective basis for the
moral law; they are part of the world of subjective, contingent
experience. According to Coleridge, both Kant and Fichte had
failed to realize that desire and inclination may be as closely
related to the rational intellect as to bodily sensation. In a discus-
sion of the psychology of pleasure, he insisted that there is a form
of pleasure which is 'the immediate consequent or accompani-
ment of the intellectual energies exerted in conformity with the
laws of the intellect and its inherent forms' and is unmistakably
good when used in the service of a higher good, that of faith and
conscience (OM iii, fos. 79–82):

I think . . . that both the philosopher of Königsburg, and his first disciple
and rival Fichte, have erred, and verged towards enthusiasm in their
confusion of . . . the *eunoya* with the *Hedone*, the desirable of the intellect
with the desirable of the body, and the exclusion of both indifferently
from the permanent objects of the rational Will. The former is not
indeed spiritual in the highest & most proper sense of that term, but still
it may be to the spirit as the body to the soul. (OM iii, fo. 82)

Coleridge saw in the Trinity a *perichoresis*, the dynamic of
which is realization through relationship—a movement through
Self–Other–Self, that is, God as Self, loving the Other who is
yet Self. Healthy self-love must reflect this relation, and therefore
be, according to its *true* nature, love of the 'Other'; it unites in
itself subject and object. The object may be the self known in
self-consciousness, or, equally, it may be the other—'Thou'—in
relation to whom alone the self is truly known. Coleridge's
repeated criticisms of Kant's psychology seem, at least in part, to
have been the result of disagreement regarding the nature of both
pleasure and self-love, and the relation of these to the rational
will. Coleridge believed self-love could only be judged to be
inconsistent with the principle of will and reason if 'self' were
taken to mean either merely the 'perpetual antecedent unity'
within each individual, or the bodily self (OM iii, fos. 50–1). The
former must of necessity be antecedent to all our sensations 'and
to all the objects, towards which they may be directed'. The

latter, he warned, may mistakenly be regarded as the true self if 'the reflections on our sensations[,] desires & objects have been habitually appropriated to it in too great a proportion' (OM iii. 51). This will be the result, he argued, if the child is given objects to pacify it, instead of the loving presence of its mother, that is, instead of, another 'self' in which to find its own self reflected (OM ii, fos. 74–81).

Coleridge insisted, however, that this false image of self 'is *not* a necessity of our nature' (OM iii, fo. 51). The infant views its mother as 'self' for a short time, and this suggests the possibility, he continued, for an individual to constitute for himself 'the representative or objective Self (as distinguished from the primary originative and subjective Self) in whatever it wills to love'. Self, in its representative sense, 'signifies only a less degree of distance[,] a determination of value by distance and the comparative narrowness of our moral view' (OM iii. 53). The individual, Coleridge maintained, unless he has totally subjected his will to the law of the senses (this would present only his body to him as the objective 'self'), is determined by a higher law than that of nature and one in which his moral freedom is confirmed: that which enables him to recognize and love 'a Self in another'.

Despite his criticisms of Kant's inadequate psychology, Coleridge frequently asserted his respect for the latter's idea of God which was inclusive of the positive attributes of will and reason. God is, for Kant, the Principle and source of that moral law or practical reason which itself bears witness to his existence; an existence unprovable by the speculative intellect.[72] Luther's faith in the Divine Humanity well-pleasing to God was confirmed, so Coleridge believed, in Kant's moral philosophy.[73] Transcendental philosophy provided insight by which a new metaphysics was seen to be necessary: that of the rational will. Yet Kant interpreted the Christian Logos as the moral perfection of earthly rational existence; for Coleridge, in contrast, though he admits that

---

[72] Kant, *Critique of Practical Reason*, tr. Lewis White Beck (New York, 1956), 144–5.

[73] Kant, *Religion within the Limits of Reason Alone*, 120. Kant wrote: 'in the appearance of the God-Man [on earth] it is not that in him which strikes the senses and can be known through experience, but rather the archetype, lying in our reason, that we attribute to him . . . which is really the object of saving faith' (p. 110).

human nature can only be adequately understood in the light of the rational will, even Kant's exploration of aesthetic experience and judgement is insufficient to bridge the gulf between the determinations of nature, and moral freedom. This can only be overcome through the relation of Persons which involves the determinations of 'otherness' together with the freedom of self-determination in a new sense—that of '*finding* a self in a Brother' (N 41, fo. 16). Only God-in-Person (Logos) can raise the mind of man to true self-knowledge on the ground of relation.

Self-Determination

An important element in the idea of person as reflected in Scholastic theology from an Aristotelian root re-emerges powerfully in the moral philosophy of Kant, Fichte, and Schelling. This is the idea of self-definition, the individual's determination of the direction of growth of his own personality. When, in Germany (1798–9), Coleridge read Christopher Meiners's work on Pico della Mirandola,[74] he recorded his interest and his intention to study Pico's writings further (*CN* i, § 374). It seems likely that Pico's views, which were representative of a Renaissance theme concerning the moral freedom of the will and its potential to define human nature in terms of the ascent towards God or the descent towards nature, were as influential on Coleridge's own thought as on German philosophy in general.

We have seen Coleridge's interest in *der Willkür*,[75] the faculty which is the condition of choice (as more than mere selection or volition) in humankind. According to his scheme, although the conditions of choice are supplied by the potentiating power of the Logos as inner Light and Life, man determines his own being by his choice for Reason or for 'Will below the influences of Reason': 'that will which is the dark root of the Animal Life' (N 41, fo. 63). For human individuals, there are *two* poles in relation to which the self may be realized. One may 'find a self' in the Will which is one with Reason, and thus be joined to the true Self—the Idea of Man (Logos). Or the will may be directed to finding a

---

[74] Christopher Meiners, *Lebens Beschreibungen berühmter Männer aus den Zeiten der Wiederherstellung der Wissenschaften* (Zurich, 1795–7): 'Ueber das Leben und die Schriften des Grafen Johannes Picus Mirandula.'
[75] See above, Ch. 3.4.

self in the natural man, in the life of the senses. The result is 'an alienation of the WILL—*i.e.* of the man himself' (*C & S* 176–7). Coleridge's '*Schema* of the total *Man*' gives (in the form of a diagram representing the 'Noetic Pentad' which has been integrated with the figure of a circle and diametrical polarities) 'the distinguishable grounds of all the Faculties, Acts, Functions, Products, & States of Man's nature as an Intelligent Will under the condition of finite existence'.[76] He emphasized that there may be a preponderance of any energy, function, or act. The proportions of the higher nature of spirit, or of the lower animal nature, will vary as man 'by the power of his Will . . . *determines* the relations of his own being & of that being to nature, and the relations of nature & of what is above nature as far as these have relation to his being'. The relation between will and Reason is crucial in this self-determination, and, here again, man's relation to the supreme reality of his own Being in the Logos is the focus of Coleridge's thought: 'The Ground of Man's nature is the Will in a form of Reason. It is this which gives the Totality, One-ness, and it is the various metamorphoses, degradations, and the varying relations of the Will, which determine the particular energies, functions & acts of his existence'.[77] Knowledge depends upon the ability to connect experiences, to relate the several parts of experience to each other: 'Can you increase your knowledge otherwise than by connecting your several experiences, so that they may reciprocally confirm and perfect each other, and form the ground and incitement to continued inquiry?'[78] Coleridge probes further: 'But if there must be a connection of knowledges, will this connection come spontaneously, i.e. without an act of your will?'

Reflection, the searching of the inner life, is a means to the growth and development of the person: 'The first step to knowledge, or rather the previous condition of all insight into truth, is to dare to commune with our very and permanent self' (*Friend*, i. 115). Yet Coleridge could not agree with Kant's assertion that we can have no ground on which to claim knowledge of any supernatural aid to our will in the endeavour to perform our duty in accordance with the moral law. Kant stated that such a claim was

---

[76] BL MS Egerton 2801, fo. 77.   [77] Ibid.
[78] Ibid., fo. 68.

hazardous and hard to reconcile with reason, though he allowed that its truth was not impossible.[79] Coleridge concurred that explanation in terms of cause and effect is impossible with regard to free will and its origin. There is no possible explanation for 'Regeneration thro' an act and energy of the diseased Arbitrement aided & fostered by a supernatural Will, or divine agency, which, in order to make this compatible with the Laws of Spirit, was first united to Humanity' (*CM* iii. 311). Free will must of its very nature be 'incomprehensible—i.e. causeless, unconditional, undetermined—else it could not be freedom'. But there is another sense of the word 'explanation' which can, in this case at least, facilitate rational belief, through the 'co-classing of this Object of Faith with analogous Objects or Facts of Experience'.

In his annotations of Kant's *Die Religion* (1794), Coleridge set out clearly his argument for the validity of analogy. He then supported his claim that the idea of a supernatural influence on the will was, at least, a reasonable response to the facts of experience by drawing an analogy between this and the 'influence of Example, of Education, in short of all the administrants and auxiliaries of the Will'. He claimed that Kant himself did not deny these forms of influence 'but on the contrary makes the cultivation of certain qualities & habits important derivative Duties on this account' (*CM* iii. 311). Our will is acted upon by many outside influences in the cultivation of its habits, not only by other human individuals, but by nature: 'Why not then an influence of influences from the Son of God with the Spirit of God, acting directly on the *Homo Νουμενον*, as well as thro' the *Homo Phaenomenon*?' Coleridge suggested that this would allow a distinction between 'Grace to Redemption' and 'Providential Aids': 'the direct action on the Noumenon would be then Grace, the Call . . . the influence on the Noumenon thro' the Homo phænomenon by the pre-arrangement of outward or bodily circumstances would be, as they are commonly called in pious language, Providences'. The concept of spiritual influence upon the will is, according to Coleridge, perfectly consistent with the demands of Reason; and for him, this is the crucial point when the proofs required by the Understanding are, by the nature of the question, impossible.

[79] Kant, *Die Religion innerhalb der Grenzen der blössen Vernunft*, 296–7.

Jacobi: On the Personality of God

Some of Coleridge's criticisms of Kant echo those made by F. H. Jacobi, particularly in their emphasis on love, desire, and feeling. Jacobi insisted that these qualities are of crucial importance in man's moral development and in his approach to God. He approved of what he took to be Kant's attribution of personality to God and, like Coleridge after him, criticized Schelling for its omission. With Kant, he emphasized the will, freedom, and intelligence of God.[80] Having distinguished between *Vernunft* (Reason) and *Verstand* (Understanding), the former being that unity of will, reason, and love which must include such faculties as faith and conscience, Jacobi insisted that:

If reason can exist only in a person, and the world must have a rational author, mover, and ruler, then must this essence be a personal essence. Such an essence we can conceive only under the form of human rationality and personality, and the characteristics which I recognise in man as the highest, viz; Love, Self-Consciousness, Understanding, Free-Will, I must attribute to him. . . . This decisive assertion Feeling makes for the religious faith.[81]

The God of the Bible, Jacobi claimed, knows, wills, and loves, and therefore cannot be conceived as an abstraction but must be recognized as the source of personality. Jacobi claimed that the idea of person is that in which the human 'I' and the divine 'Thou' are interdependently grounded. 'Without a divine Thou there is no human I, and without a human I, no divine Thou.'[82] Coleridge's emphasis on the finding of self in the other and of the interdependence of I and Thou, follows this idea closely. In the 'Essay on Faith' there are passages which seem to be a variation of Jacobi's own statement.[83] Coleridge notably omitted the second

---

[80] Kant, *Critique of Practical Reason*, 130.

[81] Jacobi, *Werke*, iva, p. xlv; tr. in A. W. Crawford, 'The Philosophy of F. H. Jacobi', *Cornell Studies in Philosophy* (New York, 1901), iv. 73.

[82] Jacobi, *Werke*, iva, p. xlii: Crawford, 'The Philosophy of F. H. Jacobi', 79.

[83] 'Now the third person could never have been distinguished from the first but by means of the second. There can be no He without a previous Thou. Much less could an I exist for us, except as it exists during the suspension of the will, as in dreams. . . . There can be no I without a Thou, and . . . a Thou is only possible by an equation in which I is taken as equal to Thou, and yet not the same. . . . The equation of Thou with I, by means of a free act, negativing the sameness in order to establish the equality, is the true definition of conscience.' The pattern of Coleridge's conception of the *perichoresis* of the Trinity is seen clearly here (*LR* iv. 428–9).

part of Jacobi's phrase, perhaps fearing to suggest what to him would be the false view that God's existence is somehow dependent on the creation of the world. The I–Thou relation is a relation of persons and is constituted by reason, conscience, faith, feeling, and love. It is clearly in these qualities of relationship (which they believed to be inseparable from the concept of the rational will and the universal moral law) that Jacobi and Coleridge differ from Kant. Coleridge's marginal notes to Jacobi's work suggest that he believed the latter to have insight into the true nature of the 'I' (that 'organ of spiritual truth' which is 'the *real* Ich that shines through the empirical Ich—the correspondence of which with the former is categorically demanded') (*CM* iii. 96). Yet he did not share Jacobi's distrust of the speculative approach to God and to the moral law. The Logos (Christ) is, claimed Coleridge, the Person of God, Will in the form of Reason, 'communicative intellect in man and deity' (*BL* i. 302). In him, the Idea of Humanity, the forms of Reason, are seen to be united with the principles of relationship, love, and feeling.

Schelling and the Dialectical 'Self'

Coleridge's views on the subject of persons have much in common with those of Schelling, who also recognized personhood to be distinction-in-unity, grounded in the freedom of the will.[84] Yet in some respects their ideas differ markedly; for example, Schelling declared: 'It is . . . certain that God's personality can only be based upon the nexus between him and nature.'[85] This was quite unacceptable to Coleridge. Other important differences emerge, particularly in the light of his later notebooks and letters (post-1818). Schelling's God must constitute himself as Person; as the living unification of contradictory principles. A dynamic interaction must take place between the light of Reason in God and the ground of the dark Will which has been expelled from him.[86] God becomes *Person* through his own self-creation and self-revelation. Coleridge's God is, in contrast, 'I AM' from eternity.

---

[84] See Schelling, *Sämmtliche Werke*, viia, 395; P. J. Gutmann, *Schelling's Of Human Freedom* (Chicago, 1936), 46–7, 74.
[85] Schelling, ibid., viia. 395: *Of Human Freedom*, 74.
[86] Schelling, *Sämmtliche Werke*, viia. 432–3.

There is no possibility of becoming in him. He is realized in the Idea, the Son, the 'Other' in whom he is, as Person. The 'I AM' exists as Person and through relation (ipsëity–alterity–community) totally independently of his Creation. Schelling had claimed: 'That principle which rises up from the depths of nature and by which man is divided from God, is the selfhood in him; but by reason of its unity with the ideal principle, this becomes *spirit*; or man as an egocentric, particularized being (divorced from God) is spirit—the very relation [to God] constitutes personality'.[87] Coleridge argued, on the contrary, that the selfhood (not to be confused with individuality as *particularity*) which emerges from nature is the false or 'phantom' self. Man's true Self is found in the divine Humanity who is never separated from but coeternally one with God.

Despite his disagreements with Schelling, Coleridge expressed admiration for the latter's work on freedom,[88] and adopted his definition of personality as consisting 'in the connection of an autonomous being with a basis which is independent of it, so that the two completely interpenetrate one another and are but one being'.[89] Coleridge copied this passage, almost word for word, in a notebook entry, without mentioning its source (*CN* iv, § 4728). Both he and Schelling were agreed that God is the highest principle of personality, but, for the latter, this personality is realized in nature, in becoming and in the appearance of man as 'other'; in Coleridge, the ideal and the real are already reconciled in the divine Idea, the Logos-alterity. In God the Ideal is supremely Real. His differences with Schelling concerning the person may be summed up in an extract from his annotations of the *System des Transcendentalen Idealismus* (1800): 'all Schelling's contradictions are reducible to the one difficulty of comprehending the co-existence of the Attributes, Agere et Pati in the same subject'. Coleridge maintained that the principle of personality is a synthesis of 'Action + Passion'.[90] Love is an example of an 'act

---

[87] Ibid. vii. 364: *Of Human Freedom*, 39.

[88] Coleridge is reported to have said that 'Schelling . . . appears greatest in his last work on *Freiheit*' (*Diary, Reminiscences, and Correspondence of Henry Crabb Robinson*, ed. T. Sadler, 3rd edn., 2 vols. (London, 1872), i. 107 (13 Aug. 1812)).

[89] Schelling, *Sämmtliche Werke*, viia. 395: *Of Human Freedom*, 74.

[90] See Coleridge's notes on Kant, *Die Metaphysik der Sitten* (Königsberg, 1797), back flyleaf in *CM* iii. 266.

which is yet a passion', the lover loves and is transformed by his love, and this *'mysterium finale'* reflects the essence of personality which both acts and is determined by its actions. The acts of will, of faith and conscience, mould and form the personality itself. Through the indwelling Idea of man (Logos), the human person is given the power to determine his or her own being.[91]

Schelling, Coleridge believed, neglected the subjective, active pole of reality. His God is an abstraction dependent upon the world of becoming for its realization. 'I AM' is therefore ultimately dependent upon 'It is'. Coleridge argued that, on the contrary, the Logos, as 'He [who] is', is dependent on, begotten by, the Father, the 'I am'; while the 'I am' is realized as Being only in this begetting of the other Self. Fichte, on the other hand, was accused by Coleridge of neglecting the 'It is', the Other; not merely that which is not-self, but that which exists in objective reality and is found in God as Logos *'deitas objectiva'*. But Fichte had usefully developed further Pico della Mirandola's idea of the self-definition of the human person, suggesting that the human person must be understood as *act*, the act of self-definition. This idea, later taken up by the existentialist philosophers, is theologically developed through Schleiermacher's emphasis on the importance of the individual response and act of faith.[92]

Coleridge's own reading of Schleiermacher was often critical (N 26, fos. 43^v–44), but both men agreed on the inwardness of the Christian experience. Both were certain of the importance of the growth of personality through self-realizing acts made possible through the indwelling Light and Life of Christ. Schleiermacher insisted that individuality was more than mere particularity,[93] and

---

[91] For Coleridge's emphasis on the priority of the 'I am', of the self-assertive act, see e.g. *CM* ii. 293, 726 and n., 745.

[92] Schleiermacher calls the 'creation [of the inner life] an act of spiritual freedom': 'If the purpose of my actions is to shape what is human in me, giving it a particular form and definite characteristics, thus contributing to the world by my own self-development and offering to the community of free spiritual beings the unique expression of my own freedom, then I see no difference whether or not my efforts are at once combined with those of others and some objective result immediately appears to greet me as part of the world order. My efforts have not been in vain, if only I myself acquire greater individuality and independence, for through such self-development I also contribute to the world' (*Monologen*; tr. H. L. Friess as *Soliloquies* (Chicago, 1926), 20).

[93] Schleiermacher contrasts to true personhood the individual who 'sees and recognizes only the outward spectacle of life instead of the spiritual activity that

was realized through a process which moves from within outward. He too denied that the true self can be identified with the biological self which only seeks satisfaction of its earthly needs. The selfhood of the other is therefore to be revered; on this both Coleridge and Schleiermacher insisted: it represents the 'Thou' which is the image of God. Coleridge found in St Paul an emphasis on 'loving-kindness' as the mark of true personhood. This 'does not ask[:] what would I do for myself? Let me do the same for my neighbour! But . . . supersedes this movement by *finding* a self in a Brother in the first instance. It is an immediate, and not a reflex act' (N 41, fo. 16). Coleridge was prepared to argue that without the recognition of 'Thou' as another self only a false and phantom 'I' exists. This is the reality of self-love, that it is interdependent with love of one's neighbour (OM iii, fo. 115). Coleridge and Schleiermacher developed their ideas of community out of these theories of individuality and of personhood. The state cannot rightly be understood as a collection of particular individuals. It is realized through the dynamic process of relationship between moral beings in whom the potentiality for self-determination (through the rational will) exists, in I–Thou relationship.

Fichte: Personhood in Act and Faith

Coleridge described one of the most important questions for Christians as '*What* within the sphere of my inward immediately [*sic*] Consciousness am I [to] call my *Self*[?]' He answered with another question: 'May the Answer be—this is the very mark & Character of thy state that thou art to determine this for thyself?' (N 41, fos. 78ᵛ). Fichte had described the act of faith by which the individual determines himself, his consciousness, and his worth as itself *truth*, that which has its origin in conscience alone.[94] This determination of consciousness by conscience is also characteristic of Coleridge's definition of 'person'. Conscience is not merely, as for Kant, concerned with the moral imperative; its force is derived from the longing of the self for completion in the

secretly stirs his inmost being . . . in the image which he constructs of himself, this very self becomes something external, like all else' (*Soliloquies*, 15; see also 20, 31).

[94] Fichte, *The Vocation of Man*, 72.

other (OM i, fo. 109). It is, wrote Coleridge, 'the Duty of Love' (*CN* ii, §3231). Hence, rather than being concerned with 'the formal truths of the pure *Science* of Morality', he affirmed the 'duties of *Men*' (N 38, fo. 31), which could not be separated from experience, feeling, and emotion (N 41, fo. 68^v). Morality is concerned with relationship to the other, to nature, and to God. The responsible will is 'the essential, indispensable ground & condition of [man's] Personality' (OM ii, fo. 158). It mirrors the divine relationships, the *perichoresis* of the Godhead, and is revealed and communicated to humanity by the living Word.

Coleridge expressed his admiration of Fichte's insight into act and faith as the starting-point of all philosophy, an insight on which his own system was grounded.[95] However, he criticized the latter's neglect of the objective pole of reality, his 'heavy mass of mere *notions*, and psychological acts of arbitrary reflection' (*BL* i. 158). Fichte's 'other' was simply and always 'not-I', and hence lost completely its objective frame of reference:

Thus his theory degenerated into a crude 'egoismus', a boastful and hyperstoic hostility to NATURE, as lifeless, godless, and altogether unholy: while his *religion* consisted in the assumption of a mere ORDO ORDINANS, which we were permitted *exoterice** to call GOD; and his *ethics* in an ascetic, and almost monkish, mortification of the natural passions and desires. (*BL*: i. 158–60)

[* 'Ordering Order . . . exoterically, popularly']

Coleridge was also critical of the interpretation of self-love which he found in Fichte's later work. This love is only an introverted act towards a 'poor *reflection*' of a self. He noted that 'In his better Days F[ichte] taught a nobler dogma—viz. the generation of the I from the Thou in all finite Minds' (*CM* ii. 596). This 'dogma' became an important feature of Coleridge's own idea of person and of the concept of relationship which is integral to it;—the 'I + He = Ye' which 'enabled *Man* to love his neighbour as himself' (*CN* iv, §4636). It is dependent on the absolute Subject in whom Self is completed and perfected through the relationship of 'alterity' (the Logos—the Word which goes forth as 'other' and yet remains). Trinity is the active self-determining relationship of distinct persons in perfect unity. This

---

[95] See *BL* i. 157–8; *CL* iv. 792.

is an outgoing love in which the objective reality of the other is more than merely 'not-I'; 'Thou' is the means by which the 'I' finds itself. Fichte failed, in Coleridge's view, to recognize the *distinction*-in-unity of the personality of Christ. He did not distinguish the personality of the Son from the 'personëity' of the Father; similarly, he neglected the reality of alterity, of objective 'otherness'. Coleridge insisted that 'there can be no personality *without* Unity, or *with* absolute Sameness'. His definition of personality is 'Ego et Alter Ego—: or A + A = A . . . without consciousness this is animal Life—with consciousness this is *Person*' (*CN* iii, § 4195). The human self mirrors God's self-realization (achieved in willing and loving the Other, the Son). The true idea of self is 'This person and the other who is nevertheless this or I, and the other I' (ibid.).

The True and Phantom 'I'

By 1827 Coleridge had reached the conclusion that the true self must be identified neither with the empirical, phenomenal self (the body), nor with mind. It was not, for example, that antecedent unity to which Kant appealed: this was itself dependent upon a higher reality. The solution of the substantial 'I', he believed, could only be found 'in the immanent Life in the communicative Logos' (N 36, fo. 2). Mind might indeed be defined as

a Subject that is its own *Object*!—but for this reason it may with no less propriety be defined an Object involving its own Subject . . . But this is not the definition of the '*I*'—this must be defined, as Subject recognising itself as a *Subject*. The 'I' therefore cannot be conceived as the *whole mind*; and tho' it is indeed the mind itself, of which the mind is conscious (ni rectius dicatur, scious*) yet it is not of necessity conscious of it *as* itself.—Something more, therefore, seems to be required for the existence of an 'I', than mind in the universal idea. What is this? (N 35, fo. 48–48ᵛ)

[* 'unless it would be more correct to say "scious"', i.e. 'con' implies shared knowledge]

The answer to this question he provided himself: will, faith, and conscience enabled the human person to find his true self in the divine Humanity, the divine Subject, God manifested as 'I am'. The Logos is the *objective* reality of the Absolute *Subject*, he who *acts* and *is*. This position, Coleridge believed, avoided the errors into which the necessity of maintaining an objective absolute Reality led Spinoza,[96] and it enabled escape 'from the unreality of the Objective in Schelling's scheme'.[97]

The true Self is discoverable, then, through faith, which responds to, and affirms, the law of conscience.[98] Coleridge's view of faith has a paradoxical quality: while 'Faith must be a Light originating in the Logos, or the substantial Reason, which is co-eternal and one with the Holy Will and which Light is at the same time the Life of men'; yet, faith is also 'the commencement of experience' (*LR* iv. 428). The leap of faith cannot in itself be dismissed as irrational, since it is the condition and first step of all knowledge and of every hypothesis; like these it is an act of will. For Coleridge, true faith will always conform to Reason (Logos):

> The opposite of Faith and its' worst enemy is Credulity if indeed it be not rather the Contrary—The Scepticism, which counteracts Faith, may be counteracted by it—nay, the Faith by being contracted may be strengthened, and obtain in intensive more than it had lost in extensive Quantity—may win in *Quality* more than it loses in quantity. But Credulity precludes Faith. Hence the well-known Fact, that Liars are almost always credulous—& the Converse is not seldom found true—. (N 37, fos. 5ᵛ–6)

Coleridge was aware of the 'Tyranny of *Dogmas*' (N 35, fo. 34ᵛ); these he claimed could be counteracted by faith because of the constituent of reason. 'How is it possible', he asks in Augustinian vein, 'that Faith, which includes Reason, should contradict it?' (*CN* iv, § 5048).

Although will and reason are the co-factors of faith, and in that sense its *ground*, yet, Coleridge argued, faith is, conversely, necessary to reason itself. Whether reasoning from experience, from 'things that are seen' to the 'One invisible', or beginning, on the other hand, from *Ideas*, such as the Idea of God, and reasoning from here to the existence of the phenomena of the

---

[96] Ibid., fo. 11.

[97] See ODI, fos. 11–17; here Coleridge criticized the use of the term 'non-being' and the opposition of negativity as cause or explanation of change and development from the Absolute to the separated finite.

[98] See Coleridge's equation of Paul's use of the term 'law' with conscience; N 35, fo. 30.

senses, human reason 'will find a Chasm, which the *Moral* Being only, which the Spirit and Religion of man alone can fill up or over-bridge' (OM ii, fo. 38).

Relationship: The Condition of Personality

Coleridge's description of his own philosophy as a restoration of that of Pythagoras and Plato (*BL* i. 263) might be seen as credible in respect, at least, of the importance which he attached to the subject of relationship, that aspect of the Greek *logos* which could be expressed as *ratio*. Pythagoras had applied this concept to both spiritual and material reality and to the area of human relationships. Iamblichus attributes to Pythagoras the statement 'Friendship is equality; equality is friendship'[99] and a strikingly similar idea is found in Coleridge's assertion that 'all true, all real . . . equality is by relation' (N 55, fo. 9). We have seen the centrality of the idea of relation (expressed as *idem et alter*, 'ipsëity' and 'alterity', as the I–Thou relation, as distinction-in-unity) in Coleridge's thought. For him, as for Pythagoras, Heraclitus, Plato, and Philo, and for the Patristic writers, *Logos* is the principle of relationship, the realization of the unity of distinctions, and the mediator between infinite and finite. Coleridge's concept of logical, epistemological, and ontological relations was always linked to that of the relationship of *persons*. He denied that the idea of the soul could be understood as an 'insulated form', insisting that its very meaning is 'unattainable by those who have not learnt the possibility of finding now a Self in another and now another yea! even an alien and an enemy, in the Self' (OM iii, fo. 54). Love itself is the act of '*finding* a self in a Brother' (N 41, fo. 16).

In his later writings, Coleridge emphasized the unity of the active and passive poles of human nature in the context of relationship. Love is a particular and mysterious synthesis of action and passion. Not only love indeed, but also the '5 or 6 Magna mysteria of human Nature' which, with love, include will, conscience, evil (as original sin), identification ('Coadunation' or

---

[99] Iamblichus, *Life of Pythagoras*, tr. Thomas Taylor (London, 1818), 118. It is clear that Coleridge had read this work of Iamblichus (see *CN* iv, § 5097); the reference here is to his reading of T. Kiessling's edition (1815–16).

spiritual Marriage), growth, and progression; all these involve a synthesis of action and passion or 'passive action' (CM iii. 266). He connected this synthesis to the principle of individuation and to that of personality. Because human consciousness in its creative, relational faculty mirrors the divine principle of *idem et alter*, in which all true being is comprehended, these two faculties are found, in human persons, as a synthesis of passive action. The 'I' which finds itself in the very act by which it distinguishes itself from the 'not-I' is yet one with that 'not-I' by which it is, in fact, determined.

Love exemplifies this form of distinction in unity. Coleridge believed that love itself is a recognition of 'Self-insufficiency', which is, paradoxically, greater in a more morally complete and developed individual. It is the desire for the completion of one's self by another (*CN* iv, § 4730). Love is 'a Passion of the whole Being in harmony', a 'co-alescence of all our Powers & Receptivities, to one particular Object' which is only possible where there is a real, or imagined, common basis, or shared sympathy with 'the inmost Being of the Beloved'. The opposition of the two individuals is reconciled in the synthesis, the passive action, of love, this common base in which the self is found in the other. It is this reciprocal self-and-other integration of passive action which Christ, as Logos, communicates to humanity. Through this love, the reconciliation of the divine and human will is effected. The supreme reality of Trinity is 'the Prothesis, or Punctum Identitatis, or One potentially involving two: or Two in One' (*CN* iv, § 5097). This is imaged in finite form in the relationship of marriage. There, love produces itself as a 'bipolar line' of reciprocal relationship, in which the husband is the 'Positive Pole or Thesis; the Wife the Negative or Antithesis'.[100]

The concept of relationship was central to every aspect of Coleridge's thought. It was essential to the idea of self-consciousness and knowledge itself, to that of the dynamic polarities operative in physical and moral life, to the individual's self-determination, and, finally, to the idea of community, to the family, Church, nation, and state. The whole of the unified system

---

[100] Coleridge was careful to emphasize the misconception of interpreting 'negative' as '*nihilative*, or the mere absence of the contrary, mere privation'; it should be understood, on the contrary, as 'an *aliquid* correlativum, the correspondent Opposite of the Power first *put*' (*CN* iv, § 5097).

which he sought to establish has as its foundation the Logos as the source, reality, and mediator of relationship. He was convinced that the Idea of Man could not be otherwise defined than in terms of these relationships.

We have seen that Coleridge used the idea of person as a focus of the reconciliation of conscience with consciousness, intellect with feeling, action with passion. This is consistent with his idea of the Logos as the Reconciler and the Person of God, as the self-realization through Love of God as Will in the form of Reason and communicated in light and life as the Word. It is clear that his concepts of 'personëity' and personality are derived from an attempted synthesis of *Gefühlsphilosophie* with aspects of the moral philosophy of Kant, Fichte, and Schelling, and with Christian doctrine. At the same time, he criticizes past theory and doctrine and offers a new theme of reconciliation. Kant's view was transformed by Coleridge's inclusion of feeling and self-love. To Jacobi's concept of person, on the other hand, he added his analysis of the Logos as *Reason*, the principle of form and distinction-in-unity imaged in human speculative intellect. Fichte's emphasis on act and faith could be redeemed, so he thought, through the idea of the '*deitas objectiva*'—the objective reality of the Self-who-is-Other. The necessary corrective to Schelling's concept of person, on the other hand, must be to understand the condition of personality as the unity of 'Action + Passion', the nature of love itself. Although Coleridge's attempt at synthesis often appears strained, in this development of the idea of person in the light of the Logos theme it is perhaps most successful. His analysis of human nature focused his attention on important psychological questions. Through his response to these, the Platonic and Kantian emphasis on the Idea or ideal of Man is transformed into a more dynamic and existential account of the human condition and of human aspirations; here relationship is seen as the condition of moral development from individual to person.

4.4. BECOMING HUMAN

Coleridge drew his Logos theme as a connecting artery through the life of the individual, the moral and intellectual evolution of the race, and the coherence and community of the nation or state. This theme is developed out of an exploration of the Logos as the Idea of history, and of the Unity of mankind. The Logos here becomes the ground of a dynamic 'theanthropology'; on this basis, any adequate understanding of human nature must acknowledge the importance of history. This approach has more in common with Judaeo-Christian anthropology than with the forms and universals of the Greek tradition. Coleridge's prophetic pronouncements concerning the potential and destiny of the human race emerge (in his later thought) always from the ground of the Logos as both the ideal and the incarnate, historical reality of Humanity.

History: The Redemptive Scheme

Coleridge's view of human history owes much to eighteenth- and early nineteenth-century concepts of universal progress and development in the natural sciences, in moral philosophy, and in social culture. He was influenced, for example, both by Lessing's idea of the educational stages of human history and by such theories as that of J. F. Blumenbach, on racial development.[101] He drew, we have seen, on the evolutionary theories of history and cultures which Vico,[102] and later Herder, had developed. Like the former, and encouraged by the political philosophy of Kant, he read history in the light of Providence, and of the progressive moral and spiritual revelation by which humanity would move towards its ideal (Logos). This idea, the revelation of the *telos* of history in and through Logos, the universal Idea of

---

[101] We have already noted the influence on Coleridge of Lessing's *Erziehung des Menschengeschlechts* (see above, Ch. 1.3). In a passage of the *Friend* he made this especially clear (i. 504). For Blumenbach's influence, see below, n. 105.

[102] There are many parallels between what Isaiah Berlin has called Vico's theory of the 'reconstructive imagination' (*Vico and Herder* (London, 1976), p. xix); and the Reason–Understanding distinction as it is emphasized in *AR*. This was published in the same year as his reading of Vico; and Coleridge's notes hint that he was himself drawing a comparison between Vico's work and his own (see *CN* iv, §§ 5204–11 and nn.). It is interesting, in the light of Vico's emphasis on history as the working-out of the will of an eternal Providence, to note that most of Coleridge's references to the Logos as Providence post-date his close study of Vico in 1825. That he found in Vico confirmation of his own concept of the role of the will in all learning is also clear (see his citation of Vico, *CN* iv, § 5204).

Humanity, incarnate in the God-Man, Christ, has much in common with that of his contemporary, Hegel, though with crucial differences.[103] Coleridge proposed a kind of synthesis of philosophy and history on the basis of Christian revelation. His own search for a unified system of knowledge led to a synthesis of two poles: on the one hand, the attempt, characteristic of Enlightenment thought, to establish universal laws of development; on the other, the evolutionary and dynamic view of history characteristic of the Judaeo-Christian tradition; a view which re-emerges strongly in Romantic theories of history. He argued that creation was a redemptive scheme. The whole of history, natural and moral, was a continuing organic process of development. Yet there are hints long before the 'logosophic' system was fully developed that he was not convinced by the idea of uninterrupted progress in moral and social development. In the *Friend*, for example, he argued for the harmlessness of this view of progress, but allowed that there are periodic retrogressions: 'The progress of the species neither is nor can be like that of a Roman road in a right line. It may be more justly compared to that of a river, which both in its smaller reaches and larger turnings, is frequently forced back towards its fountains, by objects which cannot otherwise be eluded or overcome' (*Friend*, i. 392). The 'river', Coleridge declared, will regain its course with renewed impulse in time.

He opposed Erasmus Darwin's concept of evolution (*CL* iv. 574), insisting that humanity has developed from a 'superinduced' principle of self-consciousness in an evolved higher intelligence. There is a difference not merely in degree, but in kind between each of the classes of being in nature, between mineral, vegetable, and animal, and between animal and man. But the growing sense, in his own time, of man as a historical being, and the growing awareness of evolutionary development in the physical world (Coleridge was impressed, though not totally convinced, by the theories of Charles Lyell),[104] had produced accounts of human development which he found stimulating. He often refers to the work of J. F. Blumenbach in this connection,

---

[103] See my 'Logic and Logos', pt. 1, 1–25.

[104] Coleridge's notes reflect his interest and his doubts concerning the developments of evolutionary theories (see e.g. N 51, fo. 23; *CL* iv. 574; N 65, fos. 6–7^v; OM ii, fo. 63).

with whose view his own account of the evolutionary moral and intellectual development of the human race had much in common. He is impressed, too, by Emanuel Swedenborg's account of the stages in the history of mankind's spiritual development, and by Fichte's and Schelling's accounts of the various epochs of the development of consciousness and moral freedom.[105]

Coleridge's interpretation of the Old Testament as the history of the spiritual and moral evolution of a nation guided, supported, and protected by Providence provides the background for his study. He noted that the Hebrew people had emerged from slavery only to fall into idol worship. Their constant need for repentance and for the renewal of their relationship with God was evident. Equally evident, he argued, was their gradual development (through God's revelation of himself in the Jehovah-Word) to the point where some among them were prepared for the arrival of a spiritual Messiah rather than a victorious temporal king. Eventually (here perhaps again he was thinking of the importance of this concept in Philo[106]) some had reached the stage of moral and spiritual development at which they were ready to receive the revelation of the unity-in-distinction of the Godhead which 'by a most happy Analogy they named the Word, Logos' (N 37, fo. 29ᵛ).

Coleridge saw history as the progress of the revelation of God to man through man's experience in time. History revealed God's nature as the unity of freedom and necessity: 'In natural history, God's freedom is shown in the law of necessity. . . . In moral history, God's necessity or providence is shown in man's freedom'

---

[105] Coleridge had read and annotated J. F. Blumenbach's *Über die natürlichen Verschiedenheiten im Menschengeschlechte* (Leipzig, 1798), in which the latter provided a 'pentad of races' to show the varying characteristics which he believed belonged to various races, and attempted to trace their evolutionary development through history. Coleridge traced all the racial characteristics back to the sons of Noah: Shem, Ham, and Japheth (e.g. NQ, fo. 53): he too used the figure of a pentad to express this. He believed that individuals, institutions, nations, and races could be seen to be symbolized by and to have their source in the history which the Bible revealed. His annotations of Blumenbach's work (back flyleaf) give a detailed expression of his views. For Swedenborg's views on spiritual development see e.g. *Arcana Caelestia*, § 10225; and *True Christian Religion*, 762. For Fichte's theory of the five epochs of intellectual and moral development, see *Die Grundzüge des gegenwärtigen Zeitalters* (1804–5), in *Sämmtliche Werke*, ed. I. H. Fichte (Berlin, 1845–6), vii. 11–12.

[106] See e.g. Coleridge's notes on Philo's principle of distinction-in-unity in God: *TT* ii. 291.

(*TT* ii. 231). The study of history not only revealed God as Providence; it had another great and connected purpose: 'Assuredly the great use of History is to acquaint us with the nature of Man.'[107] He repeatedly emphasized, like Hegel, the importance of understanding and interpreting history philosophically, in the light of principles and ideas, rather than merely according to facts and events in themselves: 'the science of HISTORY,—History studied in the light of philosophy, as the great drama of an ever unfolding Providence,—has a very different effect. It infuses hope and a reverence for humanity and its destiny.'[108]

History is, then, a progressive revelation of the Idea of Man (as Logos) and of the nature of finite man; the Logos, as Providence, is also seen to be working within the events of history itself (*CL* vi. 677).[109] Man's fallen nature is evidenced as much in the history of nations and tribes as in that of individuals. The Hebrew people's idol worship and devotion to the things of the senses, to earthly glory and possessions, resulted in a kind of blindness which prevented them from discerning the spiritual nature of truth. Coleridge drew a connection here with the blindness which he believed affected those devoted to the 'mechanico-corpuscular philosophy'. These attempted to find truth through the faculty of the Understanding alone, and assumed primal matter and its organization to be the origin of reality. They too were devoted to the things of the senses. They were unable, he concluded, to grasp spiritual truth, to accept history as the record and revelation of a progressive evolution of mankind towards the Light and Life which is Logos, the very source and power of the evolutionary process itself.

In a note of 1830 Coleridge drew a clear distinction between man as the *telos* of all nature (and, as such, present as the potentiating idea within all forms of nature) and man as a living

---

[107] Coleridge, *Treatise on Method* (London, 1818), 'Science of Method', 41.

[108] *C & S* 32 (see also *BL* i. 219; *SM: LS* 11, and 124 n.; *CN* ii, § 2026; *TT* i. 383). It is clear that Coleridge's concept of the Logos as Providence of history owes much to Frederick von Schlegel's *Philosophie der Geschichte* (Vienna, 1829). Schlegel constantly emphasizes the role of Providence: 'History, by laying before our eyes the march of Divine Providence—a Providence whose loving agency is apparent as well in the lives of individuals as in the social career of nations—History, I say, constitutes the fourth revelation of God' (tr. James Baron as *Philosophy of History* (London, 1846), 60).

[109] Coleridge declared boldly of the Logos, 'He became the Providence of the Church and of the World which exists only for the Church' (N 51, fo. 8ᵛ).

soul. It was based on another and transcendent distinction: on the one hand the Logos is the eternal Idea of Humanity; on the other, this same Logos is incarnate, both in the *principle* of humanity, operating as a hidden potency within the evolutionary process of all the lower forms of nature, and in the historical individual, Christ, a man among men. The Logos is not only the eternally pre-existing 'divine Humanity', but also 'the Man in all Nature working upward from the Zoophyte (all the several genera of Animals being but uterine forms and premature Births of the Human organisms, animated by the Universal *Life*)'. At the same time the Logos must be recognized as 'the *Living Soul* first in Adam inbreathed' and as the Christ of history: 'The Logos . . . dwelt, a man, among men, in order to dwell in man, as the Spirit of Truth' (N 48, fos. 26ᵛ–27).[110]

In Coleridge's theology, Adam is the representative of the universal; that is, mankind in individual form (Coleridge was careful to note here that by 'mankind' he meant both Adam and Eve: 'Hence sometimes the Hebrew has it, Adam, sometimes the Adam . . . Homo publicus, a universal Person'). In a sense, Adam 'contains' all men. He is the first living soul. Coleridge defined 'soul' as a self-conscious personal Being, a unity of distinct faculties and qualities.[111] The idea of 'soul' could not be appropriated by a single self-consciousness any more than 'the light of the sun by an individual eye'; it will only be understood by those who find the other as a Self and are able to recognize 'otherness' and alienation even within their own being. Each human individual participates to some degree, Coleridge argued, in a transcendent Selfhood; this is the source of the potential unity of mankind. Self-conscious personal being must become fully activated spiritual life before this can be realized. The individual must grow from Adam to Christ: Adam represents the psychical humanity, or soul; Christ is the spiritual humanity (N 41, fo. 8), the realization and fulfilment of the whole human personality. Coleridge divided the evolutionary progress of the idea of Man into five stages:[112]

---

[110] See N 41, fo. 7ᵛ.

[111] BL MS Egerton 2801, fo. 81.

[112] The order in which he presents these is somewhat erratic, owing to the note-form which records his often spontaneous and unrevised ideas and associations of thought.

2. the kind—1. the Individual 3. The Race. 4. the Family: 5. the
Nation or State—All; each; a Whole.—Adam = the Race and the Indi-
vidual—the Man and Man. 2. Noah + Shem, Ham, Japhet = the
Individual and the Race. 3. Abraham—Isaak. Jacob.—the Family. 4.
The Hebrew Nation—the Citizens of the Mosaic Republic, the People of
the Kingdom of David and of Solomon. (N 26, fos. 108ᵛ–109)

In 1830 his position was more clearly defined, for example, in his
notes on the book of Deuteronomy: 'Ever more and more do I
find the truth and importance of my view respecting the States
thro' which Mankind must pass in order to actualize and bring
forth the full idea of Humanity' (N 43, fo. 37ᵛ). His association of
the developmental stages with the various races of men presently
existing appears to owe much to the influence of Blumenbach's
now strange-seeming biological conclusions.[113] He described the
succession of stages of the idea of humanity revealed in the
history of the world: the race, the family, the state, nation, or
people which are under the Mosaic Law, and, finally, '[t]he
Universal individually, the Sun in the whole countless Multitude
of Drops, entire in each—the Gospel', which is the coming of
Christ in the flesh, the complete revelation of the Idea of Man.
The Logos, Coleridge declared, is the promised Healer and
Reconciler of all the stages of man, from the individual (in which
the universal is represented) to the nation (in which the many
become one individual body). Gradually and progressively, the
individual finds himself as one distinct part of a whole or unity
(the family, the nation) which eventually includes all mankind.
Since Christ is the Idea of Man, both individual and universal, in
Christ man finds that his autonomy as an individual is dependent
upon his being an integer or part of a larger unity. The potential
of the *person* is only realized as he finds himself to be part of, and
in organic relationship with, the whole. Conversely, the whole is
never actualized except by the unity of the individuals by which it
is constituted.

The five stages of man can thus also be seen as a progress from
mere individuality to personality. Within the nation which is true
to its ideal form in the Logos, the self can find its true form and
being:

---

[113] See also *CL* vi. 689.

the true Philosophy is that the Self is in & by itself a phantom, an ens non vere ens; but yet a non-ens non prorsus non ens,* because it is capable of receiving true entity by *reflection* from the *Nation* /. It *strives* to *become* by the act of radiating to the Periphery: and it actually becomes, it *is*, by the reflection, the *retroaction* of itself from the Periphery. Without the resisting & returning outline it would be lost in vague space & be for ever a mere *striving* at Being, a pure Selfness. (N 55, fo. 10)[114]

[* 'a kind of being which is not true being; but yet a non-being which is not completely without being']

As so often, Coleridge here employed the figure of the circle and the relationship between centre and circumference by which (with the *tetractys*) he frequently represented both the relations of the Trinity and, on this ground, the forms of relationship in being and mind.[115] A nation is too often, he believed, regarded as composed of independent Selves, the mere sum of which is the All. On the contrary, 'Every point [is] a center in itself yet part of a radial determined by the ideal Circumference, the Nation . . . [this is] the antithesis to the modern Political Economy of *Self* radiating towards *All*. Now the *whole* is a most living & life-giving Reality; *All* a mere Ens imaginarium, a pure empty Abstraction—the Goddess Multitudo—in Numero' (N 55, fos. 3–4). This relationship of part and whole is worked out, Coleridge argued, through all the stages of man's development, just as it is in the forms of nature. In man there is a union of solitary and gregarious instincts,[116] a manifestation of the two principles of all life: 'individuation' and 'attachment'. Man desires not only individual freedom, but 'federation', in families, communities, and nations. These two opposing tendencies in his nature are actually interdependent: each is fulfilled only by the fulfilment of the other. Human institutions, to conform to the Idea, must take this interdependence of person and community as their foundation and goal:

civilisation is itself but a mixed good, if not far more a corrupting influence, the hectic of disease, not the bloom of health, and a nation so

[114] Coleridge's agreement with Fichte is clear here; see e.g. the latter's *Sämmtliche Werke*, ii. 143.
[115] 'The Divine Power is a Sphere, whose *Center* is *everywhere* and its circumference *nowhere*' (*CN* iv, § 5406).
[116] BL Add. MS 34225, fos. 132 ff.

distinguished more fitly to be called a varnished than a polished people; where this civilisation is not grounded in *cultivation*, in the harmonious development of those qualities and faculties that characterise our *humanity*. We must be men in order to be citizens. (*C & S* 42–3, and n.)

A 'Common Sensorium'

The Logos (Christ) is the 'symbol of Humanity' (N 44, fo. 63ᵛ). Humanity, as the 'product' of the Logos, is 'a distinct, and *personal* Multi-unity (i.e. many persons as one person, & yet remaining many)' the function of which is the living harmony of one body in Christ which Coleridge saw as the great hope of mankind (*CL* ii. 1197). This would be the ideal form of the state. The symbol of the state, as One in whom the many are represented, is the king or head. The Idea from which the symbol derives its truth is Christ as the Head of the human race (N 44, fo. 64). Coleridge was convinced that 'the only possible Unity of a Nation is Will = Reason', and therefore, Logos. The nation or state would be subject to the conflict of a multitude of wills of opposing interests unless these were united by being joined in the one universal Reason: 'Christ as the filial Godhead, the *o ΩΝ εν τω Κολπου του πατρος* [the (true) Being in the bosom of the father], is essentially & from everlasting was Will = Reason.'[117] This is to be the solution which Rousseau's *Social Contract* could not provide,[118] the solution which completes Kant's philosophy of the rational will. Coleridge saw in the Old Testament the revelation of Christ as the Head of the Hebrew Commonwealth, the 'Symbol of the Unity of the Nation'. Christ, he claimed, was manifested not in a divine imposition of perfect 'Will = Reason', but in the

---

[117] Coleridge's strange capitalization of the Greek serves no obvious purpose.

[118] Coleridge gave only moderate approval to Rousseau's work. In the *Friend*, he emphasizes the difficulties and dangers which he sees in Rousseau's theory of the General Will. He admitted that Rousseau had distinguished in *theory* 'between the *Volonté de Tous* and the *Volonté generale* (i.e. between the collective will, and a casual over-balance of wills)', but believed that this distinction had not been maintained 'in the application of theory to practice'. It is clear that Coleridge's emphasis on this distinction is derived from his Logos theory. He insisted that the ideal Will–Reason unity 'applies to no one Human Being, to no Society or assemblage of Human Beings, and least of all to the mixed multitude that makes up the PEOPLE: but entirely and exclusively to REASON itself'. It 'dwells in every man *potentially*, but actually and in perfect purity is found in no man and in no body of men' (*Friend*, i. 193–4).

potential for the unity of will and reason in the nation through the 'subordination of the finite Will to the Universal Reason', and in his function as the 'actualizing influence' on this potential. This is the thinking behind his argument for a 'Clerisy' (*C & S* 46–7), leaders who will enable the nation both as a unity and in the distinctions of *persons* (a people) to recognize the potential within itself for the relationality of Logos. The clerisy will, above all, pursue and uphold what it is to be truly *human*, to be a community pursuing the unity of Reason and Will within the particularity and contingency of history.

Coleridge argued that the Will–Reason unity of the Logos is as essential to the true form of the nation as it is to the person. It is to this end that good government is directed. The monarch's institutions must correspond to the true human nature, to the Idea of humanity (*CN* iv, § 5036): 'One sure Criterion of a Government or a Party Scheme—Is it founded on the Good, the Human, on Human Nature—& its Object to aid it, call it forth, direct & marshal it in the extrication from & warfare against the *Alien*, the Evil—and has it Faith in the Good collectively & timelessly?' (*CN* iv, § 5036). Coleridge's view of the ideal State with Christ (Humanity) as its Head is the basis of his speculation regarding the potential for a social and political unity to which all the diverse and distinct parts of the 'body' would make their particular contributions. This would be the melding and organizing 'Sensorium', a unity of thought enlightened by a common living bond of Reason and Will. He suggested that Christ, who informs humanity, would be realized *in* federative humanity, as this living reality and unity of Thought which influences, and is at the same time the source of, all thought (*CM* iii. 311–13). The divine Word is, inwardly, the grace which effects redemption, and outwardly that Providence in the affairs and circumstances of men which is the unifying principle bringing about the realization of Thought or Idea in its highest form, not as Hegel's 'Logic' but as the Idea which is far more than the merely rational. This is the basis for Coleridge's hypothesis of the unity which might be attained in an ideal future state. He acknowledged it as potential rather than actual; it is none the less, for him, a reality: 'Is it an impossible Conception, that a *perfectly organized* Corpus Politicum might (*in*, and *through* that perfection) acquire a common *Sensorium*? even as the Corpus Naturale? Is not this more than hinted, as the nature of the Future State, under Christ, our *Head*, by the Apostles, John and Paul?' (*CM* iii. 678).

The need to recognize the reality of the finite world as *potential* is the root of Coleridge's insistence that the interests of different states are congruous because there is potentially (and, none the less, *really*) a Unity of Reason under Christ's Headship (ibid.): 'the Interests of all States are *really* tho' not actually congruous: i.e. they are incongruous in consequence of errors concerning their own well-being'. The Logos, as the Unity within which the distinctions of the individual personality, the family, the nation, or state subsist, is the foundation for Coleridge's claim that '[t]here is one heart for the whole mighty mass of Humanity, and every pulse in each particular vessel strives to beat in concert with it . . . what is of permanent and essential interest to one man must needs be so to all, in proportion to the means and opportunities of each' (*Friend*, i. 97–8).

The Idea of Man, for Coleridge, is an ontological as well as an intellectual reality: the Logos is both Mind and Being. Ideas reflect their Archetype, in that they are more than regulative of intellect; they are *causative* of being. The Idea of Man is not merely an abstract universal concept, but a living Reality in which the many are reconciled in the One; finite humanity contains the potential for this unity. Coleridge's social, political, and religious thought includes the ideal of the interdependent relationship between individual and state. Man as a federative being is realized as person through community, and community is realized through the relations of *persons*. Coleridge believed that humanity must also be seen in the context of evolution: its potential for unity through the rational will is actualized through the process of history. In this form of the ideal nation or state the individual would not be lost in the mere *All*, for this Community would reflect the movement of the Holy Spirit, a movement of love and relationship. It would reflect the reality of distinction-in-unity, the 'Community of Life and Love'. The state would only evolve towards its ideal form through the actualizing influence of the Logos, as individuals found themselves as *persons* and recognized that the true self was discoverable only in relationship with 'He' and 'Thou'. The individual would find the realization and fulfilment of his personality only by acknowledging the Other

(Logos, distinction, 'alterity') as the *objective* reality of the self and the whole of which he was an indispensable part.[119]

The Logos is the link through which Coleridge connected philosophy to history. On a more personal level, it was also the means by which he attempted to redefine what had been the motivating interest of his early political radicalism. We have seen that the Logos was for him the life and unfolding Providence in both natural and moral history and the 'light' to which humanity was drawn. This theme was the stimulus of his interest in history as he himself admitted: 'But for Christ, Christianity, Christendom, as the center of convergence, I should utterly want the *historic sense*' (N 51, fo. 19ᵛ). Whereas Hegel's view of history might be described as the progress and perfection of the Logos as Mind or Reason, Coleridge believed that history should be understood as the development of the relation between conscience and consciousness. The moral theme is never subsumed under the intellectual.

It is tempting, in the light of this, to see his view of history as looking back to an age which spoke of the universality of human nature and which had as yet little idea of the historicity of its own judgements. Yet many of his remarks show an awareness of the inevitable subjectivity involved in any record of history and of the fact that interpretation of the 'facts' of history was dependent upon the preoccupations and prejudices of a particular age.[120] This has to be seen alongside his emphasis on the study of history in the light of philosophic principles (in this his admiration of Edmund Burke was an important factor), and on history as prophecy, which, he believed, was too often ignored.[121] Coleridge

[119] Coleridge stated that neither King nor People have ultimate sovereign rights. He wrote of the Logos, 'this the alone rightful Sovereignty, of which all Kings, Presidents, Legislatives are but the Shrines and Symbols' (N 50, fo. 21).

[120] See e.g. Coleridge's comments on the Bible as history, referring to the '*perspective* of the Age, in which the Record was written to the way, in which the then Believers conveyed the truth to *their* Minds according to their habits of thinking' (N 42, fo. 36).

[121] Coleridge constantly insisted that history must be understood in the light of philosophy (e.g. *C & S* 32). His emphasis on the relation between history and prophecy is no less insistent (e.g. *SM: LS* 29–30, 124). Both concepts are dependent upon his view that the Logos, the prophetic 'Jehovah-Word' which is expressed in the Old Testament, is also Reason, the life and form of Ideas and of words (thus of philosophy), and the Providence who is both the goal of history and incarnate in its process.

appears to have concluded that the idea of Providence in human history was essential to the moral welfare of both individuals and society. True dedication to the principles of Reason (with all this involved of will, faith, and conscience) demanded recognition of the *Idea* of History.[122] Beneath its lofty tone, this requirement is merely consistent with Coleridge's view of human nature and of human mind; he demanded that the study of history be linked with religion and philosophy in what he saw as a fully human endeavour. Since, in his opinion, a fact unrelated to the antecedent unity of a self was as impossible as knowledge without an initial *act* of faith, to attempt to divorce facts from conscience and principle was to betray history itself. Since human history was the great scheme of the self-realization of the Logos in the hearts and mind of humanity, the consequences of this betrayal for humankind would, he believed, be both morally and philosophically disastrous.

[122] For Coleridge's references to the Idea of History, see e.g. *CL* vi. 583, N 50, fo. 39.

Conclusion: 'Logosophia'

We have explored Coleridge's Logos theme as the unifying principle which connects his theories of language and imagination, his philosophy of nature, his attempt to establish an epistemology based on the constitutive nature of ideas, and his moral philosophy and anthropology. He attempted to harmonize all these areas of discourse within the grand scheme of the reconciliation of philosophy and religion. It has been my aim to show that his claim to have developed a 'system', while the term must be more widely interpreted than usual (as involving and assuming the role of faith and of conscience; as inclusive of the idea of freedom and of reality as relational) deserves serious consideration. I have attempted to show the consistency and coherence of the 'logosophic' theme. Coleridge's emphasis on the dynamic quality and consequences of relationship in every area of being, thought, and experience provides a stimulating and thought-provoking range of theological, hermeneutical, and philosophical possibilities.[1]

He struggled hard to overcome the dichotomies and dilemmas which were increasingly alienating philosophy from religious thought, and believed he had been successful in laying the foundations of a system which would provide grounds for reconciliation. It must be admitted that, at times, the connections which he drew between different areas of thought seem forced and artificial, for example, in his notes on Jacob Böhme which attempted

---

[1] It has not been the primary aim of this study to explore ways in which Coleridge's 'logosophic' system might stimulate fruitful insights in contemporary thought. However, I have indicated directions which might be profitably explored in this connection both in the Introduction and in the concluding section of each chapter. These might include (1) the necessity of faith as inextricably involved in both perception and in the work of the speculative intellect, (2) the emphasis on attention to every aspect of human nature as the starting-point for any concept of method or system (though a dialectical approach is essential here to avoid question-begging); and (3) the living process of language as both read and written. I have suggested that these ideas are developed by Coleridge on the basis of the Logos theme.

to blend Böhme's mysticism with the chemical explorations of contemporary scientist friends such as Humphry Davy. But these over-enthusiastic syntheses are more than compensated for by the many rich insights which are regarded with a continuing and even deepening interest today.

The influence of Coleridge's ideas in his own time and in the later nineteenth century has already been briefly noted. During this period, his poetic achievement was recognized, his political and social criticism often valued, and his religious thought was reflected in the work of F. D. Maurice, J. C. Hare, and F. J. A. Hort, and in the later efforts of the contributors to *Essays and Reviews* (1860) and to *Lux Mundi* (1891). These inherited Coleridge's emphasis on relational and incarnational theology, on the centrality of the idea of person, and on the integration of reason with a progressive revelation.[2] The non-exclusive nature of the theology of the so-called 'Broad Church' and its combination of Patristic emphases with the insights of German philosophy, were distinctly Coleridgean.

Coleridge's philosophical claims were often regarded with great suspicion in his own time[3] and have been accorded scant respect until recent years. Until the middle of the twentieth century, the only area in which his work had an enduring influence was the field of literature and literary criticism. Here his ideas have remained a significant focus of debate. The idea of symbol has been well explored, as has the Romantic attempt (judged more or less a failure by present-day literary theorists) to establish the creative and constitutive power of the imagination as an aesthetic and philosophic principle of unity; though the associations of this area with, and its dependence upon, the Logos principle have rarely been comprehensively analysed.

Since the middle of this century, and aided by the publication of the *Collected Coleridge* edition of his works, the extent of Coleridge's intellectual achievement has been more widely re-

---

[2] F. D. Maurice, for example, claimed that his inspiration came primarily from Coleridge. It is easy to find evidence of this in Maurice's own emphasis on the concept of relationship, as R. Norris has shown. The latter claims that Maurice's theology calls for 'sociability in the deepest sense of the word,—relationship, connectedness, the ties between human and divine that are created in the sociability of the kingdom of God' (F. McClain, R. Norris, and J. Orens, *F. D. Maurice: A Study* (Cambridge, Mass., 1982), p. xii).

[3] See above, Intro., n. 4.

cognized, although he is still not infrequently seen as an eccentric with a tendency to obscurity and 'random eclecticism'.[4] In suggesting that his thought may be more adequately understood in the light of the Logos theme, this study has attempted to provide a new standpoint from which Coleridge's philosophical claims may be assessed and the continuing importance of his thought to the history of ideas established. In comparison with the attention paid to his poetry and literary theories, little has been given (by his compatriots, at least), until recent years, to his philosophy and religious thought; but it is easy to find many areas of his interest and concern which are still recognizable as critical issues in the areas of epistemology, religion, psychology, and hermeneutics.[5] Whatever his system may have to offer to us today, I have suggested that it can only rightly be understood if seen in the context of the issues which preoccupied him (and many) in his own time, and within the framework of the whole history of ideas on which he drew. The Logos theme was not only a search for a synthetic unity but a response to dilemmas, both personal and public, philosophic and religious.

The Logos Response

There is no doubt that Coleridge drew gradually further away from his early political and social enthusiasms, and that he became less interested in the idea of general progress (the legacy of

---

[4] Norman Fruman, seventeen years on from *Coleridge: The Damaged Archangel* (London, 1971), a work highly critical of Coleridge's thought (he calls Coleridge 'an appallingly wide-meshed sieve' (p. 418), seeing him as 'a spectacle of deception, evasion, and all manner of falsehood' (p. 420)), still maintains Coleridge's lack of coherence, his plagiarism, and the muddled nature of his thought. Fruman writes, for example, that 'Coleridge . . . had no coherent theory of the imagination' ('Ozymandias and the Reconciliation of Opposites', in Christine Gallant (ed.), *Coleridge's Theory of Imagination Today* (New York, 1989). Fruman offers a collection of other critical judgements; for example, Orsini's estimate of Coleridge's 'random eclecticism' (*Coleridge and German Idealism*, 186), and Mary Warnock's conclusion that Coleridge was 'a reader with neither historical sense nor the ability to distinguish things which are different' (*Imagination* (Los Angeles, 1976), 95).

[5] e.g. such issues as the relation between external reality and the knowing subject, the problems involved in any understanding of the past, the nature of the self, and the relation between the language of religion and that of other areas of thought and experience; all these continue to exercise the minds of modern thinkers.

the Enlightenment), whether this referred to human knowledge or human institutions. In the first twelve years of the nineteenth century, following the death of his son Berkeley in 1799, he had to face the failure of his marriage, of his closest friendship (with Wordsworth), of many of his personal ambitions, and, in many senses the most devastating loss, that, as it seemed to him, of his own will in opium addiction. Unsurprisingly, perhaps, he lost interest in positive radical political action, and even (gradually) in the power of poetry to transform. His attention was turned ever more inward, on the one hand, and backward, to the past, on the other, in an attempt to understand a twofold alienation: the sense of a loss of self, and the sense of what he saw as a loss of humanity in the wider world.[6] The intensity of his criticisms of other thinkers reflect these preoccupations, and his most strongly maintained views were developed around these concerns. This dogged determination to find some sort of framework of intelligibility for the human condition through the idea of relationship did not, however, produce a retreat to comfortable exclusiveness, whether of rationalism or of religion. He was able to accept and even to encourage the criticism of dogma, without a reactive plunge into the pessimism which was to grip Schopenhauer's thought, or the nihilism which was later to become a powerful element in the work of Nietzsche.

I have suggested that the theme of the Logos Reconciler gave to Coleridge's system such coherence as it has. I have traced this theme as it undergirds his epistemology (in his concept of the life and power of words, of the symbolic imagination, of the act of faith implicit in all knowledge), his moral philosophy (through the potential unity of will and reason which could transform individuals into persons and collective humanity into communities and states), and his study of the natural world. We have seen how the Logos theme became the ground of his rejection of the exclusive nature of the prevailing philosophical views of his time, of, for example, idealism and materialism. I have argued that his

---

[6] Coleridge saw this alienation at work socially, politically, and in the effects of the 'mechanico-corpuscular' philosophy (materialist and mechanist views). For evidence of his (at times) despairing state of mind in respect to the state of the nation (see e.g. N 55, fos. 3–13, where he ponders on the substitution of the 'All' as mere abstraction for the whole which is the realization of persons through the life of the nation). For his thoughts on the loss of ideas, see above, Ch. 3.3 n. 66.

idealism is tempered not only by the priority of the will, but by his admission of the reality of the world of nature, and his identification of Idea and Law. He claimed that he could not see 'by what exclusive right, a scheme, which commences with the assumption of *atoms*, can claim for itself exclusively or eminently the epithet of experimental, nor in truth by what right such a scheme can be appropriately called a philosophy' (OM ii, fo. 193ᵛ). Life, whether physical, intellectual, moral, or spiritual, began with an act. He described this act, and the processes by which life was manifested in the products of nature, in terms of the Logos as the source of 'light' which revealed the hope and the underlying spiritual reality of all areas of human existence, experience, and thought; and of 'life' as constituted by and through relation (beginning with the polarity of *Idem et Alter*). He was convinced that while the physical sciences used one language and method, and religion used another, the truths expressed by both were compatible and mutually supportive. Attitudes which might now be categorized as scientific and religious fundamentalism were seen by Coleridge as the result of a failure to recognize and respect the necessary difference in approach of science and religion and the equally necessary interdependence of faith and method.

We have seen that his emphasis on the Logos Reconciler was also the focus of his attack on what he saw as distortions within some of the religious views which had developed in the eighteenth century and which were still powerful in his own time. His criticism of natural theology was a rejection of what he called an over-emphasis on the 'it is'—that is, the witness of the senses, as opposed to the recognition of God as Thou and as Person—and an expression of his affirmation of feeling and encounter.[7] His criticism of certain types of mysticism, and his anxiety on this account over tendencies in the work of, for example, Irving and Swedenborg, was a result of his conviction that reason and revelation must always be mutually supportive. We have seen how important is his understanding of the Logos as Reason.[8] Again, once he had found God as distinction-in-unity, and the Logos as the principle of distinction,[9] he denounced Unitarianism as error.

---

[7] See above, e.g. Ch. 4.3.
[8] See above, Ch. 3.1.
[9] 'The force of the term, Logos, is the Distinctive Power' (N 36, fo. 64).

Unitarians became, to him, identified with the 'Alogi' (*SM: LS* 99), those who had rejected the very substance of reality. Yet despite his increasingly strongly held and vigorously expressed views on the subject of religion, there is an openness at the heart of his system. On the one hand, he uses the tools of the speculative intellect, and his arguments then are deductive, analytical, and logical; but the 'system' is grounded as much on unity, feeling, inclusiveness, and relationship. The adjective 'logosophic' is the key: Logos must be understood as a unity with *Sophia*, the feminine Wisdom principle of the Old Testament and the term by which Coleridge, drawing on and developing Philo's thought,[10] represented Spirit, Community, and Love.

The Writer and Logos

Coleridge once wrote that the writer in some sense *becomes* the Logos,[11] the implication, in the light of his theme, being that the writer brings both life and form to his creation, but also something more, a communication which is interpersonal, potentially revelatory, and reconciliatory. The writer can be seen both as *creating* the reality which he/she wishes to communicate, and as presenting the reader with a new way of looking at reality, thus reflecting the work of the Logos as the *creative* and the *revealing* Word. Coleridge seemed (consciously or not) to adopt this same role of the writer which he described. He wrote of his system as something which had never before been attempted; in this he saw himself as, in some sense, creating a world (*TT* i. 248–9). Yet he also sought to awaken the reader to a pre-existent and transcendent reality which made possible the interpersonal communication which he attempted: that of Logos. The constantly recurring titles by which he referred to the Logos seem also to be used as stimuli

---

[10] Philo constantly associates Logos and Sophia—representing them in terms of interdependent realities; see e.g. *De Fuga et Inventione*, 97; *Legum Allegoriae*, i. 65. This same interdependence can be found in the Wisdom writings of Scripture, e.g. Wisdom 9: 1.

[11] For Coleridge's use of the term 'Alogi' and related terms such as 'Alogist' and 'Alogology', see e.g. *CN* ii, § 2466, fo. 21; *CL* iii. 533; *CN* iv, §§ 4692, 4767, 4794. Coleridge is using the term 'Alogist' to mean both a philosopher who denies the reality of ideas, and one who denies the Logos; for him the latter tends inevitably towards the former.

to new thought, as themselves revelatory through a process of defamiliarization. Terms such as 'Word', 'Life and Light', and 'Idea' are, we have seen, used in a variety of senses which it seems were intended to stimulate ever deeper levels of reflection and widening circles of relational thought, sometimes through analogy, sometimes as themselves symbols.

Every part of the system is characterized by a polarity of both formal and dynamic themes; the emphasis on living process, change, and development is there in his philosophy of language, his analysis of human history, his idea of the physical world, and in his speculation on the relation between the historical individual Jesus and the eternal Logos. It is not surprising then, to discover a kind of internal dynamic relation operating in Coleridge's own work between the structural principles of the Logos theory, and the psychological, moral, and emotional relationships which are its life. If faith and conscience are implied in every act of knowledge; if 'freedom must be assumed as a *ground* of philosophy, and can never be deduced from it' (*BL* i. 280); if the I–Thou relationship is the condition of personality, then we have to understand the term 'system', as he applied it to his own work, in a different sense to that of, for example, Hegel.[12]

From 'Either–Or' to 'Both–And'

The inherent polarity by which Coleridge's system reflects what he sees as the Logos-activity makes it vulnerable to criticism;[13] but it also provides the means by which such criticisms can easily be set against each other. His work has, for example, been described as 'spiritual positivism',[14] that which exalts intuition over language; yet both his published and his unpublished works return again and again to the importance of the evolution of language, and to language as the ground of philosophical and religious thought. On the other hand, the impact of Paul de Man's criticism of what he sees as Coleridge's eventual sub-

---

[12] See App. C, below.

[13] There is no doubt that while Coleridge emphasized the appearance of contradiction as inevitable in the attempt to express the truths of Reason through the forms of the Understanding, what to him was polarity, to many of his time was sheer nonsense. See above, e.g. Intro., n. 4.

[14] Paul Hamilton, *Coleridge's Poetics* (Oxford, 1983), 196–7.

ordination of spontaneity to rationalist and positivist speculation[15] is lessened when set beside the latter's constant emphasis on the I–Thou encounter as essential to the first and every following act of self-conscious thought. This encounter, whether with the divine Person or with another human individual, always contains the possibility of the unexpected, of the transformation or the completion of the self by the other. Coleridge's thought could easily be categorized, on the one hand, as an attempt to blend Kantian rationalism with religious dogmatism, and, on the other, as a Romantic preoccupation with mysticism, imagination, and feeling, itself opposed to the rigours of philosophical thought. Both these judgements can only stand if the inherent polarities in his thought are ignored; these make it almost impossible to categorize him in this way. He himself would no doubt have seen such mutually exclusive criticisms as confirming his theory of the necessary oppositions by which ideas are expressed. Further, he saw human experience itself as constituted of polarities which sometimes created unbearable tensions. One of the most important emphases in his work is his claim that any system must be based on human nature, need, and experience. Having in earlier years seen Schelling's concept of the imagination as the reconciling force which overcame not only philosophical dichotomies but also conflicts within the human personality, from the early 1820s he was increasingly convinced that the imagination itself, if it was to avoid the dangers of fancy, must be subordinate to faith and conscience and to the I–Thou encounter of persons.

In summary, it seems appropriate to return to Coleridge's own view of his work, as expressed towards the end of his life. First, the very boldness of his claims for the system that was intended to be the 'Logosophia' is striking: 'You may not understand my system, or any given part of it,—or by a determined act of wilfulness, you may, even though perceiving a ray of light, reject it in anger and disgust:—but this I will say,—that if you once master it, or any part of it, you cannot hesitate to acknowledge it as the truth. You cannot be sceptical about it' (*TT* ii. 293).

The ground of this claim is again revealed in the reported words from his death-bed:

---

[15] See above, Ch. 1.2 n. 13; Ch. 3.1 n. 17.

Be thou sure, in whatever may be published of my posthumous works, to remember that First of all is the Absolute Good, whose Self-affirmation is the 'I AM', as the Eternal Reality in itself, and the ground and source of all other Reality. And next, that in this Idea, nevertheless, a Distinctivity is to be carefully preserved, as manifested in the person of the Logos, by whom that Reality is communicated to all other Being.[16]

It is difficult to reconcile the first undoubtedly dogmatic pronouncement with the inclusive character of the principle of distinction-in-unity, of the self–other relation, and of the priority of will, which, I have suggested, are the focus of the Logos theme in Coleridge's 'system'. The second statement, while forthright, includes within it the terms 'distinctivity' and 'person', both of which, in the light of what we have seen of the Logos idea, mitigate its severity. There is no doubt that he was committed to the search for unity and theory. Such a search has been seen by many in the post-Modernist, post-Structuralist, and Deconstructionist schools of twentieth-century thought as unprofitable. But whatever the judgement of future thinkers on this question of an intelligible order underlying thought and experience, Coleridge was responding to the dominance of the mechanistic model in all areas of eighteenth-century thought by introducing his theme of relation as the underlying reality in the natural, moral, philosophical, and personal worlds. The ongoing debates of what might be called objectivism versus relativism[17] can be traced back to issues raised by David Hume and others in the so-called Age of Reason, the age in which analysis, determinism, and materialism became increasingly dominant. We see Coleridge in his emphasis on relationship pointing in another direction altogether. That his system is in some sense a synthesis of past ideas is certain, but I suggest that it is more than this: as he draws these ideas together, they are transformed into a whole which is more than the sum of its parts.

[16] The funeral oration for Coleridge given by John A. Heraud, 8 Aug. 1834 (transcript in VCL E.2: 'Coleridgeiana 1834–39').

[17] I have used objectivism and relativism here in the same sense as Richard Bernstein (*Beyond Objectivism and Relativism: Science, Hermeneutics and Praxis* (Oxford, 1983)). Bernstein looks for a way beyond the paralysing dichotomy which he believes has gripped all methodological issues, when the choice has seemed to be between *objectivism* (which he connects with 'foundationalism, ultimate grounding of knowledge, science, philosophy and language') and *relativism* (which he links to 'skepticism, historicism, and nihilism') (pp. 2–3).

He himself, perhaps disingenuously in the light of such a huge range of influences, admitted that he did not much care to claim originality and would rather claim 'individuality':

Because I learnt the great truths of my System from no one because it rose on me in its own Light, like the Dawn, with no direct effort on my part, save that I blew away the fogs and mists and intervening Obtrusions of the Fancy and the Understanding—*therefore* I took for granted, that there had been before me men actuated by the same pure Love of Truth. (N 35, fo. 23ᵛ)

He admitted to having recognized the same Ideas 'in many Books of the Old-Times' but insisted that he 'no where [met] with the same System or Method' (ibid.). Whatever the truth concerning the extent of his debt to other thinkers, there was one, at least, who, while clearly aware of Coleridge's borrowings, nevertheless finally appears to have supported his claim. Thomas de Quincey wrote:

I will assert finally, that, after having read for thirty years in the same track as Coleridge,—that track in which few of any age will ever follow us, such as German metaphysicians, Latin Schoolmen, thaumaturgic Platonists, religious Mystics,—and having thus discovered a large variety of trivial thefts, I do, nevertheless, most heartily believe him to have been as entirely original in all his capital pretensions, as any one man that ever has existed.[18]

---

[18] Thomas de Quincey, in *Tait's Edinburgh Magazine*, 1 (1834), 512.

APPENDIX A

Coleridge, Humboldt, and the Word

Wilhelm von Humboldt's linguistic philosophy has much in common with that of Coleridge, particularly in its acceptance of both the supernatural origin and the evolutionary development of language. What exchanges may have taken place between them when the two men met in Rome in 1806 remains a matter for speculation, as does the precise nature of any mutual influence. It is clear from a note included in Coleridge's 'Essays on the Principles of Method' that the meeting made a deep impression on them both (*Friend*, i. 510). Humboldt began his intense study of linguistic origins and development in 1820 by which time Coleridge was well immersed in his theories of language.

It is interesting to note the similarity of their views, particularly on the subject of the function of words as mediating between persons and between different levels of reality. Although Humboldt did not expound in any detail the relationship between the Word of God and human language there are many indications that he too may have had this relation in mind. Christianity was to him the highest form of belief and the best expression of the 'spirit of humanity', that 'something to which, as to an ultimate aim, [a man] can subordinate all else and by which, as by an absolute standard, he can judge all else'.[1] He, like Coleridge, held language to be 'an immediate given';[2] and he too saw it as the mediation between external reality and subjective thought.[3] It is the reflection of the spiritual energy of a nation,[4] the 'formative organ of thought', and, perhaps most importantly in comparison with Coleridge, it is the enabler of the I–Thou relationship in all its forms. Humboldt wrote:

> language cannot be brought into reality by a single individual, but only socially, by the joining of one daring experiment to another. In other

[1] Wilhelm von Humboldt, 'On the Spirit of Christianity' (1797), in *Gesammelte Schriften*, 17 vols. (Berlin, 1903–36), ii. 326; tr. M. Cowan as *Humanist without Portfolio* (Detroit, 1963), 148.
[2] Wilhelm von Humboldt, 'On Comparative Linguistics with Special Reference to the Various Periods of Linguistic Development' (1820), in *Gesammelte Schriften*, iv. 14: *Humanist without Portfolio*, 239.
[3] 'On the Differences in Human Linguistic Structure and their Influence on the Spiritual Development of the Human Race' (1830–5), in *Gesammelte Schriften*, vii. 55: *Humanist without Portfolio*, 55.
[4] Ibid. vii. 53: *Humanist without Portfolio*, 287.

words, the word must gain thing-hood; language must gain extension in a listener and a responder.

This archetype of all languages is expressed by the pronoun in its differentiation of the second person from the third. *I* and *he* are really different objects and all things are actually exhausted by them because they are *I* and *not-I*. But *thou* is a *he* placed in opposition to an *I*. While *I* and *he* are based on inner and outer observation, there lies in *thou* the spontaneity of choice. It is also a *not-I* but not, like the *he*, in the sphere of all beings, but in another sphere, that of activity dependent on mutual interaction. . . . Only through the joining, effected in language, of an 'other' to an 'I' do there arise all the profounder and nobler feelings which motivate the whole man, which in friendship and in love and in every communion of mind make the connection between two beings the loftiest and the most intimate of all connections.[5]

This concept of language as manifesting, and communicating, the relation between I, he, and thou closely parallels that found, for example, in Coleridge's 'Opus Maximum' notes (iii, fos. 142–7) and in his 'Essay on Faith'. It is the basis on which he developed his theory of conscience. Having established that the perception of *I* and of *he* is dependent upon that of a *thou*, Coleridge continues: 'there can be no I without a Thou, and . . . a Thou is only possible by an equation in which I is taken as equal to Thou, and yet not the same' (*LR* iv. 428). The definition of conscience he gives as 'the equation of Thou with I, by means of a free act, negativing the sameness in order to establish the equality' (ibid. 429).

[5] 'On Duality' (1827), in *Gesammelte Schriften*, vi. 26–7: *Humanist without Portfolio*, 336–7.

APPENDIX B

The 'Cosmic Christ'

The idea of a cosmic redemption through Christ has strong roots in the doctrines of the early Church Fathers. Coleridge would have found a powerful expression of it, for example, in the writings of Origen. The latter taught that there is an ultimate restoration of the whole creation to unity with God, a reconciliation of the primal alienation of apostasy. This doctrine had its most recent exponent in the twentieth-century Jesuit scientist Pierre Teilhard de Chardin (1881–1955); J. Lyons has explored the parallels between his thought and that of Origen.[1] The details of Teilhard de Chardin's theory also have much in common with Coleridge's dynamic system, despite the century which separates them. Origen, Coleridge, and Teilhard all drew on Fourth Gospel and Pauline theology to support their arguments. All three had an interest in the integration of Hellenic and Hebraic thought; and Philo's Logos is as central to the work of both Origen and Teilhard as it is to Coleridge. All recognized in Christ the mediator and sustainer of both the rational and the irrational creation. Creation and redemption are parts of one process, which is of a wider significance than the personal salvation of the individual, since, through man's redemption, the whole cosmos is redeemed. All three expressed a belief in the evolutionary process of life and mind towards a higher goal of unity and completion in Christ.

There are both interesting parallels and significant differences between Coleridge's exploration of the natural sciences in the light of his theory of a cosmic redemption and that of Teilhard de Chardin. Coleridge's use of the principle of polarity, his theory of individuation, and insistence on the importance of the Logos principle of distinction-in-unity are all found in modified form in Teilhard's work.[2] Because both Teilhard and Coleridge belonged to that tradition which defines life as will and power, both accepted *degrees* of reality, the point on which Coleridge believed the 'Doctors of the Absolute' (the German idealists, notably Oken,

---

The heading is taken from J. A. Lyons, *The Cosmic Christ in Origen and Teilhard de Chardin: A Comparative Study* (London, 1982).

[1] J. A. Lyons, op. cit. 169.

[2] Teilhard de Chardin's concept of radial and tangential energy is one example of the importance in his work of the polarity principle (*Le Phénomène humaine* (1955); tr. B. Wall as *The Phenomenon of Man* (London, 1959), 64–6).

Steffens, Schelling, and Hegel) were in error.[3] Reality, he insisted, can be predicated of both the potential and the actual, and of all the manifestations through which the movement from the one to the other is completed; this process can be seen in the great scheme of redemption which has its first act in creation.

The evolution of nature towards mind through a process of increasing individualization is a central feature of Teilhard's *Phenomenon of Man*. He believed that this evolution was not simply a mechanistic adaptation to outward environment, but was also dependent on an *inward* tendency in all matter. Thus Teilhard, like Coleridge, asserted the reality of both an inner and an outer life. Like Coleridge, he found the evolutionary process to be directional; he denied the Darwinian view that it was random. He too understood life to subsist in qualities and relations, interdependencies, actions and reactions. The recognition of this is, according to Teilhard, 'cosmic consciousness';[4] to Coleridge it is the *philosophy* of life, attained through Reason as opposed to the Understanding. Both described the whole of creation as moving towards an ultimate unity of distinctions, a wholeness, perfection, and fulfilment in the 'Pleroma' of the Logos. This is Teilhard's 'Omega point'. We have seen that Coleridge saw creation as the first act of the great scheme of redemption, worked out through the 'superinduction' of a tendency within nature 'to supersede herself' (N 35, fos. 29–31^v; N 36, fo. 65). He attributed to Justin Martyr (with approval) the recognition that it was necessary for the life within nature to be united with human nature in order that it might be saved (*NED* ii. 209). Teilhard described humanity as 'the axis and leading shoot of evolution'.[5] Like Coleridge, he insisted that individualism and egoism must not be confused with the idea of personality.[6] The idea of person involves the idea of relationship, and the recognition and fulfilment of this is an essential part of the evolution of human being to a higher reality.

Despite the many points of convergence, Teilhard's position differs from that of Coleridge on important points. An investigation of these reveals Coleridge's creation theology to have more in common with

---

[3] See *CN* iv, § 5162; Coleridge takes up the Aristotelian and Scholastic theme of potentiality and actuality, but with a different emphasis: 'the descending power, the Principle of all Actuality' is the Logos; the Spirit 'potenziates' the chaos of non-being, and the co-activity of the Spirit and the Word creates, through the introduction of polarity in various stages, all the forms, products, and processes of life (see above, Ch. 2.2). Coleridge here connected the act of physical creation to the 'New Creation', the redeemed life of mind and spirit.

[4] Lyons has given an account of the origin of this term in Teilhard's thought (*The Cosmic Christ in Origen*, 169).

[5] Teilhard de Chardin, *The Phenomenon of Man*, 40.

[6] Ibid. 289.

Origen's understanding of cosmic redemption through Logos. For example, Coleridge established his philosophy of nature by an appeal to the 'facts' of will and conscience, showing by Kantian argument that if these are real then the conditions necessary to their reality are also real, and closely interweaving cosmology, biology, physics, and natural history with theology. The fact of a moral evil and the need for redemption is fundamental to Coleridge's philosophy, to that of his theory of life as much as to the inner life of reason, will, and conscience in the human person. Teilhard, on the other hand, optimistically asserted that:

> If the world is convergent and if Christ occupies its centre, then the Christogenesis of St Paul and St John is nothing else and nothing less than the extension, both awaited and unhoped for, of that noogenesis* in which cosmogenesis—as regards our experience—culminates. Christ invests himself organically with the very majesty of his creation.[7]

[* 'appearance/evolution/birth of mind']

Coleridge's optimism was always tempered by the awareness of danger, of doubt, and of dependence. He too looked for the ultimate restoration of all things to unity and perfection and relationship in Christ, the 'Light and Life' of the whole creation. Yet the suggestion implicit in Teilhard that Christ is in some sense *completed* by his creation is alien to Coleridge's thought. J. A. Lyons describes Teilhard's view thus: 'The relationship between Christ and his Body is reciprocal. Each contributes to the completion of the other: if Christ is like a centre seeking for itself a sphere, the cosmos is that sphere seeking a centre.'[8] Coleridge constantly reiterated in his later writings that the life of nature is the result of a response of grace and love to a 'fall' of will and to the loss of being and selfhood. He insisted that the tendency to reversion to this evil ground of self-contradiction remains in the finite creation; it is redeemed only through the redemption of humanity. Man must recognize the 'pull' of the opposite pole to the divine Will, and the constant threat of the loss of self to which he is exposed.

The 'Cosmic Christ', though Teilhard's term, is, in essence, equally central to the thought of Origen[9] and of Coleridge. In the work of all three men this concept provides a unity, coherence, and harmony between natural and moral philosophy and theology, between reason, experience, and faith. Origen and Coleridge saw the evolution of the natural world as always dependent, at every stage, on the free-agency of

---

[7] Ibid. 325.

[8] Lyons, *The Cosmic Christ in Origen*, 186.

[9] Origen also sees the Logos as both the Alpha and the Omega of all creation (*Scholia in Apocalypsin*, 7; *Commentaria in Evangelium Joannis*, i. 116; Lyons, *The Cosmic Christ in Origen*, 131).

God. The whole process of redemption concerns, ultimately, the over-coming of alienation and of evil, the restoration of the unity of the divine and human will. In Teilhard's work, the evolutionary process itself appears inevitable, and thus suggests that a universal redemption and restoration is somehow incorporated into nature and associated more closely with the development and perfection of consciousness than with that of will. In this context, the difference between Coleridge's thought and that of Teilhard echoes that between Coleridge and the *Natur-philosophen* of the early nineteenth century.

Despite the enormous historical distance between the work of Origen and that of Coleridge they are linked by a belief (in contrast to Teilhard) that not only the relationship between man and nature, but also the progress towards the reunification of all things in Christ is always as-sociated with the state of man's will and with his relationship to God.[10] Human choices and actions are crucial, if not to the final result, certainly to the rate of progress and to the number and type of set-backs. When the human will is conformed to Reason through the grace and love of God, the individual's choices, Coleridge, like Origen, believed, will be directed not merely to self-realization as a part of one organic life, but towards an *act* of conscious detachment from that evil and separative will which is the ground (though not the life) of nature. They believed that the whole of creation was, paradoxically, ultimately redeemed in this act of detachment which the God-Man, the revealing and indwelling Word, made possible. The relationship of all things in the Unity of Christ could not, for Coleridge, be realized merely in the evolution of consciousness, but, primarily, through the rational *will*.

---

[10] The mainspring of the movement of evolution towards restoration of unity in the cosmos through the Logos, is, for Origen, the *freedom* possessed by rational creatures (*De Principiis*, ii. 9. 2; Lyons, *The Cosmic Christ in Origen*, 134).

APPENDIX C

Logocentricity in Hegel and Coleridge

Coleridge's Logos principle has much in common with Hegel's idea of World Spirit. The subject of Hegel's 'Logic',[1] as Hans Küng points out, 'is none other than the *divine* Logos, the absolute divine essence'. It 'describes the first stage of God's one, infinite and timeless path. The path trodden by the divine Logos in an act of dialectically creative self-determination . . . to the absolute Idea.'[2] Küng suggests that Hegel 'richly and patiently' unfolds all the presuppositions which make a Logos in the flesh a possibility.[3] John's Gospel is, for Hegel as for Coleridge, a seminal expression of the incarnation of the Idea of God.[4] Both he and Coleridge establish a dialectical ontology on this foundation, and both seek, through the Logos principle, a means of overcoming the alienation and fragmentation in thought and experience which they recognized in their own time.[5] Hegel, like Coleridge, combines the Logos of the Fourth Gospel with that of Greek philosophy (Pythagorean, Heraclitean, Platonic, and Stoic) in his exploration of Absolute Idea or Mind. He too finds Logos to be the light and life of the world of nature and of spirit, dynamic, living, and creative Reason, the true Idea of Man realized in the divine Humanity of Christ on behalf of all men. Coleridge's principle of 'alterity' and Hegel's concept of the oppositions through which Being

For a more detailed comparison of the logocentricity of Hegel and Coleridge, see my 'Logic and Logos', 1–25, 192–215, 340–54.

[1] 'Logic' in this case refers to the subject both of Hegel's shorter *Logik*, i.e. pt. 1 of the *Encyklopedie der philosophischen Wissenschaften im Grundrisse* (1817), and of his *Wissenschaft der Logik* (1812–16); see also n. 2 below.

[2] Hans Küng, *The Incarnation of God*, tr. J. R. Stephenson, (Edinburgh, 1987), 253. See also Hegel, *Science of Logic*, tr. A. V. Miller (London, 1969), 707: 'the logical process in question would in fact be the immediate exposition of God's self-determination to being'. In his *Lectures on the Philosophy of Religion* ((Berlin, 1832), tr. E. B. Speirs and J. Burdon Sanderson, 3 vols. (London, 1968), iii. 31), Hegel refers to God's 'specific character as the Logos'. Hegel's essay 'The Spirit of Christianity' (in *Early Theological Works*, tr. and ed. T. M. Knox (Chicago, 1948), 256–71) is particularly interesting for its parallels with Coleridge's Logos theme, including the centrality of the Logos of the Fourth Gospel.

[3] See Küng, *The Incarnation of God*, 260.

[4] See also Hegel's *Introduction to the Lectures on the Philosophy of World History*, tr. H. B. Nisbet, intro. Duncan Forbes (Cambridge, 1975), 67.

[5] See above, Intro.

and Mind are realized in the unity of the Absolute both emphasize a fundamental principle of dynamic polarity the source of which is Logos.

Both philosophy and Christianity lead—on this Hegel and Coleridge were agreed—to the same truth, and the reality which unites them is that of Logos. Within this reality the oppositions which appeared to paralyse philosophy (being and becoming, the one and the many, subject and object, mind and matter) could and would be reconciled. Coleridge went further and saw the Logos as overcoming psychological and spiritual conflicts, and even as the condition for physical well-being: 'Health itself is the *Logos*, the *Law*, controlling & harmonizing the *wills* of the blind Life' (N 49, fo. 43^V). The influence of Hegel's dialectic has been immense and wide-ranging, both as inspiration and as provocation. Indirectly, it has stimulated some of the strongest insights in such disparate movements of thought as Marxism, 'Process' theology, and Phenomenology. The parallels between the systems of Hegel and Coleridge (the latter's incomplete, as regards systematic presentation at least) have been recognized,[6] and yet Coleridge's influence in the realm of philosophy has been insignificant compared to that of Hegel.

Despite their agreements, there are important differences in their Logos themes (interestingly these are often most revealing of the strengths of Coleridge's 'system'). Hegel's Absolute contains opposition; Coleridge's, we have seen, does not.[7] For him the self-realization of the Godhead is complete in a dynamic *perichoresis* of Will, Reason, and Love; the creation is not a necessary development in divine *becoming*, but is a positive act of grace and love and the first act of redemption. For Hegel, on the other hand, the polarity implicit in the Absolute has to be worked out through the forms of nature and mind; the creation is necessary to the working-out of the divine–human Spirit. The difference in their understanding of 'otherness' has important implications and consequences in the search for a unifying principle.

Hegel, like Spinoza before him, frequently identified 'otherness' (directly or indirectly) with negation.[8] His dialectic explores, for example, the Incarnation as the *death* of the abstract God; he opposed Being to nothingness, and he found limitation to be, at least in a sense, the

---

[6] For parallels between Hegel and Coleridge see e.g. K. Wheeler, 'Coleridge's Theory of Imagination: A Hegelian Solution to Kant?' (in *The Interpretation of Belief*, ed. D. Jasper (London, 1986), 16–40); see also the many references in McFarland, *Coleridge and the Pantheist Tradition*; and G. N. G. Orsini, *Coleridge and German Idealism* (Carbondale, Ill., 1969).

[7] See above, Ch. 2.2.

[8] '*Determinateness is negation*—is the absolute principle of Spinoza's philosophy' (Hegel, *Science of Logic*, 536). Spinoza writes that 'figure is but limitation [*determino*] and limitation is negation' (*The Correspondence of Spinoza*, ed. A. Wolf (London, 1966), letter L, 270).

negation of a thing. His distinction-in-unity involves opposition which, at times, appears to be indistinguishable from *contradiction*, both in consciousness and in the process of nature and of world history—a contradiction which is then resolved and reconciled as a part of the whole. Being, in the 'moment' of reflection, *is* not, and must be identified with its opposite, with its own negation. Coleridge, in his marginal notes to Hegel's *Wissenschaft der Logik*, emphatically disagreed that Being may, in any sense, be identified with Nothing.[9] Pure Being is certainly 'No Thing', but this does not mean that it *is not*. It *is*, as *Being*, only not as *Thing* (*CM* ii. 989–90). There is no first step of opposition here inherent in abstract Being. Coleridge insisted that 'Reality can have no opposite' (*CM* i. 231).

Hegel and Coleridge were agreed that being, of all kinds, is determined by 'otherness'. Coleridge too saw the Logos as the self-measure, self-determination, and self-disclosure of God. Yet there is here no hint of negation, nor of separation—only of relation, such as that between the centre and circumference of a circle and their mutual interdependence. Being, as Logos, includes limitation,[10] not in the sense of weakness, Coleridge insists, but in the Pythagorean sense of boundary, neighbourhood, relation, and form. Being in the form of infinite *Act* finds itself as Being in the form of self-consciousness, and this presupposes the limitation involved in the necessary awareness of the not-I, that is, the self-limitation which is a part of all relationship.

One of the most important differences between Hegel and Coleridge concerns the sense in which being and becoming may be predicated of God. Becoming, for Hegel, as 'the first concrete thought-term', is born out of the inherent and primary contradiction of Absolute Being and Nothing—out of the tension between them.[11] Coleridge, on the contrary, insisted that, in the only possible order of thought, it is with *will* that we must begin. Will is prior, in order of thought, to its self-realization in

---

[9] McFarland's comment on Coleridge's annotations to Hegel's *Wissenschaft der Logik* is misleading, I believe, in its claim that 'Coleridge's commitment to dialectical movement, though implied, is more tentative than that of Hegel' (*Romanticism and the Forms of Ruin*, 296). It is not the dialectic concerning which Coleridge has doubts, but its roots (as Hegel would have it) in a primary polarity of Being and Nothing. Coleridge argues that this should be Being and *Non-being*. His understanding of the Logos as the principle of polarity (*Deus alter et idem*) is the source of his commitment to the position that Reason and Ideas are communicated through dynamic polarities, not only physical and metaphysical, but also logical and ontological, historical and social.

[10] For Coleridge's idea of *positive* limit see OM i, fo. 27, and ii, fos. 279–81. Here he specifically mentions Hegel as one of those who has misunderstood the difference between limit as weakness (negative), and limit as the essence of form (positive).

[11] Hegel, *Logic*, 132.

Being, Mind, and Love as Trinity (though he emphasizes that there is of course no succession or proper order of things in the eternity of the Godhead): 'The Absolute Will is the ground and source of all being & as such is *super*-essential i.e. no-being' (N Fo, fo. 1).

Another clear disagreement between the Logos themes of the two men concerns the relation between the eternal Logos and the God-Man Jesus. While, in their youth, each believed that to deify Jesus was to devalue his example, each finally concluded that Christ is the universal divine Humanity revealed in particular form and within the particularity of history. Hegel believed Christ to be the Example which will finally be realized in all mankind in the fulfilment of World Spirit. Coleridge, in contrast, maintained that the pursuit of the rational alone is insufficient to lead mankind towards an inevitable perfection: evil and sin are real and positive facts for finite humanity, and the individual is enabled to fulfil his potential as *person* only because he is redeemed and loved, and his prayers are heard. The emphasis on the *personal* is perhaps what most distinguishes Coleridge's system (and such, I have argued, it may be called) from that of Hegel; it is grounded in his exposition of the Logos as the Person of God, and particularly, in later years, as *Deus patiens*.[12]

As a consequence of their differences concerning the reality of Logos, Hegel and Coleridge held different views on moral evil. While Hegel saw evil as the necessary first step of alienation at the birth of self-conscious thought, Coleridge saw it as a deliberate act of apostatic Will. Both sin and guilt were, for him, real human experiences and necessary to the idea of responsibility. Pure evil, according to Coleridge, is 'Will that would manifest itself as Will, not in Being (Ετεροτης [Otherness]), not in Intelligence (therefore *form*less) not in Union or Communion, the Contrary therefore of Life, even eternal Death' (*CN* iv, § 5076). This is both like and unlike Hegel's position. Hegel acknowledged that the fact of evil must be recognized for the reconciliation of the divine–human relationship to become a fact for the individual and for mankind, and in order that the fragmentation, discord, and disjunction of human being and experience might be overcome. He believed, however, that the overcoming of evil consists, paradoxically, in the knowledge that evil has already been transcended:

---

[12] Coleridge discusses Gregory Nazianzen in this context and connects 'the sufferings of "the Man of Sorrows", the word "made flesh"' with the 'great substantive Act of Love' by which the Logos entered Chaos as the principle of life, and, as incarnate in the creation, 'became flesh' in a different sense from that in which the man Jesus Christ revealed the incarnation of the Logos in history (N 50, fos. 28ᵛ–29).

A reconciliation . . . can only be achieved through a knowledge of the affirmative side of history, in which the negative is reduced to a subordinate position and transcended altogether. In other words, we must first of all know what the ultimate design of the world really is, and secondly, we must see that this design has been realised and that evil has not been able to maintain a position of equality beside it.[13]

He claimed that 'we are not concerned with overcoming Evil, for Evil has implicitly and actually been overcome'.[14] This statement accords with the orthodox Christian doctrine that Christ has already triumphed, and redemption, in an important sense, is already complete; but in Hegel's case it is primarily a philosophical position. Coleridge, on the other hand, approaches the subject of evil with awe and trepidation and from a personal awareness and experience of the positive reality of evil. He describes it as 'subjectively *actual* with the same imperfect degree of actuality as it is imperfectly *real*' (N 43, fo. 46^V) while 'essentially *potential*' (*CM* ii. 279). Evil, that is, is actual and existent for man, and in man's experience, even though, objectively, it can never attain full reality or actuality, 'Evil exists. This is a proposition which we cannot be called on to substantiate, it being included in our first postulate as a truth, the denial of which would render the whole religion purposeless' (ODI, fos. 101 ff.).

While Hegel seems finally to have identified Logos with Logic, Coleridge continued to see the Logos always in relation to the feminine principle, which he identified as 'Santa Sophia', 'Reason in Act or Energy' (*LS:SM* 206), as the spirit of 'Wisdom, life, love, beauty, the beauty of holiness' (*LR* iii. 127). This concept retains the possibility of a reconciliation of *logos* as philosophic principle with the Logos who is God in Person—the revelation of a God 'who hears and answers prayer'. There is a somewhat bleak *necessity* to Hegel's Logos, the freedom of which appears to be subordinate to the very system through which it is expressed. The Logos of Hegel's later writings is perhaps more Principle than Person; it has been finally identified with Logic. Coleridge, in contrast, centring his 'logosophic' system on the Person of God, found the highest expression of reality not in rationalist or idealist philosophy, but in the Christian religion itself, which answered his experience of need and sin. Here, he believed, God was revealed in Person as the unity of Reason and Will in Love. At the end he subordinated the relations of a dynamic ontologic to the relations of *persons*, to an intersubjectivity the source of which is the 'communicative Logos', and to a God who responds to human weakness:

---

[13] Hegel, *Introduction to the Lectures on the Philosophy of World History*, 43.
[14] Hegel, *Lectures on the Philosophy of Religion*, iii. 128.

If I give up Hope & Trust in thy *Mercy* . . . I must cease to think of thee as the Supreme Absolute Will, the Absolute *Good*—and . . . must think of thee as a *Law*—a *Fate* . . . a Fate, a pre[-] necessitating & by eternal inherent Law self[-]necessitated God, precludes all difference of Good and Evil. But O! thanksgiving with adoration of Love to thee, to the Absolute Will, the only Absolute Good, ground and cause of all true Being . . . the great I AM . . . who thro' thine only begotten Word, thy eternal *Person*, the Jehovah, the BEING, the WAY and the TRUTH has revealed thyself a God that *hearest* Prayer . . . who *seekest* that which was self-lost, and *callest*, yea, *bringest* back to thee that which had gone astray! (N 54, fos. 15–16)

BIBLIOGRAPHY

SAMUEL TAYLOR COLERIDGE

Published Works

A full list of published works can be found in each edition of *The Collected Works of Samuel Taylor Coleridge*, Bollingen Series (London and Princeton, NJ, 1969–). See also the List of Abbreviations.

A Treatise on Method (London, 1818); separately pub. as general intro., *Encyclopedia Metropolitana* (London, 1845).

'Confessio Fidei', in *LR* i. 389–95.

Logic, ed. J. R. de J. Jackson, *The Collected Works of Samuel Taylor Coleridge*, Bollingen Series, xiii (Princeton, NJ, 1980).

Unpublished Works

With grateful acknowledgement for permission to quote from the following to Victoria College Library, Toronto, the Huntington Library, San Marino, California, the New York Public Library, and the British Library.

N 26 (1826–7), BL Add. MS 47524.
N 33 (1827), BL Add. MS 47528.
N 34 (1827), BL Add. MS 47529.
N 35 (1827), BL Add. MS 47530.
N 36 (1827), BL Add. MS 47531.
N 37 (1828), BL Add. MS 47532.
N 38 (1829), BL Add. MS 47533.
N 39 (1829), BL Add. MS 47534.
N 40 (1828), BL Add. MS 47535.
N 41 (1829), BL Add. MS 47536.
N 42 (1829), BL Add. MS 47537.
N 43 (1830), BL Add. MS 47538.
N 44 (1830), BL Add. MS 47539.
N 45 (1830), BL Add. MS 47540.
N 46 (1830), BL Add. MS 47541.
N 47 (1830), BL Add. MS 47542.
N 48 (1830), BL Add. MS 47543.
N 49 (1830–2), BL Add. MS 47544.
N 50 (1831–2), BL Add. MS 47545.

N 51 (1833), BL Add. MS 47546.
N 52 (1833), BL Add. MS 47547.
N 53 (1833), BL Add. MS 47548.
N 54 (1833), BL Add. MS 47549.
N 55 (1833), BL Add. MS 47550.
N 56 (1827), VCL S MS 21.
N 59 (1827), VCL S MS 22.
N 65 (watermarked 1821), VCL S MS 27.
N Fo, Huntington Library, San Marino, Calif., HM 17299.
NQ (1833), New York Public Library, Berg Collection.
BL Add. MS 34225, notes and fragments.
BL Add. MS 36532, collection of odd notes.
BL MS Egerton 2801, notes and fragments.
VCL MS LT 2, notes transcribed by E. H. Coleridge.
VCL S MS S, card 9, notes written on back of invitation cards to 1812 lectures on literature.
VCL S MS F2.1 (watermarked 1818), transcribed by E. H. Coleridge.
VCL S MS F2.11, notebook.

Edited Selected Writings

Inquiring Spirit, ed. K. Coburn 2nd rev. edn. (London, 1989).

Works Annotated by Coleridge

BLUMENBACH, J. F., *Über die natürlichen Verschiedenheiten im Menschengeschlechte* (Leipzig, 1798).
BÖHME (Behmen), J., *The Works of Jacob Behmen*, tr. J. Sparrow, ed. G. Ward and T. Langcake, 4 vols. (London, 1764–81).
ERIUGENA, JOHN SCOTUS, *De Divisione Naturae* (Oxford, 1681).
HERMANN, J. G. J., *De Emendenda Ratione Graecae Grammaticae* (Leipzig, 1801).
JACOBI, F. H., *Ueber die Lehre des Spinoza* (Breslau, 1789).
KANT, I., *Anthropologie in pragmatischer Hinsicht abgefasst*, 2nd edn. (Königsberg, 1800).
—— *Critik der reinen Vernunft*, 5th edn. (Leipzig, 1799).
—— *Critik der Urtheilskraft*, 3rd edn. (Berlin, 1799).
—— *Die Metaphysik der Sitten* (Königsberg, 1797).
—— *Metaphysische Anfangsgründe der Naturwissenschaft*, 2nd edn. (Riga, 1787).
—— *Die Religion innerhalb der Grenzen der blössen Vernunft etc.*, 2nd edn. (Königsberg, 1794).
LESSING, G. E., *Sämmtliche Schriften*, 30 vols. (Berlin, 1791–4).

LESSING, K. G., *Gottfried Ephraim Lessings Leben, nebst seinen übrigen litterarische Nachlasse* (Berlin, 1793–5).
LUTHER, M., *Doctoris Martini Lutheri colloquia mensalis*, tr. H. Bell as *Dr. Martin Luther's Divine Discourses at his Table, etc.* (London, 1652).
MORE, H., *Theological Works* (London, 1708).
OKEN, L., *Erste Ideen zur Theorie des Lichts etc.* (Jena, 1808).
—— *Lehrbuch der Naturphilosophie* (Jena, 1809–11).
—— *Lehrbuch der Naturgeschichte* (Jena, 1813–26).
ROBINSON, R., *Miscellaneous Works* (Harlow, 1807).
SCHELLING, F. W. J., *Denkmal der Schrift von den göttlichen Dingen . . . des Herrn Friedrich Heinrich Jacobi* (Tübingen, 1812).
—— *Ideen zu einer Philosophie der Natur*, 2nd edn. (Landshut, 1803).
—— *Philosophie und Religion* (Tübingen, 1804).
—— *Philosophische Schriften* (Landshut, 1809).
—— *System des Transcendentalen Idealismus* (Leipzig, 1800).
SCHLEIERMACHER, F. D. E., *A Critical Essay on the Gospel of St Luke*, tr. Connop Thirlwall (London, 1825).
SCHUBERT, G. H. VON, *Allgemeine Naturgeschichte* (Erlangen, 1826).
SOLGER, C. W. F., *Philosophische Gespräche* (Berlin, 1817).
STEFFENS, H., *Beyträge zur innern Naturgeschichte der Erde*, 2 vols. (Leipzig, 1801).
—— *Ueber die Idee der Universitäten* (Berlin, 1809).
STILLINGFLEET, E., *Origines Sacrae* (London, 1675).
SWEDENBORG, E., *True Christian Religion*, tr. T. Hartley, 2 vols. (London, 1819).
TENNEMANN, W. G., *Geschichte der Philosophie*, 12 vols. (Leipzig, 1798–1819).
TOOKE, J. HORNE, Ἔπεα πτερόεντα; or, The Diversions of Purley, 2nd edn. (London, 1798).
VINCENT, W., *The Greek Verb Analyzed: An Hypothesis* (London, 1795).

GENERAL

ABBOTT, E. and L. CAMPBELL, *The Life and Letters of Benjamin Jowett, M.A.*, 2 vols. (London, 1897).
ABRAMS, M. H., *Natural Supernaturalism: Tradition and Revolution in Romantic Literature* (New York, 1971).
APPLEYARD, J. A., *Coleridge's Philosophy of Literature: The Development of a Concept of Poetry, 1791–1819* (Cambridge, Mass., 1965).
AUGUSTINE, BISHOP OF HIPPO, *Confessions*, tr. R. S. Pine-Coffin (London, 1961).

AUGUSTINE, BISHOP OF HIPPO, *De Genesi contra Manichaeos: Patrologiae Cursus Completus . . . Series Latina*, ed. J. P. Migne, 221 vols. (Paris, 1844–64), xxxiv.

—— *De Trinitate*; tr. S. McKenna as *Augustine: The Trinity* (Washington, DC, 1970).

—— *In Joannis Evangelium Tractatus*, tr. by John Gibb and James Innes as *Lectures or Tractates on the Gospel according to St John*, in *Nicene and Post-Nicene Fathers of the Christian Church*, ed. Philip Schaff (New York, 1888).

—— *Œuvres de Saint Augustin, Les Confessions*, ed. M. Skutela, notes by A. Solignac (Bibliothèque Augustinienne, xiv Paris, 1962).

BAADER, F. VON, *Ueber das pythagoräische Quadrat in der Natur, oder die vier Weltgegenden* (n.p., 1798).

BACON, F., *Novum Organum*, or *The New Organum*, ed. F. H. Anderson (Indianapolis, repr. 1980).

BARFIELD, O., *What Coleridge Thought* (London, 1972).

BARRETT, W., *Irrational Man* (New York, 1962).

BARTH, J. R., *Coleridge and Christian Doctrine* (New York, 1987).

—— *The Symbolic Imagination* (Princeton, NJ, 1977).

BEER, J., *Coleridge's Poetic Intelligence* (London, 1977).

—— (ed.) *Coleridge's Variety* (London, 1974).

BERKELEY, BISHOP G., *Philosophical Commentaries*, transcribed by A. A. Luce (London, 1944).

BERLIN, I., *Vico and Herder* (London, 1976).

BOULGER, J. D., *Coleridge as Religious Thinker* (New Haven, Conn., 1961).

BRAITHWAITE, R. B., *An Empiricist's View of the Nature of Religious Belief* (Cambridge, 1955).

BRUCKER, J. J., *Historia Critica Philosophiae*, 2nd edn. (Lipsiae, 1767); abridged edn. by W. Enfield (London, 1791).

BRUNO, G., *De Immensa et Innumerabilis, seu de Universo et Mundis* (Frankfurt, 1591).

—— *De la Causa, Principio et Uno* (London, 1584).

BUBER, M., *I–Thou*, tr. R. Gregor Smith, 2nd edn. (Edinburgh, 1958).

BULL, BISHOP G., *Defensio Fidei Nicaenae* (1685); tr. anon., 3 vols. (Oxford, 1852).

BULTMANN, R., *Faith and Understanding*, ed. R. W. Funk, tr. L. P. Smith (London, 1969).

BURNET, J., *Antient Metaphysics*, 6 vols. (London, 1779–99).

—— *Of the Origin and Progress of Language*, 6 vols. (Edinburgh, 1773–92).

CARLYLE, T., *Life of John Sterling* (London, 1852).

CHADWICK, H., *Lessing's Theological Writings* (London, 1956).

CHRISTENSON, J., *Coleridge's Blessed Machine of Language* (Ithaca, NY, 1981).

CLAYTON, J., 'Coleridge and the Logos: The Trinitarian Unity of Consciousness and Culture', *Journal of Religion*, 70 (1990), 213–40.

COFFMAN, R., *Coleridge's Library* (Boston, 1987).

COLLINGWOOD, R. G., *The Idea of History* (Oxford, 1946).

COPLESTON, F., *History of Philosophy*, 9 vols. (London, 1946–75).

CORRIGAN, T., *Coleridge's Language and Criticism* (Athens, Ga., 1982).

COWAN, M., *Humanist without Portfolio* (Detroit, 1963).

CRAWFORD, A. W., 'The Philosophy of F. H. Jacobi', *Cornell Studies in Philosophy* (New York, 1901).

CREUZER, G. F., *Symbolik und Mythologie der alten Völker*, 4 vols. (Leipzig, 1810–12); 2nd edn., 6 vols. (Leipzig, 1819–23).

CUDWORTH, R., *The True Intellectual System of the Universe* (1678), 2nd edn., 2 vols. (London, 1743).

CUTSINGER, J. S., 'Coleridgean Polarity and Theological Vision', *Harvard Theological Review*, 76 (1983), 91–108.

DASCAL, M., *Leibniz, Language, Signs and Thought* (Amsterdam, 1987).

DAVIDSON, G., *Coleridge's Career* (London, 1990).

DAVIES, P., *The Cosmic Blueprint* (London, 1987).

DE LUC, J. A., 'Analysis of the Galvanic Pole', *Nicholson's Journal of Natural Philosophy, Chemistry, and the Arts*, 26 (1810), 113–36.

DE MAN, P., *Blindness and Insight: Essays in the Rhetoric of Contemporary Criticism* (London, 1983).

DE QUINCEY, T., 'S. T. Coleridge', *Tait's Edinburgh Magazine*, NS I (1834).

DUFFY, J. J. (ed.), *Coleridge's American Disciples: The Selected Correspondence of James Marsh* (Amherst, Mass., 1973).

DUNS SCOTUS, J., *Duns Scoti Opera Omnia*, Vives edn. (Paris, 1891–5).

EBELING, G., *Luther: An Introduction to his Thought*, tr. R. A. Wilson (London, 1970).

ENGELL, J., *The Creative Imagination* (Cambridge, Mass., 1981).

ENTZINGER, R. L., *Divine Word: Milton and the Redemption of Language* (Pittsburgh, 1985).

FERRIER, J., 'The Plagiarisms of S. T. Coleridge', *Blackwood's Edinburgh Magazine*, 47 (1840), 287–99.

FICHTE, J. G., *Die Bestimmung des Menschen* (Berlin, 1800); tr. Peter Preuss as *The Vocation of Man* (Indianapolis, 1987).

—— *Sämmtliche Werke*, ed. I. H. Fichte (Berlin, 1845–6).

FISH, S., *Is there a Text in this Class? The Authority of Interpretive Communities* (Cambridge, Mass., 1980).

FLEISCHMANN, J., *Hegel's Theory of the Will*, Studies in Philosophy, vi (Jerusalem, 1960).

FLUDD, R., *Philosophia Moysaica* (Gouda, 1638).

FORBES, D., *Works* (Edinburgh, 1755).

FORD, S. H., 'Perichoresis and Interpenetration: Samuel Taylor Coleridge's Trinitarian Conception of Unity', *Theology*, 89 (1986), 20–4.

FRUMAN, N., *Coleridge: The Damaged Archangel* (London, 1971).

GADAMER, H.-G., *Wahrheit und Methode* (Tübingen, 1960); tr. from 2nd edn. by W. Glen-Doepel as *Truth and Method* (London, 1975).

GALLANT, C. (ed.), *Coleridge's Theory of Imagination Today* (New York, 1989).

GILLMAN, J., *Life of S. T. Coleridge* (London, 1838).

GOETHE, J. W. VON, *Farbenlehre* (Tübingen, 1810); tr. C. L. Eastlake as *Theory of Colours* (London, 1840).

—— *The Maxims and Reflections of Goethe*, tr. B. Saunders (London, 1893).

GOODENOUGH, E. R., *By Light, Light* (New Haven, Conn., 1935).

GORE, C. (ed.), *Lux Mundi* (London, 1889).

GRAVIL, R. and M. LEFEBURE (eds.), *The Coleridge Connection* (London, 1990).

GUTHRIE, W. K. C., *A History of Greek Philosophy*, 6 vols. (Cambridge, 1965–81).

—— *The Greek Philosophers from Thales to Plato* (London, 1967).

GYSI, L., *Platonism and Cartesianism in Cudworth* (Berne, 1962).

HAPPELL, S., *Coleridge's Religious Imagination* (Salzburg, 1983).

HARDING, A. J., *Coleridge and the Idea of Love* (London, 1974).

—— *Coleridge and the Inspired Word* (Montreal, c.1985).

HARDY, D., 'Coleridge on the Trinity', *Anglican Theological Review*, 69 (1987), 145–55.

HARRIS, H. S., *Hegel's Development: Night Thoughts (Jena 1801–1806)* (Oxford, 1983).

—— *Hegel's Development: Toward the Sunlight, 1770–1801* (Oxford, 1972).

HARTLEY, D., *Observations on Man*, ed. H. A. Pistorius, 3 vols. (London, 1791).

HAVEN, J. and R., and M. ADAMS (eds.), *S. T. Coleridge: An Annotated Bibliography*, 2 vols. (Boston, Mass., 1976–87).

HAVENS, M. K., 'Coleridge on the Evolution of Language', *Studies in Romanticism*, 20 (1981), 163–83.

HAWKING, S., *A Brief History of Time* (London, 1988).

HAYWARD, C. T. R., 'The Holy Name of the God of Moses and the Prologue of St John's Gospel', *New Testament Studies*, 25 (1979), 16–32.

HEGEL, G. W. F., *Early Theological Works*, tr. and ed. T. M. Knox (Chicago, 1948).

—— *Logic*, pt. 1 of *Encyclopedia of the Philosophical Sciences* (1830), tr. W. Wallace (Oxford, 1975).

—— *Introduction to the Lectures on the Philosophy of World History*, tr. H. B. Nisbet, intro. Duncan Forbes (Cambridge, 1975).

—— *Lectures on the Philosophy of Religion* (Berlin, 1832), tr. E. B. Speirs and J. Burdon Sanderson, 3 vols. (London, 1968).

—— *Science of Logic*, tr. A. V. Miller (London, 1969).

HERDER, J. G. VON, *Ueber den Ursprung der Sprache* (Berlin, 1772).

HOBBES, T., *The English Works of Thomas Hobbes*, ed. William Molesworth, 11 vols. (London, 1839–45).

HOLMES, R., *Samuel Taylor Coleridge: Early Visions* (London, 1989).

HOOKER, M. D., 'The Johannine Prologue and the Messianic Secret', *New Testament Studies*, 21 (1975), 40–58.

HORSLEY, BISHOP S., *Tracts in Controversy with Dr Priestley*, 2nd edn. (Gloucester, 1789).

HORT, F. J. A., 'Coleridge', in *Cambridge Essays* (Cambridge, 1856).

HOWARD, C., *Coleridge's Idealism and Kant* (Boston, 1924).

HUMBOLDT, W. VON, *Gesammelte Schriften*, ed. A. Leitzmann and B. Gebhardt, 17 vols. (Berlin, 1903–36); tr. M. Cowan as *Humanist without Portfolio* (Detroit, 1963).

HUME, D., *Enquiry concerning Human Understanding* (1748); ed. from 1777 edn. by L. A. Selby-Bigge, 3rd edn. (Oxford, 1975).

HUNTER, J., *The Works of John Hunter*, 4 vols. (London, 1835–7).

HURWITZ, H., *The Etymology and Syntax, in continuation of The Elements of the Hebrew Language* (London, 1831).

IAMBLICHUS, *De Mysteriis Aegyptiorum, Chaldaeorum, Assyriorum* (Geneva, 1607).

—— *Life of Pythagoras*, tr. Thomas Taylor (London, 1818).

—— *De Vita Pythagoria*, ed. T. Kiessling (London, 1815–16).

JACKSON, H., '"Turning and Turning": Coleridge on Our Knowledge of the External World', *PMLA* 101 (1986), 848–56.

JACOBI, F. H., *Werke*, 6 vols. (Leipzig, 1812–25).

JASPER, D., *Coleridge as Poet and Religious Thinker* (London, 1985).

—— 'Some Romantic Theories on Religious Symbolic Language', *Heythrop Journal*, 28 (1987), 31–9.

—— (ed.) *The Interpretation of Belief* (London, 1986).

JOHNSON, DR S., *The Works of the Late Reverend Mr. Samuel Johnson, Sometime Chaplain to the Right Honourable William, Lord Russell*, 2 vols. (London, 1710).

KANT, I., *Critique of Practical Reason* (1788), tr. Lewis White Beck (Indianapolis, 1956).

—— *Critique of Pure Reason* (1781); tr. N. Kemp Smith (London, 1989).

KANT, I., *Foundations of the Metaphysic of Morals* (1785), tr. Lewis W. Beck (Indianapolis, 1959).
—— *The Critique of Judgement* (1790); tr. Werner S. Pluhar (Indianapolis, 1987).
—— *The Metaphysics of Morals* (1797), tr. James Ellington (New York, 1964).
—— *Religion within the Limits of Reason Alone* (1794); tr. T. M. Greene and H. H. Hudson (New York, 1960).
KELLY, J. N. D., *Early Christian Doctrines*, 3rd edn. (London, 1965).
KIERKEGAARD, S., *Journals*, tr. Alexander Dru (London, 1938).
KÜNG, H., *The Incarnation of God*, tr. J. R. Stephenson (Edinburgh, 1987).
LEASK, N., *The Politics of the Imagination in Coleridge's Critical Thought* (Basingstoke, 1988).
LEIBNIZ, G. W., *Sämmtliche Schriften und Briefe*, ed. Deutschen Akademie der Wissenschaften, 11 vols. (Berlin, 1950).
LEIGHTON, ARCHBISHOP R., *Genuine Works*, 4 vols. (London, 1819).
LESSING, G. E., *Erziehung des Menschengeschlechts* (Berlin, 1780); tr. H. Chadwick as *The Education of the Human Race* (London, 1956).
LEVERE, T., *Poetry Realized in Nature: Samuel Taylor Coleridge and Early Nineteenth-Century Science* (Cambridge, 1981).
LIESKE, P. A., *Die Theologie des Logosmystik bei Origines* (Münster, 1938).
LONERGAN, B., *Method in Theology* (London, 1972).
LOUTH, A., 'Augustine on Language', *Literature and Theology*, 3 (1989), 151–8.
LOVEJOY, A. O., *The Great Chain of Being* (Cambridge, Mass., c.1964).
—— *The Reason, the Understanding and Time* (Baltimore, Oh., 1961).
LUTHER, M., *Luther's Works*, ed. J. Pelikan and H. T. Lehmann (Philadelphia, 1958).
LYONS, J. A., *The Cosmic Christ in Origen and Teilhard de Chardin: A Comparative Study* (London, 1982).
McCLAIN, R., R. NORRIS, and J. ORENS, *F. D. Maurice: A Study* (Cambridge, Mass., 1982).
McFARLAND, T., *Coleridge and the Pantheist Tradition* (Oxford, 1969).
—— *Romanticism and the Forms of Ruin* (Princeton, NJ, 1981).
McKUSICK, J. C., *Coleridge's Philosophy of Language* (New Haven, Conn., 1986).
MACQUARRIE, J., *God-Talk* (London, 1967).
MARCEL, G., *Coleridge et Schelling* (Paris, 1971).
MEINERS, C., *Lebens Beschreibungen berühmter Männer aus den Zeiten der Wiederherstellung der Wissenschaften* (Zurich, 1795–7).

MILL, J. S., *Essay on Bentham and Coleridge*, ed. F. R. Leavis (London, 1967).

MODIANO, R., *Coleridge and the Concept of Nature* (London, 1985).

MORE, H., *An Explanation of the Grand Mystery of Godliness* (London, 1660).

—— *Conjectura Cabbalistica; or, A Conjectural Essay of Interpreting the Minde of Moses according to a Three-Fold Cabbala* (London, 1653).

MUIRHEAD, J. H., *Coleridge as Philosopher* (London, 1930).

MYERS, H. A., *The Spinoza–Hegel Paradox* (Ithaca, NY, 1944).

NEUHOUSER, F., *Fichte's Theory of Subjectivity* (Cambridge, 1990).

NEWMAN, J. H., *Apologia pro Vita Sua* (London, 1891).

NEWSOME, D., *Two Classes of Men* (London, 1974).

NICHOLAS OF CUSA, *De Docta Ignorantia*, tr. G. Heron as *Of Learned Ignorance* (London, 1954).

—— *De Visione Dei*, tr. E. G. Salter as *The Vision of God* (London, 1928).

NIETZSCHE, F., *Der Will zur Macht* (1901); tr. W. Kaufmann and R. J. Hollingdale as *The Will to Power* (London, 1968).

NORMAN, F., *Henry Crabb Robinson and Goethe* (London, 1930).

O'CONNELL, R. J., *Imagination and Metaphysics in St Augustine* (Milwaukee, 1986).

O'MEARA, J., *Eriugena* (Oxford, 1988).

ORIGEN, *De Principiis*, Koetschau's text, tr. G. W. Butterworth, *On First Principles* (London, 1936).

—— *Der Scholien-Kommentar des Origines zur Apokalypse Johannis, nebst einem Stück aus Irenaeus*, ed. C. Diobouniotis and A. Harnack, bk. v, Graece Texte und Untersuchungen zur Geschichte der altchristlichen Literatur, vol. xxxviii, pt. 3 (Leipzig, 1911).

ORSINI, G. N. G., *Coleridge and German Idealism* (Carbondale, Ill., 1969).

OWEN, H. P., 'The Theology of Coleridge', *Critical Quarterly*, 4 (1962), 59–67.

PARKER, J. (ed.), *Essays and Reviews* (London, 1860).

PATER, W., 'Coleridge's Writings', *Westminster Review*, 85 (1866), 106–32.

PAULUS, H. G., *Das Leben Jesu* (Heidelberg, 1828).

PEREIRA, G., *Antoniana Margarita* (Medina del Campo, 1554).

PERKINS, M. A., 'Logic and Logos: The Search of Unity in Hegel and Coleridge', pts. 1–3, *Heythrop Journal*, 32 (1991), 1–25, 192–215, 340–54.

PHILO, *Philo*, tr. F. H. Colson, Loeb Classical Library, 10 vols., 2 supp. vols., ed. T. E. Page *et al.* (London, 1929–62).

PHILO, *Philonis Judaei omnia quae extant opera* (Paris, 1640).

PICO DELLA MIRANDOLA, *De Ente et Uno*, tr. V. M. Hamm as *Of Being and Unity* (Milwaukee, 1943).

—— *On the Dignity of Man*, tr. C. G. Wallis (Indianapolis, 1965).

PLOTINUS, *The Enneads*, tr. S. McKenna, 4th edn. (London, 1969).

POLANYI, M., *Personal Knowledge* (London, 1958).

POPE, A., *An Essay on Man* (London, 1733–4).

POQUE, S., *La Langage symbolique dans la prédication d'Augustin d'Hippone; images héroiques*, Études Augustiniennes (Paris, 1984).

POWELL, N., *Alchemy: The Ancient Science* (London, 1976).

PRICKETT, S., *Romanticism and Religion: The Tradition of Coleridge and Wordsworth in the Victorian Church* (Cambridge, 1976).

—— *Words and the Word* (Cambridge, 1986).

PRIESTLEY, J., *History of Early Opinions concerning Jesus Christ* (Birmingham, 1786).

PROCLUS, *The Commentaries of Proclus on the Timaeus of Plato*, tr. T. Taylor (London, 1820).

—— *The Philosophical and Mathematical Commentaries of Proclus etc., and A Translation from the Greek of Proclus's* Theological Elements, tr. T. Taylor (London, 1792).

PYM, D., *The Religious Thought of Samuel Taylor Coleridge* (Gerrards Cross, 1970).

RAHNER, K., *Theological Investigations*, iv. tr. K. Smith (London, 1966).

RAMSEY, I., *Religious Language* (London, 1957; 6th imp. 1982).

REID, T., *The Life, Letters, and Friendships of Richard Monckton Milnes* (London, 1890).

REINHOLT, K. L., *Briefe über die Kantische Philosophie*, 2 vols. (Leipzig, 1790–2).

ROBINSON, H. C., *Diary, Reminiscences, and Correspondence of Henry Crabb Robinson*, ed. T. Sadler, 3rd edn., 2 vols. (London, 1872).

—— *On Books and their Writers*, ed. E. J. Morley, 3 vols. (London, 1938).

RUNIA, D. T., 'God and Man in Philo of Alexandria', *Journal of Theological Studies*, 39 (1988), 48–75.

SALLIS, J., *Being and Logos* (Pittsburgh, 1975).

SANDERS, C. R., *Coleridge and the Broad Church Movement* (Durham, NC, 1942).

—— *Maurice as a Commentator on Coleridge* (New York, 1938).

SANDMEL, S., *Philo of Alexandria* (London, 1979).

SCHAFFER, E. S., 'The Hermeneutic Community: Coleridge and Schleiermacher', in Gravil and Lefebure (eds.), *The Coleridge Connection*.

SCHELLING, F. W. J., *Sämmtliche Werke*, ed. K. F. A. Schelling, 14 vols. (Stuttgart, 1857).

—— *Philosophische Untersuchungen über das Wesen der menschlichen Freiheit und die damit zusammenhängende Gegenstände* (Landshut, 1809); tr. P. J. Gutmann as *Of Human Freedom* (Chicago, 1936).

—— *System des transcendentalen Idealismus* (Leipzig, 1800); tr. Peter Heath as *System of Transcendental Idealism* (Charlottesville, Va., 1978).

SCHLEGEL, F. VON, *Philosophie der Geschichte* (Vienna, 1829); tr. J. Baron as *Philosophy of History* (London, 1846).

SCHLEIERMACHER, F. D. E., *Herakleitos der dunkle, von Ephesos, dargestellt aus den Trümmern seines Werkes und den Zeugnissen der Alten*, in *Museum der Alterthums-Wissenschaft*, ed. F. A. Wolf and P. Buttman, 2 vols. (Berlin, 1807–10).

—— *Monologen*; tr. H. L. Friess as *Soliloquies* (Chicago, 1926).

SCHOFIELD, M., and M. NUSSBAUM (eds.), *Language and Logos: Studies in Ancient Greek Philosophy* (Cambridge, 1982).

SCHOPENHAUER, A., *Die Welt als Wille und Vorstellung* (Leipzig, 1819); tr. D. F. J. Payne as *The World as Will and Representation* (New York, 1969).

SCHRICKX, W., 'Coleridge and F. H. Jacobi', *Révue belge de philologie et d'histoire*, 36 (1958), 812–50.

SEARCH, E. (alias Abraham Tucker), *The Light of Nature Pursued*, 7 vols. (London, 1768–78).

SEIDEL, G. J., *Activity and Ground: Fichte, Schelling and Hegel* (New York, 1976).

SELIGMAN, P., *Being and Not-Being: An Introduction to Plato's Sophist* (The Hague, 1974).

SINGER, D. W., *Bruno: His Life and Thought* (New York, 1950).

SNYDER, A. D., 'Coleridge and Giordano Bruno', *Modern Language Notes*, 52 (1927), 427–43.

—— *Coleridge on Logic and Learning* (New Haven, Conn., 1929).

—— (ed.), *S. T. Coleridge's Treatise on Method* (New Haven, Conn., 1934).

SOLGER, C. W. F., *Schriften—Alt und neu*, 2 vols. (Leipzig, 1821).

SPINOZA, B., *The Correspondence of Spinoza*, ed. A. Wolf (London, 1966).

—— *The Road to Inner Freedom: The Ethics* (New York, 1957).

SPITZER, L., *A Method of Interpreting Literature* (Mensha, Wis., 1949).

STANLEY, M., *Emanuel Swedenborg: Essential Readings* (Wellingborough, 1988).

STANLEY, T., *History of Philosophy*, 4th edn. (London, 1743).

STENZEL, J., *Plato's Method of Dialectic*, tr. and ed. D. J. Allen (New York, 1964).

STILLINGFLEET, E., *Origines Sacrae etc.*, 9th edn., 2 vols. (Oxford, 1797).

STIRLING, J., *The Secret of Hegel: Being the Hegelian System in Origin,*

Principle, Form and Matter (Edinburgh, 1865).

STOKOE, F. W., *German Influence in the Romantic Period 1788–1818* (Cambridge, 1926).

STUART, J. A., 'The Augustinian "Cause of Action" in Coleridge's *Rime of the Ancient Mariner'*, *Harvard Theological Review*, 60 (1967), 177–211.

SWEDENBORG, E., *Arcana Caelestia* (Heavenly Mysteries) 12 vols. (Amsterdam, 1749–1756); tr. anon. (London); cited in *Emanuel Swedenborg: Essential Readings*, ed. M. Stanley (Wellingborough, 1988).

—— *Conjugal Love* (*Delitiae Sapientiae de Amore Conjugali etc.*) (Amsterdam, 1768); tr. in *Emanuel Swedenborg: Essential Readings*, ed. M. Stanley (Wellingborough, 1988).

—— *Divine Love and Wisdom*, from *Apocalypsis Explicata* (1763); a tr. by Society of Gentlemen (Manchester, 1813); in *Emanuel Swedenborg: Essential Readings*, ed. M. Stanley (Wellingborough, 1988).

—— *Prodromus Philosophiae Ratiocinantis de Infinito* (Leipzig, 1734).

—— *Vera Christiana Religione* (Amsterdam, 1771); tr. T. Hartley as *True Christian Religion*, 2 vols. (London, 1819); tr. in *Emanuel Swedenborg: Essential Readings*, ed. M. Stanley (Wellingborough, 1988).

SWIATECKA, M. JADWIGA, *The Idea of Symbol: Some Nineteenth Century Comparisons with Coleridge* (Cambridge, 1980).

TEILHARD DE CHARDIN, P., *Le Phénomène humaine* (1955); tr. B. Wall as *The Phenomenon of Man* (London, 1959).

TILLICH, P., *Dynamics of Faith* (New York, 1957).

TILLYARD, E. M., *The Elizabethan World Picture* (London, 1943).

TORJESON, K. J., *Hermeneutical Procedure and Theological Method in Origen's Exegesis* (Berlin, 1986).

TORRANCE, T. F., *Transformation and Convergence in the Frame of Knowledge: Explorations in the Interrelations of Scientific and Theological Enterprise* (Grand Rapids, Mich., 1984).

TRIPOLITIS, A., *Origen: A Critical Reading* (New York, c.1985).

VICO, G. B., *Principj di Scienza Nuova e Vita* (Milan, 1816); *Principj di scienza nuova* tr. from 3rd. edn. by T. G. Bergin and M. H. Fisch as *The New Science of Giambattista Vico*, rev. and abridged (Ithaca, NY, 1970).

VINCENT, W., *The Origination of the Greek Verb: An Hypothesis* (London, 1794).

WALSH, W. H., *An Introduction to Philosophy of History*, 3rd edn. (London, 1976).

WARNOCK, M., *Imagination* (Los Angeles, 1976).

WATERLAND, D., *A Vindication of Christ's Divinity: Being a Defence of Some Queries Relating to Dr Clarke's Scheme of the Holy Trinity.*, 2nd edn. (Cambridge, 1719).

WELLEK, R., *Immanuel Kant in England, 1793–1838* (Princeton, NJ, 1931).

WHITAKER, J., *The Origins of Arianism Disclosed* (London, 1791).

WHITER, W., *Etymologicon Universale; or, Universal Etymological Dictionary, on a New Plan*, 3 vols. (London, 1800).

WINKELMANN, E., *Coleridge und die Kantische Philosophie* (Leipzig, 1933).

WISDOM, J., *Philosophy and Psychoanalysis* (Oxford, 1953).

WITTGENSTEIN, L., *Philosophical Investigations*, tr. G. E. M. Anscombe, 3rd edn. (Oxford, 1972).

WOLFF, C. VON, *Vernünftige Gedanken von Gott, der Welt, und der Seele des Menschen* (Halle, 1751).

WONG, H. P., *Logos-Symbol in the Christology of Karl Rahner* (Rome, 1984).

INDEX